CAMBRIDGE TEXTS IN THE
HISTORY OF POLITICAL THOUGHT

━━━━━

T. R. MALTHUS
An Essay on the Principle of Population

CAMBRIDGE TEXTS IN THE HISTORY OF POLITICAL THOUGHT

Series editors

RAYMOND GEUSS
Professor of Political Science, Columbia University

QUENTIN SKINNER
Professor of Political Science in the University of Cambridge

This series will make available to students the most important texts required for an understanding of the history of political thought. The scholarship of the present generation has greatly expanded our sense of the range of authors indispensable for such an understanding, and the series will reflect those developments. It will also include a number of less well-known works, in particular those needed to establish the intellectual contexts that in turn help to make sense of the major texts. The principal aim, however, will be to produce new versions of the major texts themselves, based on the most up-to-date scholarship. The preference will always be for complete texts, and a special feature of the series will be to complement individual texts, within the compass of a single volume, with subsidiary contextual material. Each volume will contain an introduction on the historical identity and contemporary significance of the text concerned, as well as such student aids as notes for further reading and chronologies of the principal events in a thinker's life.

For a complete list of titles published in the series, see end of book

T. R. MALTHUS

An Essay on the Principle of Population;

or

A View of its past and present Effects on
Human Happiness;

With an Inquiry into our Prospects respecting
the future Removal or Mitigation of the
Evils which it occasions

Selected and introduced by

DONALD WINCH

Professor, School of Social Sciences, University of Sussex

using the text of the 1803 edition as prepared by
Patricia James for the Royal Economic Society, 1990,
showing the additions and corrections made in the 1806, 1807,
1817, and 1826 editions

CAMBRIDGE
UNIVERSITY PRESS

Published by the Press Syndicate of the University of Cambridge
The Pitt Building, Trumpington Street, Cambridge CB2 IRP
40 West 20th Street, New York, NY 10011-4211, USA
10 Stamford Road, Oakleigh, Victoria 3166, Australia

First published 1992

Printed in Great Britain at the University Press, Cambridge

A catalogue record for this book is available from the British Library

Library of Congress cataloguing in publication data

Malthus, R. R. (Thomas Robert), 1766–1834.
An essay on the principle of population: or a view of its past and present effects on
human happiness, with an inquiry into our prospects respecting the future removal or
mitigation of the evils which it occasions / T. R. Malthus: selected and introduced by
Donald Winch using the text of the 1803 edition as prepared by Patricia James for the
Royal Economic Society, 1990, showing the additions and corrections made in the 1806,
1807, 1817, and 1826 editions.
    p.   cm. – (Cambridge texts in the history of political thought)
Includes bibliographical references and index.
ISBN 0 521 41954 9 (hbk). – ISBN 0 521 42972 2 (pbk)
1. Population.   I. Winch, Donald.   II. James, Patricia.
III. Title.   IV. Series.
HB861.E7   1992
304.6–dc20   91–38432   CIP

ISBN 0 521 41954 9 hardback
ISBN 0 521 42972 2 paperback

Contents

Introduction

I

The proverbial relationship of great rivers to small springs is well illustrated by Robert Malthus's most famous work. The *Essay on Population* surfaced in 1797 in the form of a friendly argument between the author and his father: it has continued to flow, often as a disturbing torrent, ever since. The argument originally centred on a self-consciously paradoxical essay written by the political philosopher and novelist, William Godwin, whose public reputation was at its zenith during the last half of the 1790s, largely as a result of the interest aroused by his *Enquiry Concerning Political Justice, and its Influence on Morals and Happiness.* Since Malthus's father was an ardent follower of Rousseau, it can be inferred that he was attracted by Godwin's anarchistic vision of a perfect egalitarian society without government or social hierarchy; and that he may also have been sympathetic to the conclusions of another work on human perfectibility published at this time, the Marquis de Condorcet's speculations on a future form of society reconstructed by science from above in his *Sketch for a Historical Picture of the Progress of the Human Mind.* For the sake of clarity, Robert Malthus hurriedly committed his ideas to paper, adopting a polite yet decidedly contrary position which – as he admitted – imparted a 'melancholy hue' to the subject. This was the work – now usually known as the first *Essay* – that was published as *An Essay on the Principle of Population, as it Affects the Future Improvement of Society, with Remarks on the Speculations of Mr. Godwin, M. Condorcet, and Other Writers* in 1798.

What the world still knows, accurately or not, as the 'Malthusian' position, therefore, and what was to become the basis for Malthus's

vii

entire career as an author and teacher, made its initial appearance as an anonymous pamphlet. It was the first published work of a mild-mannered country clergyman, aged 32, who was unmarried and still living with his parents while holding the curacy of a small rural parish near their home in Surrey. Apart from the fact that Malthus was born with a harelip and cleft palate, disabilities that were an impediment to advancement within the church, the most unusual thing about him at this time was his education. Although always destined for a career in the Church of England, his father had sent Robert, his second son and seventh child, to the Dissenting Academy at Warrington, where he was left in the charge of Gilbert Wakefield, a learned and controversial figure in the Unitarian movement who was later to die after being imprisoned for opposing the war with France in terms that were regarded as seditious. After Warrington, in 1784, Malthus went up to Wakefield's old college at Cambridge, Jesus College, where his tutor, William Frend, like Wakefield, was also a Unitarian and held equally unorthodox views on religion and politics that were later to lead to banishment from the university. We know nothing about Malthus's reaction to these influ-ences when he was an undergraduate, but he was always sympathetic to the main reform aim of the dissenters, the abolition of the Test and Corporation Acts which excluded them from many aspects of public life. A couple of years before he wrote the first *Essay*, he also sought to publish a pamphlet in support of the Foxite Whigs and those who opposed the repressive policies of Pitt during the early years of the war with France. The only other thing that can be said about Malthus's Cambridge education with any certainty is that he obtained a good degree in mathematics and was sufficiently well thought of by his college to be offered a non-teaching Fellowship.

In the first version of the thesis that is now linked with his name, Malthus described himself as a reluctant opponent of the radical inter-pretation of the science of politics that was then most readily associated with the French revolution and those *philosophes*, such as Condorcet, who were thought to have provided its inspiration. According to this interpretation, politics connoted the activity of human reason operating directly through positive laws and via the remodelling of political institu-tions to improve the lives of individuals and nations. Standing this proposition on its head, Malthus maintained that misery and vice were attributable to a fundamental law of nature that was impervious to institutional change and legislative contrivance. He also shifted the terms of debate from political culture towards biology by grounding his law of nature on the population principle – an ever-present propensity for population growth to outstrip the means of subsistence that placed the happiness and morals of the mass of society under persistent threat. Since any scheme of lasting improvement in the human condition had to confront the dilemma embodied in the population principle, Malthus embarked on a life-long attempt to show that those who attributed human suffering to defective social and political institutions overlooked one of its perennial sources and were guilty of fundamental error. At best the error aroused unrealizable hopes; at worst it was a recurrent source of revolutionary unrest. In either respect, it compounded difficulties that were ultimately remediable, not through constitutional innovation and egalitarian experimentation, but through the slow processes of education, a constant struggle with circumstances, and the exercise of individual prudence in personal affairs.

Such views would probably arouse controversy at any time, but Malthus's most uncompromising statement of the primacy of nature over political culture acquired some of its initial potency from the circumstances surrounding its publication in 1798. The works of Godwin and Condorcet, in their different ways, belong to a period of reflection on the experience of the French revolution, when it seemed necessary for those who had set store by this grand experiment to rescue hopes of indefinite improvement through political change from the violent realities of the revolution itself. The radiant optimism contained in the final parts of Condorcet's *Sketch* had acquired a tragic dimension when its author became a victim of the very events which he had hoped would mark a new dawn for mankind. With hindsight, therefore, Malthus's *Essay* could be seen as another sign of that scepticism or hostility towards the revolution in Britain that set in during the final years of the century and was to continue throughout the Napoleonic wars. By association at least, Malthus's work acquired a conservative or counter-revolutionary complexion that tempts comparison with Edmund Burke's *Reflections on the Revolution in France* (1790). Although that is certainly not how Malthus wished to have his work regarded – he explicitly saw himself as an arbiter between the Burkean and Godwinian extremes – the conservative reputation of Malthus's *Essay* needs to be mentioned in any account of why 'Malthusian' acquired a negative connotation in some circles during his life-time, and why the antagonism, both then and later, came from such a wide range of the political spectrum

– from 'romantics' such as Robert Southey and Samuel Taylor Coleridge, from Tory radicals such as William Cobbett, as well as from some socialists, Owenite and Marxian alike.

Malthus's opinions, despite considerable modification and expansion in the second and subsequent editions of the *Essay* published after 1803, remained controversial throughout the Napoleonic wars and during the post-war period. The difficulties connected with securing a cheap supply of domestic food for Britain's growing population, sporadic outbreaks of political unrest, and rising public expenditure on pauper support lent additional weight to Malthus's basic thesis on population. They also account for the attention Malthus paid to two bodies of legislation, the reform or extension of which was much debated during this period: the Corn Laws and the Poor Laws. With regard to the former – a system of duties and bounties designed to encourage and protect domestic production of what was then the basic subsistence good – Malthus reluctantly came to the conclusion at the end of the war in 1814–15 that a measure of protection from foreign competition should be retained. In the eyes of many of his contemporaries within the small community of political economists, adherents of Adam Smith's 'system of natural liberty' almost to a man, this constituted an act of apostasy, a departure from the general principle of free trade between nations. It therefore required some intellectual courage on Malthus's part, but was more often interpreted in the highly charged political atmosphere surrounding the subject as evidence of a corrupt allegiance or bias in favour of the interests of the land-owning aristocracy.

For a larger public, and over a far longer period, however, the policy for which Malthus was best known and least loved was that of gradual abolition of the legal right of paupers to obtain family assistance from their parish under the English Poor Law. Elizabethan in origin, this law remained the first line of defence against indigence, though the terms upon which relief was granted, especially to those classed as able-bodied paupers, underwent considerable change during the Napoleonic wars. Malthus countenanced several different short-term remedies for acute distress, but abolition of automatic relief under the Poor Law remained his long-term aim until his death in 1834, on the eve of the passage of the Poor Law Amendment Act. Despite the fact that Malthus cannot be blamed for or credited with this controversial measure of reform, by a process of ideological association his name was and remains linked with it.

An understanding of what made Malthus's *Essay* such a persistent source of dissension, therefore, requires attention first to his interpretation of the population principle itself, and secondly to the implications that he drew from it in the course of sustaining the larger role of political moralist – where the emphasis falls about equally on the adjective and noun in this description. For although the *Essay* later assumed an important place in the history of political economy, a discipline that was increasingly becoming autonomous, Malthus was more sympathetic to the view that treated this science as it had been treated by Adam Smith, namely as a subordinate branch of the science of politics and morals. Political moralist, therefore, though a term of late twentieth-century interpretative art, captures more of Malthus's intentions, interests, and methods of pursuing them than political economist or demographer, without denying the usefulness of these terms for some purposes. It also has to be borne in mind that Malthus was a sincere Christian, which means that his thinking on all questions of morals and politics has an important theological dimension – one that supported and was in turn supported by his philosophical and scientific beliefs.

II

Malthus made no claim to originality so far as his basic principle was concerned. That population depends on the availability of subsistence, and will respond to changes in that availability, was an eighteenth-century commonplace, with David Hume, Adam Smith, and Robert Wallace being the figures to whom Malthus gave most credit for his own initial understanding. The list of names grew as his own inquiries were extended (see pp. 7–8 below). Although his conclusions could have been sustained on the basis of the simpler assumption that the rate of potential population increase exceeds that of food production, Malthus imparted an added air of drama and precision to the subject by contrasting the geometric rate at which population was capable of increasing with the arithmetic rate at which subsistence could be expanded. This formulation proved intellectually significant as well as arresting and often misleading. Thus when Charles Darwin reread the *Essay* in 1838, the mathematical determinism of Malthus's geometric rate of increase enabled him to appreciate the constancy of the pressure behind the competition for food and space – a constancy essential to his own theory of species selection in nature, where the instinct to reproduce was unchecked by foresight. The arithmetic rate of increase proved equally pregnant: it developed in the hands of Malthus and others into a generalization known later as the law of diminishing returns – a law, held to be peculiar to agriculture and the mining of raw materials, that was to dominate English political economy for over half a century. It provided the basis for one of Malthus's most important contributions to classical political economy, the theory of rent advanced as an explanation for the peculiarities of the income derived from the ownership of scarce natural resources.

Such were some later biological and economic implications of Malthus's formulation of the population principle. The most distinctive feature of his position from the outset, however, was the stress placed on the 'imminent and immediate' nature of population pressure, as opposed to what Godwin and Condorcet had noted, namely its distant potential (and hence, to them, avoidable) catastrophic effects. Malthus's writings were also remarkable for their detailed exploration of the mechanisms by which various positive checks (acting via death rates) and preventive checks (operating on marriage and birth rates) regulated population growth in different societies and at different times. The first two books of the second and later editions of the *Essay* contained a large body of historical, ethnographic, and statistical evidence on the operation of checks which Malthus endeavoured to keep up to date as new information, particularly census data, appeared. Most of this empirical material has had to be omitted from this edition, but it must be remembered that one of Malthus's most telling criticisms of Godwin and Condorcet was that they had endangered the very notion of science as a progressive enterprise by infringing Newtonian precepts. In arriving at conclusions based solely on extrapolation, they had reasoned from causes to possible effects rather than from observed effects to possible causes.

Malthus's education as a mathematician was designed to produce a Newtonian scientist capable of subjecting all theories, whether those of natural or moral philosophy, to the test of observation and experiment. It encouraged him, through travel and reading, to become an assiduous collector of information on his chosen subject; and it helps to explain his pride in claiming that he confined his inferences to what the history of mankind had already revealed. Since his basic thesis was a universal one, historical investigation had to be conducted on the largest of canvases. Although centred around a single basic idea, therefore, the comparative-historical and encyclopaedic features of the *Essay* place it alongside such large-scale Enlightenment enterprises as Montesquieu's *Spirit of the Laws* (1748), Edward Gibbon's *Decline and Fall of the Roman Empire* (1776), and Adam Smith's *Wealth of Nations* (1776). It was certainly imposing enough to make Malthus the leading, if always disputed, authority on population questions for a generation or more; and it has earned him a lasting place in the pantheon of historical demography for his analysis of population response mechanisms in pre-industrial societies.

Another distinctive feature of Malthus's thinking derives from his belief that many of these mechanisms involved *delayed* responses – usually, in modern commercial societies, to wage and price signals. This accounts for a pervasive concern with cycles and irregularities in what might otherwise be continuous processes of demographic or historical adjustment. It explains why Malthus treated the living standards of those at the base of the social pyramid – those who were most vulnerable to movements in the supply-and-demand forces acting on wages and the cost of basic subsistence – as being subject to perpetual oscillation around a culturally-defined minimum standard. He was interested in short-term remedies for the effects of cycles and in long-term methods of raising minimum standards, but the fact that 'periodic misery' seemed to be the allotted fate of those who lived by labour obliged him, both as clergyman and Newtonian philosopher, to provide a means of reconciling the sombre side of his conclusions with continued belief in fixed laws of nature and the beneficence of the divine plan. Malthus argued that God had created a universe ruled by laws in which the pressure of scarcity, and the unavoidable 'partial evils' associated with this state of affairs, were necessary in order to activate man's powers of mind and overcome a natural human tendency towards indolence. The struggle to reduce evil and overcome difficulty lay at the heart of the process known as civilization. But once achieved, civilization was not something whose continuance could be guaranteed. A degree of tension between man's circumstances and wants had to be sustained if the process was not to be halted or reversed.

This feature of Malthus's thinking appears in different guises throughout his work. It can best be illustrated by reference to the single most important change of emphasis introduced into the second edition of the *Essay* in 1803, the recognition of moral restraint, alongside vice and misery, as a third category of check. This constituted a move in a more positive direction, affording greater scope to human agency in minimizing the moral and political consequences of the population threat – a move captured in the new subtitle, which stressed 'the future removal or mitigation of the evils' arising from that threat. In promoting moral restraint as the preferred response, Malthus was expanding on his earlier treatment of preventive checks that entailed prudence and foresight while at the same time divesting prudence of any vicious connotations. *Moral* restraint was strictly defined (see p. 23 n.4 below) as marriage delayed until a family could be supported, while observing strict sexual continence during the waiting period. The restraint would show itself in a rise in the average age of marriage, and hence in a reduction in the period of female fecundity. But Malthus was opposed to what might seem an equally effective remedy: the use of contraception within marriage. He believed that the widespread use of birth control, if that ever occurred, would encourage indolence. National and world population would fail to 'reach its natural and proper extent' (see p. 369 below). In short, birth control within marriage was contrary to God's beneficent design because it removed a stimulus to industry.

Here then was the source of that narrow but deep rift which separated Malthus from many later supporters of his diagnosis of mass poverty – those called neo-Malthusians – for whom artificial methods of contraception within marriage offered a means of removing population pressure from the list of barriers to social progress. As the example of John Stuart Mill illustrates, neo-Malthusians could be more welcoming to socialistic experimentation than Malthus ever found it possible to be. Malthus's acceptance of the idea of a divine plan also resolves what might otherwise be a paradox: how he could, on the one hand, be the leading opponent of attitudes and policies that favoured population growth, and yet at the same time express fears that remedies such as birth control, if effective, would run the risk of removing an essential stimulant to progress.

III

Striking a balance between negative and positive forces, defining the golden mean in both private and public conduct, characterizes much of Malthus's thinking as a political moralist. The population principle served a negative polemical purpose – more prominent in the first edition of the *Essay* – in denying that Godwin's (in some ways) appealing vision of an alternative society based on reason, sincerity, mutual benevolence, and common ownership of property (including spouses) could ever be established permanently. More positively, Malthus asserted that in order to mitigate the problems created by the inevitable resurgence of scarcity, vice, and misery in Godwin's ideal future state, it would be necessary to reinvent precisely those institutions of private property, marriage laws, and reliance on the system of personal rewards and penalties which Godwin had hoped would disappear. In this respect, while acknowledging that the status quo contained serious imperfections and injustices that ought to be redressed, Malthus was advancing a powerful defence of the most basic features of existing society. Any objective inquiry, he was asserting, would conclude that a 'society divided into a class of proprietors and a class of labourers, and with self-love for the mainspring of the great machine' (see p. 67 below) was an inescapable fact of social existence.

Malthus was, of course, criticizing Godwin for failing to see that self-interest was the only motive capable of inspiring action on the part of the mass of society, and hence for failing to recognize that his portrait of a society based purely on universal benevolence was unrealizable. But Malthus was also standing Godwin's entire moral psychology, based on the possibilities of making unalloyed reason the sole basis for future conduct, on its head. Godwin had maintained that mind would gain hegemony over matter; that the pleasures of the intellect would overcome those associated with the body; and that the disinterested pursuit of communal welfare would replace self-regarding pursuits. Malthus countered by arguing that mind was neither separate from matter nor were its pleasures inherently superior to those arising from material pursuits. Since all passions, including the passion between the sexes, had been implanted as part of the divine plan, their pursuit must be presumed as beneficial to individual and social welfare. Any dangers arose from lack of moderation in indulging the passions rather than from their existence. The close connections between intellectual and corporeal pleasures implied that actions based on conviction could never be a matter of rationality alone, divorced from actual feeling and experience – where the experience could be pleasant, as in the case of sex and conjugal affection, or painful, as in the case of punishment for crime or any other excess. Pain and evil could be reduced but not abolished. Neither reason nor institutions were capable of controlling all the results of the passions.

On this fundamental issue in moral philosophy, though not on other questions, Malthus followed the brand of theological utilitarianism patented by William Paley in his highly successful Cambridge textbook on the *Principles of Moral and Political Philosophy* (1785), believing that God had designed a world in which pleasure/pain was the reward/penalty attached to actions that were most conducive/detrimental to our happiness. The rules that should guide the conduct of individuals could also be applied as the criterion for judging legislation and social outcomes, namely that the happiness of the community should be maximized and/or the sum of misery and vice minimized. The task of the practical moralist was to draw attention to the lessons of experience and suggest realistic solutions based on an assessment of human nature and the costs and benefits of different courses of action. A balance between vice and virtue, and sometimes between the lesser of two vices, would often have to be struck, with the added complication that short-term gains or losses had to be set against expected long-term results.

The Malthusian version of this moral calculus can be illustrated by considering his arguments for moral restraint and against those influences or competing remedies that worked against its acceptance. Moral restraint was clearly the remedy intended by a beneficent deity as the optimal solution to the population dilemma: it maximized happiness and virtue and minimized misery and vice. While such an argument met the requirements of theodicy, of a system for explaining and justifying the ways of God to man, the practical moralist had to go beyond theodicy to address the likely results of partial recourse to this solution in an imperfect world. The private and social benefits derived from delaying marriage until a family could be supported accrued under various headings: the reduction of excessive toil, indigence, irregularity of employment, crime, and vicious practices, together with higher wages and lower mortality rates. Against this had to be set the costs of any additional vice associated with a later age of marriage, chiefly in the form of male promiscuity and female prostitution. But sexual vices had no special status: they took their place in the moral scale alongside other sources of misery, one of the most important of which, in Malthus's opinion, was that associated with high rates of pre-adolescent mortality.

Malthus believed that moral restraint was adapted to man as he is rather than how he ought to be or might be. With some re-education to overcome long-established prejudices in favour of early marriage and the supposed public benefits of large and rising populations, he maintained that moral restraint was within the grasp of ordinary understanding; that it did not require heroic forms of self-denial and rational foresight into distant consequences; and that its benefits did not depend on immediate and universal acceptance. All those who adopted the solution would gain, 'whatever may be the number of others who fail' (see p. 226 below). Clearly, however, the social benefits would be greater if education and personal responsibility were more widespread, and if the influence of those institutions which undermined individual prudence was removed. Chief among these institutions, in Malthus's opinion, was the English Poor Law, which attempted to guarantee a minimum level of subsistence to all those whose incomes fell short of what was necessary to support them and their families. Malthus's case against this system of legal relief was that, as a matter of principle and fact, the promise embodied in the right to subsistence had not been and could not be delivered. The effect of redistributing money income from rich to poor under conditions of acute food scarcity was simply to raise prices and spread the burden from the very poor to the poor. Attempts to raise money wages in line with the price of food had the same effect, at the greater cost of increasing unemployment. The long-term result of the Poor Law, therefore, was to encourage population without increasing the food supply, thereby raising prices, lowering real wages and spreading the disease of dependent poverty to a larger section of the lower classes. Although Malthus later acknowledged that the facts did not bear out his contention that the Poor Law encouraged early marriage and raised birth rates, he claimed that the experience of administering the system during and after the Napoleonic wars amply supported his diagnosis and long-term remedy, gradual withdrawal of the right of support.

What is equally characteristic of Malthus, however, is the way in which he consistently combined the long-term case for abolition with recognition that, along with such remedies as employment on public works, the Poor Law could be defended for its short-term benefits. He hoped that abolition would be accompanied by an increase in less regular and systematic forms of private philanthropy capable of discriminating between the idle and the industrious, and seeking to support only those who had fallen into pauperism for reasons beyond their control. Realizing that such a reform represented a major change in English provision and expectations, Malthus proposed that it should be attempted only when the process of re-education had gone further than any signs revealed that it had done so far. This was one reason why Malthus became an enthusiastic advocate of a national system of education for the lower or, as he later increasingly called them, the labouring classes. It would acquaint them with the true causes of their condition, and thereby reduce the chances of their supporting some of the more radical and revolutionary schemes that were afoot. It would encourage personal responsibility and aid the diffusion of 'personal respectability' previously associated only with the middle classes. Without education, in fact, it would be impossible to achieve another of Malthus's aims, the extension of civil and political liberty to the unpropertied in Britain.

IV

Controversial authors attract bold denunciations, inaccurate labels, and considerable misunderstanding. Malthus has suffered all of these. Despite his efforts to respond to new evidence and tone down or remove passages that had given offence (see especially the famous excision on p. 249 below), the replies to his critics published in the Appendices he added in 1806 and 1817 show that he had good reason to complain about being both misunderstood and misrepresented – in some cases, deliberately. To a large extent this has continued to be his fate, opening up a sizeable gap between his reputation and the intentions expressed in his writings. On the evidence of the *Essay*, then, how should Malthus be characterized and regarded as a social and political thinker?

Well before his death, Malthus had firmly attached his name to the population principle as an explanation for general poverty. Despite the fact that few people would now accept the inevitability of the dilemma he posed, the reputation stands. On many of the wider issues he addressed as a political moralist, however, Malthus was often following in the footsteps of earlier generations of moral philosophers and political economists and applying established perspectives to new problems. For example, Malthus was adopting the views of David Hume and Adam Smith when he held that the diffusion of commerce and manufacturing in Europe, a process that had gone furthest in Britain, had undermined the stagnation and servility of feudal society and created legal and political conditions favourable to economic growth, upward social mobility, and the diffusion of civil and political liberties. In his earliest response to Godwin, Malthus had called on Smith's analysis of self-interested behaviour, market exchange, and capital accumulation to show that the system of natural liberty provided the best means of dividing the labour and distributing the incomes of society non-coercively, without direct government intervention or unacceptable forms of paternal dependence.

Neither Smith nor Malthus treated the resulting distribution of efforts and rewards as equitable, but the system was prized for its role in creating and maintaining a large measure of personal independence and liberty of conscience and action. Challenged by the radical egalitarianism released by the French revolution, as well as by periodic unrest in Britain, Malthus gave a more forthright defence of the *necessary* connections between inequality, prosperity, and liberty than anything that can be found in the *Wealth of Nations*. He opposed all schemes based on common property, communal provision, and compulsory social insurance that held out a promise of equal security and plenty for all, regardless of merit or effort. He defended all solutions that were voluntary and adapted to individual circumstances – from moral restraint to savings banks. Egalitarian schemes, such as those put forward by Robert Owen or Thomas Spence, exacerbated the population problem and provided no incentive to exercise personal responsibility through moral restraint. Where no effective or virtuous means of controlling population growth existed, restraint would have to be imposed from above by means of a general law, the enforcement of which would entail arbitrary infringements of liberty. Malthus was advancing a more overtly Christian version of the self-interest model, in which Smith's emphasis on the pervasive desire for personal betterment was counterbalanced by the fear of falling in the social scale. Inequality supplied the rewards *and* penalties, the 'goad of necessity' as well as the positive incentives, that were needed to sustain the advance of civilization.

One could also say that Malthus put forward a more overtly Newtonian model to deal with the pressure of population on food production under conditions of diminishing returns. He demonstrated that a social and economic system based on individual property and operating through competitive markets was the only one capable of guaranteeing the production of a surplus over basic needs and raising living standards. On this topic Malthus accomplished something Smith had not felt obliged to do, namely to prove that this type of society would provide an *optimal* solution to the population dilemma by preventing production from going beyond what was economically sustainable, even when this solution fell short of the maximum level of output that was physically possible. Much of Malthus's *Essay* can be read, negatively, as a statement of the impossibility of constructing remedies for poverty that ignore market forces, or, positively, as an assertion of the capacity of the market to maintain an optimal relationship between population and resources through time.

But if a basic commitment to the wisdom of following the invisible hand in economic matters is the hallmark of an orthodox political economist, there is much in Malthus that raises doubts about his rights to membership of this club. As noted already, on at least one major policy question, the Corn Laws, Malthus rejected Smith's economic logic as well as that of his friend and fellow economist, David Ricardo. Several of the chapters in Book III of the *Essay* on agricultural and commercial systems reached their final form only in 1817, after Malthus had published pamphlets revealing his support for agricultural protection. But they began life in 1798 as a pair of chapters in the first *Essay* questioning Smith's correctness in maintaining that economic growth was invariably associated with improvements in the standard of living of the labouring classes when capital accumulation was concentrated in manufacturing as opposed to agriculture. At that time Malthus declared himself not to be 'a very determined friend' to the unstable and 'unwholesome' growth of urban manufacturing employments, suggesting that if economic growth assumed this shape higher per capita incomes were being bought at too high a price. The chapters that eventually appeared in the 1817 and 1826 editions were originally conceived as a separate treatise: they contain Malthus's speculations (and anxieties) about the unbalanced course on which the British economy was embarked under the artificial stimulus of war. They constitute, therefore, a short treatise along comparative-historical lines on the relative merits of dependence on agriculture, commerce and manufacturing, where the problems facing what is described there as a 'large landed nation' are those of Britain. Malthus became friendlier to manufacturing over time, chiefly because he came to see the spread of conveniences and luxuries to the labouring classes as an incentive system that supported moral restraint. Nevertheless, he continued to believe that it was imprudent for a country in Britain's situation to forsake the security and stability that came with being able to meet the chief food needs of her population from domestic sources. The Newtonian in Malthus was querying once more whether an optimum point was in danger of being passed.

This was not the only topic on which Malthus found himself at odds with the new orthodoxy that was forming around Ricardo's ideas, though the evidence for this is better displayed in his correspondence and his *Principles of Political Economy* (1820) than in the *Essay*. Compared with other political economists, Malthus was less confident about the self-adjusting properties of markets and more attentive to the ways in which cycles and other irregular forces created short-term disturbance, unemployment, and, possibly, long-term stagnation. It was this aspect of Malthus that led John Maynard Keynes, writing in the light of his own preoccupation with finding an explanation for unemployment in the 1930s, to regret the way in which Ricardian presumptions had defeated Malthusian ones on this question.

When Malthus proposed, as a remedy for post-Napoleonic-war depression, that effective demand could be sustained through the unproductive expenditure of those in receipt of rental incomes, it confirmed the hostile opinion of those who already suspected him of excessive tenderness towards the land-owning interests in parliament. Along with his clerical status, it helped to lay the groundwork for a set of ideological charges, later codified by Karl Marx and his followers, to the effect that Malthus had aligned himself with the anti-progressive historical forces that opposed the revolutionary potential of the emerging capitalist system, while maintaining that the best any alternative economic systems could do would be to redistribute human misery. Once more, as in the case of his early opposition to Godwin and Condorcet, Malthus's affiliations were made to seem conservative and counter-revolutionary. But does this do justice to his political opinions and other intellectual allegiances?

Malthus did not share the radical political opinions on parliamentary reform of Ricardo and his mentor in these matters, James Mill. But neither was Malthus a Burkean or anti-jacobin on political rights and constitutional reform. He remained a moderate Whig who deplored the way in which the war with France, acting in conjunction with misguided popular agitation, had become the pretext for curtailing civil liberties in Britain. The two chapters on this subject in the *Essay* (pp. 243–58 below) are written in a mood of regret that war and the threat to public order had forced those, like himself, who occupied the middle position to defend government rather than engage in the more natural pursuit of pressing for the reform of constitutional defects and keeping a close watch on executive encroachment.

The biographical evidence suggests that Malthus was temperamentally averse to controversy and opposed to extremes on all matters. Such caution and moderation could be the clue to his opposition to radicalism and utopianism, though the position also has deeper intellectual roots. These consist of a combination of the consequentialism of the utilitarian view of morals with a predilection for Newtonian analogies based on mathematics, ballistics, weights, springs, and countervailing forces. When social problems are posed as being analogous to those of the infinitesimal calculus, the choices involved in maximization or minimization become ones of balancing opposed forces, of marginal rather than all-or-nothing adjustments. In this respect, Malthus's *Essay* can be read as an applied treatise on the proper methods of reasoning in the moral or social sciences, with examples being drawn from the abundant literature on remedies for poverty to illustrate popular fallacies and erroneous inferences. As will be clear from the chapter devoted to showing why theories or general principles are essential if the fallacy of composition is to be avoided (pp. 312–24 below), Malthus's caution was not based on reverence for facts in themselves. His penchant for Newtonian analogies sometimes takes elaborate forms, as when he speaks of 'the different velocities . . . of projectiles passing through resisting media', where the principles adopted by the natural philosopher to explain such problems are treated as being equally applicable to moral and political philosophy (see p. 374 below). But Malthus's meaning and tone are just as readily captured in more homely models involving putting the hare of population growth to sleep in order to allow the tortoise of food production to pass it (see p. 230 below), or in appeals to common sense that affirm there is 'no argument so frequently and obviously fallacious as that which infers that what is good to a certain extent is good to any extent' (see p. 174 below).

Like so much else in the *Essay*, Malthus's belief that Newton's methods were applicable to the moral or social sciences proclaims his close relationship with the broader phenomenon known as the Enlightenment. Neither his clerical allegiances nor his opposition to one style of thinking that we rightly associate with radical, usually French, versions of the Enlightenment – the positivist vision of social reconstruction through the application of science to human affairs – alter this affinity. His religious beliefs were not primarily directed at preaching docility and resignation: evils remained such, whatever part they played in the larger divine scheme. On the central issues raised by Godwin and Condorcet and kept before the public eye by Paine, Owen, and each successive generation of radical reformers – the role of human institutions in generating improvement – Malthus had reached the conclusion in 1806 that: 'Though government has but little power in the direct and immediate relief of poverty, yet its indirect influence on the prosperity of its subjects is striking and incontestable' (see p. 252 below). Like the benefits derived from a wider diffusion of luxuries, equal laws and a voice in framing them were part of the process of enhancing dignity and respectability that was essential to improvement.

Malthus thought of himself as having helped to restore the 'rational expectations' that had been usurped by 'the late wild speculations' provoked by the French revolution (see pp. 325 and 331 below). Prudential checks were gradually replacing positive ones, and might later be replaced by wider recourse to moral restraint. Some progress had been made towards making mortality rates, particularly among the young, a sounder guide to the state of the nation than rising numbers alone. If the tortoise of food production overtook the hare of population growth, Malthus could envisage a state in which increasing population would be compatible with rising standards of living for all. Life's lottery would contain 'fewer blanks and more prizes' (see p. 323 below), and those who fell into a state of poverty would do so for reasons that it was impossible to control in advance. Malthus described this vision as 'very cautious', but 'far from being entirely disheartening' (see pp. 328 and 331 below). It was not, perhaps, a noble or inspiriting vision – more decent than heroic. But it does not deserve the epithet that is still repeatedly applied to it – grim – and there is, of course, no reason to think that Malthus was any less humane than those who have professed larger goals.

Acknowledgements and notes on the text

The text on which this selection and edition are based is taken from the variorum of the *Essay* prepared by Patricia James for the Royal Economic Society, and published by Cambridge University Press in two volumes in 1990. This variorum takes the 1803 edition as its base text and records the changes, additions, and deletions that were made in the 1806, 1807, 1817, and 1826 editions. It also records the incorporation of material from the first *Essay* (1798) – indicated by an asterisk at the beginning and end of the passages. The page references to this work refer to the original edition: see the facsimile version published by Macmillan for the Royal Economic Society and entitled *First Essay on Population, 1798*, London, 1966. Black dots are used to show passages that were excised or substantially rewritten.

The editor's comments in the footnotes are preceded by a parenthesis and the editorial voice in all notes is that of Patricia James, with whom – before her untimely death in 1987 – this edition was originally planned as a collaborative enterprise. In addition to the apparatus included here, the full James edition identifies all of the authorities cited by Malthus in the text.

As an indication of the scope of the work from which the selections have been made, a complete list of the chapters in the 1826 edition is given in the contents pages. As will be clear from this, the material omitted consists largely of the illustrative historical, anthropological, and statistical material in Books I and II.

While my debts to Patricia James's edition of the text will be obvious to any reader, those to the friends who made encouraging and useful comments on my introduction are known only to me. Accordingly, I should like to express my thanks to John Burrow, Stefan Collini, and Quentin Skinner for their help.

Principal events in the life of Robert Malthus

1766 Born at The Rookery, Wooton, Surrey, 13 February. Seventh child and second son of Daniel Malthus.

1782–4 Educated by Gilbert Wakefield at the Dissenting Academy at Warrington and later at Wakefield's home in Bramcote, Nottinghamshire.

1784–8 Undergraduate at Jesus College, Cambridge, where he graduated as Ninth Wrangler in the Mathematics Tripos.

1789 Ordained as Deacon and appointed curate of Okewood, near his parent's home in Surrey.

1793 Appointed Fellow of Jesus College.

1796 Wrote 'The Crisis, a View of the Present Interesting State of Great Britain, by a Friend to the Constitution' (unpublished).

1798 First *Essay on Population* published anonymously.

1799 Travel in Norway, Sweden, and Germany with friends, also collecting additional material on population.

1800 Published *An Investigation of the Causes of the High Price of Provisions.*

1803 Second and much enlarged edition of *Essay on Population.* Appointed Rector of Walesby, Lincolnshire, a living which he retained throughout his life, paying a curate to carry out the duties.

1804 Married Harriet Eckersall: first of their three children born.

1805 Appointed first Professor of General History, Politics, Commerce and Finance at East India College, Haileybury, an establishment designed to train civil servants prior to service in India.

1807 Published *A Letter to Samuel Whitbread* criticizing Whitbread's proposals for the Poor Law.

1811   Beginning of correspondence and friendship with David Ricardo.

1814   Published *Observations on the Effects of the Corn Laws*, in which he adopted an impartial approach to the merits of free trade and protection.

1815   Published *An Inquiry into the Nature and Progress of Rent* and *The Grounds of an Opinion on the Policy of Restricting the Importation of Foreign Corn*, the latter expressing a 'deliberate, yet decided opinion' in favour of import restrictions.

1820   Published *Principles of Political Economy Considered with a View to their Practical Application*, a work partly designed to embody the conclusions he had reached as a result of teaching political economy at Haileybury, and partly to answer David Ricardo's *Principles*.

1823   Published *The Measure of Value Stated and Illustrated* and the article on 'Population' for *Encyclopaedia Britannica*, later re-issued as *A Summary View of the Principle of Population* (1830).

1826   Published sixth and final edition of *Essay on Population*.

1827   Published *Definitions in Political Economy*.

1834   Founder member of London Statistical Society.

1834   Died 29 December, buried in Bath Abbey.

Biographical notes

These notes deal with the principal authors and works mentioned by Malthus in this edition. For fuller notes on all Malthus's sources the reader should consult Patricia James's edition of the *Essay*, volume II, pp. 253–357. The dates appended to the titles of works refer to the first and last date of publication during Malthus's lifetime.

CONDORCET, Jean-Antoine-Nicholas Caritat, Marquis de (1743–94), *philosophe*, mathematician and supporter of the French revolution who became one of its victims after writing the *Esquisse d'un tableau historique des progrès de l'esprit humain* (1795), one of the works criticized by Malthus in the first and all subsequent editions of the *Essay*. Condorcet figures here as a believer in organic perfectibility, the author of proposals for a form of social insurance fund, and as an advocate of what Malthus regarded as 'unnatural' methods of birth control. See p. 23 n. 4 and p. 368 below.

EDEN, Sir Frederick Morton (1766–1809), author of *The State of the Poor* (1797), a major study of the incidence of poverty. Malthus also cites the estimates of the ratio of deaths to total population in Eden's *An Estimate of the Number of Inhabitants in Great Britain and Ireland* (1800).

FRANKLIN, Benjamin (1706–90), American philosopher, scientist, and politician, whose *Political, Miscellaneous and Philosophical Pieces* (1779) contains the 'Observations Concerning the Increase of Mankind' cited by Malthus. Franklin was also responsible for the estimate of American population growth which plays an important role in Malthus's belief that the doubling of population over a period of twenty to twenty-five years represents the maximum rate at which population could grow under the most favourable of circumstances.

GODWIN, William (1756–1836). Author of the *Enquiry Concerning Political Justice* (1793–7), a work that was at the height of its popularity in radical circles when Malthus responded to it in the first edition of the *Essay* – though it was an essay 'Of Avarice and Profusion' in Godwin's *The Enquirer* (1797) that was the proximate source of Malthus's friendly quarrel with his father. After meeting and corresponding with Malthus, Godwin replied in his *Thoughts Occasioned by Dr. Parr's Spital Sermon* (1801). He endorsed Malthus's theory and findings on population, but rejected their implications for the future. Malthus replied to this work (see Book III, Chapter iii (a) below), but dropped the chapter in 1817. Godwin responded to this slight by retracting all his earlier concessions and by mounting a bitter attack on Malthus entitled *Of Population* (1820): see Malthus's curt dismissal of this work on p. 387 below.

HUME, David (1711–76). Philosopher and historian, whose political essays are cited in the *Essay*, especially the essays on the populousness of ancient nations, and on whether the British government inclines more to absolute monarchy or to a republic. Malthus accepts Hume's position on the 'euthanasia' of the British constitution in absolute monarchy, and his views on the indispensability of theory in politics. He rejects Hume's view that only indolence stands between man and a perfect future. Malthus also cites Hume's controversial *Dialogues on Natural Religion* (1779).

MONTESQUIEU, Charles-Louis de Secondat, Baron de (1689–1755). French philosopher and political scientist, all of whose chief works (*Spirit of the Laws* (1748), *Persian Letters* (1721), and *Considerations on the Causes of the Greatness of the Romans and their Decline* (1734)) are cited by Malthus.

OWEN, Robert (1771–1858). A philanthropic industrialist who had pioneered a new form of factory organization in his cotton mills at New Lanark. Malthus supported Owen's campaign for reducing the hours of work of children in factories, but criticized Owen's ideas on equality and his scheme for creating pauper communities based on common property as outlined in Owen's *A New View of Society* (1816). See pp. 75–80 below.

PALEY, William (1743–1805), theologian. The author of *Principles of Moral and Political Philosophy* (1785), a highly successful textbook that remained in use at Cambridge until the 1840s. Malthus subscribed to

Paley's basic theological utilitarianism – the doctrine that public happiness, being the object of God's beneficent design, was the ultimate test of moral obligation and any scheme of social improvement. Paley in turn announced his conversion to Malthus's view of population in *Natural Theology* (1802), another work cited by Malthus. On the subject of the dangers of the diffusion of luxury among the populace at large, however, Malthus differed from Paley (see p. 321 below).

PRICE, Richard (1723–91). A dissenting minister and moral philosopher, chiefly known for the support he gave to both the American and French revolutions, and hence, in the latter case, for provoking Edmund Burke's *Reflections on the Revolution in France* (1790). Malthus refers to Price's estimates of declining British population in *Observations on Reversionary Payments* (1771–92).

SMITH, Adam (1723–90). Moral philosopher and political economist. The author of *An Inquiry into the Nature and Causes of the Wealth of Nations* (1776–84) and the advocate of the 'system of natural liberty' with which Malthus was in general agreement and on which he based most of his teaching at Haileybury. From the first *Essay* onward, however, Malthus expressed misgivings about Smith's identification of capital accumulation with improvements in the happiness of the mass of society. He also departed from Smith's principles on the subject of the Corn Laws. There is no reference to Smith's other work as a moral philosopher, the *Theory of Moral Sentiments* (1759–90), perhaps because Malthus followed Paley's utilitarianism on morals and politics.

STEUART, Sir James (1712–80). The author of *An Inquiry into the Principles of Political Oeconomy* (1767), a work that Malthus acknowledges for its treatment of population, while criticizing Steuart's policy conclusions.

SUMNER, John Bird (1780–1862), future Archbishop of Canterbury and the author of *A Treatise on the Records of the Creation, and on the Moral Attributes of the Creator; with particular Reference to the Jewish History and to the Consistency of the Principle of Population with the Wisdom and Goodness of the Deity*, 1816. Malthus endorsed this work (p. 76 n. 5), which became influential in making Malthusianism part of official Anglican doctrine.

TOWNSEND, Joseph (1739–1816), an Anglican clergyman whose *Journey through Spain* (1791) is cited by Malthus as well as his *Dissertation on the*

Poor Laws (1817). Malthus disapproved of Townsend's proposal for compulsory savings schemes as a remedy for pauperism.

WALLACE, Robert (1697–1771). Malthus acknowledged Wallace as a precursor on the principle of population and was often accused of plagiarizing Wallace's *Various Prospects of Mankind* (1761) – a work in which Wallace predicted that a society based on common property would eventually perish through its inability to control population growth. Malthus differed from Wallace in believing that population pressure was constantly at work rather than something that could be postponed (see pp. 45–6 below).

YOUNG, Arthur (1741–1820). Secretary to the Board of Agriculture and the best-known authority on agrarian questions as a result of his *Tour of Ireland* (1780) and his *Travels in France* (1787–90). Malthus cites the latter, but was critical of Young's proposals for dealing with pauperism by means of the distribution of land and the cow system, a form of peasant proprietorship. Events in Ireland in the 1840s confirm Malthus's criticisms.

Guide to further reading

The standard biography is Patricia James, *Population Malthus; His Life and Times*, London: Routledge and Kegan Paul, 1979. This includes many letters, though for the important correspondence Malthus conducted with David Ricardo it is necessary to consult *The Works and Correspondence of David Ricardo*, edited by Piero Sraffa with the assistance of Maurice Dobb for the Royal Economic Society, Cambridge University Press, 1952–73. Another useful biographical source is Patricia James's edition of *The Travel Diaries of Robert Malthus*, Cambridge University Press, 1966.

An eight-volume complete edition of *The Works of Thomas Robert Malthus*, edited by E. A. Wrigley and David Souden, was published by Pickering and Chatto in 1986. This edition has a valuable editorial introduction and useful bibliographies in volume I. Variorum editions of Malthus's two main works, also with valuable introductions, were published by Cambridge University Press for the Royal Economic Society in 1990: the *Essay on Population* was edited by Patricia James and the *Principles of Political Economy* by John Pullen, who also compiled excellent indexes to both of these works.

The secondary literature on Malthus now tends to separate according to the modern academic division of labour, namely between works concentrating on his demographic ideas and those dealing with his political economy. The historical background and demographic inheritance figure largely in three useful collections of articles: J. Dupaquier, A. Fauve-Chamoux, and E. Grebenik (eds), *Malthus, Past and Present*, London: Academic Press, 1983; Michael Turner (ed), *Malthus and His Time*, New York: St Martin's Press, 1986; and David Coleman and

Roger Schofield (eds), *The State of Population Theory; Forward from Malthus*, Oxford: Blackwells, 1986.

Among the best of the recent general work on Malthus's political economy is that by D. P. O'Brien in his *The Classical Economists*, Oxford: Clarendon Press, 1975 and by Walter Eltis in his *The Classical Theory of Economic Growth*, London: Macmillan, 1984. For John Maynard Keynes's essay on Malthus see *Essays in Biography* in *The Collected Writings of John Maynard Keynes*, London: Macmillan for the Royal Economic Society, 1972, volume VIII. Some of the best detailed work on Malthus as an economic thinker can be found in the journal entitled *History of Political Economy* (*HOPE*). As an illustration of research that has altered our view by showing how Malthus's opinions on the subject of manufacturing evolved see Geoffrey Gilbert, 'Economic Growth and the Poor in Malthus's *Essay on Population*', *HOPE*, XII, 1980, pp. 83–96. For a short book that attempts to bridge the demography/political economy division by stressing Malthus's work as a political moralist see Donald Winch, *Malthus*, Oxford: Past Master, 1987.

Some of the most interesting work on Malthus has been written by those interested in specific topics in intellectual history or the history of social institutions and policies. On the Poor Laws, the best detailed survey is still J. R. Poynter's *Society and Pauperism: English Ideas on Poor Relief, 1795–1834*, London: Routledge, 1969; but see also the articles by Ann Digby and J. P. Huzel in Turner (ed), *Malthus and His Time*. Malthus's continuing capacity to attract unsympathetic treatment from both ends of the political spectrum is illustrated by Gertrude Himmelfarb, *The Idea of Poverty*, New York: Alfred Knopf, 1984 and Mitchell Dean, *The Constitution of Poverty*, London: Routledge, 1991.

Malthus's theology has given rise to an interesting literature: see J. M. Pullen, 'Malthus's Theological Ideas and their Influence on his Principle of Population', *HOPE*, XIII, 1981, pp. 39–54; and E. N. Santurri, 'Theodicy and Social Policy in Malthus's Thought', *Journal of the History of Ideas*, XLII, 1982, pp. 315–30; and A. M. C. Waterman, *Revolution, Economics and Religion; Christian Political Economy, 1793–1833*, Cambridge University Press, 1991.

On Malthus and the Darwinian revolution see R. M. Young, 'Malthus and the Evolutionists', *Past and Present*, XCVIII, 1969, pp. 109–45; P. Vorzimmer, 'Darwin, Malthus and the Theory of Natural Selection', *Journal of the History of Ideas*, XXX, 1969, pp. 527–42; and

P. Bowler, 'Malthus, Darwin and the Concept of Struggle', *Journal of the History of Ideas*, XXXVII, 1976, pp. 631–50.

Surveys of the controversy aroused by Malthus during the nineteenth century are often marred by their partisanship: see for example K. Smith, *The Malthusian Controversy*, London: Routledge, 1951; and Harold A. Boner, *Hungry Generations: The Nineteenth-Century Case against Malthusianism*, New York: Columbia University Press, 1955. For a compendium of Marxian criticisms of Malthus see R. L. Meek (ed), *Marx and Engels on Malthus*, London: Lawrence, 1953.

AN ESSAY

ON THE

PRINCIPLE OF POPULATION;

OR,

A VIEW OF ITS PAST AND PRESENT EFFECTS

ON

HUMAN HAPPINESS;

WITH AN INQUIRY INTO OUR PROSPECTS RESPECTING THE FUTURE
REMOVAL OR MITIGATION OF THE EVILS WHICH IT OCCASIONS.

A NEW EDITION, VERY MUCH ENLARGED.

By T. R. MALTHUS, A.M.

FELLOW OF JESUS COLLEGE, CAMBRIDGE.

LONDON:

PRINTED FOR J. JOHNSON, IN ST. PAUL'S CHURCH-YARD,

BY T. BENSLEY, HOLT COURT, FLEET STREET.

1803.

Contents

3

Contents

Book IV

Of our future Prospects respecting the Removal or Mitigation of
the Evils arising from the Principle of Population

Preface

The Essay on the Principle of Population, which I published in 1798, was suggested, as is expressed in the preface, by a paper in Mr. Godwin's Inquirer. It was written on the spur of the occasion, and from the few materials which were within my reach in a country situation.[1] The only authors from whose writings I had deduced the principle, which formed the main argument of the essay, were Hume, Wallace, Dr. Adam Smith, and Dr. Price; and my object was to apply it to try the truth of those speculations on the perfectibility of man and society, which at that time excited a considerable portion of the public attention.

In the course of the discussion, I was naturally led into some examination of the effects of this principle on the existing state of society. It appeared to account for much of that poverty and misery observable among the lower classes of people in every nation, and for those reiterated failures in the efforts of the higher classes to relieve them. The more I considered the subject in this point of view, the more importance it seemed to acquire; and this consideration, joined to the degree of public attention which the essay excited, determined me to turn my leisure reading towards an historical examination of the effects of the principle of population on the past and present state of society; that, by illustrating the subject more generally, and drawing those inferences from it, in application to the actual state of things which experience seemed to warrant, I might give it a more practical and permanent interest.

In the course of this inquiry I found that much more had been done

---

[1] [This PREFACE of 1803 was reprinted in all subsequent editions, but from 1806 onwards the word *spur* was replaced by 'impulse', and Malthus wrote of
... the few materials which were then within my reach ...

than I had been aware of, when I first published the essay. The poverty and misery arising from a too rapid increase of population had been distinctly seen, and the most violent remedies proposed, so long ago as the times of Plato and Aristotle. And of late years the subject had been treated in such a manner by some of the French Economists, occasionally by Montesquieu, and, among our own writers, by Dr. Franklin, Sir James Steuart, Mr. Arthur Young, and Mr. Townsend, as to create a natural surprise that it had not excited more of the public attention.

Much, however, remained yet to be done. Independently of the comparison between the increase of population and food, which had not perhaps been stated with sufficient force and precision, some of the most curious and interesting parts of the subject had been either wholly omitted or treated very slightly. Though it had been stated distinctly, that population must always be kept down to the level of the means of subsistence; yet few inquiries had been made into the various modes by which this level is effected; and the principle had never been sufficiently pursued to its consequences, and those practical inferences drawn from it, which a strict examination of its effects on society appears to suggest.

These are therefore the points which I have treated most in detail in the following essay. In its present shape it may be considered as a new work, and I should probably have published it as such, omitting the few parts of the former which I have retained, but that I wished it to form a whole of itself, and not to need a continual reference to the other. On this account, I trust that no apology is necessary to the purchasers of the first edition. [2]●I should hope that there are some parts of it, not reprinted in this, which may still have their use; as they were rejected, not because I thought them all of less value than what has been inserted, but because they did not suit the different plan of treating the subject which I had adopted.●[2]

To those who either understood the subject before, or saw it distinctly on the perusal of the first edition, I am fearful that I shall appear to have treated some parts of it too much in detail, and to have been guilty of unnecessary repetitions. These faults have arisen partly from want of skill, and partly from intention. In drawing similar inferences from the state of society in a number of different countries, I found it very difficult to avoid some repetitions; and in those parts of the inquiry which led to conclusions different from our usual habits of thinking, it

---

[2] [This sentence was omitted in 1806 and all subsequent editions.]

appeared to me that, with the slightest hope of producing conviction, it was necessary to present them to the reader's mind at different times and on different occasions. I was willing to sacrifice all pretensions to merit of composition to the chance of making an impression on a larger class of readers.

The main principle advanced is so incontrovertible that, if I had confined myself merely to general views, I could have entrenched myself in an impregnable fortress; and the work, in this form, would probably have had a much more masterly air. But such general views, though they may advance the cause of abstract truth, rarely tend to promote any practical good; and I thought that I should not do justice to the subject, and bring it fairly under discussion, if I refused to consider any of the consequences which appeared necessarily to flow from it, whatever these consequences might be. By pursuing this plan, however, I am aware that I have opened a door to many objections and, probably, to much severity of criticism: but I console myself with the reflection that even the errors into which I may have fallen, by affording a handle to argument, and an additional excitement to examination, may be subservient to the important end, of bringing a subject so nearly connected with the happiness of society into more general notice.

Throughout the whole of the present work, I have so far differed in principle from the former, as to suppose another check to population possible, which does not strictly come under the head either of vice or misery;[3] and, in the latter part, I have endeavoured to soften some of the harshest conclusions of the first essay. In doing this, I hope that I have not violated the principles of just reasoning, nor expressed any opinion respecting the probable improvement of society in which I am not borne out by the experience of the past. To those who shall still think that any check to population whatever would be worse than the evils which it would relieve, the conclusions of the former essay will remain in full force; and if we adopt this opinion, we shall be compelled to acknowledge that the poverty and misery which prevail among the lower classes of society are absolutely irremediable.

I have taken as much pains as I could to avoid any errors in the facts and calculations which have been produced in the course of the work.

[3] [In 1817 this was altered:

... as to suppose the action of another check to population which does not come under the head either of vice or misery ...

Should any of them nevertheless turn out to be false, the reader will see that they will not materially affect the general tenour of the reasoning.

From the crowd of materials which presented themselves in illustration of the first branch of the subject, I dare not flatter myself that I have selected the best, or arranged them in the most perspicuous method. To those who take an interest in moral and political questions, I hope that the novelty and importance of the subject will compensate the imperfections of its execution.

London, June 8th, 1803

Preface to the fifth edition[1]

This Essay was first published at a period of extensive warfare, combined, from peculiar circumstances, with a most prosperous foreign commerce.

It came before the public, therefore, at a time when there would be an extraordinary demand for men, and very little disposition to suppose the possibility of any evil arising from the redundancy of population. Its success, under these disadvantages, was greater than could have been reasonably expected; and it may be presumed that it will not lose its interest after a period of a different description has succeeded, which has in the most marked manner illustrated its principles, and confirmed its conclusions.

On account therefore of the nature of the subject, which it must be allowed is one of permanent interest, as well as of the attention likely to be directed to it in future, I am bound to correct those errors of my work, of which subsequent experience and information may have convinced me, and to make such additions and alterations as appear calculated to improve it and promote its utility.

It would have been easy to have added many further historical illustrations of the first part of the subject; but as I was unable to supply the want I once alluded to, of accounts of sufficient accuracy to ascertain what part of the natural power of increase each particular check destroys, it appeared to me that the conclusion, which I had before drawn from very ample evidence of the only kind that could be obtained, would hardly receive much additional force by the accumulation of more, precisely of the same description.

[1] [In 1817 this PREFACE was printed immediately after that of 1803, the ADVERTISEMENTS of 1806 and 1807 being omitted.]

In the two first books, therefore, the only additions are a new chapter on France, and one on England, chiefly in reference to facts which have occurred since the publication of the last edition.[2]

In the third book I have given an additional chapter on the Poor-Laws;[3] and as it appeared to me that the chapters on the Agricultural and Commercial Systems, and the Effects of increasing Wealth on the Poor, were not either so well arranged, or so immediately applicable to the main subject, as they ought to be; and as I further wished to make some alterations in the chapter on Bounties upon Exportation, and add something on the subject of Restrictions upon Importation, I have recast and rewritten the chapters which stand the 8th, 9th, 10th, 11th, 12th, 13th, in the present edition; and given a new title, and added two or three passages to the 14th, and last chapter of the same book.

In the fourth book, I have added a new chapter to the one entitled *Effects of the Knowledge of the principal Cause of Poverty on Civil Liberty*; and another to the chapter on *the different Plans of employing the Poor*; and I have made a considerable addition to the Appendix, in reply to some writers on the Principles of Population whose works have appeared since the last edition.

These are the principal additions and alterations made in the present edition. They consist in a considerable degree of the application of the general principles of the Essay to the present state of things.

For the accommodation of the purchasers of the former editions, these additions and alterations will be published in a separate volume.

East-India College, June 7th, 1817

[2] [Chapters ix and xi of Book II – not included in this edition.]
[3] [Chapter vii of Book III in this edition.]

ESSAY, &c

BOOK I

OF THE CHECKS TO POPULATION IN THE LESS CIVILIZED PARTS OF THE WORLD, AND IN PAST TIMES

CHAPTER I

Statement of the Subject. Ratios of the Increase of Population and Food

In an inquiry concerning the future improvement of society,[1] the mode of conducting the subject which naturally presents itself, is

1. An investigation of the causes that have hitherto impeded the progress of mankind towards happiness; and
2. An examination into the probability of the total or partial removal of these causes in future.

To enter fully into this question, and to enumerate all the causes that have hitherto influenced human improvement, would be much beyond the power of an individual. The principal object of the present essay is to examine the effects of one great cause intimately united with the very nature of man; which, though it has been constantly and powerfully operating since the commencement of society, has been little noticed by the writers who have treated this subject. The facts which establish the existence of this cause have, indeed, been repeatedly stated and acknowledged; but its natural and necessary effects have been almost totally overlooked; though probably among these effects may be reckoned a very considerable portion of that vice and misery, and of that unequal distribution of the bounties of nature, which it has been the unceasing object of the enlightened philanthropist in all ages to correct.

---

[1] [In 1806 Malthus altered this to:
In an inquiry concerning the improvement of society ...

The cause to which I allude is the constant tendency in all animated life to increase beyond the nourishment prepared for it.

It is observed by Dr. Franklin that there is no bound to the prolific nature of plants or animals but what is made by their crowding and interfering with each other's means of subsistence. Were the face of the earth, he says, vacant of other plants, it might be gradually sowed and overspread with one kind only; as, for instance, with fennel: and were it empty of other inhabitants, it might in a few ages be replenished from one nation only; as, for instance, with Englishmen.[2]

[3]*This is incontrovertibly true. Through the animal and vegetable kingdoms Nature has scattered the seeds of life abroad with the most profuse and liberal hand; but has been comparatively sparing in the room and the nourishment necessary to rear them. The germs of existence contained in this spot of earth, with ample food, and ample room to expand in, would fill millions of worlds in the course of a few thousand years. Necessity, that imperious all-pervading law of nature, restrains them within the prescribed bounds. The race of plants and the race of animals shrink under this great restrictive law; and the race of man cannot by any efforts of reason escape from it.*[3]

[4]*In plants and animals the view of the subject is simple. They are all impelled by a powerful instinct to the increase of their species; and this instinct is interrupted by no reasoning or doubts about providing for their offspring. Wherever, therefore, there is liberty, the power of increase is exerted; and the superabundant effects are repressed afterwards by want of room and nourishment, which is common to plants and animals; and among animals, by their becoming the prey of each other.*[4]

The effects of this check on man are more complicated. Impelled to the increase of his species by an equally powerful instinct, reason

---

[2] Franklin's Miscell. p. 9. [For full bibliographical details of this and all such references see Patricia James's edition published by Cambridge University Press for the Royal Economic Society in 1990.]

[3] [This paragraph is taken almost verbatim from p. 15 of the 1798 *Essay*, but in 1806 Malthus altered the third sentence:

The germs of existence contained in this earth, if they could freely develop themselves, would fill millions of worlds ...

[4] [This is from p. 27 of the 1798 *Essay*. However, in 1806 Malthus made three alterations; the paragraph then read:

In plants and irrational animals ... this instinct is interrupted by no doubts about providing for their offspring.
[The concluding words were:
... by want of room and nourishment.

interrupts his career, and asks him whether he may not bring beings into the world for whom he cannot provide the means of support. If he attend to this natural suggestion, the restriction too frequently produces vice. If he hear it not, the human race will be constantly endeavouring to increase beyond the means of subsistence. But as by that law of our nature which makes food necessary to the life of man, population can never actually increase beyond the lowest nourishment capable of supporting it; a strong check on population, from the difficulty of acquiring food, must be constantly in operation. This difficulty must fall somewhere, and must necessarily be severely felt in some or other of the various forms of misery, or the fear of misery, by a large portion of mankind.

That population has this constant tendency to increase beyond the means of subsistence, and that it is kept to its necessary level by these causes, will sufficiently appear from a review of the different states of society in which man has existed. But before we proceed to this review the subject will, perhaps, be seen in a clearer light if we endeavour to ascertain what would be the natural increase of population if left to exert itself with perfect freedom; and what might be expected to be the rate of increase in the productions of the earth under the most favourable circumstances of human industry. [5]●A comparison of these two rates of increase will enable us to judge of the force of that tendency in population to increase beyond the means of subsistence, which has been stated to exist.●[5]

[6]*It will be allowed, that no country has hitherto been known where the manners were so pure and simple, and the means of subsistence so abundant, that no check whatever has existed to early marriages from the difficulty of providing for a family, and that no waste of the human

---

[5] [This sentence was omitted in 1806.]

[6] [This sentence, and the two preceding paragraphs, are based on pp. 18–20 of the 1798 *Essay*.] [A footnote was added in 1806:

It appears from some recent calculations and estimates that, from the first settlement of America to the year 1800, the periods of doubling have been but very little above twenty years. See a note on the increase of American population in Book II, chap. xi [not included in this edition].

[At the same time Malthus considerably altered the actual text of the whole paragraph:

In the northern states of America ... the population has been found to double itself, for above a century and a half successively, in less than twenty-five years. Yet ... in some of the towns the deaths exceeded the births, a circumstance which clearly proves that, in those parts of the country which supplied this deficiency, the increase must have been much more rapid than the general average.

species has been occasioned by vicious customs, by towns, by unhealthy occupations, or too severe labour. Consequently in no state that we have yet known has the power of population been left to exert itself with perfect freedom.

Whether the law of marriage be instituted or not, the dictate of nature and virtue seems to be an early attachment to one woman; and where there were no impediments of any kind in the way of an union to which such an attachment would lead, and no causes of depopulation afterwards, the increase of the human species would be evidently much greater than any increase which has been hitherto known.

In the northern states of America, where the means of subsistence have been more ample, the manners of the people more pure, and the checks to early marriages fewer, than in any of the modern states of Europe, the population was found to double itself for some successive periods every twenty-five years.*[6] Yet even during these periods, in some of the towns, the deaths exceeded the births;[7] and they consequently required a continued supply from the country to support their population.

In the back settlements, where the sole employment was agriculture, and vicious customs and unwholesome occupations were unknown, the population was found to double itself in fifteen years.[8] Even this extraordinary rate of increase is probably short of the utmost power of population. Very severe labour is requisite to clear a fresh country; such situations are not in general considered as particularly healthy; and the inhabitants were probably occasionally subject to the incursions of the Indians, which might destroy some lives, or at any rate diminish the fruits of their industry.

According to a table of Euler, calculated on a mortality of 1 in 36, if the births be to the deaths in the proportion of 3 to 1, the period of doubling will be only $12\frac{4}{5}$ years.[9] And these proportions are not only possible suppositions, but have actually occurred for short periods in more countries than one.

[7] Price's Observ. on Revers. Pay. vol. i. p. 274.
[8] Ibid. p. 282. [In 1806 this sentence was changed:
    In the back settlements, where the sole employment is agriculture, and vicious customs and unwholesome occupations are little known, the population has been found to double itself ...
[The present tense was continued throughout the paragraph:
    ... probably are occasionally subject to the incursions of the Indians, which may destroy some lives ...
[9] See this table at the end of chap. iv, book ii [not included in this edition].

Sir William Petty supposes a doubling possible in so short a time as ten years.[10]

But to be perfectly sure that we are far within the truth, we will take the slowest of these rates of increase; a rate, in which all concurring testimonies agree, and which has been repeatedly ascertained to be from procreation only.

[11]*It may safely be pronounced therefore, that population when unchecked goes on doubling itself every twenty-five years, or increases in a geometrical ratio.*[11]

The rate according to which the productions of the earth may be supposed to increase, it will not be so easy to determine. Of this, however, we may be perfectly certain, that the ratio of their increase must be of a totally different nature from the ratio of the increase of population. A thousand millions are just as easily doubled every twenty-five years by the power of population as a thousand. But the food to support the increase from the greater number will by no means be obtained with the same facility. Man is necessarily confined in room. When acre has been added to acre till all the fertile land is occupied, the yearly increase of food must depend upon the amelioration of the land already in possession. This is a stream[12] which, from the nature of all soils, instead of increasing, must be gradually diminishing. But population, could it be supplied with food, would go on with unexhausted vigour; and the increase of one period would furnish the power of a greater increase the next, and this without any limit.

From the accounts we have of China and Japan, it may be fairly doubted whether the best-directed efforts of human industry could double the produce of these countries even once in any number of years. There are many parts of the globe, indeed, hitherto uncultivated, and almost unoccupied; but the right of exterminating, or driving into a corner where they must starve, even the inhabitants of these thinly-peopled regions, will be questioned in a moral view. The process of improving their minds and directing their industry would necessarily be slow; and during this time, as population would regularly keep pace with the increasing produce, it would rarely happen that a great degree of knowledge and industry would have to operate at once upon rich unappropriated soil. Even where this might take place, as it does sometimes in new colonies, a geometrical ratio increases with such

---

[10] Polit. Arith. p. 14.   [11] [This is on p. 21 of the 1798 *Essay*.]
[12] [In 1817 the word *stream* was replaced by 'fund'.]

extraordinary rapidity that the advantage could not last long. [13]●If America continue increasing, which she certainly will do, though not with the same rapidity as formerly, the Indians will be driven further and further back into the country, till the whole race is ultimately exterminated.●[13]

These observations are, in a degree, applicable to all the parts of the earth, where the soil is imperfectly cultivated. To exterminate the inhabitants of the greatest part of Asia and Africa is a thought that could not be admitted for a moment. To civilize and direct the industry of the various tribes of Tartars and Negroes would certainly be a work of considerable time, and of variable and uncertain success.

Europe is by no means so fully peopled as it might be. In Europe there is the fairest chance that human industry may receive its best direction. The science of agriculture has been much studied in England and Scotland; and there is still a great portion of uncultivated land in these countries. Let us consider at what rate the produce of this island might be supposed to increase under circumstances the most favourable to improvement.

[14]*If it be allowed, that by the best possible policy, and great encouragements to agriculture, the average produce of the island could be doubled in the first twenty-five years, it will be allowing probably a greater increase than could with reason be expected.

In the next twenty-five years, it is impossible to suppose that the produce could be quadrupled. It would be contrary to all our knowledge of the properties of land.*[14] The improvement of the barren parts would be a work of time and labour; and it must be evident to those who have the slightest acquaintance with agricultural subjects that, in proportion as cultivation extended, the additions that could yearly be made to the former average produce must be gradually and regularly diminishing. That we may be the better able to compare the increase of population and food, let us make a supposition which, without pretending to accuracy, is clearly more favourable to the power of production in the earth than any experience that we have had of its qualities will warrant.

---

[13] [This sentence was altered in 1817:

  If the United States of America continue increasing, which they certainly will do, though not with the same rapidity as formerly, the Indians will be driven further and further back into the country, till the whole race is ultimately exterminated, and the territory is incapable of further extension.

[14] [These two sentences and the preceding paragraph are from pp. 21–2 of the 1798 *Essay*.]

[15]*Let us suppose that the yearly additions which might be made to the former average produce, instead of decreasing, which they certainly would do, were to remain the same; and that the produce of this island might be increased every twenty-five years by a quantity equal to what it at present produces: the most enthusiastic speculator cannot suppose a greater increase than this. In a few centuries it would make every acre of land in the island like a garden.

If this supposition be applied to the whole earth, and if it be allowed that the subsistence for man which the earth affords might be increased every twenty-five years by a quantity equal to what it at present produces, this will be supposing a rate of increase much greater than we can imagine that any possible exertions of mankind could make it.

It may be fairly pronounced therefore, that, considering the present average state of the earth, the means of subsistence, under circumstances the most favourable to human industry, could not possibly be made to increase faster than in an arithmetical ratio.

The necessary effects of these two different rates of increase, when brought together, will be very striking. Let us call the population of this island eleven millions; and suppose the present produce equal to the easy support of such a number. In the first twenty-five years the population would be twenty-two millions, and the food being also doubled, the means of subsistence would be equal to this increase. In the next twenty-five years, the population would be forty-four millions, and the means of subsistence only equal to the support of thirty-three millions. In the next period the population would be eighty-eight millions, and the means of subsistence just equal to the support of half of that number. And at the conclusion of the first century, the population would be a hundred and seventy-six millions, and the means of subsistence only equal to the support of fifty-five millions; leaving a population of a hundred and twenty-one millions totally unprovided for.

Taking the whole earth instead of this island, emigration would of course be excluded; and supposing the present population equal to a thousand millions, the human species would increase as the numbers 1, 2, 4, 8, 16, 32, 64, 128, 256, and subsistence as 1, 2, 3, 4, 5, 6, 7, 8, 9. In two centuries the population would be to the means of subsistence as 256 to 9; in three centuries as 4096 to 13, and in two thousand years the difference would be almost incalculable.

[15] [The concluding paragraphs of this chapter are based on pp. 22–6 of the 1798 *Essay*.]

In this supposition no limits whatever are placed to the produce of the earth. It may increase for ever, and be greater than any assignable quantity; yet still the power of population being in every period so much superior, the increase of the human species can only be kept down to the level of the means of subsistence by the constant operation of the strong law of necessity acting as a check upon the greater power.*[15]

CHAPTER II

Of the general Checks to Population, and the Mode of their Operation

[From 1806 this chapter began thus:

The ultimate check to population appears then to be a want of food, arising necessarily from the different ratios according to which population and food increase. But this ultimate check is never the immediate check, except in cases of actual famine.

The immediate check may be stated to consist in all those customs, and all those diseases, which seem to be generated by a scarcity of the means of subsistence; and all those causes, independent of this scarcity, whether of a moral or physical nature, which tend prematurely to weaken and destroy the human frame.

These checks to population, which are constantly operating with more or less force in every society, and keep down the number to the level of the means of subsistence, may be classed under two general heads – the preventive and the positive checks.

The preventive check, as far as it is voluntary, is peculiar to man, and arises from that distinctive superiority in his reasoning faculties which enables him to calculate distant consequences. The checks to the indefinite increase of plants and irrational animals are all either positive, or, if preventive, involuntary. But man cannot look around him and see the distress . . .

The checks to population, which are constantly operating with more or less force in every society, and keep down the number to the level of the means of subsistence, may be classed under two general heads; the preventive, and the positive checks.

The preventive check is peculiar to man, and arises from that distinctive superiority in his reasoning faculties, which enables him to calculate distant consequences. Plants and animals have apparently no doubts about the future support of their offspring. The checks to their indefinite increase, therefore, are all positive. But man cannot look around him, and see the distress which frequently presses upon those who have large families; he cannot contemplate his present possessions or earnings, which he now nearly consumes himself, and calculate the amount of each share, when with very little addition they must be divided, perhaps, among seven or eight, without feeling a doubt, whether if he follow the bent of his inclinations, he may be able to support the offspring which he will probably bring into the world.[1] *In a state of equality, if such can exist, this would be the simple question. In the present state of society other considerations occur. Will he not lower his rank in life, and be obliged to give up in great measure his former society?[a] Does any mode of employment present itself by which he may reasonably hope to maintain a family? Will he not at any rate subject himself to greater difficulties, and more severe labour than in his single state? Will he not be unable to transmit to his children the same advantages of education and improvement that he had himself possessed? Does he even feel secure that, should he have a large family, his utmost exertions can save them from rags, and squalid poverty, and their consequent degradation in the community? And may he not be reduced to the grating necessity of forfeiting his independence, and of being obliged to the sparing hand of charity for support?

These considerations are calculated to prevent, and certainly do prevent, a great number of persons in all civilized nations from pursuing the dictate of nature in an early attachment to one woman.*[1]

[2] ● If this restraint do not produce vice, as in many instances is the case, and very generally so among the middle and higher classes of women, it is undoubtedly the least evil that can arise from the principle of population. Considered as a restraint on an inclination otherwise innocent, and always natural, it must be allowed to produce a certain degree of temporary unhappiness; but evidently slight, compared with the evils which result from any of the other checks to population.

When this restraint produces vice, as it does most frequently among

[1] [These sentences are based on pp. 28–9 of the 1798 *Essay.*]
[a] [Here, however, Malthus simply wrote:
  Will he not lower his rank in life?
  [In 1806 he altered this again:
  Will he not lower his rank in life, and be obliged in great measure to give up his former habits?
[2] [From 1806 this passage read thus:
  If this restraint do not produce vice, it is undoubtedly the least evil that can arise from the principle of population. Considered as a restraint on a strong natural inclination, it must be allowed to produce a certain degree of temporary unhappiness; but evidently slight, compared with the evils which result from any of the other checks to population; and merely of the same nature as many other sacrifices of temporary to permanent gratification, which it is the business of a moral agent continually to make.
  When this restraint produces vice, the evils which follow are but too conspicuous.

men, and among a numerous class of females, the evils which follow are but too conspicuous. ●[2]

A promiscuous intercourse to such a degree as to prevent the birth of children, seems to lower in the most marked manner the dignity of human nature. It cannot be without its effect on men, and nothing can be more obvious than its tendency to degrade the female character, and to destroy all its most amiable and distinguishing characteristics. Add to which, that among those unfortunate females with which all great towns abound, more real distress and aggravated misery are perhaps to be found than in any other department of human life.

When a general corruption of morals, with regard to the sex, pervades all the classes of society, its effects must necessarily be to poison the springs of domestic happiness, to weaken conjugal and parental affection, and to lessen the united exertions and ardour of parents in the care and education of their children; effects which cannot take place without a decided diminution of the general happiness and virtue of the society; particularly as the necessity of art in the accomplishment and conduct of intrigues, and in the concealment of their consequences, necessarily leads to many other vices.

The positive checks to population are extremely various, and include every cause, whether arising from vice or misery, which in any degree contributes to shorten the natural duration of human life. Under this head therefore may be enumerated, all unwholesome occupations, severe labour and exposure to the seasons, extreme poverty, bad nursing of children, great towns, excesses of all kinds, the whole train of common diseases and epidemics, wars, pestilence,[3] plague, and famine.

On examining these obstacles to the increase of population which I have classed under the heads of preventive and positive checks, it will appear that they are all resolvable into moral restraint, vice, and misery.

Of the preventive checks, the restraint from marriage which is not followed by irregular gratifications may properly be termed moral restraint.[4]

[3] [The word *pestilence* was omitted in 1806.]
[4] [In 1806 this footnote was added:
    It will be observed that I here use the term *moral* in its most confined sense. By moral restraint I would be understood to mean a restraint from marriage from prudential motives, with a conduct strictly moral during the period of this restraint; and I have never intentionally deviated from this sense. When I have wished to consider the restraint from marriage unconnected with its consequences, I have either called it prudential restraint, or a part of the preventive check, of which indeed it forms the principal branch.

Promiscuous intercourse, unnatural passions, violations of the marriage bed, and improper arts to conceal the consequences of irregular connexions,[5] clearly come under the head of vice.

Of the positive checks, those which appear to arise unavoidably from the laws of nature may be called exclusively misery; and those which we obviously bring upon ourselves, such as wars, excesses, and many others which it would be in our power to avoid, are of a mixed nature. They are brought upon us by vice, and their consequences are misery.[6]

In my review of the different stages of society, I have been accused of not allowing sufficient weight in the prevention of population to moral restraint; but when the confined sense of the term, which I have here explained, is adverted to, I am fearful that I shall not be found to have erred much in this respect. I should be very glad to believe myself mistaken.

[5] [From 1806 this read:
   ... irregular connections are preventive checks that clearly come under the head of vice.

[6] As the general consequence of vice is misery, and as this consequence is the precise reason why an action is termed vicious, it may appear that the term misery alone would be here sufficient, and that it is superfluous to use both. But the rejection of the term vice would introduce a considerable confusion into our language and ideas. We want it particularly to distinguish that class of actions, the general tendency of which is to produce misery, but which, in their immediate or individual effects, may produce perhaps exactly the contrary. The gratification of all our passions in its immediate effect is happiness, not misery; and in individual instances even the remote consequences (at least in this life) come under the same denomination. I have little doubt that there have been some irregular connexions with women which have added to the happiness of both parties, and have injured no one. These individual actions therefore cannot come under the head of misery. But they are still evidently vicious, because an action is so denominated, the general tendency of which is to produce misery, whatever may be its individual effect; and no person can doubt the general tendency of an illicit intercourse between the sexes to injure the happiness of society.

[Malthus did not amend this controversial footnote until 1817; the third sentence then read:
   We want it particularly to distinguish those actions, the general tendency of which is to produce misery, and which are therefore prohibited by the commands of the Creator, and the precepts of the moralist, although in their immediate or individual effects they may produce exactly the contrary.

[Instead of saying *I have little doubt that there have been some irregular connections* ... Malthus wrote in 1817:
   There may have been some irregular connections ...

[Of individual actions which 'cannot come under the head of misery' he continued:
   But they are still evidently vicious, because an action is so denominated which violates an express precept, founded upon its general tendency to produce misery, whatever may be its individual effect ...

[This paragraph was inserted here in 1806:

The sum of all these preventive and positive checks, taken together, forms the immediate check to population; and it is evident that, in every country where the whole of the procreative power cannot be called into action, the preventive and the positive checks must vary inversely as each other; that is, in countries either naturally unhealthy, or subject to a great mortality, from whatever cause it may arise, the preventive check will prevail very little. In those countries, on the contrary, which are naturally healthy, and where the preventive check is found to prevail with considerable force, the positive check will prevail very little, or the mortality be very small.

In every country some of these checks are, with more or less force, in constant operation; yet notwithstanding their general prevalence, there are few states in which there is not a constant effort in the population to increase beyond the means of subsistence. This constant effort as constantly tends to subject the lower classes of society to distress, and to prevent any great permanent amelioration of their condition.

[7]*These effects, in the present state of society, seem to be produced in the following manner. We will suppose the means of subsistence in any country just equal to the easy support of its inhabitants. The constant effort towards population, which is found to act even in the most vicious societies, increases the number of people before the means of subsistence are increased. The food, therefore, which before supported eleven mill- ions, must now be divided among eleven millions and a half. The poor consequently must live much worse, and many of them be reduced to severe distress. The number of labourers also being above the proportion of work in the market, the price of labour must tend to fall, while the price of provisions would at the same time tend to rise. The labourer therefore must do more work to earn the same as he did before. During this season of distress, the discouragements to marriage and the difficulty of rearing a family are so great, that population is nearly at a stand.[8] In the meantime, the cheapness of labour, the plenty of labourers, and the necessity of an increased industry among them, encourage cultivators to employ more labour upon their land, to turn up fresh soil, and to manure and improve more completely what is already in tillage, till ultimately the

---

[7] [These passages, beginning with 'These effects ...' are based on pp. 29–32 of the 1798 *Essay*. In 1798, however, Malthus added that:

A satisfactory history of this kind ... would require the constant and minute attention of an observing mind during a long life.

[8] [In 1826 this was altered to:

... that the progress of population is retarded ...

means of subsistence may become in the same proportion to the population as at the period from which we set out. The situation of the labourer being then again tolerably comfortable, the restraints to population are in some degree loosened; and, after a short period, the same retrograde and progressive movements, with respect to happiness, are repeated.

This sort of oscillation will not probably be obvious to common view; and it may be difficult even for the most attentive observer to calculate its periods. Yet that, in the generality of old states, some such vibration does exist,[9] though in a much less marked, and in a much more irregular manner, than I have described it, no reflecting man who considers the subject deeply can well doubt.

One principal reason why this oscillation has been less remarked, and less decidedly confirmed by experience than might naturally be expected, is that the histories of mankind which we possess are, in general, histories only of the higher classes. We have not many accounts that can be depended upon of the manners and customs of that part of mankind where these retrograde and progressive movements chiefly take place. A satisfactory history of this kind, of one people and of one period, would require the constant and minute attention of many observing minds in local and general remarks on the state of the lower classes of society, and the causes that influenced it; and to draw accurate inferences upon this subject, a succession of such historians for some centuries would be necessary.*[7] This branch of statistical knowledge has of late years been attended to in some countries,[10] and we may promise ourselves a clearer

---

[9] [Changed in 1817 to:
 ... some alternation of this kind does exist, ...

[10] The judicious questions which Sir John Sinclair circulated in Scotland, and the very valuable accounts which he has collected in that part of the island, do him the highest honour; and these accounts will ever remain an extraordinary monument of the learning, good sense, and general information of the clergy of Scotland. It is to be regretted that the adjoining parishes are not put together in the work, which would have assisted the memory both in attaining and recollecting the state of particular districts. The repetitions and contradictory opinions which occur are not in my opinion so objectionable, as, to the result of such testimony, more faith may be given than we could possibly give to the testimony of any individual. Even were this result drawn for us by some master hand, though much valuable time would undoubtedly be saved, the information would not be so satisfactory. If, with a few subordinate improvements, this work had contained accurate and complete registers for the last 150 years, it would have been inestimable, and would have exhibited a better picture of the internal state of a country than has yet been presented to the world. But this last most essential improvement no diligence could have effected.

insight into the internal structure of human society from the progress of these inquiries. But the science may be said yet to be in its infancy, and many of the objects, on which it would be desirable to have information, have been either omitted or not stated with sufficient accuracy. Among these perhaps may be reckoned the proportion of the number of adults to the number of marriages; the extent to which vicious customs have prevailed in consequence of the restraints upon matrimony; the comparative mortality among the children of the most distressed part of the community, and of those who live rather more at their ease; the variations in the real price of labour; the observable differences in the state of the lower classes of society, with respect to ease and happiness, at different times during a certain period; and very accurate registers of births, deaths, and marriages, which are of the utmost importance in this subject.

A faithful history, including such particulars, would tend greatly to elucidate the manner in which the constant check upon population acts; and would probably prove the existence of the retrograde and progressive movements that have been mentioned; though the times of their vibration must necessarily be rendered irregular from the operation of many interrupting causes; such as, the introduction or failure of certain manufactures, a greater or less prevalent spirit of agricultural enterprize; years of plenty or years of scarcity; wars, sickly seasons, poor laws, emigration, and other causes of a similar nature.

A circumstance which has, perhaps, more than any other, contributed to conceal this oscillation from common view, is the difference between the nominal and real price of labour. It very rarely happens that the nominal price of labour universally falls; but we well know that it frequently remains the same while the nominal price of provisions has been gradually rising.

[The two following sentences, together with footnote 11, were inserted in 1817:

This, indeed, will generally be the case if the increase of manufactures and commerce be sufficient to employ the new labourers that are thrown into the market, and to prevent the increased supply from lowering the money-price.[11]

[11] If the new labourers thrown yearly into the market should find no employment but in agriculture, their competition might so lower the money-price of labour as to prevent the increase of population from occasioning an effective demand for more corn; or, in other words, if the landlords and farmers could get nothing but an

But an increased number of labourers receiving the same money-wages will necessarily, by their competition, increase the money-price of corn.

This is, in fact, a real fall in the price of labour; and, during this period, the condition of the lower classes of the community must be gradually growing worse. But the farmers and capitalists are growing rich from the real cheapness of labour. Their increasing capitals enable them to employ a greater number of men; and, as the population had probably suffered some check from the greater difficulty of supporting a family, the demand for labour, after a certain period, would be great in proportion to the supply, and its price would of course rise, if left to find its natural level; and thus the wages of labour, and consequently the condition of the lower classes of society, might have progressive and retrograde movements, though the price of labour might never nominally fall.

In savage life, where there is no regular price of labour, it is little to be doubted that similar oscillations take place. When population has increased nearly to the utmost limits of the food, all the preventive and the positive checks will naturally operate with increased force. Vicious habits with respect to the sex will be more general, the exposing of children more frequent, and both the probability and fatality of wars and epidemics, will be considerably greater; and these causes will probably continue their operation till the population is sunk below the level of the food; and then the return to comparative plenty will again produce an increase, and, after a certain period, its further progress will again be checked by the same causes.[12]

But without attempting to establish these progressive and retrograde movements in different countries, which would evidently require more minute histories than we possess,[13] the following propositions are intended to be proved:

1.   Population is necessarily limited by the means of subsistence.

additional quantity of agricultural labour in exchange for any additional produce which they could raise, they might not be tempted to raise it.

[12] Sir James Steuart very justly compares the generative faculty to a spring loaded with a variable weight, (Polit. Econ. vol. i. b. i. c. 4. p. 20.) which would of course produce exactly that kind of oscillation which has been mentioned. In the first book of his Political Economy, he has explained many parts of the subject of population very ably.

[13] [From 1806 this read:
   ... require more minute histories than we possess, and which the progress of civilisation naturally tends to counteract, ...

2. Population invariably increases, where the means of subsistence increase, unless prevented by some very powerful and obvious checks.[14]

3. These checks, and the checks which repress the superior power of population, and keep its effects on a level with the means of subsistence, are all resolvable into moral restraint, vice, and misery.

The first of these propositions scarcely needs illustration. The second and third will be sufficiently established by a review of the past and present state of society.[15]

This review will be the subject of the following chapters.

[Chapters iii to xiv omitted from this edition.]

[14] [In 1806 Malthus added a footnote here:

I have expressed myself in this cautious manner, because I believe there are a very few instances, such as the negroes in the West Indies, and one or two others, where population does not keep up to the level of subsistence. But these are extreme cases; and generally speaking it might be said (and the propositions in this form would be more neatly and distinctly expressed) that,

2. Population always increases where the means of subsistence increase.

3. The checks which repress the superior power of population, and keep its effects on a level with the means of subsistence, are all resolvable into moral restraint, vice, and misery.

[In 1807 Malthus deleted the passage in brackets.]

[In 1817 he altered the first paragraph of this note:

I have expressed myself in this cautious manner, because I believe there are some instances where population does not keep up to the level of subsistence. But these are extreme cases ...

[Also in 1817, he added another paragraph to the footnote:

It should be observed that, by an increase in the means of subsistence is here meant such an increase as will enable the mass of society to command more food. An increase might certainly take place, which in the actual state of a particular society would not be distributed to the lower classes, and consequently would give no stimulus to population.

[15] [This sentence was altered in 1806:

The second and third will be sufficiently established by a review of the immediate checks to population in the past and present state of society.

ESSAY, &c

BOOK II

OF THE CHECKS TO POPULATION IN THE DIFFERENT STATES OF MODERN EUROPE

[Chapters i to xii omitted from this edition.]

CHAPTER XIII

General deductions from the preceding view of Society[1]

That the checks which have been mentioned are the true[2] causes of the slow increase of population, and that these checks result principally from an insufficiency of subsistence, will be evident from the comparatively rapid increase which has invariably taken place whenever, by some sudden enlargement in the means of subsistence, these checks have been in any considerable degree removed.

It has been universally remarked that all new colonies, settled in healthy countries, where room and food were abundant, have constantly made a rapid progress in population. Many of the colonies from ancient Greece, in the course of one or two centuries, appear to have rivalled, and even surpassed, their mother cities. Syracuse and Agrigentum in Sicily; Tarentum and Locri in Italy; Ephesus and Miletus in Lesser Asia; were, by all accounts, at least equal to any of the cities of ancient Greece.[3] All these colonies had established themselves in countries inhabited by savage and barbarous nations which easily gave place to the new settlers who had of course plenty of good land. It is calculated that the Israelites, though they increased very slowly while they were wandering in the land of Canaan, on settling in a fertile district of Egypt doubled their numbers every fifteen years during the whole period of their stay.[4] But not to dwell on remote instances, the European settlements in America bear ample testimony to the truth of a remark that has never, I believe, been doubted. Plenty of rich land, to be had for little or nothing, is so powerful a cause of population as generally to overcome all obstacles.

No settlements could easily have been worse managed than those of Spain, in Mexico, Peru, and Quito. The tyranny, superstition, and vices of the mother country were introduced in ample quantities among her children. Exorbitant taxes were exacted by the crown; the most arbitrary restrictions were imposed on their trade; and the governors were not

---

[1] [This was chapter xi of Book II in the quarto, 1806 and 1807; it became chapter xiii in 1817 and 1826.]

[2] [In 1806 *true* was changed to 'immediate'.]

[3] Smith's Wealth of Nations, vol. ii. p. 360. [Also in 1806 this footnote was omitted.]

[4] Short's New Observ. on Bills of Mortality, p. 259, 8vo. 1750.

behindhand, in rapacity and extortion for themselves as well as their master. Yet under all these difficulties, the colonies made a quick progress in population. The city of Quito, which was but a hamlet of Indians, is represented by Ulloa as containing fifty or sixty thousand inhabitants above fifty years ago.[5] Lima, which was founded since the conquest, is mentioned by the same author as equally or more populous, before the fatal earthquake in 1746. Mexico is said to contain a hundred thousand inhabitants which, notwithstanding the exaggerations of the Spanish writers, is supposed to be five times greater than what it contained in the time of Montezuma.[6]

In the Portuguese colony of Brazil, governed with almost equal tyranny, there were supposed to be, above thirty years ago, six hundred thousand inhabitants of European extraction.[7]

The Dutch and French colonies, though under the government of exclusive companies of merchants, [8]●which, as Dr. Smith justly observes, is the worst of all possible governments,●[8] still persisted in thriving under every disadvantage.[9]

But the English North American colonies, now the powerful people of the United States of America, far outstripped all the others in the progress of their population. To the quantity of rich land, which they possessed in common with the Spanish and Portuguese colonies, they added a greater degree of liberty and equality. Though not without some restrictions on their foreign commerce, they were allowed the liberty of managing their own internal affairs. The political institutions which prevailed were favourable to the alienation and division of property. Lands which were not cultivated by the proprietor within a limited time were declared grantable to any other person. In Pennsylvania there was no right of primogeniture and, in the provinces of New England, the eldest son had only a double share. There were no tythes in any of the States, and scarcely any taxes. And on account of the extreme cheapness of good land,[10] a capital could not be more advantageously employed than in agriculture which, at the same time that it affords the greatest quantity of healthy work, supplies the most valuable produce to the society.

[5] Voy. d'Ulloa, tom. i. liv. v. ch. v. p. 229. 4to. 1752.
[6] Smith's Wealth of Nations, vol. ii. b. iv. ch. vii. p. 363.
[7] Id. p. 365.   [8] [In 1807 this clause was omitted.]
[9] Smith's Wealth of Nations, vol. ii. pp. 368, 369.
[10] [In 1826 Malthus inserted here:
　　... and a situation favourable to the export of grain, ...

The consequence of these favourable circumstances united was a rapidity of increase almost without parallel in history. Throughout all the northern provinces the population was found to double itself in 25 years. The original number of persons which had settled in the four provinces of New England in 1643 was 21 200. Afterwards, it was calculated, that more left them than went to them. In the year 1760, they were increased to half a million. They had, therefore, all along, doubled their number in 25 years. In New Jersey the period of doubling appeared to be 22 years; and in Rhode Island still less. In the back settlements, where the inhabitants applied themselves solely to agriculture, and luxury was not known, they were supposed to double their number in fifteen years. Along the sea-coast, which would naturally be first inhabited, the period of doubling was about 35 years, and in some of the maritime towns the population was absolutely at a stand.[11] From the late census made in America it appears that, taking all the States together, they have still continued to double their numbers every 25

---

[11] Price's Observ. on Revers. Paym. vol. i. p. 282, 283, and vol. ii. p. 260. I have lately had an opportunity of seeing some extracts from the sermon of Dr. Styles, from which Dr. Price has taken these facts. Speaking of Rhode Island, Dr. Styles says that though the period of doubling for the whole colony is 25 years, yet that it is different in different parts, and within land is 20 and 15 years. The five towns of Gloucester, Situate, Coventry, Westgreenwich, and Exeter, were 5033, A.D. 1748, and 6986 A.D. 1755; which implies a period of doubling of 15 years only. He mentions afterwards that the county of Kent doubles in 20 years; and the county of Providence in 18 years.

●I have also lately seen a paper of *Facts and calculations respecting the population of the United States*, which makes the period of doubling for the whole of the States, since their first settlement, only 20 years. I know not of what authority this paper is; but far as it goes upon public facts and enumerations, I should think that it must be to be depended on. One period is very striking. From a return to Congress in 1782, the population appeared to be 2 389 300, and in the census of 1790, 4 000 000: increase in 9 years, 1 610 700: from which deduct ten thousand per annum for European settlers, which will be 90 000; and allow for their increase at 5 per cent. for 4½ years, which will be 20 250: the remaining increase during these 9 years, from procreation only, will be 1 500 450, which is very nearly 7 per cent.; and consequently the period of doubling at this rate would be less than 16 years.

If this calculation for the whole population of the States be in any degree near the truth, it cannot be doubted that, in particular districts, the period of doubling from procreation only has often been less than 15 years. The period immediately succeeding the war was likely to be a period of very rapid increase.●

[The last two paragraphs of this note were omitted in 1826. The 'paper' was probably a 7-page octavo pamphlet entitled *Facts and Calculations respecting the Population and Territory of the United States of America*. According to Charles Evans's *American Bibliography* (vol. 13, 36051) it was published in Boston, 'printed by Russell for John Peck', on paper watermarked 1799.]

years,[12] and, as the whole population is now so great as not to be materially affected by the emigrations from Europe; and as it is known that in some of the towns and districts near the sea-coast, the progress of population has been comparatively slow; it is evident that in the interior of the country in general the period of doubling, from procreation only, must have been considerably less than 25 years.

The population of the United States of America, according to the late census, is 5 172 312.[13] We have no reason to believe that Great Britain is less populous, at present, for the emigration of the small parent stock which produced these numbers. On the contrary a certain degree of emigration is known to be favourable to the population of the mother country. It has been particularly remarked that the two Spanish provinces from which the greatest number of people emigrated to America became in consequence more populous.

Whatever was the original number of British emigrants which increased so fast in North America, let us ask, Why does not an equal number produce an equal increase in the same time in Great Britain? The obvious reason to be assigned is the want of food; and that this want is the most efficient cause of the three great[14] checks to population which have been observed to prevail in all societies is evident from the rapidity with which even old states recover the desolations of war, pestilence, famine, and the convulsions of nature. They are then, for a short time, placed a little in the situation of new colonies, and the effect is always answerable to what might be expected. If the industry of the inhabitants be not destroyed, subsistence will soon increase beyond the wants of the reduced numbers; and the invariable consequence will be that population which before, perhaps, was nearly stationary, will begin immediately to

[12] [In 1826 a footnote was added here:

  See an article in the Supplement to the Encyclopædia Britannica on Population, p. 308; and a curious table, p. 310, calculated by Mr. Milne, Actuary to the Sun Life Assurance Office, which strikingly confirms and illustrates the computed rate of increase in the United States, and shows that it cannot be essentially affected by immigrations.

  [The article on Population was written by Malthus himself.]

[13] One small State is mentioned as being omitted in the census; and I understand that the population is generally considered at above this number. It is said to approach towards 6 000 000. But such vague opinions cannot of course be much relied on.

  [This footnote was omitted in 1826 and the relevant sentence amended:

  The population of the United States of America, according to the fourth census, in 1820, was 7 861 710.

[14] [In 1806 *great* was changed to 'immediate'].

increase, and will continue its progress till the former population is recovered.

The fertile province of Flanders, which has been so often the seat of the most destructive wars, after a respite of a few years, has always appeared as rich and as populous as ever. The undiminished population of France, which has before been noticed, is an instance very strongly in point. The tables of Susmilch afford continual proofs of a very rapid increase, after great mortalities; and the table for Prussia and Lithuania which I have inserted is particularly striking in this respect. The effects of the dreadful plague in London, in 1666, were not perceptible 15 or 20 years afterwards. It may even be doubted whether Turkey or Egypt are, upon an average, much less populous for the plagues which periodically lay them waste. If the number of people which they contain be considerably less now, than formerly, it is rather to be attributed to the tyranny and oppression of the governments under which they groan, and the consequent discouragements to agriculture, than to the losses which they sustain by the plague. The traces of the most destructive famines in China, Indostan, Egypt, and other countries, are by all accounts very soon obliterated; and the most tremendous convulsions of nature, such as volcanic eruptions and earthquakes, if they do not happen so frequently as to drive away the inhabitants, or destroy their spirit of industry, have been found to produce but a trifling effect on the average population of any state.[15]

It has appeared from the registers of different countries, which have already been produced, that the progress of their population is checked by the periodical though irregular returns of plagues and sickly seasons. Dr. Short, in his curious researches into bills of mortality, often uses the expression of 'terrible correctives of the redundance of mankind',[16] and in a table of all the plagues, pestilences, and famines, of which he could collect accounts, shews the constancy and universality of their operation.

The epidemical years in his table, or the years in which the plague or some great and wasting epidemic prevailed, for smaller sickly seasons seem not to be included, are 431,[17] of which 32 were before the Christian aera.[18] If we divide, therefore, the years of the present aera by 399, it will

---

[15] [Up to this point in this chapter, Malthus followed very closely pp. 100–12 of the 1798 *Essay*.]

[16] New Observ. on Bills of Mortality, p. 96.

[17] Hist. of Air, Seasons, &c. vol. ii. p. 366.

[18] Id. vol. ii. p. 202.

appear that the periodical returns of such epidemics, to some countries that we are acquainted with, have been on an average only at the interval of about 4½ years.

Of the 254 great famines and dearths enumerated in the table, 15 were before the Christian aera,[19] beginning with that which occurred in Palestine in the time of Abraham. If, subtracting these 15, we divide the years of the present aera by the remainder, it will appear that the average interval between the visits of this dreadful scourge has been only about 7½ years.

How far these 'terrible correctives to the redundance of mankind', have been occasioned by the too rapid increase of population, is a point which it would be very difficult to determine with any degree of precision. The causes of most of our diseases appear to us to be so mysterious, and probably are really so various, that it would be rashness to lay too much stress on any single one: but it will not perhaps be too much to say that, *among* these causes, we ought certainly to rank crowded houses, and insufficient or unwholesome food, which are the natural consequences of an increase of population faster than the accommodations of a country with respect to habitations and food, will allow.

Almost all the histories of epidemics which we possess tend to confirm this supposition, by describing them in general as making their principal ravages among the lower classes of people. In Dr. Short's tables this circumstance is frequently mentioned;[20] and it further appears that a very considerable proportion of the epidemic years either followed or were accompanied by seasons of dearth and bad food.[21] In other places he also mentions great plagues as diminishing particularly the number of the lower or servile sort of people,[22] and, in speaking of different diseases, he observes that those which are occasioned by bad and unwholesome food generally last the longest.[23]

We know from constant experience that fevers are generated in our jails, our manufactories, our crowded workhouses, and in the narrow and close streets of our large towns; all which situations appear to be similar in their effects to squalid poverty: and we cannot doubt that causes of this kind, aggravated in degree, contributed to the production and prevalence of those great and wasting plagues formerly so common in Europe, but which now, from the mitigation of these causes, are every-

---

[19] Id. vol. ii. p. 206.   [20] Hist. of Air, Seasons, &c. vol. ii. p. 206. et seq.
[21] Ibid. and p. 366.   [22] New Observ. p. 125.   [23] Id. p. 108.

where considerably abated, and in many places appear to be completely extirpated.

Of the other great scourge of mankind, famine, it may be observed that it is not in the nature of things that the increase of population should absolutely produce one. This increase, though rapid, is necessarily gradual; and as the human frame cannot be supported, even for a very short time, without food, it is evident that no more human beings can grow up than there is provision to maintain. But though the principle of population cannot absolutely produce a famine, it prepares the way for one in the most complete manner; and, by obliging all the lower classes of people to subsist nearly on the smallest quantity of food that will support life,[24] turns even a slight deficiency from the failure of the seasons into a severe dearth; and may be fairly said, therefore, to be one of the principal causes of famine. Among the signs of an approaching dearth, Dr. Short mentions one or more years of luxuriant crops together,[25] and this observation is probably just, as we know that the general effect of years of cheapness and abundance is to dispose a greater number of persons to marry, and under such circumstances the return to a year, merely of an average crop might produce a scarcity.

The small-pox, which at present may be considered as the most prevalent and fatal epidemic in Europe,[26] is of all others, perhaps, the most difficult to account for, though the periods of its return are in many places regular.[27] Dr. Short observes, that from the histories of this disorder, it seems to have very little dependence upon the past or present constitution of the weather or seasons, and that it appears epidemically at all times, and in all states of the air, though not so frequently in a hard frost. We know of no instances, I believe, of its being clearly generated under any circumstances of situation. I do not mean therefore to insinuate that poverty and crowded houses ever absolutely produced it; but I may be allowed to remark that in those places where its returns are regular, and its ravages among children, particularly among those of the lower class, are considerable, it necessarily follows that these circumstances, in a greater degree than usual, must always precede and accom-

[24] [In 1826 Malthus altered this:
    ... cannot absolutely produce a famine, it prepares a way for one; and by frequently obliging the lower classes of people to subsist on the smallest quantity of food ...
[25] Hist. of Air, Seasons, &c. vol. ii. p. 367.
[26] [In 1826 the words *at present* were deleted.]
[27] Hist of Air, Seasons, &c. vol. ii. p. 411.

pany its appearance; that is, from the time of its last visit, the average number of children will be increasing, the people will in consequence be growing poorer, and the houses will be more crowded, till another visit removes this superabundant population.

In all these cases, how little soever force we may be disposed to attribute to the effects of the principle of population in the actual production of disorders, we cannot avoid allowing their force as predisposing causes to the reception of contagion, and as giving very great additional force to the extensiveness and fatality of its ravages.

It is observed by Dr. Short that a severe mortal epidemic is generally succeeded by an uncommon healthiness, from the late distemper having carried off most of the declining worn-out constitutions.[28] It is probable, also, that another cause of it may be the greater plenty of room and food, and the consequently ameliorated condition of the lower classes of the people. Sometimes, according to Dr. Short, a very fruitful year is followed by a very mortal and sickly one, and mortal ones often succeeded by very fruitful, as if Nature sought either to prevent or quickly repair the loss by death. In general the next year after sickly and mortal ones is prolific in proportion to the breeders left.[29]

This last effect we have seen most strikingly exemplified in the table for Prussia and Lithuania. And from this and other tables of Susmilch, it also appears that when the increasing produce of a country and the increasing demand for labour so far ameliorate the condition of the labourer as greatly to encourage marriage, the custom of early marriages is generally continued till the population has gone beyond the increased produce, and sickly seasons appear to be the natural and necessary consequence. The continental registers exhibit many instances of rapid increase interrupted in this manner by mortal diseases; and the inference seems to be that those countries where subsistence is increasing sufficiently to encourage population, but not to answer all its demands, will be more subject to periodical epidemics than those where the increase of population is more nearly accommodated to the average produce.

The converse of this will of course be true. In those countries which are subject to periodical sicknesses, the increase of population, or the excess of births above the deaths, will be greater, in the intervals of these periods than is usual in countries not so much subject to these diseases. If Turkey and Egypt have been nearly stationary in their average

---

[28] Id. vol. ii. p. 344.   [29] New Observ. p. 191.

population for the last century in the intervals of their periodical plagues, the births must have exceeded the deaths in a much greater proportion than in such countries as France and England.

It is for these reasons that no estimates of future population or depopulation, formed from any existing rate of increase or decrease, can be depended upon. Sir William Petty calculated that in the year 1800 the city of London would contain 5 359 000 inhabitants,[30] instead of which it does not now contain a fifth part of that number. And Mr. Eton has lately prophesied the extinction of the population of the Turkish empire in another century,[31] an event which will certainly fail of taking place. If America were to continue increasing at the same rate as at present, for the next 150 years, her population would exceed the population of China; but though prophecies are dangerous, I will venture to say that such an increase will not take place in that time, though it may perhaps in five or six hundred years.

Europe was, without doubt, formerly more subject to plagues and wasting epidemics than at present, and this will account, in great measure, for the greater proportion of births to deaths in former times, mentioned by many authors, as it has always been a common practice to estimate these proportions from too short periods, and generally to reject the years of plague as accidental.

The highest average proportion of births to deaths in England may be considered as about 12 to 10, or 120 to 100.[32] The proportion in France for ten years, ending in 1780, was about 115 to 100.[33] Though these proportions undoubtedly varied at different periods during the century, yet we have reason to think that they did not vary in any very considerable degree; and it will appear, therefore, that the population of France and England had accommodated itself more nearly to the average produce of each country than many other states.[34]*The operation of the preventive check, vicious manners,[35] wars, the silent, though certain, destruction of life in large towns and manufactories, and the close habitations and insufficient food of many of the poor, prevent population

---

[30] Political Arithmetick, p. 17.   [31] Survey of the Turkish Empire, c. vii. p. 281.

[32] [In 1817 this sentence read:

The average proportion of births to deaths in England during the last century may be considered . . .

[33] Necker, de l'Administration des Finances, tom. i. c. ix. p. 255.

[34] [From the beginning of this sentence until the word 'misery?' on p. 43 Malthus has closely followed pp. 125–41 of the 1798 *Essay*.]

[35] [In 1806 the words *vicious manners* were deleted.]

from outrunning the means of subsistence; and if I may use an expression, which certainly at first appears strange, supersede the necessity of great and ravaging epidemics to destroy what is redundant. If a wasting plague were to sweep off two millions in England, and six millions in France, it cannot be doubted that, after the inhabitants had recovered from the dreadful shock, the proportion of births to deaths would rise much above the usual average in either country during the last century.[36]

In New Jersey the proportion of births to deaths, on an average of 7 years, ending 1743, was 300 to 100. In France and England, the average proportion cannot be reckoned at more than 120 to 100. Great and astonishing as this difference is, we ought not to be so wonder-struck at it as to attribute it to the miraculous interposition of heaven. The causes of it are not remote, latent, and mysterious, but near us, round about us, and open to the investigation of every inquiring mind. It accords with the most liberal spirit of philosophy to believe that no stone can fall, or plant rise, without the immediate agency of divine power. But we know from experience that these operations of what we call nature have been conducted almost according to fixed laws. And since the world began, the causes of population and depopulation have been probably as constant as any of the laws of nature with which we are acquainted.

The passion between the sexes has appeared in every age to be so nearly the same that it may always be considered, in algebraic language, as a given quantity. The great law of necessity which prevents population from increasing in any country beyond the food which it can either produce or acquire, is a law so open to our view, so obvious and evident to our understandings, that we cannot for a moment doubt it. The different modes which nature takes to repress a redundant population do not indeed appear to us so certain and regular; but though we cannot always predict the mode, we may with certainty predict the fact. If the proportion of the births to the deaths for a few years indicates an increase of numbers much beyond the proportional increased or acquired food of the country, we may be perfectly certain that, unless an emigration take place, the deaths will shortly exceed the births, and that the increase that had been observed for a few years, cannot be the real average increase of the population of the country. If there were no other depopulating causes, and if the preventive check did not operate very strongly, every

[36] This remark has been, to a certain degree, verified of late in France, by the increase of births which has taken place since the revolution. [In 1817 this footnote was omitted.]

country would without doubt be subject to periodical plagues or famines.

The only true criterion of a real and permanent increase in the population of any country is the increase of the means of subsistence. But even this criterion is subject to some slight variations, which however are completely open to our observation. In some countries population seems to have been forced; that is, the people have been habituated, by degrees, to live almost upon the smallest possible quantity of food. There must have been periods in such countries when population increased permanently without an increase in the means of subsistence. China, India, and the countries possessed by the Bedoween Arabs, as we have seen in the former part of this work, appear to answer to this description. The average produce of these countries seems to be but barely sufficient to support the lives of the inhabitants, and of course any deficiency from the badness of the seasons must be fatal. Nations in this state must necessarily be subject to famines.

In America, where the reward of labour is at present so liberal, the lower classes might retrench very considerably in a year of scarcity, without materially distressing themselves. A famine, therefore, seems to be almost impossible. It may be expected, that in the progress of the population of America, the labourers will in time be much less liberally rewarded. The numbers will in this case permanently increase without a proportional increase in the means of subsistence.

In the different countries of Europe, there must be some variations in the proportion of the number of inhabitants and the quantity of food consumed, arising from the different habits of living which prevail in each state. The labourers of the south of England are so accustomed to eat fine wheaten bread, that they will suffer themselves to be half-starved before they will submit to live like the Scotch peasants. They might perhaps, in time, by the constant operation of the hard law of necessity, be reduced to live even like the lower classes of the Chinese, and the country would then with the same quantity of food support a greater population. But to effect this must always be a difficult and, every friend to humanity will hope, an abortive attempt.

I have mentioned some cases where population may permanently increase without a proportional increase in the means of subsistence. But it is evident that the variation in different states, between the food and the numbers supported by it, is restricted to a limit beyond which it cannot pass. In every country, the population of which is not absolutely decreasing, the food must be necessarily sufficient to support and to continue the race of labourers.

Other circumstances being the same, it may be affirmed that countries are populous according to the quantity of human food which they produce or can acquire; and happy according to the liberality with which this food is divided, or the quantity which a day's labour will purchase. Corn countries are more populous than pasture countries, and rice countries more populous than corn countries. But their happiness does not depend either upon their being thinly or fully inhabited, upon their poverty or their riches, their youth or their age; but on the proportion which the population and the food bear to each other. This proportion is generally the most favourable in new colonies, where the knowledge and industry of an old state operate on the fertile unappropriated land of a new one. In other cases the youth or the age of a state is not, in this respect, of great importance. It is probable that the food of Great Britain is divided in more liberal shares to her inhabitants at the present period than it was two thousand, three thousand, or four thousand years ago. And it has appeared that the poor and thinly-inhabited tracts of the Scotch Highlands are more distressed by a redundant population than the most populous parts of Europe.

If a country were never to be over-run by a people more advanced in arts, but left to its own natural progress in civilization; from the time that its produce might be considered as an unit, to the time that it might be considered as a million, during the lapse of many thousand years, there would[37] not be a single period when the mass of the people could be said to be free from distress, either directly or indirectly, for want of food. In every state in Europe, since we have first had accounts of it, millions and millions of human existences have been repressed from this simple cause, though perhaps in some of these states an absolute famine may never have been known.

[38]●Famine seems to be the last, the most dreadful resource of nature. The power of population is so superior to the power in the earth to produce subsistence for man that, unless arrested by the preventive check, premature death must in some shape or other visit the human race. The vices of mankind are active and able ministers of depopulation. They are the precursors in the great army of destruction, and often finish

---

[37] [In 1826 *would* was changed to 'might'.]

[38] [In 1807 this paragraph was omitted. It is taken verbatim from pp. 139–40 of the 1798 *Essay*.]

the dreadful work themselves. But should they fail in this war of extermination, sickly seasons, epidemics, pestilence, and plague, advance in terrific array, and sweep off their thousands and ten thousands. Should success be still incomplete, gigantic inevitable famine stalks in the rear and, with one mighty blow, levels the population with the food of the world. ●[38]

Must it not then be acknowledged, by an attentive examiner of the histories of mankind, that in every age, and in every state, in which man has existed, or does now exist,

The increase of population is necessarily limited by the means of subsistence:

Population invariably increases when the means of subsistence increase,[39] unless prevented by powerful and obvious checks:

These checks, and the checks which keep the population down to the level of the means of subsistence, are, moral restraint, vice, and misery?*

In comparing the state of society which has been considered in this second book with that which formed the subject of the first, I think it appears that in modern Europe the positive checks to population prevail less, and the preventive checks more, than in past times, and in the more uncivilized parts of the world.

War, the predominant check to the population of savage nations, has certainly abated, even including the late unhappy revolutionary contests: and since the prevalence of a greater degree of personal cleanliness, of better modes of clearing and building towns, and of a more equable distribution of the products of the soil from improving knowledge in political economy, plagues, violent diseases, and famines have been certainly mitigated, and have become less frequent.

With regard to the preventive checks to population, though it must be acknowledged, that moral restraint does not at present prevail much among the male part of society;[40] yet I am strongly disposed to believe

[39] [In 1817 a footnote was added here:
By an increase in the means of subsistence, as the expression is used here, is always meant such an increase as the mass of the population can command: otherwise it can be of no avail in encouraging an increase of people.

[40] [In 1817 Malthus altered this sentence:
With regard to the preventive check to population, though it must be acknowledged that that branch of it which comes under the head of moral restraint,[(a)] does not at present prevail much ...
[He added a footnote:
[(a)] The reader will recollect the confined sense in which I use this term.
[The reader must here refer to note 4 of chapter ii of Book I, added in 1806.]

that it prevails more than in those states which were first considered; and it can scarcely be doubted that, in modern Europe, a much larger proportion of women pass a considerable part of their lives in the exercise of this virtue than in past times and among uncivilized nations. But however this may be, taking the preventive check in its general acceptation, as implying an infrequency of the marriage union from the fear of a family, without reference to its producing vice, it may be considered in this light as the most powerful of the checks which in modern Europe keep down the population to the level of the means of subsistence.[41]

[41] [This final sentence was amended twice. In 1806 it read:
But however this may be, if we consider only the general term which implies principally an infrequency of the marriage union from the fear of a family, without reference to consequences, it may be considered ...
[In 1817 this was changed to:
But however this may be, if we consider only the general term which implies principally a delay of the marriage union from prudential considerations, without reference to consequences, it may be considered ...

ESSAY, &c

BOOK III

OF THE DIFFERENT SYSTEMS OR EXPEDIENTS
WHICH HAVE BEEN PROPOSED OR HAVE
PREVAILED IN SOCIETY, AS THEY AFFECT THE
EVILS ARISING FROM THE PRINCIPLE OF
POPULATION

CHAPTER I

Of Systems of Equality. Wallace. Condorcet[1]

To a person who views the past and present states of mankind in the light in which they have appeared in the two preceding books, it cannot but be a matter of astonishment, that all the writers on the perfectibility of man and of society, who have noticed the argument of the principle of population, treat it always very slightly,[2] and invariably represent the difficulties arising from it, as at a great, and almost immeasurable distance. Even Mr. Wallace, who thought the argument itself of so much weight as to destroy his whole system of equality, did not seem to be aware that any difficulty would arise from this cause till the whole earth had been cultivated like a garden, and was incapable of any further increase of produce. Were this really the case, and were a beautiful system of equality in other respects practicable, I cannot think that our ardour in the pursuit of such a scheme ought to be damped by the contemplation of so remote a difficulty. An event at such a distance might fairly be left to providence. But the truth is, that if the view of the argument given in this essay be just, the difficulty, so far from being remote, would be[3] imminent and immediate. At every period during the

---

[1] [The whole of this chapter is based on pp. 142–72 of the 1798 *Essay*, chapters viii and ix.]

[2] [In 1817 this was altered to:
 ... very lightly.

[3] [In 1817 *would be* was changed to 'is'.

45

progress of cultivation, from the present moment to the time when the whole earth was become like a garden, the distress for want of food would be constantly pressing on all mankind, if they were equal. Though the produce of the earth would be increasing every year, population would be increasing much faster,[4] and the redundancy must necessarily be checked by the periodical or constant action of moral restraint, vice, or misery.

M. Condorcet's *Esquisse d'un tableau historique des progrès de l'esprit humain* was written, it is said, under the pressure of that cruel proscription which terminated in his death. If he had no hopes of its been seen during his life, and of its interesting France in his favour, it is a singular instance of the attachment of a man to principles which every day's experience was, so fatally for himself, contradicting. To see the human mind, in one of the most enlightened nations of the world, debased by such a fermentation of disgusting passions, of fear, cruelty, malice, revenge, ambition, madness, and folly, as would have disgraced the most savage nations in the most barbarous age, must have been such a tremendous shock to his ideas of the necessary and inevitable progress of the human mind, that nothing but the firmest conviction of the truth of his principles, in spite of all appearances, could have withstood.

This posthumous publication is only a sketch of a much larger work which he proposed should be executed. It necessarily wants, therefore, that detail and application which can alone prove the truth of any theory. A few observations will be sufficient to shew how completely this theory is contradicted, when it is applied to the real and not to an imaginary state of things.

In the last division of the work, which treats of the future progress of man towards perfection, M. Condorcet says, that, comparing in the different civilized nations of Europe the actual population with the extent of territory; and observing their cultivation, their industry, their divisions of labour, and their means of subsistence, we shall see that it would be impossible to preserve the same means of subsistence, and consequently the same population, without a number of individuals who have no other means of supplying their wants than their industry.

Having allowed the necessity of such a class of men, and adverting

---

[4] [In 1817 this sentence was altered:

   Though the produce of the earth would be increasing every year, population
would have the power of increasing much faster, and this superior power must
necessarily be checked ...

afterwards to the precarious revenue of those families that would depend so entirely on the life and health of their chief,[5] he says very justly: 'There exists then a necessary cause of inequality, of dependence, and even of misery, which menaces without ceasing the most numerous and active class of our societies.' The difficulty is just, and well stated; but his mode of removing it will, I fear, be found totally inefficacious.

By the application of calculations to the probabilities of life, and the interest of money, he proposes that a fund should be established, which should assure to the old an assistance produced in part by their own former savings, and in part by the savings of individuals who, in making the same sacrifice, die before they reap the benefit of it. The same, or a similar fund, should give assistance to women and children who lose their husbands or fathers; and afford a capital to those who were of an age to found a new family, sufficient for the development of their industry. These establishments, he observes, might be made in the name and under the protection of the society. Going still further, he says that, by the just application of calculations, means might be found of more completely preserving a state of equality, by preventing credit from being the exclusive privilege of great fortunes, and yet giving it a basis equally solid, and by rendering the progress of industry and the activity of commerce less dependent on great capitalists.

Such establishments and calculations may appear very promising upon paper; but when applied to real life they will be found to be absolutely nugatory. M. Condorcet allows that a class of people which maintains itself entirely by industry is necessary to every state. Why does he allow this? No other reason can well be assigned than because he conceives that the labour necessary to procure subsistence for an extended population will not be performed without the goad of necessity. If by establishments upon the plans that have been mentioned, this spur to industry be removed; if the idle and negligent be placed upon the same footing with regard to their credit, and the future support of their wives and families, as the active and industrious, can we expect to see men exert that animated activity in bettering their condition, which now forms the master-spring of public prosperity? If an inquisition were to

[5] To save time and long quotations, I shall here give the substance of some of M. Condorcet's sentiments, and I hope that I shall not misrepresent them; but I refer the reader to the work itself, which will amuse if it do not convince him. [In Dr Johnson's Dictionary (posthumous edition of 1792) 'to amuse' meant 'to entertain in tranquillity'; the verb had no risible connotation.]

be established to examine the claims of each individual, and to determine whether he had or had not exerted himself to the utmost, and to grant or refuse assistance accordingly, this would be little else than a repetition upon a larger scale of the English poor laws, and would be completely destructive of the true principles of liberty and equality.

But independently of this great objection to these establishments, and supposing for a moment that they would give no check to production, the greatest difficulty remains yet behind.

Were every man sure of a comfortable provision for a family, almost every man would have one; and were the rising generation free from the 'killing frost' of misery, population must increase with unusual rapidity.[6] Of this, M. Condorcet seems to be fully aware himself; and, after having described further improvements, he says,

'But in this progress of industry and happiness, each generation will be called to more extended enjoyments, and in consequence, by the physical constitution of the human frame, to an increase in the number of individuals. Must not there arrive a period then, when these laws, equally necessary, shall counteract each other; when the increase of the number of men surpassing their means of subsistence, the necessary result must be either a continual diminution of happiness and population – a movement truly retrograde; or, at least a kind of oscillation between good and evil? In societies arrived at this term, will not this oscillation be a constantly subsisting cause of periodical misery? Will it not mark the limit when all further amelioration will become impossible, and point out that term to the perfectibility of the human race, which it may reach in the course of ages, but can never pass?' He then adds,

'There is no person who does not see how very distant such a period is from us. But shall we ever arrive at it? It is equally impossible to pronounce for, or against, the future realization of an event which cannot take place but at an era when the human race will have attained improvements of which we can, at present, scarcely form a conception.'

M. Condorcet's picture of what may be expected to happen, when the number of men shall surpass their means of subsistence, is justly drawn. The oscillation which he describes will certainly take place, and will without doubt be a constantly subsisting cause of periodical misery. The

---

[6] [In 1817 this sentence was altered:

If every man were sure of a comfortable provision for a family, almost every man would have one; and if the rising generation were free from the fear of poverty, population must increase with unusual rapidity.

only point in which I differ from M. Condorcet in this description is with regard to the period when it may be applied to the human race. M. Condorcet thinks that it cannot possibly be applicable but at an era extremely distant. If the proportion between the natural increase of population and food,[7] which was stated in the beginning of this essay, and which has received considerable confirmation from the poverty that has been found to prevail in every stage and department of human society, be in any degree near the truth; it will appear, on the contrary, that the period when the number of men surpass their means of subsistence,[8] has long since arrived; and that this necessary oscillation, this constantly subsisting cause of periodical misery, has existed ever since we have had any histories of mankind, does exist at present, and will for ever continue to exist, unless some decided change take place in the physical constitution of our nature.[9]

M. Condorcet, however, goes on to say, that should the period which he conceives to be so distant ever arrive, the human race, and the advocates of the perfectibility of man, need not be alarmed at it. He then proceeds to remove the difficulty in a manner which I profess not to understand. Having observed that the ridiculous prejudices of super-stition would by that time have ceased to throw over morals a corrupt and degrading austerity, he alludes either to a promiscuous concubinage, which would prevent breeding, or to something else as unnatural. To remove the difficulty in this way will surely, in the opinion of most men, be to destroy that virtue and purity of manners which the advocates of equality, and of the perfectibility of man, profess to be the end and object of their views.

The last question which M. Condorcet proposes for examination is the organic perfectibility of man. He observes, that if the proofs which have been already given, and which, in their development, will receive greater force in the work itself, are sufficient to establish the indefinite

---

[7] [In 1826 a qualification was introduced here:
   If the proportion between the natural increase of population and of food in a limited territory, which was stated ...
[8] [In 1817 this was changed to:
   ... surpass their means of easy subsistence, ...
[9] [In 1806 Malthus amended this sentence, which he had taken verbatim from p. 153 of the 1798 *Essay*:
   ... cause of periodical misery, has existed ever since we have had any histories of mankind, and continues to exist at the present moment.
   [In 1817 he altered it again:
   ... misery, has existed in most countries ever since we have had any histories ...

perfectibility of man, upon the supposition of the same natural faculties and the same organization which he has at present; what will be the certainty, what the extent of our hopes, if this organization, these natural faculties themselves, be susceptible of melioration?

From the improvement of medicine; from the use of more wholesome food and habitations; from a manner of living which will improve the strength of the body by exercise, without impairing it by excess; from the destruction of the two great causes of the degradation of man, misery, and too great riches; from the gradual removal of transmissible and contagious disorders by the improvement of physical knowledge, rendered more efficacious, by the progress of reason and of social order; he infers, that though man will not absolutely become immortal, yet that the duration between his birth and natural death will increase without ceasing, will have no assignable term, and may properly be expressed by the word indefinite. He then defines this word to mean either a constant approach to an unlimited extent, without ever reaching it; or an increase in the immensity of ages to an extent greater than any assignable quantity.

But surely the application of this term in either of these senses to the duration of human life is in the highest degree unphilosophical, and totally unwarranted by any appearances in the laws of nature. Variations from different causes are essentially distinct from a regular and unretrograde increase. The average duration of human life will, to a certain degree, vary from healthy or unhealthy climates, from wholesome or unwholesome food, from virtuous or vicious manners, and other causes; but it may be fairly doubted, whether there has been really the smallest perceptible advance in the natural duration of human life since first we had any authentic history of man. The prejudices of all ages have indeed been directly contrary to this supposition; and though I would not lay much stress upon these prejudices, they will in some measure tend to prove[10] that there has been no marked advance in an opposite direction.

It may perhaps be said that the world is yet so young, so completely in its infancy, that it ought not to be expected that any difference should appear so soon.

If this be the case, there is at once an end of all human science. The whole train of reasonings from effects to causes will be destroyed. We may shut our eyes to the book of nature, as it will no longer be of any use

---

[10] [In 1817 this was changed to:
    ... they must have some tendency to prove ...

to read it. The wildest and most improbable conjectures may be advanced with as much certainty as the most just and sublime theories founded on careful and reiterated experiments. We may return again to the old mode of philosophising, and make facts bend to systems, instead of establishing systems upon facts. The grand and consistent theory of Newton, will be placed upon the same footing as the wild and eccentric hypotheses of Descartes. In short, if the laws of nature be thus fickle and inconstant; if it can be affirmed, and be believed, that they will change, when for ages and ages they have appeared immutable; the human mind will no longer have any incitements to inquiry, but must remain fixed[11] in inactive torpor, or amuse itself only in bewildering dreams and extravagant fancies.

The constancy of the laws of nature, and of effects and causes, is the foundation of all human knowledge; and if, without any previous observable symptoms or indications of a change, we can infer that a change will take place, we may as well make any assertion whatever, and think it as unreasonable to be contradicted, in affirming that the moon will come in contact with the earth to-morrow, as in saying that the sun will rise at its appointed time.[12]

With regard to the duration of human life, there does not appear to have existed, from the earliest ages of the world to the present moment, the smallest permanent symptom or indication of increasing prolongation. The observable effects of climate, habit, diet, and other causes, on length of life, have furnished the pretext for asserting its indefinite extension; and the sandy foundation on which the argument rests is, that because the limit of human life is undefined; because you cannot mark its precise term, and say so far exactly shall it go, and no further; that therefore its extent may increase for ever, and be properly termed indefinite or unlimited. But the fallacy and absurdity of this argument will sufficiently appear from a slight examination of what M. Condorcet calls the organic perfectibility or degeneration of the race of plants and

---

[11] [In 1817 *fixed* was changed to 'sunk'.

[12] [After following the 1798 *Essay* very closely, Malthus omitted here a passage from pp. 159–60:

... the foundation of all human knowledge; though far be it from me to say, that the same power which framed and executes the laws of nature, may not change them all in a moment, in the twinkling of an eye. Such a change may undoubtedly happen. All that I mean to say is that it is impossible to infer it from reasoning. If without any previous observable symptoms ...

[In 1817 Malthus wrote:

... the sun will rise at its expected time.

animals, which, he says, may be regarded as one of the general laws of nature.

I am told that it is a maxim among the improvers of cattle,[13] that you may breed to any degree of nicety you please; and they found this maxim upon another, which is, that some of the offspring will possess the desirable qualities of the parents in a greater degree. In the famous Leicestershire breed of sheep, the object is to procure them with small heads and small legs. Proceeding upon these breeding maxims, it is evident that we might go on till the heads and legs were evanescent quantities; but this is so palpable an absurdity that we may be quite sure that the premises are not just, and that there really is a limit, though we cannot see it, or say exactly where it is. In this case, the point of the greatest degree of improvement, or the smallest size of the head and legs, may be said to be undefined; but this is very different from unlimited, or from indefinite, in M. Condorcet's acceptation of the term. Though I may not be able, in the present instance, to mark the limit at which further improvement will stop, I can very easily mention a point at which it will not arrive. I should not scruple to assert, that were the breeding to continue for ever, the heads and legs of these sheep would never be so small as the head and legs of a rat.

It cannot be true, therefore, that among animals, some of the offspring will possess the desirable qualities of the parents in a greater degree; or that animals are indefinitely perfectible.

The progress of a wild plant to a beautiful garden flower is perhaps more marked and striking than any thing that takes place among animals; yet even here, it would be the height of absurdity to assert that the progress was unlimited or indefinite. One of the most obvious features of the improvement is the increase of size. The flower has grown gradually larger by cultivation. If the progress were really unlimited, it might be increased ad infinitum; but this is so gross an absurdity that we may be quite sure that among plants, as well as among animals, there is a limit to improvement, though we do not exactly know where it is. It is probable that the gardeners who contend for flower-prizes have often applied stronger dressing without success. At the same time, it would be highly presumptuous in any man to say that he had seen the finest carnation or anemone that could ever be made to grow. He might however assert without the smallest chance of being contradicted by a future fact, that

---

[13] [In 1806 this was changed to:
    I have been told that it is a maxim among some of the improvers of cattle . . .

no carnation or anemone could ever by cultivation be increased to the size of a large cabbage; and yet there are assignable quantities greater than a cabbage. No man can say that he has seen the largest ear of wheat, or the largest oak that could ever grow; but he might easily, and with perfect certainty, name a point of magnitude at which they would not arrive. In all these cases, therefore, a careful distinction should be made between an unlimited progress, and a progress where the limit is merely undefined.

It will be said, perhaps, that the reason why plants and animals cannot increase indefinitely in size is that they would fall by their own weight. I answer, how do we know this but from experience? from experience of the degree of strength with which these bodies are formed. I know that a carnation, long before it reached the size of a cabbage, would not be supported by its stalk; but I only know this from my experience of the weakness, and want of tenacity in the materials of a carnation stalk. There are many substances in nature, of the same size, that would support as large a head as a cabbage.[14]

The reasons of the mortality of plants are at present perfectly unknown to us. No man can say why such a plant is annual, another biennial, and another endures for ages. The whole affair in all these cases, in plants, animals, and in the human race, is an affair of experience; and I only conclude that man is mortal, because the invariable experience of all ages has proved the mortality of those materials of which his visible body is made.[15]

What can we reason but from what we know?

Sound philosophy will not authorize me to alter this opinion of the mortality of man on earth till it can be clearly proved that the human race has made, and is making, a decided progress towards an illimitable extent of life. And the chief reason why I adduced the two particular instances from animals and plants was to expose and illustrate, if I could, the fallacy of that argument which infers an unlimited progress merely because some partial improvement has taken place, and that the limit of this improvement cannot be precisely ascertained.

The capacity of improvement in plants and animals, to a certain

[14] [In 1806 Malthus was more cautious:
　There might be substances of the same size that would support as large a head as a cabbage.
[15] [In 1817 this was altered to:
　... the mortality of that organised substance of which his visible body is made.

degree, no person can possibly doubt. A clear and decided progress has already been made; and yet I think it appears that it would be highly absurd to say that this progress has no limits. In human life, though there are great variations from different causes, it may be doubted whether, since the world began, any organic improvement whatever of the human frame can be clearly ascertained. The foundations, therefore, on which the arguments for the organic perfectibility of man rest, are unusually weak, and can only be considered as mere conjectures. It does not, however, by any means seem impossible that, by an attention to breed, a certain degree of improvement, similar to that among animals, might take place among men. Whether intellect could be communicated may be a matter of doubt: but size, strength, beauty, complexion, and perhaps even longevity, are in a degree transmissible. The error does not seem to lie in supposing a small degree of improvement possible,[16] but in not discriminating between a small improvement, the limit of which is undefined, and an improvement really unlimited. As the human race, however, could not be improved in this way without condemning all the bad specimens to celibacy, it is not probable that an attention to breed should ever become general; indeed I know of no well-directed attempts of the kind, except in the ancient family of the Bickerstaffs, who are said to have been very successful in whitening the skins, and increasing the height of their race by prudent marriages, particularly by that very judicious cross with Maud the milk-maid, by which some capital defects in the constitutions of the family were corrected.

It will not be necessary, I think, in order more completely to shew the improbability of any approach in man towards immortality on earth, to urge the very great additional weight that an increase in the duration of life would give to the argument of population.

M. Condorcet's book may be considered not only as a sketch of the opinions of a celebrated individual, but of many of the literary men in France at the beginning of the revolution. As such, though merely a sketch, it seems worthy of attention.

Many, I doubt not, will think that the attempting gravely to controvert so absurd a paradox as the immortality of man on earth, or indeed, even the perfectibility of man and society, is a waste of time and words; and that such unfounded conjectures are best answered by neglect. I profess, however, to be of a different opinion. When paradoxes

---

[16] [In 1817 this became:

The error does not lie in supposing ...

of this kind are advanced by ingenious and able men, neglect has no tendency to convince them of their mistakes. Priding themselves on what they conceive to be a mark of the reach and size of their own understandings, of the extent and comprehensiveness of their views; they will look upon this neglect merely as an indication of poverty and narrowness in the mental exertions of their contemporaries; and only think that the world is not yet prepared to receive their sublime truths.

On the contrary, a candid investigation of these subjects accompanied with a perfect readiness to adopt any theory warranted by sound philosophy, may have a tendency to convince them that, in forming improbable and unfounded hypotheses, so far from enlarging the bounds of human science, they are contracting it; so far from promoting the improvement of the human mind, they are obstructing it: they are throwing us back again almost into the infancy of knowledge; and weakening the foundations of that mode of philosophising, under the auspices of which science has of late made such rapid advances. The late rage for wide and unrestrained speculation[17] seems to have been a kind of mental intoxication, arising, perhaps, from the great and unexpected discoveries which had been made in various branches of science. To men elate and giddy with such successes, everything appeared to be within the grasp of human powers; and under this illusion they confounded subjects where no real progress could be proved with those where the progress had been marked, certain, and acknowledged. Could they be persuaded to sober themselves with a little severe and chastized thinking, they would see that the cause of truth and of sound philosophy cannot but suffer, by substituting wild flights and unsupported assertions, for patient investigation and well authenticated proofs.[18]

[17] [In 1798 (footnote, p. 162) Malthus had written:
    The present rage ...
[18] [In 1817 *well authenticated proofs* was changed to:
    ... well-supported proofs.

CHAPTER II

Of Systems of Equality. Godwin[1]

In reading Mr. Godwin's ingenious work on political justice, it is impossible not to be struck with the spirit and energy of his style, the force and precision of some of his reasonings, the ardent tone of his thoughts, and particularly with that impressive earnestness of manner which gives an air of truth to the whole. At the same time it must be confessed that he has not proceeded in his inquiries with the caution that sound philosophy requires. His conclusions are often unwarranted by his premises. He fails sometimes in removing objections which he himself brings forward. He relies too much on general and abstract propositions which will not admit of application. And his conjectures certainly far outstrip the modesty of nature.

The system of equality which Mr. Godwin proposes is, on a first view, the most beautiful and engaging of any that has yet appeared. An amelioration of society to be produced merely by reason and conviction gives more promise of permanence than any change effected and maintained by force. The unlimited exercise of private judgement is a doctrine grand and captivating, and has a vast superiority over those systems where every individual is in a manner the slave of the public. The substitution of benevolence, as the masterspring and moving principle of society, instead of self-love, appears at first sight to be a consummation devoutly to be wished. In short, it is impossible to contemplate the whole of this fair picture without emotions of delight and admiration, accompanied with an ardent longing for the period of its accomplishment. But alas! that moment can never arrive. The whole is little better than a dream – a phantom of the imagination. These 'gorgeous palaces' of happiness and immortality, these 'solemn temples' of truth and virtue, will dissolve, 'like the baseless fabric of a vision', when we awaken to real life and contemplate the genuine situation of man on earth.

Mr. Godwin, at the conclusion of the third chapter of his eighth book, speaking of population, says: 'There is a principle in human society, by

[1] [This chapter follows closely chapter x (pp. 173–209) of the 1798 *Essay*.]

which population is perpetually kept down to the level of the means of subsistence. Thus, among the wandering tribes of America and Asia, we never find, through the lapse of ages, that population has so increased as to render necessary the cultivation of the earth.'[2] This principle, which Mr. Godwin thus mentions as some mysterious and occult cause, and which he does not attempt to investigate, has appeared to be the grinding law[3] of necessity – misery, and the fear of misery.

The great error under which Mr. Godwin labours throughout his whole work is the attributing of almost all the vices and misery that prevail in civil society to human institutions. Political regulations and the established administration of property are, with him, the fruitful sources of all evil, the hotbeds of all the crimes that degrade mankind. Were this really a true state of the case, it would not seem an absolutely hopeless task, to remove evil completely from the world; and reason seems to be the proper and adequate instrument for effecting so great a purpose. But the truth is, that though human institutions appear to be the obvious and obtrusive causes of much mischief to mankind, they are, in reality, light and superficial in comparison with those deeper-seated causes of evil which result from the laws of nature.[4]

In a chapter on the benefits attendant upon a system of equality, Mr. Godwin says: 'The spirit of oppression, the spirit of servility, and the spirit of fraud, these are the immediate growth of the established administration of property. They are alike hostile to intellectual improvement.[5] The other vices of envy, malice, and revenge, are their inseparable companions. In a state of society where men lived in the midst of plenty, and where all shared alike the bounties of nature, these sentiments would inevitably expire. The narrow principle of selfishness would vanish. No man being obliged to guard his little store, or provide with anxiety and pain for his restless wants, each would lose his individual existence in the thought of the general good. No man would be an enemy to his neighbours, for they would have no subject of

---

[2] P. 460. 8vo. 2nd edit.   [3] [In 1817 the word *grinding* was omitted.]

[4] [In 1807 (Vol. II, pp. 24–5) this sentence was altered:

But the truth is, that though human institutions appear to be, and indeed often are, the obvious and obtrusive causes of much mischief to society, they are, in reality, light and superficial in comparison with those deeper-seated causes of evil which result from the laws of nature and the passions of mankind.

[5] [Professor Antony Flew points out in the Pelican edition of the 1798 *Essay* (p. 280) that what Godwin actually wrote was 'hostile to intellectual and moral improvement'.]

contention: and of consequence philanthropy would resume the empire which reason assigns her. Mind would be delivered from her perpetual anxiety about corporal support, and free to expatiate in the field of thought which is congenial to her. Each would assist the inquiries of all.'[6]

This would indeed be a happy state. But that it is merely an imaginary picture, with scarcely a feature near the truth, the reader, I am afraid, is already too well convinced.

Man cannot live in the midst of plenty. All cannot share alike the bounties of nature. Were there no established administration of property, every man would be obliged to guard with force his little store. Selfishness would be triumphant. The subjects of contention would be perpetual. Every individual would be under a constant anxiety about corporal support, and not a single intellect would be left free to expatiate in the field of thought.

How little Mr. Godwin has turned his attention to the real state of human society will sufficiently appear from the manner in which he endeavours to remove the difficulty of an overcharged population.[7] He says: 'The obvious answer to this objection is, that to reason thus is to foresee difficulties at a great distance. Three-fourths of the habitable globe is now uncultivated. The parts already cultivated are capable of immeasurable improvement. Myriads of centuries of still increasing population may pass away, and the earth be still found sufficient for the subsistence of its inhabitants.'[8]

I have already pointed out the error of supposing that no distress or difficulty would arise from a redundant population before the earth absolutely refused to produce any more. But let us imagine, for a moment, Mr. Godwin's system of equality realized in its utmost extent,[9] and see how soon this difficulty might be expected to press, under so perfect a form of society. A theory that will not admit of application cannot possibly be just.

Let us suppose all the causes of vice and misery in this island removed. War and contention cease. Unwholesome trades and manufactories do not exist. Crowds no longer collect together in great and pestilent cities for purposes of court intrigue, of commerce, and vicious gratification.

---

[6] Political Justice, b. viii. c. iii. p. 458.
[7] [In 1817 this was changed to:
    ... a superabundant population.
[8] Polit. Justice, b. viii. c. ix. p. 510.
[9] [In 1826 the words *in its utmost extent* were excised.]

Simple, healthy, and rational amusements take place of drinking, gaming, and debauchery. There are no towns sufficiently large to have any prejudicial effects on the human constitution. The greater part of the happy inhabitants of this terrestrial paradise live in hamlets and farm-houses scattered over the face of the country. All men are equal. The labours of luxury are at an end; and the necessary labours of agriculture are shared amicably among all. The number of persons and the produce of the island we suppose to be the same as at present. The spirit of benevolence guided by impartial justice will divide this produce among all the members of society according to their wants. Though it would be impossible that they should all have animal food every day, yet vegetable food, with meat occasionally, would satisfy the desires of a frugal people, and would be sufficient to preserve them in health, strength, and spirits.

Mr. Godwin considers marriage as a fraud and a monopoly.[10] Let us suppose the commerce of the sexes established upon principles of the most perfect freedom. Mr. Godwin does not think himself that this freedom would lead to a promiscuous intercourse; and in this I perfectly agree with him. The love of variety is a vicious, corrupt, and unnatural taste, and could not prevail in any great degree in a simple and virtuous state of society. Each man would probably select for himself a partner, to whom he would adhere, as long as that adherence continued to be the choice of both parties. It would be of little consequence, according to Mr. Godwin, how many children a woman had, or to whom they belonged. Provisions and assistance would spontaneously flow from the quarter in which they abounded, to the quarter in which they were deficient.[11] And every man, according to his capacity, would be ready to furnish instruction to the rising generation.

I cannot conceive a form of society so favourable, upon the whole, to population. The irremediableness of marriage, as it is at present consti-tuted, undoubtedly deters many from entering into this state. An unshackled intercourse, on the contrary, would be a most powerful incitement to early attachments: and as we are supposing no anxiety about the future support of children to exist, I do not conceive that there would be one woman in a hundred, of twenty-three years of age, without a family.

With these extraordinary encouragements to population, and every cause of depopulation, as we have supposed, removed, the numbers

---

[10] Polit. Justice, b. viii. c. viii. p. 498. et seq.   [11] Id. b. viii. c. viii. p. 504.

would necessarily increase faster than in any society that has ever yet been known. I have before mentioned that the inhabitants of the back settlements of America appear to double their numbers in fifteen years. England is certainly a more healthy country than the back settlements of America; and as we have supposed every house in the island to be airy and wholesome, and the encouragements to have a family greater even than in America, no probable reason can be assigned why the population should not double itself in less, if possible, than fifteen years. But to be quite sure that we do not go beyond the truth, we will only suppose the period of doubling to be twenty-five years; a ratio of increase which is well known to have taken place throughout all the northern states of America.[12]

There can be little doubt, that the equalization of property which we have supposed, added to the circumstance of the labour of the whole community being directed chiefly to agriculture, would tend greatly to augment the produce of the country. But to answer the demands of a population increasing so rapidly, Mr. Godwin's calculation of half an hour a day would certainly not be sufficient. It is probable that the half of every man's time must be employed for this purpose. Yet with such or much greater exertions, a person who is acquainted with the nature of the soil in this country, and who reflects on the fertility of the lands already in cultivation, and the barrenness of those that are not cultivated, will be very much disposed to doubt whether the whole average produce could possibly be doubled in twenty-five years from the present period. The only chance of success would be from the ploughing up most of the grazing countries, and putting an end almost entirely to animal food. Yet this scheme would probably defeat itself. The soil of England will not produce much without dressing; and cattle seem to be necessary to make that species of manure which best suits the land.

Difficult however as it might be to double the average produce of the island in twenty-five years, let us suppose it effected. At the expiration of the first period therefore, the food, though almost entirely vegetable, would be sufficient to support in health the doubled population of 22 millions.[13]

[12] [In 1817 this was changed to:
     . . . all the United States of America.
[13] [In 1826 this was altered to:
     . . . to support in health the population increased from 11 to 22 millions.
   [A footnote was added:
     The numbers here mentioned refer to the enumeration of 1800.

During the next period, where will the food be found to satisfy the importunate demands of the increasing numbers? Where is the fresh land to turn up? Where is the dressing necessary to improve that which is already in cultivation? There is no person with the smallest knowledge of land, but would say that it was impossible that the average produce of the country could be increased during the second twenty-five years by a quantity equal to what it at present yields. Yet we will suppose this increase, however improbable, to take place. The exuberant strength of the argument allows of almost any concession. Even with this concession, however, there would be eleven millions at the expiration of the second term unprovided for. A quantity equal to the frugal support of 33 millions would be to be divided among 44 millions.

Alas! what becomes of the picture where men lived in the midst of plenty, where no man was obliged to provide with anxiety and pain for his restless wants; where the narrow principle of selfishness did not exist; where the mind was delivered from her perpetual anxiety about corporeal support, and free to expatiate in the field of thought which is congenial to her? This beautiful fabric of the imagination vanishes at the severe touch of truth. The spirit of benevolence, cherished and invigorated by plenty, is repressed by the chilling breath of want. The hateful passions that had vanished reappear. The mighty law of self-preservation expels all the softer and more exalted emotions of the soul. The temptations to evil are too strong for human nature to resist. The corn is plucked before it is ripe, or secreted in unfair proportions; and the whole black train of vices that belong to falsehood are immediately generated. Provisions no longer flow in for the support of a mother with a large family. The children are sickly from insufficient food. The rosy flush of health gives place to the pallid cheek and hollow eye of misery. Benevolence, yet lingering in a few bosoms, makes some faint expiring struggles, till at length self-love resumes his wonted empire and lords it triumphant over the world.

No human institutions here existed, to the perverseness of which Mr. Godwin ascribes the original sin of the worst men.[14] No opposition had been produced by them between public and private good. No monopoly had been created of those advantages which reason directs to be left in common. No man had been goaded to the breach of order by unjust laws. Benevolence had established her reign in all hearts. And yet in so short a

---

[14] Polit. Justice, b. viii. c. iii. p. 340.

period as fifty years, violence, oppression, falsehood, misery, every hateful vice and every form of distress, which degrade and sadden the present state of society, seem to have been generated by the most imperious circumstances, by laws inherent in the nature of man, and absolutely independent of all human regulations.

If we be not yet too well convinced of the reality of this melancholy picture, let us look for a moment into the next period of twenty-five years, and we shall see 44 millions of human beings without the means of support: and at the conclusion of the first century, the population would be 176 millions, and the food only sufficient for 55 millions, leaving 121 millions unprovided for. In these ages, want, indeed, would be triumphant, and rapine and murder must reign at large:[15] and yet all this time we are supposing the produce of the earth absolutely unlimited, and the yearly increase greater than the boldest speculator can imagine.

This is undoubtedly a very different view of the difficulty arising from the principle of population from that which Mr. Godwin gives, when he says: 'Myriads of centuries of still increasing population may pass away, and the earth be still found sufficient for the subsistence of its inhabitants.'

I am sufficiently aware that the redundant millions which I have mentioned could never have existed. It is a perfectly just observation of Mr. Godwin, that 'there is a principle in human society by which population is perpetually kept down to the level of the means of subsistence.' The sole question is, what is this principle? Is it some obscure and occult cause? Is it some mysterious interference of heaven, which at a certain period strikes the men with impotence and the women with barrenness? Or is it a cause open to our researches, within our view; a cause which has constantly been observed to operate, though with varied force, in every state in which man has been placed? Is it not misery, and the fear of misery, the necessary and inevitable results of the laws of nature,[16] which

---

[15] [In 1817 this paragraph was substantially altered:
   ... let us but look for a moment into the next period of twenty-five years, and we shall see that, according to the natural increase of population, 44 millions of human beings would be without the means of support; and at the conclusion of the first century the population would have had the power of increasing to 176 millions, while the food was only sufficient for 55 millions, leaving 121 millions unprovided for; and yet all this time we are supposing the produce of the earth absolutely unlimited ...

[16] [In 1817 there was a qualifying insertion here:
   ... inevitable results of the laws of nature, in the present state of man's existence, which human institutions ...

human institutions, so far from aggravating, have tended considerably to mitigate, though they can never remove?

It may be curious to observe, in the case that we have been supposing, how some of the principal laws which at present govern civilized society would be successively dictated by the most imperious necessity. As man, according to Mr. Godwin, is the creature of the impressions to which he is subject, the goadings of want could not continue long before some violations of public or private stock would necessarily take place. As these violations increased in number and extent, the more active and comprehensive intellects of the society would soon perceive that, while population was fast increasing, the yearly produce of the country would shortly begin to diminish. The urgency of the case would suggest the necessity of some immediate measures being taken for the general safety. Some kind of convention would then be called, and the dangerous situation of the country stated in the strongest terms. It would be observed that while they lived in the midst of plenty, it was of little consequence who laboured the least, or who possessed the least, as every man was perfectly willing and ready to supply the wants of his neighbour. But that the question was no longer whether one man should give to another that which he did not use himself; but whether he should give to his neighbour the food which was absolutely necessary to his own existence. It would be represented that the number of those who were in want very greatly exceeded the number and means of those who should supply them; that these pressing wants, which from the state of the produce of the country could not all be gratified, had occasioned some flagrant violations of justice; that these violations had already checked the increase of food, and would, if they were not by some means or other prevented, throw the whole community into confusion; that imperious necessity seemed to dictate that a yearly increase of produce should, if possible, be obtained at all events; that, in order to effect this first great and indispensable purpose, it would be advisable to make a more complete division of land, and to secure every man's property against violation, by the most powerful sanctions.

It might be urged perhaps by some objectors, that, as the fertility of the land increased, and various accidents occurred, the shares of some men might be much more than sufficient for their support; and that, when the reign of self-love was once established, they would not distribute their surplus produce without some compensation in return. It would be observed in answer that this was an inconvenience greatly to be lamented; but that it was an evil which would bear no comparison to the black train of distresses which would inevitably be occasioned by the insecurity of property; that the quantity of food which one man could consume was necessarily limited by the narrow capacity of the human stomach; that it was certainly not probable that he should throw away the rest; and if he exchanged his surplus produce for the labour of others, this would be better than that these others should absolutely starve.

It seems highly probable, therefore, that an administration of property, not very different from that which prevails in civilized states at present, would be established, as the best (though inadequate) remedy, for the evils which were pressing on the society.

The next subject which would come under discussion, intimately connected with the preceding, is the commerce of the sexes. It would be urged by those who had turned their attention to the true cause of the difficulties under which the community laboured, that while every man felt secure that all his children would be well provided for by general benevolence, the powers of the earth would be absolutely inadequate to produce food for the population which would inevitably ensue;[17] that even if the whole attention and labour of the society were directed to this sole point, and if by the most perfect security of property, and every other encouragement that could be thought of, the greatest possible increase of produce were yearly obtained; yet still the increase of food would by no means keep pace with the much more rapid increase of population; that some check to population, therefore, was imperiously called for; that the most natural and obvious check seemed to be to make every man provide for his own children; that this would operate in some respect as a measure and a guide in the increase of population, as it might be expected that no man would bring beings into the world for whom he could not find the means of support; that, where this notwithstanding was the case, it seemed necessary, for the example of others, that the disgrace and inconvenience attending such a conduct should fall upon that individual who had thus inconsiderately plunged himself and his innocent children into want and misery.

The institution of marriage, or at least of some express or implied obligation on every man to support his own children, seems to be the natural result of these reasonings in a community under the difficulties that we have supposed.

---

[17] [In 1807 the word *inevitably* was omitted.]

The view of these difficulties presents us with a very natural reason why the disgrace which attends a breach of chastity should be greater in a woman than in a man. It could not be expected that women should have resources sufficient to support their own children. When, therefore, a woman had lived with a man, who had entered into no compact to maintain her children; and aware of the inconveniences that he might bring upon himself, had deserted her, these children must necessarily fall upon the society for support, or starve. And to prevent the frequent recurrence of such an inconvenience, as it would be highly unjust to punish so natural a fault by personal restraint or infliction, the men might agree to punish it with disgrace. The offence is, besides, more obvious and conspicuous in the woman, and less liable to any mistake. The father of a child may not always be known; but the same uncertainty cannot easily exist with regard to the mother. Where the evidence of the offence was most complete, and the inconvenience to the society, at the same time, the greatest, there it was agreed that the largest share of blame should fall. The obligation on every man to support his children, the society would enforce by positive laws; and the greater degree of inconvenience or labour to which a family would necessarily subject him, added to some portion of disgrace which every human being must incur, who leads another into unhappiness, might be considered as a sufficient punishment for the man.

That a woman should, at present, be almost driven from society for an offence which men commit nearly with impunity, seems undoubtedly to be a breach of natural justice. But the origin of the custom, as the most obvious and effectual method of preventing the frequent recurrence of a serious inconvenience to a community, appears to be natural, though not perhaps perfectly justifiable. This origin is now lost in the new train of ideas that the custom has since generated. What at first might be dictated by state necessity is now supported by female delicacy; and operates with the greatest force on that part of the society where, if the original intention of the custom were preserved, there is the least real occasion for it.

When these two fundamental laws of society, the security of property and the institution of marriage, were once established, inequality of conditions must necessarily follow. Those who were born after the division of property would come into a world already possessed. If their parents, from having too large a family, were unable to give them sufficient for their support, what could they do in a world where everything was appropriated? We have seen the fatal effects that would result to society if every man had a valid claim to an equal share of the produce of the earth. The members of a family which was grown too large for the original division of land appropriated to it could not then demand a part of the surplus produce of others as a debt of justice. It has appeared that, from the inevitable laws of human nature, some human beings will be exposed to want. These are the unhappy persons who in the great lottery of life have drawn a blank. The number of these persons would soon exceed the ability of the surplus produce to supply. Moral merit is a very difficult criterion, except in extreme cases. The owners of surplus produce would in general seek some more obvious mark of distinction; and it seems to be both natural and just that, except upon particular occasions, their choice should fall upon those, who were able, and professed themselves willing, to exert their strength in procuring a further surplus produce, which would at once benefit the community and enable the proprietors to afford assistance to greater numbers. All who were in want of food would be urged by imperious necessity[18] to offer their labour in exchange for this article, so absolutely necessary to existence. The fund appropriated to the maintenance of labour would be the aggregate quantity of food possessed by the owners of land beyond their own consumption. When the demands upon this fund were great and numerous, it would naturally be divided into very small shares. Labour would be ill paid. Men would offer to work for a bare subsistence; and the rearing of families would be checked by sickness and misery. On the contrary, when this fund was increasing fast; when it was great in proportion to the number of claimants, it would be divided in much larger shares. No man would exchange his labour without receiving an ample quantity of food in return. Labourers would live in ease and comfort, and would consequently be able to rear a numerous and vigorous offspring.

On the state of this fund, the happiness, or the degree of misery, prevailing among the lower classes of people, in every known state, at present chiefly depends; and on this happiness, or degree of misery, depends principally the increase, stationariness, or decrease, of population.

And thus it appears that a society constituted according to the most beautiful form that imagination can conceive, with benevolence for its

---

[18] [In 1817 the word *imperious* was excised.]

moving principle, instead of self-love, and with every evil disposition in all its members corrected by reason, not force, would, from the inevitable laws of nature, and not from any original depravity of man or of human institutions,[19] degenerate in a very short period into a society constructed upon a plan not essentially different from that which prevails in every known state at present; a society divided into a class of proprietors and a class of labourers, and with self-love for the mainspring of the great machine.

In the supposition which I have made, I have undoubtedly taken the increase of population smaller, and the increase of produce greater, than they really would be. No reason can be assigned why, under the circumstances supposed, population should not increase faster than in any known instance. If, then, we were to take the period of doubling at fifteen years instead of twenty-five years, and reflect upon the labour necessary to double the produce in so short a time, even if we allow it possible; we may venture to pronounce with certainty that, if Mr. Godwin's system of society were established in its utmost perfection,[20] instead of myriads of centuries, not thirty years could elapse before its utter destruction from the simple principle of population.

I have taken no notice of emigration in this place, for obvious reasons. If such societies were instituted in other parts of Europe, these countries would be under the same difficulties with regard to population, and could admit no fresh members into their bosoms. If this beautiful society were confined to our island, it must have degenerated strangely from its original purity, and administer but a very small portion of the happiness it proposed, before any of its members would voluntarily consent to leave it, and live under such governments as at present exist in Europe, or submit to the extreme hardships of first settlers in new regions.

[19] [This wording is that of the 1798 *Essay* (p. 207). In 1817 it was altered:
    ... from the inevitable laws of nature, and not from any fault in human institutions, degenerate ...
[20] [In 1826 the words *in its utmost perfection* were excised.]

Observations on the Reply of Mr. Godwin

Mr. Godwin, in a late publication, has replied to those parts of the Essay on the Principle of Population which he thinks bear the hardest on his system. A few remarks on this reply will be sufficient.

In a note to an early part of his pamphlet, he observes that the main attack of the essay is not directed against the principles of his work, but its conclusion.[1] It may be true indeed that, as Mr. Godwin had dedicated one particular chapter towards the conclusion of his work, to the consideration of the objections to his system from the principle of population, this particular chapter is most frequently alluded to: but certainly if the great principle of the essay be admitted, it affects his whole work, and essentially alters the foundations of political justice. A great part of Mr. Godwin's book consists of an abuse of human institutions, as productive of all, or most of, the evils which afflict society. The acknowledgment of a new and totally unconsidered cause of misery would evidently alter the state of these arguments, and make it absolutely necessary that they should be either newly modified or entirely rejected.

In the first book of Political Justice, chap. iii. entitled: 'The Spirit of Political Institutions', Mr. Godwin observes, that: 'Two of the greatest abuses relative to the interior policy of nations which at this time prevail in the world, consist in the irregular transfer of property, either first by violence, or secondly by fraud.' And he goes on to say that if there existed no desire in individuals to possess themselves of the substance of others, and if every man could, with perfect facility, obtain the necessaries of life, civil society might become what poetry has feigned of the golden age. Let us inquire, he says, into the principles to which these evils are indebted for existence. After acknowledging the truth of the principal argument in the essay on population, I do not think he could stop in this inquiry at mere human institutions. Many other parts of his work would be affected by this consideration in a similar manner.

As Mr. Godwin seems disposed to understand, and candidly to admit

---

[1] Reply to the attacks of Dr. Parr, Mr. Mackintosh, the author of an Essay on Population, and others, p. 10.

the truth of the principal argument in the essay, I feel the more mortified that he should think it a fair inference from my positions, that the political superintendents of a community are bound to exercise a paternal vigilance and care over the two great means of advantage and safety to mankind, misery and vice; and that no evil is more to be dreaded than that we should have too little of them in the world, to confine the principle of population within its proper sphere.[2] I am at a loss to conceive what class of evils Mr. Godwin imagines is yet behind, which these salutary checks are to prevent. For my own part, I know of no stronger or more general terms than vice and misery; and the sole question is respecting a greater or less degree of them.[3] The only reason why I object to Mr. Godwin's system is my full conviction that an attempt to execute it would very greatly increase the quantity of vice and misery in society. If Mr. Godwin will undo this conviction and prove to me, though it be only in theory, provided that theory be consistent, and founded on a knowledge of human nature, that his system will really tend to drive vice and misery from the earth, he may depend upon having me one of its steadiest and warmest advocates.

Mr. Godwin observes that he should naturally be disposed to pronounce that man strangely indifferent to schemes of extraordinary improvement in society, who made it a conclusive argument against them that, when they were realized, they might peradventure be of no permanence and duration. And yet what is morality, individual or political, according to Mr. Godwin's own definition of it, but a calculation of consequences? Is the physician the patron of pain, who advises his patient to bear a present evil, rather than betake himself to a remedy which, though it might give momentary relief, would afterwards greatly aggravate all the symptoms? Is the moralist to be called an enemy to pleasure, because he recommends to a young man just entering into life, not to ruin his health and patrimony in a few years, by an excess of present gratifications, but to economize his enjoyments, that he may spread them over a longer period? Of Mr. Godwin's system, according to the present arguments by which it is supported, it is not enough to say, *peradventure* it will be of no permanence; but we can pronounce with *certainty* that it will be of no permanence: and under such circumstances

---

[2] Reply, &c. p. 60.
[3] [In 1806 this sentence was amended:

For my own part, I know of no greater evils than vice and misery; and the sole question is respecting the most effectual mode of diminishing them.

an attempt to execute it would unquestionably be a great political immorality.

Mr. Godwin observes, that after recovering from the first impression made by the Essay on Population, the first thing that is apt to strike every reflecting mind, is that the excess of power in the principle of population over the principle of subsistence has never, in any past instance, in any quarter or age of the world, produced those great and astonishing effects, that total breaking-up of all the structures and maxims of society, which the essay lead us to expect from it in certain cases in future.[4] This is undoubtedly true; and the reason is that in no past instance, nor in any quarter or age of the world, has an attempt been made to establish such a system as Mr. Godwin's, and without an attempt of this nature, none of these great effects will follow. The convulsions of the social system, described in the last chapter, appeared by a kind of irresistible necessity to terminate in the establishment of the laws of property and marriage; but in countries where these laws are already established, as they are in all the common constitutions of society with which we are acquainted, the operation of the principle of population will always be silent and gradual, and not different to what we daily see in our own country. Other persons besides Mr. Godwin have imagined that I looked to certain periods in the future, when population would exceed the means of subsistence in a much greater degree that at present, and that the evils arising from the principle of population were rather in contemplation than in existence; but this is a total misconception of the argument.[5] Poverty, and not absolute famine, is the specific effect of the principle of population, as I have before endeavoured to show. Many countries are now suffering all the evils that can ever be expected to flow from this principle, and even if we were arrived at the absolute limit to all further increase of produce, a point which we shall certainly never reach, I should by no means expect that these evils would be in any marked manner aggravated. The increase of produce in most European countries is so very slow, compared with what would be required to support an unrestricted increase of people, that the checks which are constantly in action to repress the population to the level of a produce increasing so slowly would have very little more to do in wearing it down to a produce absolutely stationary.

But Mr. Godwin says, that if he looks into the past history of the

[4] Reply, p. 70.
[5] In other parts of his Reply, Mr. Godwin does not fall into this error.

world, he does not see that increasing population has been controlled and confined by vice and misery alone. In this observation I cannot agree with him. I will thank Mr. Godwin to name to me any check which in past ages has contributed to keep down the population to the level of the means of subsistence, that does not fairly come under some form of vice or misery; except indeed the check of moral restraint, which I have mentioned in the course of this work; and which, to say the truth, whatever hopes we may entertain of its prevalence in future, has undoubtedly in past ages operated with very inconsiderable force.[6]

I do not think that I should find it difficult to justify myself in the eyes of my readers from the imputation of being the patron of vice and misery; but I am not clear that Mr. Godwin would find such a justification so easy. For though he has positively declared that he does not 'regard them with complacency', and 'hopes that it may not be considered as a taste absolutely singular in him that he should entertain no vehement partialities for vice and misery';[7] yet he has certainly exposed himself to the suspicion of having this singular taste, by suggesting the organization of a very large portion of them for the benefit of society in general. On this subject I need only observe that I have always ranked the two checks[8] which he first mentions among the worst forms of vice and misery.

In one part of his Reply, Mr. Godwin makes a supposition respecting

[6] [In 1806 Malthus added a footnote here:
   It should be recollected always, that by moral restraint I mean a restraint from marriage from prudential motives, which is not followed by irregular gratifications. In this sense, I am inclined to believe that the expression I have here used is not too strong.

[7] *Reply*, p. 76.

[8] Mr. Godwin does not acknowledge the justice of Hume's observation respecting infanticide; and yet the extreme population and poverty in China, where this custom prevails, tends strongly to confirm the observation. It is still, however, true, as Mr. Godwin observes, that the expedient is, in its own nature, adequate to the end for which it was cited (p. 66.); but, to make it so in fact, it must be done by the magistrate, and not left to the parents. The almost invariable tendency of this custom to increase population, when it depends entirely on the parents, shews the extreme pain which they must feel, in making such a sacrifice, even when the distress arising from excessive poverty may be supposed to have deadened in great measure their sensibility. What must this pain be then, upon the supposition of the interference of a magistrate or of a positive law, to make parents destroy a child, which they feel the desire, and think they possess the power, of supporting? The permission of infanticide is bad enough, and cannot but have a bad effect on the moral sensibility of a nation; but, I cannot conceive anything much more detestable, or shocking to the feelings, than any direct regulation of this kind, although sanctioned by the names of Plato and Aristotle.

the number of children that might be allowed to each prolific marriage; but as he has not entered into the detail of the mode by which a greater number might be prevented, I shall not notice it further than merely to observe that, although he professes to acknowledge the geometrical and arithmetical ratios of population and food, yet in this place he appears to think that, practically applied, these different ratios of increase are not of a nature to make the evil resulting from them urgent, or alarmingly to confine the natural progress of population.[9] This observation seems to contradict his former acknowledgment.

The last check which Mr. Godwin mentions, and which, I am persuaded, is the only one which he would seriously recommend, is, 'that sentiment, whether virtue, prudence, or pride, which continually restrains the universality and frequent repetition of the marriage contract'.[10] On this sentiment, which I have already noticed under the name of moral restraint, and of the more comprehensive title, the preventive check, it will appear that in the sequel of this work I shall lay considerable stress.[11] Of this check therefore itself, I entirely approve; but I do not think that Mr. Godwin's system of political justice is by any means favourable to its prevalence. The tendency to early marriages is so strong that we want every possible help that we can get to counteract it; and a system which in any way whatever tends to weaken the foundation of private property, and to lessen in any degree the full advantage and superiority which each individual may derive from his prudence, must remove the only counteracting weight to the passion of love that can be depended upon for any essential effect. Mr. Godwin acknowledges that in his system 'the ill consequences of a numerous family will not come so coarsely home to each man's individual interest as they do at present'.[12] But I am sorry to say that, from what we know hitherto of the human character, we can have no rational hopes of success, without this coarse application to individual interest which Mr. Godwin rejects. If the whole effect were to depend merely on a sense of duty, considering the powerful antagonist that is to be contended with in the present case, I confess that I should absolutely despair. At the same time, I am strongly of opinion that a sense of duty, superadded to a sense of interest, would

---

[9] Reply, p. 70.   [10] Reply, p. 72.
[11] [In 1806 this sentence was altered:
    On this sentiment, which I have already noticed, it will appear that in the sequel
    of this work I shall lay considerable stress.
[12] Reply, p. 74.

by no means be without its effect. There are many noble and disinterested spirits who, though aware of the inconveniences which they may bring upon themselves by the indulgence of an early and virtuous passion, feel a kind of repugnance to listen to the dictates of mere worldly prudence, and a pride in rejecting these low considerations. There is a kind of romantic gallantry in sacrificing all for love, naturally fascinating to a young mind; and to say the truth, if all is to be sacrificed, I do not know in what better cause it can be done. But if a strong sense of duty could, in these instances, be added to prudential suggestions, the whole question might wear a different colour. In delaying the gratification of passion from a sense of duty, the most disinterested spirit, the most delicate honour, might be satisfied. The romantic pride might take a different direction, and the dictates of worldly prudence might be followed with the cheerful consciousness of making a virtuous sacrifice.

If we were to remove or weaken the motive of interest, which would be the case in Mr. Godwin's system, I fear we should have but a weak substitute in a sense of duty. But if to the present beneficial effects, known to result from a sense of interest, we could superadd a sense of duty, which is the object of the latter part of this work, it does not seem absolutely hopeless that some partial improvement in society should result from it.

CHAPTER III(B)

Of Systems of Equality (continued)[1]

It was suggested to me some years since by persons for whose judgment I have a high respect, that it might be advisable, in a new edition, to throw out the matter relative to systems of equality, to Wallace, Condorcet and Godwin, as having in a considerable degree lost its interest, and as not being strictly connected with the main subject of the Essay, which is an explanation and illustration of the theory of population. But independently of its being natural for me to have some little partiality for that part of the work which led to those inquiries on which the main subject rests; I really think that there should be somewhere on record an answer to systems of equality founded on the principle of population; and perhaps such an answer is as appropriately placed, and is likely to have as much effect, among the illustrations and applications of the principle of population, as in any other situation to which it could be assigned.

The appearances in all human societies, particularly in all those which are the furthest advanced in civilization and improvement, will ever be such as to inspire superficial observers with a belief that a prodigious change for the better might be effected by the introduction of a system of equality and of common property. They see abundance in some quarters, and want in others; and the natural and obvious remedy seems to be an equal division of the produce. They see a prodigious quantity of human exertion wasted upon trivial, useless, and sometimes pernicious objects, which might either be wholly saved or more effectively employed. They see invention after invention in machinery brought forward, which is seemingly calculated, in the most marked manner, to abate the sum of human toil. Yet with these apparent means of giving plenty, leisure and happiness to all, they still see the labours of the great mass of society undiminished, and their condition, if not deteriorated, in no very striking and palpable manner improved.

Under these circumstances, it cannot be a matter of wonder that proposals for systems of equality should be continually reviving. After

[1] [This chapter, in 1817, replaced chapter iii (a) of Book III, which had appeared in 1803, 1806 and 1807.]

74

periods when the subject has undergone a thorough discussion, or when some great experiment in improvement has failed, it is likely that the question should lie dormant for a time, and that the opinions of the advocates of equality should be ranked among those errors which had passed away, to be heard of no more. But it is probable that if the world were to last for any number of thousand years, systems of equality would be among those errors, which like the tunes of a barrel organ, to use the illustration of Dugald Stewart,[2] will never cease to return at certain intervals.

I am induced to make these remarks, and to add a little to what I have already said on systems of equality, instead of leaving out the whole discussion, by a tendency to a revival of this kind at the present moment.[3]

A gentleman for whom I have a very sincere respect, Mr. Owen of Lanark, has lately published a work entitled *A New View of Society*, which is intended to prepare the public mind for the introduction of a system involving a community of labour and of goods. It is also generally known that an idea has lately prevailed among some of the lower classes of society, that the land is the people's farm, the rent of which ought to be equally divided among them; and that they have been deprived of the benefits which belong to them from this their natural inheritance, by the injustice and oppression of their stewards, the landlords.

Mr. Owen is, I believe, a man of real benevolence, who has done much good; and every friend to humanity[4] must heartily wish him success in his endeavours to procure an Act of Parliament for limiting the hours of working among the children in the cotton manufactories, and preventing them from being employed at too early an age. He is further entitled to great attention on all subjects relating to education, from the experience and knowledge which he must have gained in an intercourse of many years with two thousand manufacturers, and from the success which is said to have resulted from his modes of management. A theory professed to be founded on such experience is no doubt worthy of much more consideration than one formed in a closet.

The claims to attention possessed by the author of the new doctrines

---

[2] Preliminary Dissertation to Supplement to the Encyclopædia Britannica, p. 121.
[3] [In 1826 a footnote was added:
    Written in 1817.
[4] [In 1826 this was changed to:
    ... every friend of humanity.

relating to land are certainly very slender; and the doctrines themselves indicate a very great degree of ignorance; but the errors of the labouring classes of society are always entitled to great indulgence and consideration. They are the natural and pardonable results of their liability to be deceived by first appearances, and by the arts of designing men, owing to the nature of their situation, and the scanty knowledge which in general falls to their share. And, except in extreme cases, it must always be the wish of those who are better informed, that they should be brought to a sense of the truth, rather by patience and the gradual diffusion of education and knowledge, than by any harsher methods.

After what I have already said on systems of equality in the preceding chapters, I shall not think it necessary to enter into a long and elaborate refutation of these doctrines. I merely mean to give an additional reason for leaving on record an answer to systems of equality, founded on the principle of population, together with a concise restatement of this answer for practical application.

Of the two decisive arguments against such systems, one is the unsuitableness of a state of equality, both according to experience and theory, to the production of those stimulants to exertion which can alone overcome the natural indolence of man, and prompt him to the proper cultivation of the earth and the fabrication of those conveniences and comforts which are necessary to his happiness.

And the other, the inevitable and necessary poverty and misery in which every system of equality must shortly terminate from the acknowledged tendency of the human race to increase faster than the means of subsistence, unless such increase be prevented by means infinitely more cruel than those which result from the laws of private property, and the moral obligations imposed on every man by the commands of God and nature to support his own children.

The first of these arguments has, I confess, always appeared to my own mind sufficiently conclusive. A state, in which an inequality of conditions offers the natural rewards of good conduct, and inspires widely and generally the hopes of rising and the fears of falling in society, is unquestionably the best calculated to develop the energies and faculties of man, and the best suited to the exercise and improvement of human virtue.[5] And history, in every case of equality that has yet

---

[5] See this subject very ably treated in a work on the Records of the Creation, and the Moral Attributes of the Creator, by the Rev. John Bird Sumner, not long since

occurred, has uniformly borne witness to the depressing and deadening effects which arise from the want of this stimulus. But still perhaps it may be true that neither experience nor theory on this subject is quite so decisive as to preclude all plausible arguments on the other side. It may be said that the instances which history records of systems of equality really carried into execution are so few, and those in societies so little advanced from a state of barbarism, as to afford no fair conclusions relative to periods of great civilization and improvement; that in other instances in ancient times, where approaches were made toward a tolerable equality of conditions, examples of considerable energy of character in some lines of exertion are not unfrequent; and that in modern times some societies, particularly of Moravians,[6] are known to have had much of their property in common without occasioning the destruction of their industry. It may be said that, allowing the stimulus of inequality of conditions to have been necessary, in order to raise man from the indolence and apathy of the savage to the activity and intelligence of civilized life, it does not follow that the continuance of the same stimulus should be necessary when this activity and energy of mind has been once gained. It may *then* be allowable quietly to enjoy the benefit of a regimen which, like many other stimulants, having produced its proper effect at a certain point must be left off, or exhaustion, disease and death will follow.

These observations are certainly not of a nature to produce conviction in those who have studied the human character; but they are to a certain degree plausible, and do not admit of so definite and decisive an answer as to make the proposal for an experiment in modern times utterly absurd and unreasonable.

The peculiar advantage of the other argument against systems of equality, that which is founded on the principle of population, is, that it is not only still more generally and uniformly confirmed by experience, in every age and in every part of the world, but it is so pre-eminently clear in theory, that no tolerably plausible answer can be given to it; and consequently no decent pretence can be brought forward for an experi-

published; a work of very great merit, which I hope soon to see in as extensive circulation as it deserves.

[6] [Moravia is the English name for part of Bohemia (in the Austro-Hungarian Empire in Malthus's time) whence a Protestant episcopal sect spread to Germany, England and North America, as the result of renewed persecution in the early eighteenth century. Malthus would have known of them as outstandingly successful settlers in the United States.]

ment. The affair is a matter of the most simple calculation applied to the known properties of land, and the proportion of births to deaths which takes place in almost every country village. There are many parishes in England, where, notwithstanding the actual difficulties attending the support of a family which must *necessarily* occur in every well-peopled country, and making no allowances for omissions in the registers, the births are to the deaths in the proportion of 2 to 1. This proportion, with the usual rate of mortality in country places, of about 1 in 50, would continue doubling the population in 41 years, if there were no emigrations from the parish. But in any system of equality, either such as that proposed by Mr. Owen, or in parochial partnerships in land, not only would there be no means of emigration to other parishes with any prospect of relief, but the rate of increase at first would of course be much greater than in the present state of society. What then, I would ask, is to prevent the division of the produce of the soil to each individual from becoming every year less and less, till the whole society and every individual member of it are pressed down by want and misery?[7]

This is a very simple and intelligible question. And surely no man ought to propose or support a system of equality, who is not able to give a rational answer to it, at least in theory. But even in theory, I have never yet heard any thing approaching to a rational answer to it.

It is a very superficial observation which has sometimes been made, that it is a contradiction to lay great stress upon the efficacy of moral restraint in an improved and improving state of society, according to the present structure of it, and yet to suppose that it would not act with sufficient force in a system of equality, which almost always presupposes a great diffusion of information and a great improvement of the human mind. Those who have made this observation do not see that the encouragement and motive to moral restraint are at once destroyed in a system of equality and community of goods.

---

[7] In the Spencean system, as published by the secretary of the Society of Spencean Philanthropists, it unfortunately happens that after the *proposed allowances* have been made for the expenses of the government, and of the other bodies in the state which are intended to be supported, there would be absolutely no remainder; and the people would not derive a single sixpence from their estate, even at first, and on the supposition of the national debt being entirely abolished, without the slightest compensation to the national creditors.

The annual rent of the land, houses, mines and fisheries, is estimated at 150 millions, about three times its real amount; yet, even upon this extravagant estimate, it is calculated that the division would only come to about four pounds a head, not

Let us suppose that in a system of equality, in spite of the best exertions to procure more food, the population is pressing hard against the limits of subsistence, and all are becoming very poor. It is evidently necessary under these circumstances, in order to prevent the society from starving, that the rate at which the population increases should be retarded. But who are the persons that are to exercise the restraint thus called for, and either to marry late or not at all? It does not seem to be a necessary consequence of a system of equality that all the human passions should be at once extinguished by it; but if not, those who might wish to marry would feel it hard that they should be among the number forced to restrain their inclinations. As all would be equal, and in similar circumstances, there would be no reason whatever why one individual should think himself obliged to practise the duty of restraint more than another. The thing however must be done, with any hope of avoiding universal misery; and in a state of equality, the necessary restraint could only be effected by some general law. But how is this law to be supported, and how are the violations of it to be punished? Is the man who marries early to be pointed at with the finger of scorn? is he to be whipped at the cart's tail? is he to be confined for years in a prison? is he to have his children exposed? Are not all direct punishments for an offence of this kind shocking and unnatural to the last degree? And yet, if it be absolutely necessary, in order to prevent the most overwhelming wretchedness, that there should be some restraint on the tendency to early marriages, when the resources of the country are only sufficient to support a slow rate of increase, can the most fertile imagination conceive one at once so natural, so just, so consonant to the laws of God and to the best laws framed by the most enlightened men, as that each individual should be responsible for the maintenance of his own children; that is, that he should be subjected to the natural inconveniences and difficulties arising from the indulgence of his inclinations, and to no other whatever?

That this natural check to early marriages arising from a view of the difficulty attending the support of a large family operates very widely throughout all classes of society in every civilized state, and may be expected to be still more effective, as the lower classes of people continue to improve in knowledge and prudence, cannot admit of the slightest doubt. But the operation of this natural check depends exclusively upon the existence of the laws of property, and succession; and in a state of

more than is sometimes given to individuals from the poor's rates; a miserable provision! and yet constantly diminishing.

equality and community of property could only be replaced by some artificial regulation of a very different stamp, and a much more unnatural character. Of this Mr. Owen is fully sensible, and has in consequence taxed his ingenuity to the utmost to invent some mode by which the difficulties arising from the progress of population could be got rid of, in the state of society to which he looks forward. His absolute inability to suggest any mode of accomplishing this object that is not unnatural, immoral, or cruel in a high degree, together with the same want of success in every other person, ancient[8] or modern, who has made a similar attempt, seem to shew that the argument against systems of equality founded on the principle of population does not admit of a plausible answer, even in theory. The fact of the tendency of population to increase beyond the means of subsistence may be seen in almost every register of a country parish in the kingdom. The unavoidable effect of this tendency to depress the whole body of the people in want and misery, unless the progress of the population be somehow or other retarded, is equally obvious; and the impossibility of checking the rate of increase in a state of equality, without resorting to regulations that are unnatural, immoral or cruel, forms an argument at once conclusive against every such system.

[8] The reader has already seen in ch. xiii bk. i. the detestable means of checking population proposed by some ancient lawgivers in order to support their systems of equality. [This is the chapter about Greece – not included in this edition.]

CHAPTER IV

Of Emigration

Although the resource of emigration seems to be excluded from such a society as Mr. Godwin has imagined;[1] yet in that partial degree of improvement which alone can rationally be expected, it may fairly enter into our consideration. And as it is not probable that human industry should begin to receive its best direction throughout all the nations of the earth at the same time, it may be said that, in the case of a redundant population in the more cultivated parts of the world, the natural and obvious remedy that presents itself is emigration to those parts that are uncultivated. As these parts are of great extent and very thinly peopled, this resource might appear, on a first view of the subject, an adequate remedy, or at least of a nature to remove the evil to a distant period: but, when we advert to experience, and to the actual state of the uncivilized parts of the globe, instead of any thing like an adequate remedy, it will appear but a very weak palliative.[2]

In the accounts which we have received of the peopling of new countries, the dangers, difficulties, and hardships that the first settlers have had to struggle with,[3] appear to be even greater than we can well imagine that they could be exposed to in their parent state. The endeavour to avoid that degree of unhappiness arising from the difficulty of supporting a family might long have left the new world of America unpeopled by Europeans, if those more powerful passions, the thirst of gain, the spirit of adventure, and religious enthusiasm, had not directed and animated the enterprize. These passions enabled the first adventurers to triumph over every obstacle; but in many instances in a way to make humanity shudder, and to defeat the true end of emigration.

---

[1] [In 1817 following the substitution of chapter iii(b) for chapter iii(a) on Godwin's *Reply*, this opening was altered:

Although the resource of emigration seems to be excluded from such perfect societies as the advocates of equality generally contemplate, yet in that imperfect state of improvement, which alone can rationally be expected, ...

[2] [In 1806 this was changed to:

... but a slight palliative.

[3] [In 1806 this was amended to:

... hardships with which the first settlers have had to struggle, ...

Whatever may be the character of the Spanish inhabitants of Mexico and Peru at the present moment, we cannot read the accounts of the first conquests of these countries without feeling strongly that the race destroyed was, in moral worth as well as numbers, highly superior[4] to the race of their destroyers.

The parts of America settled by the English, from being thinly peopled, were better adapted to the establishment of new colonies; yet even here the most formidable difficulties presented themselves. In the settlement of Virginia, begun by Sir Walter Raleigh, and established by Lord Delaware, three attempts completely failed. Nearly half of the first colony was destroyed by the savages, and the rest, consumed and worn down by fatigue and famine, deserted the country and returned home in despair. The second colony was cut off to a man, in a manner unknown; but they were supposed to be destroyed by the Indians. The third experienced the same dismal fate; and the remains of the fourth, after it had been reduced by famine and disease, in the course of six months, from 500 to 60 persons, were returning in a famishing and desperate condition to England, when they were met in the mouth of the Chesapeak bay by Lord Delaware, with a squadron loaded with provisions, and every thing for their relief and defence.[5]

The first puritan settlers in New England were few in number. They landed in a bad season, and they were only supported by their private funds. The winter was premature, and terribly cold; the country was covered with wood, and afforded very little for the refreshment of persons sickly with such a voyage, or for the sustenance of an infant people. Nearly half of them perished by the scurvy, by want, and the severity of the climate; yet those who survived were not dispirited by their hardships; but, supported by their energy of character, and the satisfaction of finding themselves out of the reach of the spiritual arm, reduced this savage country by degrees to yield them a comfortable subsistence.[6]

Even the plantation of Barbadoes, which increased afterwards with such extraordinary rapidity, had at first to contend with a country utterly desolate, an extreme want of provisions, a difficulty in clearing the ground unusually great from the uncommon size and hardness of the

---

[4] [In 1806 the word *highly* was omitted.]
[5] Burke's America, vol. ii. p. 219. Robertson, b. ix. p. 83, 86.
[6] Id. vol. ii. p. 144.

trees, a most disheartening scantiness and poverty in their first crops, and a slow and precarious supply of provisions from England.[7]

The attempt of the French, in 1663, to form at once a powerful colony in Guiana, was attended with the most disastrous consequences. Twelve thousand men were landed in the rainy season, and placed under tents and miserable sheds. In this situation, inactive, weary of existence, and in want of all necessaries, exposed to contagious distempers, which are always occasioned by bad provisions, and to all the irregularities which idleness produces among the lower classes of society, almost the whole of them ended their lives in all the horrors of despair. The attempt was completely abortive. Two thousand men, whose robust constitutions had enabled them to resist the inclemency of the climate, and the miseries to which they had been exposed, were brought back to France; and the 25 000 000 of livres which had been expended in the expedition were totally lost.[8]

In the last settlement at Port Jackson, in New Holland, a melancholy and affecting picture is drawn by Collins of the extreme hardships with which, for some years, the infant colony had to struggle before the produce was equal to its support. These distresses were undoubtedly aggravated by the character of the settlers; but those which were caused by the unhealthiness of a newly-cleared country, the failure of first crops, and the uncertainty of supplies from so distant a mother country, were of themselves sufficiently disheartening to place in a strong point of view the necessity of great resources, as well as unconquerable perseverance, in the colonization of savage countries.

The establishment of colonies in the more thinly peopled regions of Europe and Asia would evidently require still greater resources. From the power and warlike character of the inhabitants of these countries, a considerable military force would be necessary to prevent their utter and immediate destruction. Even the frontier provinces of the most powerful states are defended with considerable difficulty from such restless neighbours; and the peaceful labours of the cultivator are continually interrupted by their predatory incursions. The late Empress Catharine of Russia found it necessary to protect, by regular fortresses, the colonies which she had established in the districts near the Wolga; and the calamities which her subjects suffered by the incursions of the Crim Tartars

[7] Id. p. 85.
[8] Raynal, Hist. des Indes, tom. vii. liv. xiii. p. 43. 10 vols 8vo. 1795. [In 1807 this figure was corrected to 26 000 000.]

furnished a pretext, and perhaps a just one, for taking possession of the whole of the Crimea, and expelling the greatest part of these turbulent neighbours, and reducing the rest to a more tranquil mode of life.

The difficulties attending a first establishment, from soil, climate, and the want of proper conveniences, are of course nearly the same in these regions as in America. Mr. Eton, in his account of the Turkish Empire, says that 75 000 Christians were obliged by Russia to emigrate from the Crimea, and sent to inhabit the country abandoned by the Nogai Tartars; but the winter coming on before the houses built for them were ready, a great part of them had no other shelter from the cold, than what was afforded them by holes dug in the ground, covered with what they could procure, and the greatest part of them perished. Only seven thousand remained a few years afterwards. Another colony from Italy to the banks of the Borysthenes had, he says, no better fate, owing to the bad management of those who were commissioned to provide for them.

It is needless to add to these instances, as the accounts given of the difficulties experienced in new settlements are all nearly similar. It has been justly observed, by a correspondent of Dr. Franklin, that one of the reasons why we have seen so many fruitless attempts to settle colonies at an immense public and private expense, by several of the powers of Europe is, that the moral and mechanical habits adapted to the mother country are frequently not so to the new-settled one, and to external events, many of which are unforeseen; and that it is to be remarked that none of the English colonies became any way considerable, till the necessary manners were born and grew up in the country. Pallas particularly notices the want of proper habits in the colonies established by Russia as one of the causes why they did not increase so fast as might have been expected.

In addition to this, it may be observed that the first establishment of a new colony generally presents an instance of a country peopled considerably beyond its actual produce; and the natural consequence seems to be that this population, if not amply supplied by the mother country, should at the commencement be diminished to the level of the first scanty productions, and not begin permanently to increase till the remaining numbers had so far cultivated the soil as to make it yield a quantity of food more than sufficient for their own support; and which consequently they could divide with a family. The frequent failures in the establishment of new colonies tend strongly to show the order of precedence between food and population.

It must be acknowledged, then, that the class of people on whom the distress arising from a too rapidly increasing population would principally fall could not possibly begin a new colony in a distant country. From the nature of their situation, they must necessarily be deficient in those resources which alone could ensure success: and unless they could find leaders among the higher classes, urged by the spirit of avarice or enterprize; or of religious or political discontent; or were furnished with means and support by government; whatever degree of misery they might suffer in their own country from the scarcity of subsistence, they would be absolutely unable to take possession of any of those uncultivated regions, of which there is yet such an extent on the earth.[9]

When new colonies have been once securely established, the difficulty of emigration is indeed very considerably diminished; yet, even then, some resources are necessary to provide vessels for the voyage, and support and assistance till the emigrants can settle themselves, and find employment in their adopted country. How far it is incumbent upon a government to furnish these resources may be a question; but whatever be its duty in this particular, perhaps it is too much to expect that, except where any particular colonial advantages are proposed, emigration should be actively assisted.

The necessary resources for transport and maintenance are, however, frequently furnished by individuals or private companies. For many years before the American war, and for some few since, the facilities of emigration to this new world, and the probable advantages in view, were unusually great; and it must be considered undoubtedly as a very happy circumstance for any country to have so comfortable an asylum for its redundant population. But I would ask whether, even during these periods, the distress among the common people in this country was little or nothing, and whether every man felt secure before he ventured on marriage that, however large his family might be, he should find no difficulty in supporting it without parish assistance? The answer, I fear, could not be in the affirmative.

It will be said that, when an opportunity of advantageous emigration is offered, it is the fault of the people themselves if, instead of accepting it, they prefer a life of celibacy or extreme poverty in their own country. Is it then a fault for a man to feel an attachment to his native soil, to love the parents that nurtured him, his kindred, his friends, and the companions

[9] [In 1806 the word *yet* was omitted.]

of his early years? Or is it no evil that he suffers, because he consents to bear it, rather than snap these cords which nature has wound in close and intricate folds round the human heart? The great plan of providence seems to require, indeed, that these ties should sometimes be broken; but the separation does not, on that account, give less pain; and though the general good may be promoted by it, it does not cease to be an individual evil. Besides, doubts and uncertainty must ever attend all distant emigrations, particularly in the apprehensions of the lower classes of people. They cannot feel quite secure that the representations made to them of the high price of labour, or the cheapness of land, are accurately true. They are placing themselves in the power of the persons who are to furnish them with the means of transport and maintenance, who may perhaps have an interest in deceiving them; and the sea which they are to pass appears to them like the separation of death from all their former connexions, and in a manner to preclude the possibility of return in case of failure, as they cannot expect the offer of the same means to bring them back. We cannot be surprised then, that, except where a spirit of enterprise is added to the uneasiness of poverty, the consideration of these circumstances should frequently

> Make them rather bear the ills they suffer,
> Than fly to others which they know not of.

If a tract of rich land as large as this island were suddenly annexed to it, and sold in small lots, or let out in small farms, the case would be very different, and the amelioration of the state of the common people would be sudden and striking; though the rich would be continually complaining of the high price of labour, the pride of the lower classes, and the difficulty of getting work done. These, I understand, are not unfrequent complaints among the men of property in America.

Every resource, however, from emigration, if used effectually, as this would be, must be of short duration. There is scarcely a state in Europe, except perhaps Russia, the inhabitants of which do not often endeavour to better their condition by removing to other countries. As these states therefore have nearly all rather a redundant than deficient population, in proportion to their produce, they cannot be supposed to afford any effectual resources of emigration to each other. Let us suppose for a moment that, in this more enlightened part of the globe, the internal economy of each state were so admirably regulated that no checks existed to population, and the different governments provided every facility for emigration. Taking the population of Europe, excluding Russia, at a hundred millions, and allowing a greater increase of produce than is probable, or even possible, in the mother countries, the redundancy of parent stock in a single century would be eleven hundred millions, which, added to the natural increase of the colonies during the same time, would be more than double what has been supposed to be the present population of the whole earth.

Can we imagine that in the uncultivated parts of Asia, Africa, or America, the greatest exertions and the best directed endeavours could, in so short a period, prepare a quantity of land sufficient for the support of such a population? If any sanguine person should feel a doubt upon the subject, let him only add 25 or 50 years more, and every doubt must be crushed in overwhelming conviction.

It is evident, therefore, that the reason why the resource of emigration has so long continued to be held out as a remedy to redundant population is because, from the natural unwillingness of people to desert their native country, and the difficulty of clearing and cultivating fresh soil, it never is or can be adequately adopted. If this remedy were indeed really effectual, and had power so far to relieve the disorders of vice and misery in old states, as to place them in the condition of the most prosperous new colonies, we should soon see the phial exhausted, and when the disorders returned with increased virulence, every hope from this quarter would be for ever closed.

It is clear, therefore, that with any view of making room for an unrestricted increase of population, emigration is perfectly inadequate; but as a partial and temporary expedient, and with a view to the more general cultivation of the earth, and the wider spread of civilization, it seems to be both useful and proper; and if it cannot be proved that governments are bound actively to encourage it, it is not only strikingly unjust, but in the highest degree impolitic in them to prevent it. There are no fears so totally ill-grounded as the fears of depopulation from emigration. The *vis inertiæ* of people in general,[10] and their attachment to their homes, are qualities so strong and general, that we may rest assured that they will not emigrate unless, from political discontents or extreme poverty, they are in such a state as will make it as much for the advantage of their country as of themselves that they should go out of it. The

---

[10] [In 1817 *people in general* was changed to:
    ... the great body of the people, ...

complaints of high wages in consequence of emigrations are of all others the most unreasonable, and ought the least to be attended to. If the wages of labour in any country be such as to enable the lower classes of people to live with tolerable comfort, we may be quite certain that they will not emigrate; and if they be not such, it is cruelty and injustice to detain them.

[In 1817 the following long paragraph was added:

In all countries the progress of wealth must depend mainly upon the industry, skill and success of individuals, and upon the state and demands of other countries. Consequently, in all countries, great variations may take place at different times in the rate at which wealth increases, and in the demand for labour. But though the progress of population is mainly regulated by the effective demand for labour, it is obvious that the number of people cannot conform itself immediately to the state of this demand. Some time is required to bring more labour into the market when it is wanted; and some time to check the supply when it is flowing in with too great rapidity. If these variations amount to no more than that natural sort of oscillation noticed in an early part of this work, which seems almost always to accompany the progress of population and food, they should be submitted to as a part of the usual course of things. But circumstances may occasionally give them great force, and then, during the period that the supply of labour is increasing faster than the demand, the labouring classes are subject to the most severe distress. If, for instance, from a combination of external and internal causes, a very great stimulus should be given to the population of a country for ten or twelve years together, and it should then comparatively cease, it is clear that labour will continue flowing into the market, with almost undiminished rapidity, while the means of employing and paying it have been essentially contracted. It is precisely under these circumstances that emigration is most useful as a temporary relief; and it is in these circumstances that Great Britain finds herself placed at present.[11] Though no emigration should take place, the population will by degrees conform itself to the state of the demand for labour; but the interval must be marked by the most severe distress, the amount of which can scarcely be reduced by any human efforts; because, though it may be mitigated at particular periods, and as it affects particular classes, it will be proportionably extended over a larger space of time and a greater number of people. The only real relief in such a case is emigration; and the subject at the present moment is well worthy the attention of the government, both as a matter of humanity and policy.

[11] 1816 and 1817.

CHAPTER V

Of the English Poor Laws[1]

To remedy the frequent distresses of the poor, laws to enforce their relief have been instituted; and in the establishment of a general system of this kind, England has particularly distinguished herself. But it is to be feared that, though it may have alleviated a little the intensity of individual misfortune, it has spread the evil over a much larger surface.

It is a subject often started in conversation, and mentioned always as a matter of great surprise, that, notwithstanding the immense sum which is annually collected for the poor in this country, there is still so much distress among them. Some think that the money must be embezzled for private use; others, that the churchwardens and overseers consume the greatest part of it in feasting. All agree that somehow or other it must be very ill managed. In short the fact that, even before the late scarcities, three millions were collected annually for the poor, and yet that their distresses were not removed, is the subject of continual astonishment. But a man who looks a little below the surface of things would be much more astonished if the fact were otherwise than it is observed to be; or even if a collection universally of eighteen shillings in the pound, instead of four, were materially to alter it.

Suppose, that by a subscription of the rich, the eighteen-pence or two shillings, which men earn now, were made up to five shillings; it might be imagined, perhaps, that they would then be able to live comfortably, and have a piece of meat every day for their dinner. But this would be a very false conclusion. The transfer of three additional shillings a day to each labourer would not increase the quantity of meat in the country. There is not at present enough for all to have a moderate share. What

---

[1] [In 1806 this chapter became simply 'Of Poor Laws'. The first eight paragraphs are based on pp. 74–82 of the 1798 *Essay*. The English Poor Laws dated from the 43rd year of the reign of Elizabeth I (1601) and did not apply to Scotland, which was then a separate kingdom; in that year parliament made permanent and compulsory certain practices which had developed gradually in different parts of the country during the previous three decades. The unit of civil administration was the ecclesiastical parish, of which there were some 15 000. Each parish was obliged to appoint Overseers of the Poor, who were to levy a rate to support the helpless and to provide work for the unemployed.]

would then be the consequence? The competition among the buyers in the market of meat would rapidly raise the price from eight-pence or nine-pence to two or three shillings in the pound, and the commodity would not be divided among many more than it is at present. When an article is scarce, and cannot be distributed to all, he that can show the most valid patent, that is, he that offers the most money, becomes the possessor. If we can suppose the competition among the buyers of meat to continue long enough for a greater number of cattle to be reared annually, this could only be done at the expense of the corn, which would be a very disadvantageous exchange; for it is well known that the country could not then support the same population; and when subsistence is scarce in proportion to the number of people, it is of little consequence whether the lowest members of the society possess two shillings or five. They must, at all events, be reduced to live upon the hardest fare and in the smallest quantity.

It might be said, perhaps, that the increased number of purchasers in every article would give a spur to productive industry, and that the whole produce of the island would be increased. But the spur that these fancied riches would give to population would more than counterbalance it; and the increased produce would be to be divided among a more than proportionably increased number of people.

A collection from the rich, of eighteen shillings in the pound, even if distributed in the most judicious manner, would have an effect similar to that resulting from the supposition which I have just made; and no possible sacrifices of the rich, particularly in money, could for any time prevent the recurrence of distress among the lower members of society, whoever they were. Great changes might indeed be made. The rich might become poor, and some of the poor rich; but while the present proportion between population and food continues, a part of society must necessarily find it difficult to support a family, and this difficulty will naturally fall on the least fortunate members.

It may at first appear strange, but I believe it is true, that I cannot by means of money raise the condition of a poor man, and enable him to live much better than he did before, without proportionably depressing others in the same class. If I retrench the quantity of food consumed in my house, and give him what I have cut off, I then benefit him without depressing any but myself and family, who perhaps may be well able to bear it. If I turn up a piece of uncultivated land, and give him the produce, I then benefit both him and all the members of society, because what he before consumed is thrown into the common stock, and probably some of the new produce with it. But if I only give him money, supposing the produce of the country to remain the same, I give him a title to a larger share of that produce than formerly, which share he cannot receive without diminishing the shares of others. It is evident that this effect in individual instances must be so small as to be totally imperceptible; but still it must exist, as many other effects do, which, like some of the insects that people the air, elude our grosser perceptions.

Supposing the quantity of food in any country to remain the same for many years together, it is evident that this food must be divided according to the value of each man's patent, or the sum of money which he can afford to spend in this commodity so universally in request. It is a demonstrative truth, therefore, that the patents of one set of men could not be increased in value without diminishing the value of the patents of some other set of men. If the rich were to subscribe, and give five shillings a day to five hundred thousand men, without retrenching their own tables, no doubt can exist that as these men would live more at their ease, and consume a greater quantity of provisions, there would be less food remaining to divide among the rest; and consequently, each man's patent would be diminished in value, or the same number of pieces of silver would purchase a smaller quantity of subsistence, and the price of provisions would universally rise.

These general reasonings have been strikingly confirmed during the late scarcities.[2] The supposition which I have made, of a collection from the rich of eighteen shillings in the pound, has been nearly realized; and the effect has been such as might have been expected. If the same distribution had been made when no scarcity existed, a considerable advance in the price of provisions would have been a necessary consequence; but following as it did a scarcity, its effect must have been doubly powerful. No person, I believe, will venture to doubt that, if we were to give three additional shillings a day to every labouring man in the kingdom, as I before supposed, in order that he might have meat for his dinner, the price of meat would rise in the most rapid and unexampled manner. But surely, in a deficiency of corn, which renders it impossible for every man to have his usual share, if we still continue to furnish each person with the means of purchasing the same quantity as before, the effect must be in every respect similar.

[2] [Here Malthus departs from the 1798 *Essay*. In 1817 a footnote was added:
The scarcities referred to in this chapter were those of 1800 and 1801.

It seems, in great measure, to have escaped observation that the price
of corn, in a scarcity, will depend much more upon the obstinacy with
which the same degree of consumption is persevered in, than on the
degree of the actual deficiency. A deficiency of one half of a crop, if the
people could immediately consent to consume only one half of what they
did before, would produce little or no effect on the price of corn. A
deficiency of one twelfth, if exactly the same consumption were to
continue for ten or eleven months, might raise the price of corn to almost
any height. The more is given in parish assistance, the more power is
furnished of persevering in the same consumption; and, of course, the
higher will the price rise before the necessary diminution of consumption
is effected.

It has been asserted by some people that high prices do not diminish
consumption. If this were really true, we should see the price of a bushel
of corn at a hundred pounds or more, in every deficiency which could not
be fully and completely remedied by importation. But the fact is that
high prices do ultimately diminish consumption; but, on account of the
riches of the country, the unwillingness of the people to resort to
substitutes, and the immense sums which are distributed by parishes,
this object cannot be attained till the prices become excessive, and force
even the middle classes of society, or at least those immediately above the
poor, to save in the article of bread from the actual inability of purchasing it in the usual quantity. The poor who were assisted by their parishes
had no reason whatever to complain of the high price of grain; because it
was the excessiveness of this price, and this alone, which, by enforcing
such a saving, left a greater quantity of corn for the consumption of the
lowest classes, which corn the parish allowances enabled them to
command. The greatest sufferers in the scarcity were undoubtedly the
classes immediately above the poor; and these were in the most marked
manner depressed by the excessive bounties given to those below them.
Almost all poverty is relative; and I much doubt whether these people
would have been rendered so poor, if a sum equal to half of these
bounties had been taken directly out of their pockets, as they were by
that new distribution of the money of the society which actually took
place.[3] This distribution, by giving to the poorer classes a command of

---

[3] Supposing the lower classes to earn on an average ten shillings a week, and the
classes just above them, twenty, it is not to be doubted that, in a scarcity, these latter
would be more straightened in their power of commanding the necessaries of life, by
a donation of ten shillings a week to those below them, than by the subtraction of five

food so much greater than their degree of skill and industry entitled them to,[4] in the actual circumstances of the country, diminished, exactly in the same proportion, that command over the necessaries of life which the classes above them, by their superior skill and industry, would naturally possess; and it may be a question whether the degree of assistance which the poor received, and which prevented them from resorting to the use of those substitutes which, in every other country on such occasions, the great law of necessity teaches, was not more than overbalanced by the severity of the pressure on so large a body of people from the extreme high prices, and the permanent evil which must result from forcing so many persons on the parish, who before thought themselves almost out of the reach of want.

If we were to double the fortunes of all those who possess above a hundred a year, the effect on the price of grain would be slow and inconsiderable; but if we were to double the price of labour throughout the kingdom, the effect in raising the price of grain would be rapid and great. The general principles on this subject will not admit of dispute; and that in the particular case which we have been considering, the bounties to the poor were of a magnitude to operate very powerfully in this manner will sufficiently appear, if we recollect that before the late scarcities the sum collected for the poor was estimated at three millions, and that during the year 1801 it was said to be ten millions. An additional seven millions acting at the bottom of the scale,[5] and employed exclus-

shillings a week from their own earnings. In the one case, they would be all reduced to a level; the price of provisions would rise in an extraordinary manner from the greatness of the competition; and all would be straightened for subsistence. In the other case, the classes above the poor would still maintain a considerable part of their relative superiority; the price of provisions would by no means rise in the same degree; and their remaining fifteen shillings would purchase much more than their twenty shillings in the former case.

[4] [In 1806 this was amended to:
    ... so much greater than that to which their degree of skill and industry entitled them ...
[In 1826 this was changed to:
    ... degree of skill and industry entitle them ...

[5] See a small pamphlet published in November 1800, entitled, *An investigation of the cause of the present high price of provisions.* This pamphlet was mistaken by some for an inquiry into the cause of the scarcity, and as such it would naturally appear to be incomplete, adverting, as it does, principally to a single cause. But the sole object of the pamphlet was to give the principal reason for the extreme high price of provisions, in proportion to the degree of the scarcity, admitting the deficiency of one fourth, as stated in the Duke of Portland's letter which, I am much inclined to think, was very near the truth.
[The pamphlet, published anonymously, was by Malthus himself.]

ively in the purchase of provisions, joined to a considerable advance in the price of wages in many parts of the kingdom, and increased by a prodigious sum expended in voluntary charity, must have had a most powerful effect in raising the price of the necessaries of life, if any reliance can be placed on the clearest general principles, confirmed as much as possible by appearances. A man with a family has received, to my knowledge, fourteen shillings a week from the parish. His common earnings were ten shillings a week, and his weekly revenue, therefore, twenty-four. Before the scarcity, he had been in the habit of purchasing a bushel of flour a week with eight shillings, perhaps, and consequently had two shillings out of his ten to spare for other necessaries. During the scarcity, he was enabled to purchase the same quantity at nearly three times the price. He paid twenty-two shillings for his bushel of flour and had, as before, two shillings remaining for other wants. Such instances could not possibly have been universal without raising the price of wheat very much higher than it really was during any part of the dearth. But similar instances were by no means infrequent, and the system itself, of measuring the relief given by the price of grain, was general.

If the circulation of the country had consisted entirely of specie, which could not have been immediately increased, it would have been impossible to have given such an additional sum as seven millions to the poor without embarrassing, to a great degree, the operations of commerce.[6] On the commencement, therefore, of this extensive relief, which would necessarily occasion a proportionate expenditure in provisions throughout all the ranks of society, a great demand would be felt for an increased circulating medium. The nature of the medium then principally in use was such that it could be created immediately on demand. From the accounts of the bank of England,[7] as laid before Parliament, it appeared that no very great additional issues of paper took place from this quarter. The three millions and a half added to its former average issues were not probably much above what was sufficient to supply the quantity of specie that had been withdrawn from the circulation. If this supposition be true (and the small quantity of gold which made its appearance at that time,

---

[6] [This and the four subsequent paragraphs follow very closely pp. 23–5 of Malthus's anonymous pamphlet *An Investigation of the Cause of the present High Price of Provisions* (London, 1800). In February 1797, following rumours of a French invasion and a run on gold, the Bank Act was suspended: this meant that the Bank of England was no longer obliged to pay out gold coins, on demand, in exchange for its own notes of the equivalent face value.]

[7] [Not until 1826 did the Bank of England merit a capital B.]

furnishes the strongest reason for believing that as much as this must have been withdrawn) it would follow that the part of the circulation originating in the bank of England, though changed in its nature, had not been increased in its quantity;[8] and with regard to the effect of the circulating medium on the price of all commodities, it cannot be doubted that it would be precisely the same, whether it were made up principally of guineas, or of pound notes and shillings, which would pass current for guineas.

The demand, therefore, for an increased circulating medium was left to be supplied by the country banks,[9] and it could not be expected that they should hesitate in taking advantage of so profitable an opportunity. The paper issues of a country bank are, as I conceive, measured by the quantity of its notes which will remain in circulation; and this quantity is again measured, supposing a confidence to be established, by the sum of what is wanted to carry on all the money transactions of the neighbour-hood. From the high price of provisions, all these transactions became more expensive. In the single article of the weekly payment of labourers' wages, including the parish allowances, it is evident that a very great addition to the circulating medium of the neighbourhood would be wanted.[10] Had the country banks attempted to issue the same quantity of paper without such a particular demand for it, they would quickly have been admonished of their error by its rapid and pressing return upon them; but at this time it was wanted for immediate and daily use, and was therefore eagerly absorbed into the circulation.

It may even admit of a question, whether, under similar circum-stances, the country banks would not have issued nearly the same quantity of paper if the bank of England had not been restricted from payment in specie. Before this event, the issues of the country banks in

---

[8] [In 1806 this was modified:
   ... furnishes the strongest reason for believing that nearly as much as this must have been withdrawn) ... the part of the circulation originating in the bank of England ... had not been much increased in its quantity ...

[9] [In 1806 this was changed to:
   ... left to be supplied principally by the country banks ...

[10] A rise of wages or of parish allowances, amounting to any particular sum, would occasion a much greater demand for the current circulating medium than an increase of commercial transactions to the same amount; because, in the first case, it is the common currency alone which can be used; in the latter, much is done by the bills of exchange, &c.; in the first also, much money is actually wanted, in proportion to the amount of the increased payments; in the latter, a little will go a great way. [In 1806 this footnote was omitted.]

paper were regulated by the quantity which the circulation would take up; and after, as well as before, they were obliged to pay the notes which returned upon them in bank of England circulation. The difference in the two cases would arise principally from the pernicious custom, adopted since the restriction of the bank, of issuing one and two pound notes, and from the little preference that many people might feel, if they could not get gold, between country bank paper and bank of England paper.

The very great issue of country bank paper during the years 1800 and 1801 was evidently, therefore, in its origin, rather a consequence than a cause of the high price of provisions; but being once absorbed into the circulation, it must necessarily affect the price of all commodities, and throw very great obstacles in the way of returning cheapness.[11] This is the great mischief of the system. During the scarcity itself, it is not to be doubted that the increased circulation, by preventing the embarrass-ments which commerce and speculation must otherwise have felt, enabled the country to continue all the branches of its trade with less interruption, and to import a much greater quantity of grain, than it could have done otherwise; but to overbalance these temporary advan-tages, a lasting evil might be entailed upon the community, and the prices of a time of scarcity might become permanent, from the difficulty of re-absorbing this increased circulation.

In this respect, however, it is much better that the great issue of paper should have come from the country banks, than from the bank of England. During the restriction of payment in specie, there is no possibility of forcing the bank to retake its notes when too abundant; but with regard to the country banks, as soon as their notes are not wanted in the circulation, they will be returned; and if the bank of England notes be not increased, which they probably will not be,[12] the whole circulating medium will thus be diminished.

We may consider ourselves as peculiarly fortunate that the two years of scarcity were succeeded by two events the best calculated to restore plenty and cheapness – an abundant harvest, and a peace;[13] which,

---

[11] It does not appear to me that Mr. Thornton, in his valuable publication on paper credit, has taken sufficient notice of the effects of the great paper issues of the country banks, in raising the price of commodities, and producing an unfavourable state of exchange with foreigners. [In 1806 this footnote was omitted.]

[12] [In 1806 this clause, *which they probably will not be,* was excised.]

[13] [This was the Peace of Amiens, which lasted from March 1802 until May 1803.]

together, produced a general conviction of plenty in the minds both of buyers and sellers; and by rendering the first slow to purchase, and the others eager to sell, occasioned a glut in the market and a consequent rapid fall of price, which has enabled parishes to take off their allowances to the poor, and thus to prevent a return of high prices when the alarm among the sellers was over.

If the two years of scarcity had been succeeded merely by years of average crops, I am strongly disposed to believe that, as no glut would have taken place in the market, the price of grain would have fallen only in an inconsiderable degree, the parish allowances could not have been resumed,[14] the increased quantity of paper would still have been wanted, and the prices of all commodities might by degrees have been regulated permanently according to the increased circulating medium.

If instead of giving the temporary assistance of parish allowances, which might be withdrawn on the first fall of price, we had raised universally the wages of labour, it is evident that the obstacles to a diminution of the circulation, and to returning cheapness, would have been still further increased; and the high price of labour would have become permanent, without any advantage whatever to the labourer.

There is no one that more ardently desires to see a real advance in the price of labour than myself; but the attempt to effect this object by forcibly raising the nominal price, which was practised to a certain degree, and recommended almost universally during the late scarcities, every thinking man must reprobate as puerile and ineffectual.

The price of labour, when left to find its natural level, is a most important political barometer, expressing the relation between the supply of provisions, and the demand for them; between the quantity to be consumed, and the number of consumers; and taken on the average, independently of accidental circumstances, it further expresses clearly the wants of society respecting population; that is, whatever may be the number of children to a marriage necessary to maintain exactly the present population, the price of labour will be just sufficient to support this number, or be above it, or below it, according to the state of the real funds for the maintenance of labour, whether stationary, progressive, or retrograde. Instead, however, of considering it in this light, we consider it as something which we may raise or depress at pleasure, something

---

[14] [*Resumed* here means to take back (or take off) something previously given or granted.]

which depends principally upon His Majesty's justices of the peace. When an advance in the price of provisions already expresses that the demand is too great for the supply, in order to put the labourer in the same condition as before, we raise the price of labour, that is, we increase the demand, and are then much surprised that the price of provisions continues rising. In this, we act much in the same manner, as if, when the quicksilver in the common weather-glass stood at *stormy*, we were to raise it by some forcible pressure to *settled fair*,[15] and then be greatly astonished that it continued raining.

Dr. Smith has clearly shown that the natural tendency of a year of scarcity is either to throw a number of labourers out of employment, or to oblige them to work for less than they did before, from the inability of masters to employ the same number at the same price. The raising of the price of wages tends necessarily to throw more out of employment, and completely to prevent the good effects which, he says, sometimes arise from a year of moderate scarcity, that of making the lower classes of people do more work, and become more careful and industrious. The number of servants out of place, and of manufacturers wanting employment during the late scarcities, were melancholy proofs of the truth of these reasonings. If a general rise in the wages of labour had taken place proportioned to the price of provisions, none but farmers and a few gentlemen could have afforded to employ the same number of workmen as before. Additional crowds of servants and manufacturers would have been turned off; and those who were thus thrown out of employment would of course have no other refuge than the parish. In the natural order of things, a scarcity must tend to lower, instead of to raise, the price of labour.

After the publication and general circulation of such a work as Dr. Smith's, I confess that it appears to me strange that so many men, who would yet aspire to be thought political economists, should still think that it is in the power of the justices of the peace, or even of the omnipotence of parliament, to alter by a *fiat* the whole circumstances of the country; and when the demand for provisions is greater than the supply, by publishing a particular edict, to make the supply at once equal to or greater than the demand. Many men who would shrink at the proposal of a maximum, would propose themselves that the price of

---

[15] [In 1806 this was changed to:
    ... raise it by some mechanical pressure ...

labour should be proportioned to the price of provisions, and do not seem to be aware that the two proposals are very nearly of the same nature, and that both tend directly to famine. It matters not whether we enable the labourer to purchase the same quantity of provisions which he did before, by fixing their price, or by raising in proportion the price of labour. The only advantage on the side of raising the price of labour is that the rise in the price of provisions, which necessarily follows it, encourages importation: but putting importation out of the question, which might possibly be prevented by war, or other circumstances, a universal rise of wages in proportion to the price of provisions, aided by adequate parish allowances to those who were thrown out of work, would, by preventing any kind of saving, in the same manner as a maximum, cause the whole crop to be consumed in nine months, which ought to have lasted twelve, and thus produce a famine.

[In 1806 Malthus added a passage here:

At the same time we must not forget that both humanity and true policy imperiously require that we should give every assistance to the poor on these occasions that the nature of the case will admit. If provisions were to continue at the price of scarcity, the wages of labour must necessarily rise, or sickness and famine would quickly diminish the number of labourers; and the supply of labour being unequal to the demand, its price would soon rise in a still greater proportion than the price of provisions. But even one or two years of scarcity, if the poor were left entirely to shift for themselves, might produce some effect of this kind, and consequently it is our interest, as well as our duty, to give them temporary aid in such seasons of distress. It is on such occasions that every cheap substitute for bread and every mode of economising food should be resorted to. Nor should we be too ready to complain of that high price of corn, which by encouraging importation increases the supply.

As the inefficacy of poor laws, and of attempts forcibly to raise the price of labour, is most conspicuous in a scarcity, I have thought myself justified in considering them under this view; and as these causes of increased price received great additional force during the late scarcity from the increase of the circulating medium, I trust that the few observations which I have made on this subject, will be considered as an allowable digression.

CHAPTER VI

Subject of Poor Laws continued[1]

Independently of any considerations respecting a year of deficient crops, it is evident that an increase of population, without a proportional increase of food, must lower the value of each man's earnings. The food must necessarily be distributed in smaller quantities, and consequently, a day's labour will purchase a smaller quantity of provisions. An increase in the price of provisions will arise, either from an increase of population faster than the means of subsistence, or from a different distribution of the money of the society. The food of a country which has been long peopled, if it be increasing, increases slowly and regularly, and cannot be made to answer any sudden demands; but variations in the distribution of the money of the society are not unfrequently occurring, and are undoubtedly among the causes which occasion the continual variations in the prices of provisions.

The poor laws of England tend to depress the general condition of the poor in these two ways. Their first obvious tendency is to increase population without increasing the food for its support. A poor man may marry with little or no prospect of being able to support a family without parish assistance. They may be said, therefore, to create the poor which they maintain; and as the provisions of the country must, in consequence of the increased population, be distributed to every man in smaller proportions, it is evident that the labour of those who are not supported by parish assistance will purchase a smaller quantity of provisions than before, and consequently more of them must be driven to apply for assistance.

Secondly, the quantity of provisions consumed in workhouses, upon a part of the society that cannot in general be considered as the most valuable part, diminishes the shares that would otherwise belong to more industrious and more worthy members, and thus, in the same manner, forces more to become dependent. If the poor in the workhouses were to

---

[1] [In 1817 this chapter became simply 'Of Poor-Laws (continued)'. Here Malthus returns again to the 1798 *Essay* (pp. 82–94) and follows it closely for the first 13 paragraphs of this chapter.]

live better than they do now, this new distribution of the money of the society would tend more conspicuously to depress the condition of those out of the workhouses by occasioning an advance in the price of provisions.

Fortunately for England, a spirit of independence still remains among the peasantry. The poor laws are strongly calculated to eradicate this spirit. They have succeeded in part; but had they succeeded as completely as might have been expected, their pernicious tendency would not have been so long concealed.

Hard as it may appear in individual instances, dependent poverty ought to be held disgraceful. Such a stimulus seems to be absolutely necessary to promote the happiness of the great mass of mankind; and every general attempt to weaken this stimulus, however benevolent its apparent intention, will always defeat its own purpose. If men be induced to marry from the mere prospect of parish provision, they are not only unjustly tempted to bring unhappiness and dependence upon themselves and children, but they are tempted, without knowing it, to injure all in the same class with themselves.

The parish laws of England[2] appear to have contributed to raise the price of provisions, and to lower the real price of labour. They have therefore contributed to impoverish that class of people whose only possession is their labour. It is also difficult to suppose that they have not powerfully contributed to generate that carelessness and want of frugality observable among the poor, so contrary to the disposition generally to be remarked among petty tradesmen and small farmers. The labouring poor, to use a vulgar expression, seem always to live from hand to mouth. Their present wants employ their whole attention; and they seldom think of the future. Even when they have an opportunity of saving, they seldom exercise it; but all that they earn beyond their present necessities goes, generally speaking, to the alehouse. The poor laws may, therefore, be said to diminish both the power and the will to save among the common people, and thus to weaken one of the strongest incentives to sobriety and industry, and consequently to happiness.

It is a general complaint among master manufacturers that high wages ruin all their workmen; but it is difficult to conceive that these men would not save a part of their high wages for the future support of their families, instead of spending it in drunkenness and dissipation, if they

[2] [In 1807 this was changed to:
The poor laws of England ...

did not rely on parish assistance for support in case of accidents. And that the poor employed in manufactures consider this assistance as a reason why they may spend all the wages which they earn, and enjoy themselves while they can, appears to be evident from the number of families that, upon the failure of any great manufactory, immediately fall upon the parish; when, perhaps, the wages earned in this manufactory while it flourished were sufficiently above the price of common country labour to have allowed them to save enough for their support, till they could find some other channel for their industry.

A man who might not be deterred from going to the alehouse, from the consideration that, on his death or sickness, he should leave his wife and family upon the parish, might yet hesitate in thus dissipating his earnings, if he were assured that in either of these cases his family must starve, or be left to the support of casual bounty.

The mass of happiness among the common people cannot but be diminished, when one of the strongest checks to idleness and dissipation is thus removed; and positive institutions, which render dependent poverty so general, weaken that disgrace which for the best and most humane reasons ought to be attached to it.

The poor laws of England were undoubtedly instituted for the most benevolent purpose; but it is evident that they have failed in attaining it. They certainly mitigate some cases of severe distress which might otherwise occur, though the state of the poor who are supported by parishes, considered in all its circumstances, is very miserable. But one of the principal objections to the system, is, that for the assistance which some of the poor receive, in itself almost a doubtful blessing, the whole class of the common people of England is subjected to a set of grating, inconvenient, and tyrannical laws, totally inconsistent with the genuine spirit of the constitution. The whole business of settlements, even in its present amended state, is contradictory to all ideas of freedom. The parish persecution of men whose families are likely to become chargeable, and of poor women who are near lying-in, is a most disgraceful and disgusting tyranny. And the obstructions continually occasioned in the market of labour, by these laws, have a constant tendency to add to the difficulties of those who are struggling to support themselves without assistance.

These evils attendant on the poor laws seem to be irremediable. If assistance be to be distributed to a certain class of people, a power must be lodged somewhere of discriminating the proper objects, and of managing the concerns of the institutions that are necessary; but any great interference with the affairs of other people is a species of tyranny; and, in the common course of things, the exercise of this power may be expected to become grating to those who are driven to ask for support. The tyranny of justices, churchwardens, and overseers, is a common complaint among the poor;[3] but the fault does not lie so much in these persons who, probably, before they were in power, were not worse than other people, but in the nature of all such institutions.

It will scarcely admit of a doubt,[4] that if the poor laws had never existed in this country, though there might have been a few more instances of very severe distress, the aggregate mass of happiness among the common people would have been much greater than it is at present.

The radical defect of all systems of the kind is that of tending to increase population, without increasing the means for its support, and by thus depressing the condition of those that are not relieved by parishes, to create more poor.[5] If, indeed, we examine some of our statutes, strictly with reference to the principle of population, we shall find that they attempt an absolute impossibility; and we cannot be surprised, therefore, that they should constantly fail in the attainment of their object.

The famous 43rd of Elizabeth, which has been so often referred to and admired, enacts that the overseers of the poor, 'shall take order from time to time, by and with the consent of two or more justices, for setting to work the children of all such whose parents shall not, by the said persons, be thought able to keep and maintain their children; and also such persons married or unmarried, as, having no means to maintain them, use no ordinary and daily trade of life to get their living by. And also to raise, weekly or otherwise, by taxation of every inhabitant, and every occupier of lands in the said parish, (in such competent sums as they shall think fit,) a convenient stock of flax, hemp, wool, thread, iron, and other necessary ware and stuff, to set the poor to work.'

What is this but saying that the funds for the maintenance of labour in this country may be increased at will, and without limit, by a *fiat* of government or an assessment of the overseers? Strictly speaking, this

---

[3] [In 1807 the *justices* were omitted; the sentence began:
   The tyranny of churchwardens and overseers is a common complaint ...
[4] [In 1806 this was altered to:
   I feel persuaded that ...
[5] [In 1807 this sentence was re-written:
   The radical defect of all systems of the kind is that of tending to depress the condition of those that are not relieved by parishes, and to create more poor.

clause is as arrogant and as absurd as if it had enacted that two ears of wheat should in future grow where one only had grown before. Canute, when he commanded the waves not to wet his princely foot, did not in reality assume a greater power over the laws of nature. No directions are given to the overseers how to increase the funds for the maintenance of labour; the necessity of industry, economy, and enlightened exertion in the management of agricultural and commercial capital is not insisted on for this purpose; but it is expected that a miraculous increase of these funds should immediately follow an edict of the government, used at the discretion of some ignorant parish officers.

If this clause were really and *bona fide* put in execution, and the shame attending the receiving of parish assistance worn off, every labouring man might marry as early as he pleased, under the certain prospect of having all his children properly provided for; and as, according to the supposition, there would be no check to population from the consequences of poverty after marriage, the increase of people would be rapid beyond example in old states. After what has been said in the former parts of this work, it is submitted to the reader, whether the utmost exertions of the most enlightened government could, in this case, make the food keep pace with the population, much less a mere arbitrary edict, the tendency of which is certainly rather to diminish than to increase the funds for the maintenance of productive labour.

In the actual circumstances of every country, the principle of population[6] seems to be always ready to exert nearly its full force; but, within the limit of possibility, there is nothing perhaps more improbable, or more out of the power of any government to effect,[7] than the direction of the industry of its subjects in such a manner as to produce the greatest quantity of human sustenance that the earth could bear. It evidently could not be done without the most complete violation of the law of property, from which everything that is valuable to man has hitherto arisen. Such is the disposition to marry, particularly in very young people, that if the difficulties of providing for a family were entirely removed, very few would remain single at twenty-two. But what statesman or rational government could propose that all animal food should be prohibited, that no horses should be used for business or pleasure, that

---

[6] [In 1806 *the principle of population* was altered to:
    ... the prolific power of nature ...

[7] [On the same page, Malthus also changed *out of the power of any government* to:
    ... out of the reach of any government ...

all the people should live upon potatoes, and that the whole industry of the nation should be exerted in the production of them, except what was required for the mere necessaries of clothing and houses. Could such a revolution be effected, would it be desirable? Particularly as in a few years, notwithstanding all these exertions, want, with less resource than ever, would inevitably recur.

After a country has once ceased to be in the peculiar situation of a new colony, we shall always find that, in the actual state of its cultivation, or in that state which may rationally be expected from the most enlightened government, the increase of its food can never allow, for any length of time, an unrestricted increase of population; and therefore the due execution of the clause in the 43rd of Elizabeth, as a permanent law, is a physical impossibility.

It will be said, perhaps, that the fact contradicts the theory, and that the clause in question has remained in force, and has been executed, during the last two hundred years. In answer to this I should say without hesitation that it has not really been executed; and that it is merely owing to its incomplete execution that it remains on our statute book at present.

The scanty relief granted to persons in distress, the capricious and insulting manner in which it is sometimes distributed by the overseers, and the natural and becoming pride not yet quite extinct among the peasantry of England, have deterred the more thinking and virtuous part of them from venturing on marriage, without some better prospect of maintaining their families than mere parish assistance. The desire of bettering our condition and the fear of making it worse, like the *vis medicatrix naturæ* in physic, is the *vis medicatrix reipublicæ* in politics, and is continually counteracting the disorders arising from narrow human institutions. In spite of the prejudices in favour of population, and the direct encouragements to marriage from the poor laws, it operates as a preventive check to increase; and happy for this country is it that it does so.

[In 1806 Malthus added a passage here:

But besides that spirit of independence and prudence which checks the frequency of marriage, notwithstanding the encouragements of the poor-laws, these laws themselves occasion a check of no inconsiderable magnitude, and thus counteract with one hand what they encourage with the other. As each parish is obliged to maintain its own poor, it is naturally fearful of increasing their number; and every landholder is in consequence more inclined to pull down than to build cottages, (except when the demand for labourers is really urgent.) This deficiency of cottages operates necessarily as a strong check to marriage; and this check is probably the principal reason why we have been able to continue the system of the poor-laws so long.

[The clause given in brackets here was inserted in 1807 without brackets.]

Those who are not deterred for a time from marriage, by considerations of this nature,[8] are either relieved very scantily at their own homes, where they suffer all the consequences arising from squalid poverty; or they are crowded together in close and unwholesome workhouses, where a great mortality almost universally takes place, particularly among the young children. The dreadful account given by Jonas Hanway of the treatment of parish children in London, is too well known to need a comment; and it appears from Mr. Howlett, and other writers, that in some parts of the country they are not very much better off.[9] A great part of the redundant population occasioned by the poor laws is thus taken off by the operation of the laws themselves, or at least by their ill execution. The remaining part which survives, by causing the funds for the maintenance of labour to be divided among a greater number than can be properly maintained by them, and by turning a considerable share from the support of the diligent and careful workman to the support of the idle and the negligent, depresses the condition of all those who are out of the workhouses, forces more every year into them, and has ultimately produced the enormous evil which we all so justly deplore, that of the great and unnatural proportion of the people which is now become dependent upon charity.

If this be a just representation of the manner in which the clause in question has been executed, and of the effects which it has produced, it must be allowed that we have practised an unpardonable deceit upon the poor, and have promised what we have been very far from performing. [10]●It may be asserted, without danger of exaggeration, that the poor laws have destroyed many more lives than they have preserved.●[10]

[8] [In 1806 this was changed to:
    Those who are not prevented for a time from marrying by these causes, are either
. . .
[9] [In 1806 this was altered to:
    The dreadful account given by Jonas Hanway of the treatment of parish children in London is well known; and it appears from Mr Howlett and other writers, that in some parts of the country their situation is not very much better.
[10] [In 1807 this sentence was excised.]

The attempts to employ the poor on any great scale in manufactures have almost invariably failed, and the stock and materials have been wasted. In those few parishes which, by better management or larger funds, have been enabled to persevere in this system, the effect of these new manufactures in the market must have been to throw out of employment many independent workmen who were before engaged in fabrications of a similar nature. This effect has been placed in a strong point of view by Daniel de Foe, in an address to parliament, entitled *Giving alms no charity*. Speaking of the employment of parish children in manufactures, he says: 'For every skein of worsted these poor children spin, there must be a skein the less spun by some poor family that spun it before; and for every piece of baize so made in London, there must be a piece the less made at Colchester, or somewhere else.'[11] Sir F. M. Eden, on the same subject, observes that 'whether mops and brooms are made by parish children, or by private workmen, no more can be sold than the public is in want of'.[12]

It will be said, perhaps, that the same reasoning might be applied to any new capital brought into competition in a particular trade or manufacture, which can rarely be done without injuring, in some degree, those that were engaged in it before. But there is a material difference in the two cases. In this the competition is perfectly fair, and what every man on entering into business must lay his account to. He may rest secure that he will not be supplanted unless his competitor possess superior skill and industry. In the other case, the competition is supported by a great bounty; by which means, notwithstanding very inferior skill and industry on the part of his competitors, the independent workman may be undersold, and unjustly excluded from the market. He himself, perhaps, is made to contribute to this competition against his own earnings; and the funds for the maintenance of labour are thus

---

[11] See extracts from Daniel de Foe, in Sir F. M. Eden's valuable work on the poor, vol. i. p. 261.

[12] Sir F. Eden, speaking of the supposed right of the poor to be supplied with employment while able to work, and with a maintenance when incapacitated from labour, very justly remarks, 'It may, however, be doubted whether any right, the gratification of which seems to be impracticable, can be said to exist', vol. i. p. 447. No man has collected so many materials for forming a judgment on the effects of the poor laws as Sir F. Eden, and the result he thus expresses: 'Upon the whole, therefore, there seems to be just grounds for concluding that the sum of good to be expected from a compulsory maintenance of the poor will be far outbalanced by the sum of evil which it will inevitably create', vol. i. p. 467. I am happy to have the sanction of so practical an inquirer to my opinion of the poor laws.

turned, from the support of a trade which yields a proper profit, to one which cannot maintain itself without a bounty. It should be observed, in general, that when a fund for the maintenance of labour is raised by assessment, the greatest part of it is not a new capital brought into trade, but an old one, which before was much more profitably employed, turned into a new channel. The farmer pays to the poor's rates, for the encouragement of a bad and unprofitable manufacture, what he would have employed on his land with infinitely more advantage to his country. In the one case, the funds for the maintenance of labour are daily diminished; in the other, daily increased. And this obvious tendency of assessments for the employment of the poor to decrease the real funds for the maintenance of labour in any country, aggravates the absurdity of supposing that it is in the power of a government to find employment for all its subjects, however fast they may increase.

It is not intended that these reasonings should be applied against every mode of employing the poor on a limited scale, and with such restrictions, as may not encourage, at the same time, their increase. I would never wish to push general principles too far, though I think that they ought to be kept in view. In particular cases, the individual good to be obtained may be so great, and the general evil so slight, that the former may clearly overbalance the latter.

The intention is merely to show[13] that the poor laws, as a general system, are founded on a gross error; and that the common declamation on the subject of the poor, which we see so often in print, and hear continually in conversation, namely that the market price of labour ought always to be sufficient decently to support a family, and that employment ought to be found for all those who are willing to work, is in effect to say that the funds for the maintenance of labour, in this country, are not only infinite, [14]•but might be made to increase with such rapidity that, supposing us to have at present six millions of labourers, including their families, we might have 96 millions in another century; or if these funds

[13] [In 1817 this paragraph began:
   My intention is merely to show . . .
[14] [In 1817 this concluding paragraph finished thus:
   . . . are not only infinite, but not subject to variation; and that, whether the resources of a country be rapidly progressive, slowly progressive, stationary, or declining, the power of giving full employment and good wages to the labouring classes must always remain exactly the same – a conclusion which contradicts the plainest and most obvious principles of supply and demand, and involves the absurd position that a definite quantity of territory can maintain an infinite population.

had been properly managed since the beginning of the reign of Edward I, supposing that there were then only two millions of labourers, we might now have possessed above four million millions of labourers, or about four thousand times as many labourers as it has been calculated that there are people now on the face of the earth.●[14]

CHAPTER VII

Of Poor-Laws, continued

The remarks made in the last chapter on the nature and effects of the poor-laws have been in the most striking manner confirmed by the experience of the years 1815, 1816 and 1817.[1] During these years, two points of the very highest importance have been established, so as no longer to admit of a doubt in the mind of any rational man.

The first is that the country does not in point of fact fulfil the promise which it makes to the poor in the poor-laws, to maintain and find in employment, by means of parish assessments, those who are unable to support themselves or their families, either from want of work or any other cause.

And secondly, that with a very great increase of legal parish assessments, aided by the most liberal and praiseworthy contributions of voluntary charity, the country has been wholly unable to find adequate employment for the numerous labourers and artificers who were able as well as willing to work.

It can no longer surely be contended that the poor-laws really perform what they promise, when it is known that many almost starving families have been found in London and other great towns, who are deterred from going on the parish by the crowded, unhealthy and horrible state of the workhouses into which they would be received, if indeed they could be received at all; when it is known that many parishes have been absolutely unable to raise the necessary assessments, the increase of which, according to the existing laws, have tended only to bring more and more persons upon the parish, and to make what was collected less and less effectual; and when it is known that there has been an almost universal cry from one end of the kingdom to the other for voluntary charity to come in aid of the parochial assessments.

These strong indications of the inefficiency of the poor-laws may merely[2] be considered not only as incontrovertible proofs of the fact that

---

[1] [In 1826 a footnote was added here:
This chapter was written in 1817.
[2] [In 1826 the word *merely* was omitted.]

they do not perform what they promise, but as affording the strongest presumption that they cannot do it. The best of all reasons for the breach of a promise is the absolute impossibility of executing it; indeed it is the only plea that can ever be considered as valid. But though it may be fairly pardonable not to execute an impossibility, it is unpardonable knowingly to promise one. And if it be still thought advisable to act upon these statutes as far as is practicable, it would surely be wise so to alter the terms in which they are expressed, and the general interpretation given to them, as not to convey to the poor a false notion of what really is within the range of practicability.

It has appeared further as a matter of fact, that very large voluntary contributions, combined with greatly increased parochial assessments, and aided by the most able and incessant exertions of individuals, have failed to give the necessary employment to those who have been thrown out of work by the sudden falling off of demand which has occurred during the last two or three years.

It might perhaps have been foreseen that, as the great movements of society, the great causes which render a nation progressive, stationary or declining, for longer or shorter periods, cannot be supposed to depend much upon parochial assessments or the contributions of charity, it could not be expected that any efforts of this kind should have power to create in a stationary or declining state of things that effective demand for labour which only belongs to a progressive state. But to those who did not see this truth before, the melancholy experience of the last two years[3] must have brought it home with an overpowering conviction.

It does not however by any means follow that the exertions which have been made to relieve the present distresses have been ill directed. On the contrary, they have not only been prompted by the most praiseworthy motives; they have not only fulfilled the great moral duty of assisting our fellow-creatures in distress; but they have in point of fact done great good, or at least prevented great evil. Their partial failure does not necessarily indicate either a want of energy or a want of skill in those who

---

[3] [In 1826 a footnote was added here:
    The years 1816 and 1817.
[The very wet summer of 1816 resulted in a bad harvest and an epidemic of typhus; the cessation of the Napoleonic wars led to a steep fall in demand, for labour, and for such commodities as had already been manufactured in anticipation of high profits. There were outbreaks of destructive violence all over the country, as well as more rational agitation for parliamentary reform.]

have taken the lead in these efforts, but merely that a part only of what has been attempted is practicable.

It is practicable to mitigate the violence and relieve the severe pressure of the present distress, so as to carry the sufferers through to better times, though even this can only be done at the expense of some sacrifices, not merely of the rich, but of other classes of the poor. But it is impracticable by any exertions, either individual or national, to restore at once that brisk demand for commodities and labour which has been lost by events that, however, they may have originated, are now beyond the power of control.

The whole subject is surrounded on all sides by the most formidable difficulties, and in no state of things is it so necessary to recollect the saying of Daniel de Foe quoted in the last chapter. The manufacturers all over the country, and the Spitalfields weavers in particular, are in a state of the deepest distress, occasioned immediately and directly by the want of demand for the produce of their industry, and the consequent necessity felt by the masters of turning off many of their workmen, in order to proportion the supply to the contracted demand. It is proposed however, by some well-meaning people, to raise by subscription a fund for the express purpose of setting to work again those who have been turned off by their masters, the effect of which can only be to continue glutting a market already much too fully supplied. This is most naturally and justly objected to by the masters, as it prevents them from withdrawing the supply, and taking the only course which can prevent the total destruction of their capitals, and the necessity of turning off all their men instead of a part.

On the other hand, some classes of merchants and manufacturers clamour very loudly for the prohibition of all foreign commodities which may enter into competition with domestic products, and interfere, as they intimate, with the employment of British industry. But this is most naturally and most justly deprecated by other classes of British subjects, who are employed to a very great extent in preparing and manufacturing those commodities which are to purchase our imports from foreign countries. And it must be allowed to be perfectly true that a court-ball, at which only British stuffs are admitted, may be the means of throwing out of employment in one quarter of the country just as many persons as it furnishes with employment in another.

Still, it would be desirable if possible to employ those that are out of work, if it were merely to avoid the bad moral effects of idleness, and of the evil habits which might be generated by depending for a considerable time on mere alms. But the difficulties just stated will show that we ought to proceed in this part of the attempt with great caution, and that the kinds of employment which ought to be chosen are those, the results of which will not interfere with existing capitals. Such are public works of all descriptions, the making and repairing of roads, bridges, railways,[4] canals, &c.; and now perhaps, since the great loss of agricultural capital, almost every sort of labour upon the land, which could be carried on by public subscription.

Yet even in this way of employing labour, the benefit to some must bring with it disadvantages to others. That portion of each person's revenue, which might go in subscriptions of this kind, must of course be lost to the various sorts of labour which its expenditure in the usual channels would have supported; and the want of demand thus occasioned in these channels must cause the pressure of distress to be felt in quarters which might otherwise have escaped it. But this is an effect which, in such cases, it is impossible to avoid; and, as a temporary measure, it is not only charitable but just to spread the evil over a larger surface, in order that its violence on particular parts may be so mitigated as to be made bearable by all.

The great object to be kept in view, is to support the people through their present distresses, in the hope (and I trust a just one) of better times. The difficulty is without doubt considerably aggravated by the prodigious stimulus which has been given to the population of the country of late years, the effects of which cannot suddenly subside. But it will be seen probably, when the next returns of the population are made, that the marriages and births have diminished, and the deaths increased in a still greater degree than in 1800 and 1801; and the continuance of this effect to a certain degree for a few years will retard the progress of the population, and combined with the increasing wants of Europe and America from their increasing riches, and the adaptation of the supply of commodities at home to the new distribution of wealth occasioned by the alteration of the circulating medium, will again give life and energy to all

---

[4] [In 1817 there were about 160 miles of rail-road in the United Kingdom, used mainly for the transport of coal, timber, limestone and iron-ore, in wagons pulled by horses. Malthus would certainly have heard of the early experiments with steam locomotives, made by Trevithick and Hedley in 1804 and 1813; their inventions were to some extent stimulated by the war-time shortage of horses and fodder.]

our mercantile and agricultural transactions, and restore the labouring classes to full employment and good wages.[5]

On the subject of the distresses of the poor, and particularly the increase of pauperism of late years, the most erroneous opinions have been circulated. During the progress of the war, the increase in the proportion of persons requiring parish assistance was attributed chiefly to the high price of the necessaries of life. We have seen these necessaries of life experience a great and sudden fall, and yet at the same time a still larger proportion of the population requiring parish assistance.

It is now said that taxation is the sole cause of their distresses, and of the extraordinary stagnation in the demand for labour; yet I feel the firmest conviction that if the whole of the taxes were removed to-morrow, this stagnation, instead of being at an end, would be considerably aggravated. Such an event would cause another great and general rise in the value of the circulating medium, and bring with it that discouragement to industry with which such a convulsion in society must ever be attended. If, as has been represented, the labouring classes now pay more than half of what they receive in taxes, he must know very little indeed of the principles on which the wages of labour are regulated, who can for a moment suppose that, when the commodities on which they are expended have fallen one half by the removal of taxes, these wages themselves would still continue of the same nominal value. Were they to remain but for a short time the same, while all commodities had fallen, and the circulating medium had been reduced in proportion, it would be quickly seen that multitudes of them would be at once thrown out of employment.

The effects of taxation are no doubt in many cases pernicious in a very high degree; but it may be laid down as a rule which has few exceptions, that the relief obtained by taking off a tax is in no respect equal to the injury inflicted in laying it on; and generally it may be said that the specific evil of taxation consists in the check which it gives to production,

[5] [In 1826 a footnote was added here:

1825. This has, in a considerable degree, taken place; but it has been owing rather to the latter causes noticed than to the former. It appeared, by the returns of 1821, that the scarce years of 1817 and 1818 had but a slight effect in diminishing the number of marriages and births, compared with the effect of the great proportion of plentiful years in increasing them; so that the population proceeded with great rapidity during the ten years ending with 1820. But this great increase of the population has prevented the labouring classes from being so fully employed as might have been expected from the prosperity of commerce and agriculture during the last two or three years.

rather than the diminution which it occasions in demand. With regard to all commodities indeed of home production and home demand, it is quite certain that the conversion of capital into revenue, which is the effect of loans, must necessarily increase the proportion of demand to the supply; and the conversion of the revenue of individuals into the revenue of the government, which is the effect of taxes properly imposed, however hard upon the individuals so taxed, can have no tendency to diminish the general amount of demand. It will of course diminish the demands of the persons taxed by diminishing their powers of purchasing; but to the exact amount that the powers of these persons are diminished, will the powers of the government and of those employed by it be increased. If an estate of five thousand a year has a mortgage upon it of two thousand, two families, both in very good circumstances, may be living upon the rents of it, and both have considerable demands for houses, furniture, carriages, broad-cloth, silks, cottons, &c. The man who owns the estate is certainly much worse off than if the mortgage-deed was burnt, but the manufacturers and labourers who supply the silks, broad-cloth, cottons, &c., are so far from being likely to be benefited by such burning, that it would be a considerable time before the new wants and tastes of the enriched owner had restored the former demand; and if he were to take a fancy to spend his additional income in horses, hounds and menial servants, which is probable, not only would the manufacturers and labourers who had before supplied their silks, cloths and cottons be thrown out of employment, but the substituted demand would be very much less favourable to the increase of the capital and general resources of the country.

The foregoing illustration represents more nearly than may generally be imagined the effects of a national debt on the labouring classes of society, and the very great mistake of supposing that, because the demands of a considerable portion of the community would be increased by the extinction of the debt, these increased demands would not be balanced, and often more than balanced, by the loss of the demand from the fundholders[6] and government.

It is by no means intended by these observations to intimate that a

---

[6] [The fund-holders were those who had money invested in government stock. In 1751 a number of public securities had been consolidated into a single fund, bearing interest at 3 per cent; those who derived their income from this source were regarded as parasites on the rest of the community by William Cobbett and other radical writers.]

national debt may not be so heavy as to be extremely prejudicial to a state. The division and distribution of property, which is so beneficial when carried only to a certain extent, is fatal to production when pushed to extremity. The division of an estate of five thousand a year will generally tend to increase demand, stimulate production and improve the structure of society; but the division of an estate of eighty pounds a year will generally be attended with effects directly the reverse.

But, besides the probability that the division of property occasioned by a national debt may in many cases be pushed too far, the process of the division is effected by means which sometimes greatly embarrass production. This embarrassment must necessarily take place to a certain extent in almost every species of taxation; but under favourable circumstances it is overcome by the stimulus given to demand.[7] During the late war, from the prodigious increase of produce and population, it may fairly be presumed that the power of production was not essentially impeded, notwithstanding the enormous amount of taxation; but in the state of things which has occurred since the peace, and under a most extraordinary fall of the exchangeable value of the raw produce of the land, and a great consequent diminution of the circulating medium, the very sudden increase of the weight and pressure of taxation must greatly aggravate the other causes which discourage production. This effect has been felt to a considerable extent on the land; but the distress in this quarter is already much mitigated;[8] and among the mercantile and manufacturing classes, where the greatest numbers are without employment, the evil obviously arises not so much from the want of capital and the means of production, as the want of a market for the commodity when produced – a want for which the removal of taxes, however proper, and indeed absolutely necessary as a permanent measure, is certainly not the immediate and specific remedy.

The principal causes of the increase of pauperism, independently of the present crisis, are, first, the general increase of the manufacturing system and the unavoidable variations of manufacturing labour; and secondly, and more particularly, the practice which has been adopted in some counties, and is now spreading pretty generally all over the

---

[7] [In 1826 Malthus inserted three words here:
    ... stimulus given to demand compared with supply.
[8] [In 1826 a footnote was added here:
    Written in 1817. It increased again afterwards from another great fall in the price of corn, subsequent to 1818.

kingdom, of paying a considerable portion of what ought to be the wages of labour out of the parish rates. During the war, when the demand for labour was great and increasing, it is quite certain that nothing but a practice of this kind could for any time have prevented the wages of labour from rising fully in proportion to the necessaries of life, in whatever degree these necessaries might have been raised by taxation. It was seen, consequently, that in those parts of Great Britain where this practice prevailed the least, the wages of labour rose the most. This was the case in Scotland, and some parts of the North of England, where the improvement in the condition of the labouring classes, and their increased command over the necessaries and conveniences of life, were particularly remarkable. And if, in some other parts of the country, where the practice did not greatly prevail, and especially in the towns, wages did not rise in the same degree, it was owing to the influx and competition of the cheaply raised population of the surrounding counties.

It is a just remark of Adam Smith, that the attempts of the legislature to raise the pay of curates had always been ineffectual, on account of the cheap and abundant supply of them, occasioned by the bounties given to young persons educated for the church at the universities. And it is equally true that no human efforts can keep up the price of day-labour so as to enable a man to support on his earnings a family of a moderate size, so long as those who have more than two children are considered as having a valid claim to parish assistance.

If this system were to become universal, and I own it appears to me that the poor-laws naturally lead to it, there is no reason whatever why parish assistance should not by degrees begin earlier and earlier; and I do not hesitate to assert that, if the government and constitution of the country were in all other respects as perfect as the wildest visionary thinks he could make them; if parliaments were annual, suffrage universal, wars, taxes and pensions unknown, and the civil list fifteen hundred a year,[9] the great body of the community might still be a collection of paupers.

[9] [The word *pension* here does not refer to the modern retirement pension, but to 'regular payments to persons of rank, royal favourites, etc., to enable them to maintain their state' (O.E.D.). The civil list was formerly a list of the charges to be defrayed by the government; in Malthus's time it meant the sum voted by parliament for what were traditionally the personal expenses of the monarch, including the payment of pensions, as above. Like the fund-holders (see n.6) the pensioners were not popular.]

I have been accused of proposing a law to prohibit the poor from marrying.[10] This is not true. So far from proposing such a law, I have distinctly said that, if any person chooses to marry without having a prospect of being able to maintain a family, he ought to have the most perfect liberty so to do; and whenever any prohibitory propositions have been suggested to me as advisable by persons who have drawn wrong inferences from what I have said, I have steadily and uniformly reprobated them. I am indeed most decidedly of opinion that any positive law to limit the age of marriage would be both unjust and immoral; and my greatest objection to a system of equality and the system of the poor-laws (two systems which, however different in their outset, are of a nature calculated to produce the same results) is, that the society in which they are effectively carried into execution, will ultimately be reduced to the miserable alternative of choosing between universal want and the enactment of *direct* laws against marriage.

What I have really proposed is a very different measure. It is the *gradual* and *very gradual* abolition of the poor-laws.[11] And the reason why I have ventured to suggest a proposition of this kind for consideration is my firm conviction that they have lowered very decidedly the wages of the labouring classes, and made their general condition essentially worse than it would have been if these laws had never existed. Their operation is every where depressing; but it falls peculiarly hard upon the labouring classes in great towns. In country parishes the poor do really receive some compensation for their low wages; their children, beyond a certain number, are really supported by the parish; and though it must be a most grating reflection to a labouring man, that it is scarcely possible for him to marry without becoming the father of paupers; yet if he can reconcile himself to this prospect, the compensation, such as it is, is no doubt made to him. But in London and all the great towns of the kingdom, the evil is suffered without the compensation. The population raised by bounties in the country naturally and necessarily flows into the towns, and as naturally and necessarily tends to lower wages in them; while, in point of fact, those who marry in towns, and have large families, receive no assistance from their parishes unless they are actually starving; and

---

[10] [In this and the following paragraph Malthus virtually assumes that readers of this chapter are familiar with earlier editions of the *Essay*, and know already about the plan for the gradual abolition of the poor laws which he had put forward in the quarto, chapter viii of Book iv in this edition.]

[11] So gradual as not to affect any individuals at present alive, or who will be born within the next two years.

altogether the assistance which the manufacturing classes obtain for the support of their families, in aid of their lowered wages, is perfectly inconsiderable.

To remedy the effects of this competition from the country, the artificers and manufacturers in towns have been apt to combine, with a view to keep up the price of labour and to prevent persons from working below a certain rate. But such combinations are not only illegal,[12] but irrational and ineffectual; and if the supply of workmen in any particular branch of trade be such as would naturally lower wages, the keeping them up forcibly must have the effect of throwing so many out of employment, as to make the expense of their support fully equal to the gain acquired by the higher wages, and thus render these higher wages in reference to the whole body perfectly futile.

It may be distinctly stated to be an *absolute impossibility* that all the different classes of society should be both well paid and fully employed, if the supply of labour on the whole exceed the demand; and as the poor-laws tend in the most marked manner to make the supply of labour exceed the demand for it, their effect must be, either to lower universally all wages, or, if some are kept up artificially, to throw great numbers of workmen out of employment, and thus constantly to increase the poverty and distress of the labouring classes of society.

If these things be so (and I am firmly convinced that they are) it cannot but be a subject of the deepest regret to those who are anxious for the happiness of the great mass of the community, that the writers which are now most extensively read among the common people should have selected for the subject of reprobation exactly that line of conduct which can alone generally improve their condition, and for the subject of approbation that system which must inevitably depress them in poverty and wretchedness.

---

[12] [In 1826 a footnote was added here:

This has since been altered; but the subsequent part of the passage is particularly applicable to the present time – the end of the year 1825. The workmen are beginning to find that, if they could raise their wages above what the state of the demand and the prices of goods will warrant, it is absolutely impossible that all, or nearly all, should be employed. The masters could not employ the same number as before without inevitable ruin.

[The Combination Acts of 1799 and 1800 had amounted to a general law against all trade unions; there had previously been many statutes forbidding combinations of workmen in particular trades. All such Acts were repealed in 1825. Malthus himself had given evidence, in May 1824, to the Select Committee on Artisans and

They are taught that there is no occasion whatever for them to put any sort of restraint upon their inclinations, or exercise any degree of prudence in the affair of marriage; because the parish is bound to provide for all that are born. They are taught that there is as little occasion to cultivate habits of economy, and make use of the means afforded them by saving-banks, to lay by their earnings while they are single, in order to furnish a cottage when they marry, and enable them to set out in life with decency and comfort; because, I suppose, the parish is bound to cover their nakedness, and to find them a bed and a chair in a work-house.

They are taught that any endeavour on the part of the higher classes of society to inculcate the duties of prudence and economy can only arise from a desire to save the money which they pay in poor-rates; although it is absolutely certain that the *only* mode, consistent with the laws of morality and religion, of giving to the poor the largest share of the property of the rich, without sinking the whole community in misery, is the exercise on the part of the poor of prudence in marriage, and of economy both before and after it.

They are taught that the command of the Creator to increase and multiply is meant to contradict those laws which he has himself appointed for the increase and multiplication of the human race; and that it is equally the duty of a person to marry early, when, from the impossibility of adding to the food of the country in which he lives, the greater part of his offspring must die prematurely, and consequently no multiplication follow from it, as when the children of such marriages can all be well maintained, and there is room and food for a great and rapid increase of population.

They are taught that, in relation to the condition of the labouring classes, there is no other difference between such a country as England, which has been long well peopled, and where the land which is not yet taken into cultivation is comparatively barren, and such a country as America, where millions and millions of acres of fine land are yet to be had for a trifle, except what arises from taxation.

And they are taught, O monstrous absurdity! that the only reason why the American labourer earns a dollar a day, and the English labourer earns two shillings, is that the English labourer pays a great part of these two shillings in taxes.

Some of these doctrines are so grossly absurd that I have no doubt

Machinery that recommended the abolition of these restrictive laws, laws which were in any case almost impossible to enforce.]

they are rejected at once by the common sense of many of the labouring classes. It cannot but strike them that, if their main dependence for the support of their children is to be on the parish, they can only expect parish fare, parish clothing, parish furniture, a parish house and parish government, and they must know that persons living in this way cannot possibly be in a happy and prosperous state.

It can scarcely escape the notice of the common mechanic, that the scarcer workmen are upon any occasion, the greater share do they retain of the value of what they produce for their masters; and it is a most natural inference, that prudence in marriage, which is the only moral means of preventing an excess of workmen above the demand, can be the only mode of giving to the poor permanently a large share of all that is produced in the country.

A common man, who has read his Bible, must be convinced that a command given to a rational being by a merciful God cannot be intended so as to be interpreted as to produce only disease and death instead of multiplication; and a plain sound understanding would make him to see that if, in a country in which little or no increase of food is to be obtained, every man were to marry at eighteen or twenty, when he generally feels most inclined to it, the consequence must be increased poverty, increased disease and increased mortality, and not increased numbers, as long at least as it continues to be true (which he will hardly be disposed to doubt) that additional numbers cannot live without additional food.

A moderately shrewd judgment would prompt any labourer acquainted with the nature of land to suspect that there must be some great difference, quite independent of taxation, between a country such as America, which might easily be made to support fifty times as many inhabitants as it contains at present, and a country such as England, which could not without extraordinary exertions be made to support two or three times as many. He would at least see that there would be a prodigious difference in the power of maintaining an additional number of cattle, between a small farm already well stocked, and a very large one which had not the fiftieth part of what it might be made to maintain; and as he would know that both rich and poor must live upon the produce of the earth as well as all other animals, he would be disposed to conclude that what was so obviously true in one case could not be false in the other. These considerations might make him think it natural and prob- able that in those countries where there was a great want of people, the wages of labour would be such as to encourage early marriages and large families, for the best of all possible reasons, because all that are born may be very easily and comfortably supported; but that in those countries which were already nearly full, the wages of labour cannot be such as to give the same encouragement to early marriages, for a reason surely not much worse, because the persons so brought into the world cannot be properly supported.

There are few of our mechanics and labourers who have not heard of the high prices of bread, meat and labour in this country compared with the nations of the continent, and they have generally heard at the same time that these high prices were chiefly occasioned by taxation, which, though it had raised among other things the money wages of labour, had done harm rather than good to the labourer, because it had before raised the price of the bread and beer and other articles on which he spent his earnings. With this amount of information, the meanest understanding would revolt at the idea that the very same cause which had kept the money price of labour in all the nations of Europe much lower than in England, namely, the absence of taxation, had been the means of raising it to more than double in America. He would feel quite convinced that, whatever might be the cause of the high money wages of labour in America, which he might not perhaps readily understand, it must be something very different indeed from the mere absence of taxation, which could only have an effect exactly opposite.

With regard to the improved condition of the lower classes of people in France since the revolution, which has also been much insisted upon; if the circumstances accompanying it were told at the same time, it would afford the strongest presumption against the doctrines which have been lately promulgated. The improved condition of the labouring classes in France since the revolution has been accompanied by a greatly diminished proportion of births, which has had its natural and necessary effect in giving to these classes a greater share of the produce of the country, and has kept up the advantage arising from the sale of the church lands and other national domains, which would otherwise have been lost in a short time. The effect of the revolution in France has been to make every person depend more upon himself and less upon others. The labouring classes are therefore become more industrious, more saving and more prudent in marriage than formerly; and it is quite certain that without these effects the revolution would have done nothing for them. An improved government has, no doubt, a natural tendency to produce these effects, and thus to improve the condition of the poor. But if an extensive system of parochial relief, and such doctrines as have lately been inculcated, counteract them, and prevent the labouring classes from depending upon their own prudence and industry, then any change for the better in other respects becomes comparatively a matter of very little importance; and, under the best form of government imaginable, there may be thousands on thousands out of employment and half starved.

If it be taught that all who are born have a *right* to support on the land, whatever be their number, and that there is no occasion to exercise any prudence in the affair of marriage so as to check this number, the temptations, according to all the known principles of human nature, will inevitably be yielded to, and more and more will gradually become dependent on parish assistance. There cannot therefore be a greater inconsistency and contradiction than that those who maintain these doctrines respecting the poor should still complain of the number of paupers. Such doctrines and a crowd of paupers are unavoidably united; and it is utterly beyond the power of any revolution or change of government to separate them.

CHAPTER VIII

Of the Agricultural System[1]

As it is the nature of agriculture to produce subsistence for a greater number of families than can be employed in the business of cultivation, it might perhaps be supposed that a nation which strictly pursued an agricultural system would always have more food than was necessary for its inhabitants, and that its population could never be checked from the want of the means of subsistence.

It is indeed obviously true that the increase of such a country is not immediately checked, either by the want of power to produce, or even by the deficiency of the actual produce of the soil compared with the population. Yet if we examine the condition of its labouring classes, we shall find that the real wages of their labour are such as essentially to check and regulate their increase, by checking and regulating their command over the means of subsistence.

A country under certain circumstances of soil and situation, and with a deficient capital, may find it advantageous to purchase foreign commodities with its raw produce rather than manufacture them at home: and in this case it will necessarily grow more raw produce than it consumes. But this state of things is very little connected either with the permanent condition of the lower classes of the society or the rate of their increase; and in a country where the agricultural system entirely predominates, and the general mass of its industry is directed towards the land, the condition of the people is subject to almost every degree of variation.

Under the agricultural system perhaps are to be found the two extremes in the condition of the poor; instances where they are in the best state, and instances where they are in the worst state of any of which we have accounts.

In a country where there is an abundance of good land, where there are no difficulties in the way of its purchase and distribution, and where there is an easy foreign vent for raw produce, both the profits of stock

---

[1] [The next six chapters replaced in 1817 the four chapters in Book III which were numbered vii–x in previous editions.]

and the wages of labour will be high. These high profits and high wages, if habits of economy pretty generally prevail, will furnish the means of a rapid accumulation of capital and a great and continued demand for labour, while the rapid increase of population which will ensue will maintain undiminished the demand for produce, and check the fall of profits. If the extent of territory be considerable, and the population comparatively inconsiderable, the land may remain understocked both with capital and people for some length of time, notwithstanding a rapid increase of both; and it is under these circumstances of the agricultural system that labour is able to command the greatest portion of the necessaries of life, and that the condition of the labouring classes of society is the best.

The only drawback to the wealth of the labouring classes under these circumstances is the relatively low value of the raw produce.

If a considerable part of the manufactured commodities used in such a country be purchased by the export of its raw produce, it follows as a necessary consequence that the relative value of its raw produce will be lower, and of its manufactured produce higher, than in the countries with which such a trade is carried on. But where a given portion of raw produce will not command so much of manufactured and foreign commodities as in other countries, the condition of the labourer cannot be exactly measured by the quantity of raw produce which falls to his share. If, for instance, in one country the yearly earnings of a labourer amount in money value to fifteen quarters of wheat, and in another to nine, it would be incorrect to infer that their relative condition, and the comforts which they enjoy, were in the same proportion, because the whole of a labourer's earnings are not spent in food; and if that part which is not so spent will, in the country where the value of fifteen quarters is earned, not go near so far in the purchase of clothes and other conveniences as in the countries where the value of nine quarters is earned, it is clear that altogether the situation of the labourer in the latter country may approach nearer to that of the labourer in the former than might at first be supposed.

At the same time it should be recollected that *quantity* always tends powerfully to counterbalance any deficiency of value; and the labourer who earns the greatest number of quarters may still command the greatest quantity of necessaries and conveniences combined, though not to the extent implied by the proportions of the raw produce.

America affords a practical instance of the agricultural system in a state the most favourable to the condition of the labouring classes. [2]●The nature of the country has been such as to make it answer to employ a very large proportion of its capital in agriculture; and the consequence has been a very rapid increase of stock. This rapid increase of stock has kept up a steady and continued demand for labour.●[2] The labouring classes have in consequence been peculiarly well paid. They have been able to command an unusual quantity of the necessaries of life, and the progress of population has been unusually rapid.

Yet even here, some little drawback has been felt from the relative cheapness of corn. As America till the late war imported the greatest part of its manufactures from England, and as England imported flour and wheat from America, the value of food in America compared with manufactures must have been decidedly less than in England. Nor would this effect take place merely with relation to the foreign commodities imported into America, but also to those of its home manufactures, in which it has no particular advantage. In agriculture, the abundance of good land would counterbalance the high wages of labour and high profits of stock, and keep the price of corn moderate, notwithstanding the great expense of these two elements of price. But in the production of manufactured commodities they must necessarily tell, without any particular advantage to counterbalance them, and must in general occasion in home goods, as well as foreign, a high price compared with food.

Under these circumstances, the condition of the labouring classes of society cannot in point of conveniences and comforts be so much better than that of the labourers of other countries as the relative quantity of food which they earn might seem to indicate; and this conclusion is sufficiently confirmed by experience. In some very intelligent Travels through a great part of England, written in 1810 and 1811 by Mr. Simond, a French gentleman, who had resided above twenty years in America, the author seems to have been evidently much struck with the air of convenience and comfort in the houses of our peasantry, and the neatness and cleanliness of their dress. In some parts of his tour he saw so many neat cottages, so much good clothing, and so little appearance of poverty and distress, that he could not help wondering where the poor of

---

[2] [In 1826 this passage was altered:

   The nature of the country is such as to make it answer to employ a very large proportion of its capital in agriculture; and the consequence has been a very rapid increase of it. This rapid increase both of the quantity and value of capital has kept up a steady and continued demand for labour.

England and their dwellings were concealed. These observations, coming from an able, accurate and apparently most impartial observer, just landed from America and visiting England for the first time, are . curious and instructive; and the facts which they notice, though they may arise in part from the different habits and modes of life prevailing in the two countries, must be occasioned in a considerable degree by the causes above mentioned.

A very striking instance of the disadvantageous effect of a low relative price of food on the consumption of the poor may be observed in Ireland. [3]● In Ireland the funds for the maintenance of labour have increased so rapidly during the last century, and so large a portion of that sort of food which forms the principal support of the lower classes of society has been awarded to them, that the increase of population has been more rapid that in almost any known country,●[3] except America. The Irish labourer paid in potatoes has earned perhaps the means of subsistence for double the number of persons that could be supported by the earnings of an English labourer paid in wheat; and the increase of population in the two countries during the last century has been nearly in proportion to the relative quantity of the customary food awarded to the labourers in each. But their general condition with respect to conveniences and comforts are very far indeed from being in a similar proportion. The great quantity of food which land will bear when planted with potatoes, and the consequent cheapness of the labour supported by them, tends rather to raise than to lower the rents of land, and as far as rent goes, to keep up the price of the materials of manufactures and all other sorts of raw produce, except potatoes. [4]● In the raw materials of home manufactures, therefore, a great relative disadvantage will be suffered, and a still greater both in the raw and manufactured produce of foreign countries. The exchangeable value of the food which the Irish labourer earns,●[4] above what he and his family consume, will go but a very little way in the

---

[3] [In 1826 this sentence was changed:
　The food of Ireland has increased so rapidly during the last century, and so large a portion of that which forms the principal support of the lower classes of society has been obtained by them, that the increase of population has been more rapid than in almost any known country ...
[4] [In 1826 this passage was altered:
　The indolence and want of skill which usually accompany such a state of things tend further to render all wrought commodities comparatively dear. In home manufactures, therefore, a great relative disadvantage will be suffered, and a still greater both in the raw and manufactured produce of foreign countries. The value of the food which the Irish labourer earns ...

purchase of clothing, lodging and other conveniences; and the consequence is that his condition in these respects is extremely miserable, at the same time that his means of subsistence, such as they are, may be comparatively abundant.

In Ireland the money price of labour is not much more than the half of what it is in England. The quantity of food earned by no means makes up for its deficient value.[5] A certain portion, therefore, of the Irish labourer's wages (a fourth or a fifth for instance) will go but a very little way in the purchase of manufactures and foreign produce. In America,[6] on the other hand, even the money wages of labour are nearly double those of England. Though the American labourer, therefore, cannot purchase manufactures and foreign produce with the food that he earns so cheap as the English labourer, yet the greater quantity of this food makes up for its deficiency of relative value.[7] His condition, compared with the labouring classes of England, though it may not be so much superior as their relative means of subsistence might indicate, must still on the whole have decidedly the advantage; and altogether, perhaps, America[8] may be produced as an instance of the agricultural system in which the condition of the labouring classes is the best of any that we know.

The instances where, under the agricultural system, the condition of the lower classes of society is very wretched, are more frequent. When the accumulation of capital stops, whatever may be the cause, the population, before it comes to a stand, will always be pressed on as near to the limits of the actual means of subsistence as the habits of the lower classes of the society will allow; that is, the real wages of labour will sink till they are only just sufficient to maintain a stationary population. Should this happen, as it frequently does, while land is still in abundance and capital scarce, the profits of stock will naturally be high; but corn will be very cheap, owing to the goodness and plenty of the land, and the stationary demand for it, notwithstanding the high profits of stock; while these high profits, together with the usual want of skill and proper

---

[5] [In 1826 *deficient value* was changed to:
   ... very low price.
[6] [In 1826 'the United States' was substituted for *America*.]
[7] [In 1826 this sentence was altered:
   ... English labourer, yet the greater quantity of this food more than makes up for its lower price.
[8] [In 1826 *America* was again changed to 'the United States'.]

division of labour, which attend a scanty capital,[9] will render all domestic manufactured commodities comparatively very dear. This state of things will naturally be unfavourable to the generation of those habits of prudential restraint which most frequently arise from the custom of enjoying conveniences and comforts, and it is to be expected that the population will not stop till the wages of labour, estimated even in food, are very low. But in a country where the wages of labour estimated in food are low, and that food is relatively of a very low value, both with regard to domestic and foreign manufactures, the condition of the labouring classes of society must be the worst possible.

Poland, and some parts of Russia, Siberia and European Turkey, afford instances of this kind. In Poland the population seems to be almost stationary or very slowly progressive; and as both the population and produce are scanty, compared with the extent of territory, we may infer with certainty that its capital is scanty, and yet slowly progressive. It follows, therefore, that the demand for labour increases very slowly, and that the real wages of labour, or the command of the labouring classes over the necessaries and conveniences of life, are such as to keep the population down to the level of the slowly increasing quantity that is awarded to them. And as from the state of the country the peasantry cannot have been much accustomed to conveniences and comforts, the checks to its population are more likely to be of the positive than of the preventive kind.

Yet here corn is in abundance, and great quantities of it are yearly exported. [10]●But it appears clearly that it is not either the power of the country to produce food, or even what it actually produces, that limits and regulates the progress of population, but the quantity which in the actual state of things is awarded to the labourer, and the rate at which the funds so appropriated increase.●[10]

In the present case the demand for labour is very small; and though the population is inconsiderable, it is greater than the scanty capital of

---

[9] [In 1826 this was altered to:
    ... while these high profits, together with the want of skill and proper division of labour, which usually attend a scanty capital ...
[10] [In 1826 this sentence was re-written:
    Hence it appears that it is not either the power of the country to produce food, or even what it actually produces, that limits and regulates the progress of population, but the quantity and value of the food which in the actual state of things is awarded to the labourer, and the rate at which these funds appropriated increase.

the country can fully employ; the condition of the labourer therefore is depressed by his being able to command only such a quantity of food as will maintain a stationary or very slowly increasing population. It is further depressed by the low relative value of the food that he earns, which gives to any surplus he may possess a very small power in the purchase of manufactured commodities or foreign produce.

Under these circumstances, we cannot be surprised that all accounts of Poland should represent the condition of the lower classes of society as extremely miserable; and the other parts of Europe, which resemble Poland in the state of their land and capital, resemble it in the condition of their people.

In justice, however, to the agricultural system, it should be observed that the premature check to the capital and the demand for labour, which occurs in some of the countries of Europe, while land continues in considerable plenty, is not occasioned by the particular direction of their industry, but by the vices of the government and the structure of the society, which prevent its full and fair development in that direction.

Poland is continually brought forward as an example of the miserable effects of the agricultural system. But nothing surely can be less fair. The misery of Poland does not arise from its directing its industry chiefly to agriculture, but from the little encouragement given to industry of any kind, owing to the state of property and the servile condition of the people. While the land is cultivated by boors, the produce of whose exertions belongs entirely to their masters, and the whole society consists mainly of these degraded beings and the lords and owners of great tracts of territory, there will evidently be no class of persons possessed of the means either of furnishing an adequate demand at home for the surplus produce of the soil, or of accumulating fresh capital and increasing the demand for labour. In this miserable state of things, the best remedy would unquestionably be the introduction of manufactures and commerce; because the introduction of manufactures and commerce could alone liberate the mass of the people from slavery and give the necessary stimulus to industry and accumulation. But were the people already free and industrious, and landed property easily divisible and alienable, it might still answer to such a country as Poland to purchase its finer manufactures from foreign countries by means of its raw products, and thus to continue agricultural for many years. Under these new circumstances, however, it would present a totally different picture from that which it exhibits at present; and the condition of the people would more resemble that of the inhabitants of the United States of America than of the inhabitants of the unimproved countries of Europe.

Indeed America is perhaps the only modern instance of the fair operation of the agricultural system. In every country of Europe, and in most of its colonies in other parts of the world, formidable obstacles still exist to the employment of capital upon the land, arising from the remains of the feudal system. But these obstacles, which have essentially impeded cultivation, have been very far indeed from proportionably encouraging other branches of industry. Commerce and manufactures are necessary to agriculture; but agriculture is still more necessary to commerce and manufactures. It must ever be true that the surplus produce of the cultivators, taken in its most enlarged sense, measures and limits the growth of that part of the society which is not employed upon the land. Throughout the whole world the number of manufacturers, of merchants, of proprietors and of persons engaged in the various civil and military professions, must be exactly proportioned to this surplus produce, and cannot in the nature of things increase beyond it.

If the earth had been so niggardly of her produce as to oblige all her inhabitants to labour for it, no manufacturers or idle persons could ever have existed. But her first intercourse with man was a voluntary present, not very large indeed, but sufficient as a fund for his subsistence till he could procure a greater. And the power to procure a greater was given to him in that quality of the earth by which it may be made to yield a much larger quantity of food, and of the materials of clothing and lodging, than is necessary to feed, clothe and lodge the persons employed in the cultivation of the soil. This quality is the foundation of that surplus produce which peculiarly distinguishes the industry employed upon the land. In proportion as the labour and ingenuity of man exercised upon the land have increased this surplus produce, leisure has been given to a greater number of persons to employ themselves in all the inventions which embellish civilized life; while the desire to profit by these inventions has continued to stimulate the cultivators to increase their surplus produce. This desire indeed may be considered as almost absolutely necessary to give it its proper value, and to encourage its further extension; but still the order of precedence is, strictly speaking, the surplus produce; because the funds for the subsistence of the manufacturer must be advanced to him before he can complete his work; and no step can be taken in any other sort of industry unless the cultivators obtain from the soil more than they themselves consume.

If in asserting the peculiar productiveness of the labour employed upon the land, we look only to the clear moneyed rent yielded to a certain number of proprietors, we undoubtedly consider the subject in a very contracted point of view. In the advanced stages of society, this rent forms indeed the most prominent portion of the surplus produce here meant; but it may exist equally in the shape of high wages and profits during the earlier periods of cultivation, when there is little or no rent. The labourer who earns a value equal to fifteen[11] quarters of corn in the year may have only a family of three or four children, and not consume in kind above five or six quarters; and the owner of the farming stock, which yields high profits, may consume but a very moderate proportion of them in food and raw materials. All the rest, whether in the shape of wages and profits, or of rents, may be considered as a surplus produce from the soil, which affords the means of subsistence and the materials of clothing and lodging to a certain number of people according to its extent, some of whom may live without manual exertions, and others employ themselves in modifying the raw materials obtained from the earth into the forms best suited to the gratification of man.[12]

It will depend of course entirely upon its answering to a country to exchange a part of the surplus produce for foreign commodities, instead of consuming it at home, whether it is to be considered as mainly agricultural or otherwise. And such an exchange of raw produce for manufactures, or peculiar foreign products, may for a period of some extent suit a state which might resemble Poland in scarcely any other feature but that of exporting corn.

It appears, then, that countries in which the industry of the inhabitants is principally directed towards the land, and in which corn continues to be exported, may enjoy great abundance or experience great want, according to the particular circumstances in which they are placed. They will in general not be much exposed to the temporary evils of scarcity arising from the variations of the seasons; but the quantity of food permanently awarded to the labourer may be such as not to allow of an increase of population; and their state, in respect to their being progressive, stationary or declining, will depend upon other causes than that of directing their attention principally to agriculture.

[11] [In 1826 Malthus altered this to:
     ... fifteen or twenty quarters of corn in the year ...
[12] [Malthus repeats this in chapter x, n.2.]

CHAPTER IX

Of the Commercial System

A country which excels in commerce and manufactures may purchase corn from a great variety of others; and it may be supposed perhaps that, proceeding upon this system, it may continue to purchase an increasing quantity, and to maintain a rapidly increasing population, till the lands of all the nations with which it trades are fully cultivated. As this is an event necessarily at a great distance, it may appear that the population of such a country will not be checked from the difficulty of procuring subsistence till after the lapse of a great number of ages.

There are, however, causes constantly in operation, which will occasion the pressure of this difficulty long before the event here contemplated has taken place, and while the means of raising food in the surrounding countries may still be comparatively abundant.

In the first place, advantages which depend exclusively upon capital and skill, and the present possession of particular channels of commerce, cannot in their nature be permanent. We know how difficult it is to confine improvements in machinery to a single spot; we know that it is the constant object, both of individuals and countries, to increase their capital; and we know, from the past history of commercial states, that the channels of trade are not unfrequently taking a different direction. It is unreasonable therefore to expect that any one country, merely by the force of skill and capital, should remain in possession of markets uninterrupted by foreign competition. But, when a powerful foreign competition takes place, the exportable commodities of the country in question must soon fall to prices which will essentially reduce profits; and the fall of profits will diminish both the power and the will to save. Under these circumstances the accumulation of capital will be slow, and the demand for labour proportionably slow, till it comes nearly to a stand; while perhaps the new competitors, either by raising their own raw materials or by some other advantages, may still be increasing their capitals and population with some degree of rapidity.

But secondly, even if it were possible for a considerable time to exclude any formidable foreign competition, it is found that domestic competition produces almost unavoidably the same effects. If a machine be invented in a particular country, by the aid of which one man can do the work of ten, the possessors of it will of course at first make very unusual profits; but as soon as the invention is generally known, so much capital and industry will be brought into this new and profitable employment as to make its products greatly exceed both the foreign and domestic demand at the old prices. These prices, therefore, will continue to fall, till the stock and labour employed in this direction cease to yield unusual profits. In this case it is evident that, though in an early period of such a manufacture, the product of the industry of one man for a day might have been exchanged for such a portion of food as would support forty or fifty persons; yet, at a subsequent period, the product of the same industry might not purchase the support of ten.

In the cotton trade of this country, which has extended itself so wonderfully during the last twenty-five years, very little effect has hitherto been produced by foreign competition.[1] The very great fall which has taken place in the prices of cotton goods has been almost exclusively owing to domestic competition; and this competition has so glutted both the home and foreign markets, that the present capitals employed in the trade, notwithstanding the very peculiar advantages which they possess from the saving of labour, have ceased to possess any advantage whatever in the general rate of their profits. Although, by means of the admirable machinery used in the spinning of cotton, one boy or girl can now do as much as many grown persons could do formerly; yet neither the wages of the labourer, nor the profits of his master, are higher than in those employments where no machinery is used, and no saving of labour accomplished.

The country has, however, in the mean time, been very greatly benefited. Not only have all its inhabitants been enabled to obtain a superior fabric for clothing, at a less expense of labour and property, which must be considered as a great and permanent advantage; but the high temporary profits of the trade have occasioned a great accumulation of capital, and consequently a great demand for labour; while the extending markets abroad and the new values thrown into the market at home, have created such a demand for the products of every species of industry, agricultural and colonial, as well as commercial and manufacturing, as to prevent a fall of profits.

[1] 1816.

This country, from the extent of its lands, and its rich colonial possessions, has a large *arena* for the employment of an increasing capital; and the general rate of its profits are not, as it appears, very easily and rapidly reduced by accumulation. But a country, such as we are considering, engaged principally in manufactures, and unable to direct its industry to the same variety of pursuits, would sooner find its rate of profits diminished by an increase of capital, and no ingenuity in machinery[2] could save it, after a certain period, from low profits and low wages, and their natural consequences, a check to population.

Thirdly, a country which is obliged to purchase both the raw materials of its manufactures, and the means of subsistence for its population, from foreign countries, is almost entirely dependent for the increase of its wealth and population on the increasing wealth and demands of the countries with which it trades.

It has been sometimes said that a manufacturing country is no more dependent upon the country which supplies it with food and raw materials, than the agricultural country is on that which manufactures for it; but this is really an abuse of terms. A country with great resources in land may find it decidedly for its advantage to employ the main part of its capital in cultivation and to import its manufactures. In so doing, it will often employ the whole of its industry most productively, and most rapidly increase its stock. But, if the slackness of its neighbours in manufacturing, or any other case, should either considerably check or altogether prevent the importation of manufactures, a country with food and raw materials provided at home cannot be long at a loss. For a time it would not certainly be so well supplied; but manufacturers and artisans would soon be found, and would soon acquire tolerable skill;[3] and though the capital and population of the country might not, under the new circumstances in which it was placed, increase so rapidly as before, it would still have the power of increasing in both to a great and almost undefinable extent.[4]

On the other hand, if food and raw materials were denied to a nation merely manufacturing, it is obvious that it could not longer exist. But not only does the absolute existence of such a nation, on an extreme

---

[2] [In 1826 a clause was inserted here:

    ... no ingenuity in machinery which was not continually progressive could save
  it ...

[3] This has been fully exemplified in America (1816).

[4] [In 1826 the words *and almost undefinable* were deleted.]

supposition, depend upon its foreign commerce, but its progress in wealth must be almost entirely measured by the progress and demand of the countries which deal with it. However skilful, industrious and saving such a nation might be, if its customers, from indolence and want of accumulation, would not or could not take off a yearly increasing value of its commodities, the effects of its skill and machinery would be but of very short duration.

That the cheapness of manufactured commodities, occasioned by skill and machinery in one country, is calculated to encourage an increase of raw produce in others, no person can doubt; but we know at the same time that high profits may continue for a considerable period in an indolent and ill-governed state, without producing an increase of wealth; yet, unless such an increase of wealth and demand were produced in the surrounding countries, the increasing ingenuity and exertions of the manufacturing and commercial state would be lost in continually falling prices. It would not only be obliged, as its skill and capital increased, to give a larger quantity of manufactured produce for the raw produce which it received in return; but it might be unable, even with the temptation of reduced prices, to stimulate its customers to such purchases as would allow of an increasing importation of food and raw materials; and without such an increasing importation, it is quite obvious that the population must become stationary.

It would come to the same thing, whether this inability to obtain an increasing quantity of food were occasioned by the advancing money price of corn or the falling money price of manufactures. In either case the effect would be the same; and it is certain that this effect might take place in either way, from increasing competition and accumulation in the manufacturing nation, and the want of them in the agricultural, long before any essential increase of difficulty had occurred in the production of corn.

Fourthly. A nation which is obliged to purchase from others nearly the whole of its raw materials, and the means of its subsistence, is not only dependent entirely upon the demands of its customers, as they may be variously affected by indolence, industry or caprice, but it is subjected to a necessary and unavoidable diminution of demand in the natural progress of these countries towards that proportion of skill and capital which they may reasonably be expected after a certain time to possess. It is generally an accidental and temporary, not a natural and permanent division of labour, which constitutes one state the manufacturer and the carrier of others. While in these landed nations agricultural profits continue very high, it may fully answer to them to pay others as their manufacturers and carriers; but when the profits on land fall, or the tenures on which it can be held are not such as to encourage the investment of an accumulating capital, the owner of this capital will naturally look towards commerce and manufactures for its employment; and, according to the just reasoning of Adam Smith and the Economists,[5] finding at home both the materials of manufactures, the means of subsistence, and the power of carrying on their own trade with foreign countries, they will probably be able to conduct the business of manufacturing and carrying for themselves at a cheaper rate than if they allowed it to continue in the hands of others. As long as the agricultural nations continued to apply their increasing capital principally to the land, this increase of capital would be of the greatest possible advantage to the manufacturing and commercial nation. It would be indeed the main cause and great regulator of its progress in wealth and population. But after they had turned their attention to manufactures and commerce, their further increase of capital would be the signal of decay and destruction to the manufactures and commerce which they had before supported. And thus, in the natural progress of national improvement, and without the competition of superior skill and capital, a purely commercial state must be undersold and driven out of the markets by those who possess the advantage of land.

In the distribution of wealth during the progress of improvement, the interests of an independent state are essentially different from those of a province, a point which has not been sufficiently attended to.[6] If agricultural capital increases and agricultural profits diminish in Sussex, the overflowing stock will go to London, Manchester, Liverpool, or some other place where it can probably be engaged in manufactures or commerce more advantageously than at home. But if Sussex were an independent kingdom, this could not take place; and the corn which is now sent to London must be withdrawn to support manufacturers and traders living within its confines. If England, therefore, had continued to be separated into the seven kingdoms of the Heptarchy, London could

[5] [Malthus here means the French *Economistes* or *Physiocrates.*]
[6] [In 1826 this sentence was altered:

In the distribution of wealth during the progress of improvement, the interests of an independent state in relation to others are essentially different from those of a particular province, in relation to the kingdom to which it belongs, a point which has not been sufficiently attended to.

not possibly have been what it is; and that distribution of wealth and population which takes place at present, and which we may fairly presume is the most beneficial to the whole of the realm, would have been essentially changed, if the object had been to accumulate the greatest quantity of wealth and population in particular districts instead of the whole island. But at all times the interest of each independent state is to accumulate the greatest quantity of wealth within its limits. Consequently, the interest of an independent state, with regard to the countries with which it trades, can rarely be the same as the interest of a province with regard to the empire to which it belongs; and the accumulation of capital which would occasion the withdrawing of the exports of corn in the one case, would leave them perfectly undisturbed in the other.

If, from the operation of one or more of the causes above enumerated, the importation of corn into a manufacturing and commercial country should be essentially checked, and should either actually decrease, or be prevented from increasing, it is quite evident that its population must be checked nearly in the same proportion.

Venice presents a striking instance of a commercial state at once stopped in its progress to wealth and population by foreign competition. The discovery made by the Portuguese of a passage to India by the Cape of Good Hope completely turned the channel of the Indian trade. The high profits of the Venetians, which had been the foundation of their rapidly increasing wealth and of their extraordinary preponderance as a naval and commercial power, were not only suddenly reduced; but the trade itself, on which these high profits had been made, was almost annihilated, and their power and wealth were shortly contracted to those more confined limits which suited their natural resources.

In the middle of the 15th century, Bruges in Flanders was the great *entrepôt* of the trade between the north and the south of Europe. Early in the 16th century its commerce began to decline under the competition of Antwerp. Many English and foreign merchants in consequence left the declining city, to settle in that which was rapidly increasing in commerce and wealth. About the middle of the 16th century Antwerp was at the zenith of its power. It contained above a hundred thousand inhabitants, and was universally allowed to be the most illustrious mercantile city, and to carry on the most extensive and richest commerce of any in the north of Europe.

The rising greatness of Amsterdam was favoured by the unfortunate siege and capture of Antwerp by the duke of Parma; and the competition of the extraordinary industry and persevering exertions of the Hollanders not only prevented Antwerp from recovering her commerce, but gave a severe blow to the foreign trade of almost all the other Hanse Towns.[7]

The subsequent decline of the trade of Amsterdam itself was caused partly by the low profits arising from home competition and abundance of capital; partly by excessive taxation, which raised the price of the necessaries of life; but more than either, perhaps, by the progress of other nations possessing greater natural advantages, and being able, even with inferior skill, industry and capital, beneficially to carry on much of that trade which had before fallen almost exclusively into the hands of the Dutch.

As early as 1669 and 1670, when Sir William Temple was in Holland, the effects of abundance of capital and domestic competition were such that most of the foreign trades were losing ones, except the Indian, and that none of them gave a profit of more than two or three per cent.[8] In such a state of things both the power and the will to save must be greatly diminished. The accumulation of capital must have been either stationary or declining, or at the best very slowly progressive. In fact, Sir William Temple gives it as his opinion that the trade of Holland had for some years passed its meridian, and begun sensibly to decay.[9] Subsequently, when the progress of other nations was still more marked, it appeared from undoubted documents that most of the trades of Holland, as well as its fisheries, had decidedly fallen off, and that no branch of its commerce had retained its former vigour, except the American and African trades, and that of the Rhine and Maese, which are independent of foreign power and competition.

---

[7] [The siege and capture of Antwerp in 1585, by the Duke of Parma, was 'unfortunate' because it represented a victory for Roman Catholic Spain over the Protestant inhabitants. The reasons for the decline of Antwerp were many: by the Treaty of Münster in 1648 the United Provinces became independent of Spain, but the river Scheldt was closed to navigation; this meant that Antwerp ceased to be an international port (until it was re-opened by the French in 1795) and towns with better access to the sea naturally increased in prosperity at Antwerp's expense.

The Hanseatic League was a medieval *ad hoc* confederation of cities, headed by Lübeck; in the fourteenth century it monopolised the Baltic trade, and later it maintained agencies all over Europe, and as far east as Novgorod. It gradually became less important after the discovery of America, and the last formal Assembly of the Hansa at Lübeck took place in 1669.]

[8] Temple's Works, vol. i. p. 69 fol.   [9] Id. p. 67.

In 1669, the whole population of Holland and West Friezeland was estimated by John de Witt at 2 400 000.[10] In 1778, the population of the seven provinces was estimated only at 2 000 000;[11] and thus, in the course of above a hundred years, the population, instead of increasing, as is usual, had greatly diminished.

In all these cases of commercial states, the progress of wealth and population seems to have been checked by one or more of the causes above mentioned, which must necessarily affect more or less the power of commanding the means of subsistence.

Universally it may be observed that if, from any cause or causes whatever, the funds for the maintenance of labour in any country cease to be progressive, the effective demand for labour will also cease to be progressive; and wages will be reduced to that sum which, under the existing prices of provisions, and the existing habits of the people, will just keep up, and no more than keep up, a stationary population. A state so circumstanced is under a moral impossibility of increasing, whatever may be the plenty of corn, or however high may be the profits of stock in other countries.[12] It may indeed at a subsequent period, and under new circumstances, begin to increase again. If by some happy invention in mechanics, the discovery of some new channel of trade, or an unusual increase of agricultural wealth and population in the surrounding countries, its exports, of whatever kind, were to become unusually in demand, it might again import an increasing quantity of corn, and might again increase its population. But as long as it is unable to make yearly additions to its imports of food, it will evidently be unable to furnish the means of support to an increasing population; and it will necessarily experience this inability when, from the state of its commercial transactions, the funds for the maintenance of its labour become stationary or begin to decline.

---

[10] Interest of Holland, vol. i. p. 9.

[11] Richesse de la Hollande, vol. ii. p. 349.

[12] It is a curious fact, that among the causes of the decline of the Dutch trade, Sir William Temple reckons the cheapness of corn, which, he says, 'has been for these dozen years, or more, general in these parts of Europe'. (vol. i. p. 69) This cheapness, he says, impeded the vent of spices and other Indian commodities among the Baltic nations, by diminishing their power of purchasing.

CHAPTER X

Of Systems of Agriculture and Commerce combined

In a country the most exclusively confined to agriculture, some of its raw materials will always be worked up for domestic use. In the most commercial state, not absolutely confined to the walls of a town, some part of the food of its inhabitants, or of its cattle, will be drawn from the small territory in its neighbourhood. But, in speaking of systems of agriculture and commerce combined, something much further than this kind of combination is intended; and it is meant to refer to countries where the resources in land, and the capitals employed in commerce and manufactures, are both considerable, and neither preponderating greatly over the other.

A country so circumstanced possesses the advantages of both systems, while at the same time it is free from the peculiar evils which belong to each, taken separately.

The prosperity of manufactures and commerce in any state implies at once that it has freed itself from the worst parts of the feudal system. It shows that the great body of the people are not in a state of servitude; that they have both the power and the will to save; that when capital accumulates it can find the means of secure employment, and consequently that the government is such as to afford the necessary protection to property. Under these circumstances, it is scarcely possible that it should ever experience that premature stagnation in the demand for labour, and the produce of the soil, which at times has marked the history of most of the nations of Europe. In a country in which manufactures and commerce flourish, the produce of the soil will always find a ready market at home; and such a market is peculiarly favourable to the progressive increase of capital. But the progressive increase of capital, and of the funds for the maintenance of labour, is the great cause of a demand for labour, and of high corn wages,[1] while the high relative

---

[1] [In 1826 this sentence was amended thus:

But the progressive increase of capital, and particularly of the quantity and value of the funds for the maintenance of labour, is the great cause of a demand for labour, and of good corn wages, ...

price of corn, occasioned by the improved machinery and extended capital employed in manufactures, together with the prosperity of foreign commerce, enables the labourer to exchange any given portion of his earnings in corn for a large proportion both of domestic and foreign conveniences and luxuries. Even when the effective demand for labour begins to slacken, and the corn wages to be reduced, still the high relative value of corn keeps up comparatively the condition of the labouring classes; and though their increase is checked, yet a very considerable body of them may still be well lodged and well clothed, and able to indulge themselves in the conveniences and luxuries of foreign produce. Nor can they ever be reduced to the miserable condition of the poor in those countries where, at the same time that the demand for labour is stationary, the value of corn, compared with manufactures and foreign commodities, is extremely low.

All the peculiar disadvantages therefore of a purely agricultural country are avoided by the growth and prosperity of manufactures and commerce.

In the same manner it will be found that the peculiar disadvantages attending states merely manufacturing and commercial will be avoided by the possession of resources in land.

A country which raises its own food cannot by any sort of foreign competition be reduced at once to a necessarily declining population. If the exports of a merely commercial country be essentially diminished by foreign competition, it may lose, in a very short time, its power of supporting the same number of people; but if the exports of a country which has resources in land be diminished, it will merely lose some of its foreign conveniences and luxuries; and the great and most important of all trades, the domestic trade carried on between the towns and the country, will remain comparatively undisturbed. It may indeed be checked in the rate of its progress, for a time, by the want of the same stimulus; but there is no reason for its becoming retrograde; and there is no doubt that the capital thrown out of employment by the loss of foreign trade will not lie idle. It will find some channel in which it can be employed with advantage, though not with the same advantage as before; and will be able to maintain an increasing population, though not increasing at the same rate as under the stimulus of a prosperous foreign trade.

The effects of home competition will in like manner be very different in the two states we are comparing.

In a state merely manufacturing and commercial, home competition and abundance of capital may so reduce the price of manufactured compared with raw produce, that the increased capital employed in manufactures may not procure in exchange an increased quantity of food. In a country where there are resources in land this cannot happen; and though from improvements in machinery and the decreasing fertility of the new land taken into cultivation, a greater quantity of manufactures will be given for raw produce, yet the mass of manufactures can never fall in value, owing to a competition of capital in this species of industry, unaccompanied by a correspondent competition of capital on land.

It should also be observed that in a state, the revenue of which consists solely in profits and wages, the diminution of profits and wages may greatly impair its disposable income. The increase in the amount of capital and in the number of labourers may in many cases not be sufficient to make up for the diminished rate of profits and wages. But where the revenue of the country consists of rents as well as profits and wages, a great part of what is lost in profits and wages is gained in rents, and the disposable income remains comparatively unimpaired.

Another eminent advantage possessed by a nation which is rich in land, as well as in commerce and manufactures, is, that the progress of its wealth and population is in a comparatively slight degree dependent upon the state and progress of other countries. A nation, whose wealth depends exclusively on manufactures and commerce, cannot increase without an increase in the raw products of the countries with which it trades; or taking away a share of what they have been in the habit of actually consuming, which will rarely be parted with; and thus the ignorance and indolence of others may not only be prejudicial, but fatal to its progress.

A country with resources in land can never be exposed to these inconveniences; and if its industry, ingenuity and economy increase, its wealth and population will increase, whatever may be the situation and conduct of the nations with which it trades. When its manufacturing capital becomes redundant, and manufactured commodities are too cheap, it will have no occasion to wait for the increasing raw products of its neighbours. The transfer of its own redundant capital to its own land will raise fresh products, against which its manufactures may be exchanged, and by the double operation of diminishing comparatively the supply, and increasing the demand, enhance their price. A similar operation, when raw produce is too abundant, will restore the level between the profits of agriculture and manufactures. And upon the same principle, the stock of the country will be distributed through its various and distant provinces, according to the advantages presented by each situation for the employment either of agricultural or manufacturing capital.

A country in which in this manner agriculture, manufactures, and commerce, and all the different parts of a large territory, act and re-act upon each other in turn, might evidently go on increasing in riches and strength, although surrounded by Bishop Berkeley's wall of brass. Such a country would naturally make the most of its foreign commerce, whatever might be the actual state of it; and its increase or decrease would be the addition or removal of a powerful stimulus to its own produce; but still the increase of this produce, to a very considerable extent, would be independent of foreign countries; and though it might be retarded by a failure of foreign commerce, it could not either be stopped or be made retrograde.

A fourth advantage derived from the union of agriculture and manufactures, particularly when they are nearly balanced, is that the capital and population of such a country can never be forced to make a retrograde movement, merely by the natural progress of other countries to that state of improvement to which they are all constantly tending.

According to all general principles, it will finally answer to most landed nations, both to manufacture for themselves, and to conduct their own commerce. That raw cottons should be shipped in America, carried some thousands of miles to another country, unshipped there, to be manufactured and shipped again for the American market, is a state of things which cannot be permanent. That it may last for some time, there can be no doubt; and I am very far from meaning to insinuate that an advantage, while it lasts, should not be used, merely because it will not continue for ever. But if the advantage be in its nature temporary, it is surely prudent to have this in view, and to use it in such a way that when it ceases it may not have been productive, on the whole, of more evil than good.

If a country, owing to temporary advantages of this kind, should have its commerce and manufactures so greatly preponderate as to make it necessary to support a large portion of its people on foreign corn, it is certain that the progressive improvement of foreign countries in manufactures and commerce might, after a time, subject it to a period of poverty and of retrograde movements in capital and population, which might more than counterbalance the temporary benefits before enjoyed. While a nation in which the commercial and manufacturing population continued to be supported by its agriculture might receive a very considerable stimulus to both, from such temporary advantages, without being exposed to any essential evil on their ceasing.

The countries which thus unite great landed resources with a prosperous state of commerce and manufactures, and in which the commercial part of the population never essentially exceeds the agricultural part, are eminently secure from sudden reverses. Their increasing wealth seems to be out of the reach of all common accidents; and there is no reason to say that they might not go on increasing in riches and population for hundreds, nay, almost thousands of years.

We must not, however, imagine that there is no limit to this progress though it is distant, and has certainly not been attained by any large landed nation yet known.

We have already seen that the limit to the population of commercial nations is the period when, from the actual state of foreign markets, they are unable regularly to import an increasing quantity of food. And the limit to the population of a nation which raises the whole of its food on its own territory is when the land has been so fully occupied and worked, that the employment of another labourer on it will not on an average raise an additional quantity of food sufficient to support a family of such a size as will admit of an increase of population.

This is evidently the extreme practical limit to the progress of population, which no nation has ever yet reached, nor indeed ever will; since no allowance has been here made either for other necessaries besides food, or for the profits of stock, both of which, however low, must always be something not inconsiderable.

Yet even this limit is very far short of what the earth is capable of producing, if all were employed upon it who were not employed in the production of other necessaries; that is, if soldiers, sailors, menial servants and all the artificers of luxuries, were made to labour upon the land. They would not indeed produce the support of a family, and ultimately not even of themselves; but till the earth absolutely refused to yield any more, they would continue to add something to the common stock and by increasing the means of subsistence, would afford the means of supporting an increasing population. The whole people of a country might thus be employed during their whole time in the production of mere necessaries, and no leisure be left for other pursuits of any kind. But this state of things could only be effected by the forced direction of the national industry into one channel by public authority. Upon the principle of private property, which it may be fairly presumed will always prevail in society, it could never happen. With a view to the individual interest, either of a landlord or farmer, no labourer can ever be employed on the soil who does not produce more than the value of his wages; and if these wages be not on an average sufficient to maintain a wife, and rear two children to the age of marriage, it is evident that both the population and produce must come to a stand. Consequently, at the most extreme practical limit of population, the state of the land must be such as to enable the last employed labourers to produce the maintenance of as many, probably, as four persons.

And it is happy for mankind that such are the laws of nature. If the competition for the necessaries of life, in the progress of population, could reduce the whole human race to the necessity of incessant labour for them, man would be continually tending to a state of degradation; and all the improvements which had marked the middle stages of his career would be completely lost at the end of it; but in reality, and according to the universal principle of private property, at the period when it will cease to answer to employ more labour upon the land, the excess of raw produce, not actually consumed by the cultivators, will, in the shape of rents, profits, and wages, particularly the first, bear nearly as great a proportion to the whole as at any previous period, and, at all events, sufficient to support a large part of the society living either without manual labour, or employing themselves in modifying the raw materials of the land into the forms best suited to the gratification of man.[2]

When we refer therefore to the practical limits of population, it is of great importance to recollect that they must be always very far short of the utmost power of the earth to produce food.

It is also of great importance to recollect that, long before this practical limit is attained in any country, the rate of the increase of population will gradually diminish. When the capital of a country becomes stationary from bad government, indolence, extravagance, or a sudden shock to commerce, it is just possible that the check to population may in some degree be sudden, though in that case it cannot take place without a considerable convulsion. But when the capital of a country comes to a

---

[2] [This is a repetition of what Malthus has said before; see chapter viii, n.12.]

stop from the continued progress of accumulation and the exhaustion of the cultivable land, both the profits of stock and the wages of labour must have been gradually diminishing for a long period, till they are both ultimately so low as to afford no further encouragement to an increase of stock, and no further means for the support of an increasing population. If we could suppose that the capital employed upon the land was, at all times, as great as could possibly be applied with the same profit, and there were no agricultural improvements to save labour, it is obvious that, as accumulation proceeded, profits and wages would regularly fall, and the diminished rate in the progress of population would be quite regular. But practically this can never happen; and various causes, both natural and artificial, will concur to prevent this regularity, and occasion great variations at different times in the rate at which the population proceeds towards its final limit.

In the first place, land is practically almost always understocked with capital. This arises partly from the usual tenures on which farms are held, which, by discouraging the transfer of capital from commerce and manufactures, leaves it principally to be generated on the land; and partly from the very nature of much of the soil of almost all large countries, which is such that the employment of a small capital upon it may be little productive, while the employment of a large capital in draining, or in changing the character of the soil by a sufficient quantity of natural and artificial manures, may be productive in a high degree; and partly also from the circumstance that, after every fall of profits and wages there will often be room for the employment of a much greater capital upon the land than is at the command of those who, by being in the actual occupation of farms, can alone so employ it.

Secondly; improvements in agriculture. If new and superior modes of cultivation be invented, by which not only the land is better managed, but is worked with less labour, it is obvious that inferior land may be cultivated at higher profits than could be obtained from richer land before; and an improved system of culture, with the use of better instruments, may, for a long period, more than counterbalance the tendency of an extended cultivation and a great increase of capital to yield smaller proportionate returns.

Thirdly; improvements in manufactures. When by increased skill and the invention of improved machinery in manufactures one man becomes capable of doing as much as eight or ten could before, it is well known that, from the principle of home competition and the consequent great increase of quantity, the prices of such manufactures will greatly fall; and, as far as they include the necessaries and accustomed conveniences of labourers and farmers, they must tend to diminish that portion of the value of the whole produce which is consumed necessarily on the land, and leave a larger remainder. From this larger remainder may be drawn a higher rate of profits, notwithstanding the increase of capital and extension of cultivation.

Fourthly; the prosperity of foreign commerce. If from a prosperous foreign commerce our labour and domestic commodities rise considerably in price, while foreign commodities are advanced comparatively very little, an event which is very common, it is evident that the farmer or labourer will be able to obtain the tea, sugar, cottons, linens, leather, tallow, timber, &c., which he stands in need of, for a smaller quantity of corn or labour than before; and this increased power of purchasing foreign commodities will have precisely the same effect, in allowing the means of an extended cultivation without a fall of profits, as the improvements in manufactures just referred to.

Fifthly; a temporary increase in the relative price of raw produce from increased demand. Allowing, what is certainly not true, that a rise in the price of raw produce will, after a certain number of years, occasion a proportionate rise in labour[3] and other commodities; yet, during the time that the price of raw produce takes the lead, it is obvious that the profits of cultivation may increase under an extended agriculture and a continued accumulation of capital. And these intervals, it should be observed, must be of infinite importance in the progress of the wealth of a landed nation, particularly with reference to the causes of deficient capital upon the land before mentioned. If the land, for the most part, generates the new capital which is employed in extending its cultivation; and if the employment of a considerable capital for a certain period will often put land in such a state that it can be cultivated afterwards at comparatively little expense; a period of high agricultural profits, though it may last only eight or ten years, may often be the means of giving to a country what is equivalent to a fresh quantity of land.

Though it is unquestionably and necessarily true, therefore, that the

---

[3] A rise, which is occasioned exclusively by the increased quantity of labour which may be required in the progress of society to raise a given quantity of corn on the last land taken into cultivation must, of course, be peculiar to raw produce, and will not be communicated to those commodities in the production of which there is no increase of labour.

tendency of a continually increasing capital and extending cultivation is to occasion a progressive fall both of profits and wages; yet the causes above enumerated are evidently sufficient to account for great and long irregularities in this progress.

We see in consequence, in all the states of Europe, great variations at different periods in the progress of their capital and population. After slumbering for years in a state almost stationary, some countries have made a sudden start, and have begun increasing at a rate almost approaching to new colonies.[4] Russia and parts of Prussia have afforded instances of this kind, and have continued this rate of progress after the accumulation of capital and the extension of cultivation had been proceeding with great rapidity for many years.

From the operation of the same causes we have seen similar variations in our own country. About the middle of last century the interest of money was at 3 per cent.; and we may conclude that the profits of stock were nearly in proportion. At that time, as far as can be collected from the births and marriages, the population was increasing but slowly. From 1720 to 1750, a period of 30 years, the increase is calculated to have been only about 900 000 on a population of 5 565 000.[5] Since this period it cannot be doubted that the capital of the country has been prodigiously enlarged, and its cultivation very greatly extended; yet, during the last twenty years, we have seen the interest of money at above 5 per cent., with profits in proportion; and, from 1800 to 1811, an increase of population equal to 1 200 000 on 9 287 000, a rate of increase about two and a half times as great as at the former period.

But, notwithstanding these causes of irregularity in the progress of capital and population, it is quite certain that they cannot reach their necessary practical limit but by a very gradual process. Before the accumulation of capital comes to a stop from *necessity*, the profits of stock must, for a long time, have been so low as to afford scarcely any encouragement to an excess of saving above expenditure; and before the progress of population is finally stopped, the real wages of labour must have been gradually diminishing till, under the existing habits of the people, they could only support such families as would just keep up, and no more than keep up, the actual population.

[4] [In 1826 this was amended to:
    ... increasing at a rate almost approaching to that of new colonies.
[5] Population Abstracts, Preliminary Observations, table, p. xxv.
    [This reference is to the volume published in 1812.]

It appears then, that it is the union of the agricultural and commercial systems, and not either of them taken separately, that is calculated to produce the greatest national prosperity; that a country with an extensive and rich territory, the cultivation of which is stimulated by improvements in agriculture, manufactures and foreign commerce, has such various and abundant resources that it is extremely difficult to say when they will reach their limits. That there is, however, a limit which, if the capital and population of a country continue increasing, they must ultimately reach, and cannot pass; and that this limit, upon the principle of private property, must be far short of the utmost power of the earth to produce food.

CHAPTER XI

Of Corn-Laws. Bounties upon Exportation

It has been observed that some countries, with great resources in land, and an evident power of supporting a greatly increased population from their own soil, have yet been in the habit of importing large quantities of foreign corn, and have become dependent upon other states for a great part of their supplies.

The causes which may lead to this state of things seem to be chiefly the following:

First; any obstacles which the laws, constitutions and customs of a country present to the accumulation of capital on the land, which do not apply with equal force to the increasing employment of capital in commerce and manufactures.

In every state in which the feudal system has prevailed there are laws and customs of this kind, which prevent the free division and alienation of land like other property, and render the preparations for an extension of cultivation often both very difficult and very expensive. Improvements in such countries are chiefly carried on by tenants, a large part of whom have not leases, or at least leases of any length; and though their wealth and respectability have of late years very greatly increased, yet it is not possible to put them on a footing with enterprising owners, and to give them the same independence, and the same encouragement to employ their capitals with spirit, as merchants and manufacturers.

Secondly; a system of direct or indirect taxation, of such a nature as to throw a weight upon the agriculture of a country, which is either unequal, or, from peculiar circumstances, can be better borne by commerce and manufactures.

It is universally allowed that a direct tax on corn grown at home, if not counterbalanced by a corresponding tax on the importation of it, might be such as to destroy at once the cultivation of grain, and make a country import the whole of its consumption; and a partial effect of the same kind would follow if, by a system of indirect taxation, the general price of labour were raised, and yet by means of drawbacks on home and foreign commodities, by an abundance of colonial produce, and by those peculiar articles,[1] the demand for which abroad would not be much affected by the increase of price, the value of the whole of the exports, though not the quantity, might admit of increase.

Thirdly; improved machinery, combined with extensive capital and a very advantageous division of labour.

If in any country, by means of capital and machinery, one man be enabled to do the work of ten, it is quite obvious that before the same advantages are extended to other countries, a rise in the price of labour will but very little interfere with the power of selling those sorts of commodities in the production of which the capital and machinery are so effectively applied. It is quite true that an advance in the necessary wages of labour, which increases the expense of raising corn, may have the same effect upon many commodities besides corn; and if there were no others, no encouragement would be given to the importation of foreign grain, as there might be no means by which it could be purchased cheaper abroad.

But a large class of the exportable commodities of a commercial country are of a different description. They are either articles in a considerable degree peculiar to the country and its dependencies, or such as have been produced by superior capital and machinery, the prices of which are determined rather by domestic than foreign competition. All commodities of this kind will evidently be able to support without essential injury an advance in the price of labour, some permanently, and others for a considerable time. The rise in the price of the commodity so occasioned, or rather the prevention of that fall which would otherwise have taken place, may always indeed have the effect of decreasing in some degree the *quantity* of the commodity exported; but it by no means follows that it will diminish the whole of its bullion value in the foreign country, which is precisely what determines the bullion value, and generally the quantity of the returns. If cottons in this country were now to fall to half their present price, we should undoubtedly export a greater quantity than we do at present; but I very much doubt whether we should export double the quantity,[2] and yet we must do this to enable us to command as much foreign produce as before. In this case, as in numerous others of the same kind, quantity and value go together to a

---

[1] A rise in the price of labour in China would certainly increase the returns which it receives for its teas.

[2] [In 1826 Malthus qualified this:

... but I very much doubt whether we should export double the quantity, at least for many years, and yet we must ...

certain point, though not at an equal pace; but, beyond this point, a further increase of quantity only diminishes the whole value produced, and the amount of the returns that can be obtained for it.

It is obvious then that a country, notwithstanding a high comparative price of labour and of materials, may easily stand a competition with foreigners in those commodities to which it can apply a superior capital and machinery with great effect; although such a price of labour and materials might give an undisputed advantage to foreigners in agriculture and some other sorts of produce, where the same saving of labour cannot take place. Consequently such a country may find it cheaper to purchase a considerable part of its supplies of grain from abroad, with its manufactures and peculiar products, than to grow the whole at home.

If, from all or any of these causes, a nation becomes habitually dependent on foreign countries for the support of a considerable portion of its population, it must evidently be subjected, while such dependence lasts, to some of those evils which belong to a nation purely manufacturing and commercial. In one respect, indeed, it will still continue to have a great superiority. It will possess resources in land which may be resorted to when its manufactures and commerce, either from foreign competition or any other causes, begin to fail. But, to balance this advantage, it will be subjected, during the time that large importations are necessary, to much greater fluctuations in its supplies of corn, than countries wholly manufacturing and commercial. The demands of Holland and Hamburgh may be known with considerable accuracy by the merchants who supply them. If they increase, they increase gradually; and, not being subject from year to year to any great and sudden variations, it might be safe and practicable to make regular contracts for the average quantity wanted. But it is otherwise with such countries as England and Spain. Their wants are necessarily very variable, from the variableness of the seasons; and if the merchants were to contract with exporting countries for the quantity required in average years, two or three abundant seasons might ruin them. They must necessarily wait to see the state of the crops in each year, in order safely to regulate their proceedings; and though it is certainly true that it is only the deficiency from the average crop, and not the whole deficiency, which may be considered altogether in the light of a new demand in Europe; yet the largeness and previous uncertainty of this whole deficiency, the danger of making contracts for a stated quantity annually, and the greater chance of hostile combinations against large and warlike states, must greatly aggravate the

difficulties of procuring a steady supply; and if it be true that unfavourable seasons are not unfrequently general, it is impossible to conceive
that they should not occasionally be subject to great variations of price.

It has been sometimes stated that scarcities are partial, not general,
and that a deficiency in one country is always compensated by a plentiful
supply in others. But this seems to be quite an unfounded supposition.
In the evidence brought before the Committee of the House of
Commons in 1814, relating to the corn-laws, one of the corn merchants
being asked whether it frequently happened that crops in the countries
bordering upon the Baltic failed, when they failed here, replied: 'When
crops are unfavourable in one part of Europe, it generally happens that
they are more or less so in another.'³ If any person will take the trouble to
examine the contemporaneous prices of corn in the different countries of
Europe for some length of time, he will be convinced that the answer
here given is perfectly just. In the last hundred and fifty years, above
twenty will be found in which the rise of prices is common to France and
England, although there was seldom much intercourse between them in
the trade of corn: and Spain and the Baltic nations, as far as their prices
have been collected, appear frequently to have shared in the same general
deficiency. Even within the last five years, two have occurred, the years
1811–12, and 1816–17, in which, with extraordinary high prices in this
country, the imports have been comparatively inconsiderable; which can
only have arisen from those scarcities having been general over the
greatest part of Europe.

Under these circumstances let us suppose that two million quarters of
foreign grain were the average quantity annually wanted in this country,
and suppose, at the same time, that a million quarters were deficient
from a bad season; the whole deficiency to be supplied would then be
three millions.

If the scarcity were general in Europe, it may fairly be concluded that
some states would prohibit the export of their corn entirely, and others
tax it very highly; and if we could obtain a million or fifteen hundred
thousand quarters, it is probably as much as we could reasonably expect.
We should then, however, be two millions or fifteen hundred thousand
quarters deficient. On the other hand, if we had habitually grown our
own consumption, and were deficient a million of quarters from a bad
season, it is scarcely probable that, notwithstanding a general scarcity,

³ Report, p. 93.

we should not be able to obtain three or four hundred thousand quarters in consequence of our advanced prices; particularly if the usual prices of our corn and labour were higher than in the rest of Europe. And in this case the sum of our whole deficiency would only be six or seven hundred thousand quarters, instead of fifteen hundred thousand or two millions of quarters. If the present year (1816–17) had found us in a state in which our growth of corn had been habitually far short of our consumption, the distresses of the country would have been dreadfully aggravated.

To provide against accidents of this kind, and to secure a more abundant and, at the time, a more steady supply of grain, a system of corn-laws has been recommended, the object of which is to discourage by duties or prohibitions the importation of foreign corn, and encourage by bounties the exportation of corn of home growth.

A system of this kind was completed in our own country in 1688,[4] the policy of which has been treated of at some length by Adam Smith.

In whatever way the general question may be finally decided, it must be allowed, by all those who acknowledge the efficacy of the great principle of supply and demand, that the line of argument taken by the author of the *Wealth of Nations* against the system is essentially erroneous.

He first states that, whatever extension of the foreign market can be occasioned by the bounty, must in every particular year be altogether at the expense of the home market, as every bushel of corn which is exported by means of the bounty, and which would not have been exported without the bounty, would have remained in the home market to increase the consumption, and to lower the price of that commodity.[5]

---

[4] Though the object here stated may not have been the specific object of the law of 1688, it is certainly the object for which the system has been subsequently recommended.

[This footnote is difficult to understand. There had been corn laws in England since the time of Richard II (1377–99) to facilitate exports and prevent cheap imports, in the interest of both the farmers and the sovereign: armies could not be raised without a plentiful supply of home-grown food, and the insurrections which followed a scarcity were a threat to the throne.

A systematic bounty on the export of corn was first introduced during the reign of Charles II (1660–85) and made permanent after the Glorious Revolution of 1688: the subsidy on the export of wheat was 5s. a quarter, as long as the home price of wheat did not exceed 48s., which it seldom did during the eighteenth century, but the object of the scheme was to encourage farmers to keep land in tillage and to help them to 'dump' their surplus grain abroad in the event of a glut.]

[5] Vol. ii. b. iv. c. 5.

In this observation he evidently misapplies the term market. Because, by selling a commodity lower, it is easy to get rid of a greater quantity of it, in any particular market, than would have gone off otherwise, it cannot justly be said that by this process such a market is proportionally extended. Though the removal of the two taxes mentioned by Adam Smith as paid on account of the bounty would certainly increase the power of the lower classes to purchase, yet in each particular year the consumption must ultimately be limited by the population, and the increase of consumption from the removal of these taxes would by no means be sufficient to give the same encouragement to cultivation as the addition of the foreign demand. If the price of British corn in the home market rise in consequence of the bounty, before the price of production is increased (and an immediate rise is distinctly acknowledged by Adam Smith), it is an unanswerable proof that the effectual demand for British corn is extended by it; and that the diminution of demand at home, whatever it may be, is more than counterbalanced by the extension of demand abroad.

Adam Smith goes on to say that the two taxes paid by the people on account of the bounty, namely, the one to the government to pay this bounty, and the other paid in the advanced price of the commodity, must either reduce the subsistence of the labouring poor, or occasion an augmentation in their pecuniary wages proportioned to that in the pecuniary price of their subsistence. So far as it operates in the one way, it must reduce the ability of the labouring poor to educate and bring up their children, and must so far tend to restrain the population of the country. So far as it operates in the other, it must reduce the ability of the employers of the poor to employ so great a number as they otherwise might do, and must so far tend to restrain the industry of the country.

It will be readily allowed that the tax occasioned by the bounty will have the one or the other of the effects here contemplated; but it cannot be allowed that it will have both. Yet it is observed, that though the tax, which that institution imposes upon the whole body of the people be very burdensome to those who pay it, it is of very little advantage to those who receive it. This is surely a contradiction. If the price of labour rise in proportion to the price of wheat, as is subsequently asserted, how is the labourer rendered less competent to support a family? If the price of labour do not rise in proportion to the price of wheat, how is it possible to maintain that the landlords and farmers are not able to employ more labourers on their land? Yet in this contradiction the author of the *Wealth of Nations* has had respectable followers; and some of those who have agreed with him in his opinion that corn regulates the prices of labour, and of all other commodities, still insist on the injury done to the labouring classes of society by a rise in the price of corn, and the benefit they would derive from a fall.

The main argument, however, which Adam Smith adduces against the bounty, is that as the money price of corn regulates that of all other home-made commodities, the advantage to the proprietor from the increase of money price is merely apparent, and not real; since what he gains in his sales he must lose in his purchases.

This position, though true to a certain extent, is by no means true to the extent of preventing the movement of capital to or from the land, which is the precise point in question. The money price of corn in a particular country is undoubtedly by far the most powerful ingredient in regulating the price of labour, and of all other commodities; but it is not enough for Adam Smith's position that it should be the most powerful ingredient; it must be shown that, other causes remaining the same, the price of every article will rise and fall exactly in proportion to the price of corn, and this is very far from being the case. Adam Smith himself excepts all foreign commodities; but when we reflect upon the vast amount of our imports, and the quantity of foreign articles used in our manufactures, this exception alone is of the greatest importance. Wool and raw hides, two most important materials of home growth, do not, according to Adam Smith's own reasonings (Book I. c. xi. p. 363, et seq.) depend much upon the price of corn and the rent of land; and the prices of flax, tallow, and leather, are of course greatly influenced by the quantity we import. But woollen cloths, cotton and linen goods, leather, soap, candles, tea, sugar &c., which are comprehended in the above-named articles, form almost the whole of the clothing and luxuries of the industrious classes of society.

It should be further observed that in all countries, the industry of which is greatly assisted by fixed capital, the part of the price of the wrought commodity which pays the profits of such capital will not necessarily rise in consequence of an advance in the price of corn, except as it requires gradual renovation; and the advantage derived from machinery which has been constructed before the advance in the price of labour will naturally last for some years.

In the case also of great and numerous taxes on consumption, a rise or fall in the price of corn, though it would increase or decrease that part of the wages of labour which resolves itself into food, evidently would not increase or decrease that part which is destined for the payment of taxes.

It cannot then be admitted as a general position that the money price of corn in any country is a just measure of the real value of silver in that country. But all these considerations, though of great weight to the owners of land, will not influence the farmers beyond the present leases. At the expiration of a lease, any particular advantage which a farmer had received from a favourable proportion between the price of corn and of labour would be taken from him, and any disadvantage from an unfavourable proportion be made up to him. The sole cause which would determine the proportion of capital employed in agriculture, would be the extent of the effectual demand for corn; and if the bounty had really enlarged this demand, which it certainly would have done, it is impossible to suppose that more capital would not be employed upon the land.

When Adam Smith says that the nature of things has stamped upon corn a real value, which cannot be altered by merely altering the money price, and that no bounty upon exportation, no monopoly of the home market, can raise that value, nor the freest competition lower it, it is obvious that he changes the question from the profits of the growers of corn, or of the proprietors of the land, to the physical and absolute value of corn itself.[6] I certainly do not mean to say that the bounty alters the physical value of corn, and makes a bushel of it support equally well a greater number of labourers than it did before; but I certainly do mean to say that the bounty to the British cultivator does, in the actual state of things, really increase the demand for British corn, and thus encourage him to sow more than he otherwise would do, and enables him in consequence to employ more bushels of corn in the maintenance of a greater number of labourers.

If Adam Smith's theory were true, and the real price of corn were unchangeable,[7] or not capable of experiencing a relative increase or decrease of value compared with labour and other commodities, agriculture would indeed be in an unfortunate situation. It would be at once excluded from the operation of that principle so beautifully explained in

---

[6] [In 1826 this read:
    ... to the physical value of corn itself.
[7] [In 1826 this paragraph began:
    If Adam Smith's theory were true, and what he calls the real price of corn were unchangeable ...

the *Wealth of Nations*, by which capital flows from one employment to another, according to the various and necessarily fluctuating wants of society. But surely we cannot doubt that the real price of corn varies, though it may not vary so much as the real price of other commodities; and that there are periods when all wrought commodities are cheaper, and periods when they are dearer, in proportion to the price of corn; and in the one case capital flows from manufactures to agriculture, and in the other from agriculture to manufactures. To overlook these periods, or consider them of slight importance, is not allowable; because in every branch of trade these periods form the grand encouragement to an increase of supply. Undoubtedly the profits of trade in any particular branch of industry can never long remain higher than in others; but how are they lowered except by the influx of capital occasioned by these high profits? It never can be a national object permanently to increase the profits of any particular set of dealers. The national object is the increase of supply; but this object cannot be attained except by previously increasing the profits of these dealers, and thus determining a greater quantity of capital to this particular employment. The ship-owners and sailors of Great Britain do not make greater profits now than they did before the Navigation Act; but the object of the nation was not to increase the profits of ship-owners and sailors, but the quantity of shipping and seamen; and this could not be done but by a law which, by increasing the demand for them, raised the profits of the capital before employed in this way, and determined a greater quantity to flow into the same channel. The object of a nation in the establishment of a bounty is, not to increase the profits of the farmers or the rents of the landlords, but to determine a greater quantity of the national capital to the land, and consequently to increase supply; and though, in the case of an advance in the price of corn from an increased demand, the rise of wages, the rise of rents and the fall of silver tend, in some degree, to obscure our view of the subject; yet we cannot refuse to acknowledge that the real price of corn varies during periods sufficiently long to affect the determination of capital, or we shall be reduced to the dilemma of owning that no possible degree of demand can encourage the growth of corn.

It must be allowed then that the peculiar argument relating to the nature of corn brought forward by Adam Smith upon this occasion cannot be maintained; and that a bounty upon the exportation of corn must enlarge the demand for it and encourage its production in the same manner, if not in the same degree, as a bounty upon the exportation of any other commodity.

But it has been urged further, that this increased production of corn must necessarily occasion permanent cheapness; and a period of considerable length, during the first 64 years of the last century, while a bounty was in full operation in this country, has been advanced as a proof of it. In this conclusion, however, it may be reasonably suspected that an effect, in its nature temporary, though it may be of some duration, has been mistaken for one which is necessarily permanent.

According to the theory of demand and supply, the bounty might be expected to operate in the following manner:

It is frequently stated in the *Wealth of Nations* that a great demand is followed by a great supply; a great scarcity by a great plenty; an unusual dearness by an unusual cheapness. A great and indefinite demand is indeed generally found to produce a supply more than proportioned to it. This supply as naturally occasions unusual cheapness; but this cheapness, when it comes, must in its turn check the production of the commodity; and this check, upon the same principle, is apt to continue longer than necessary, and again to occasion a return to high prices.

This appears to be the manner in which a bounty upon the exportation of corn, if granted under circumstances favourable to its efficiency, might be expected to operate, and this seems to have been the manner in which it really did operate in the only instance where it has been fairly tried.

Without meaning to deny the concurrence of other causes, or attempting to estimate the relative efficiency of the bounty, it is impossible not to acknowledge that when the growing price of corn was, according to Adam Smith, only 28 shillings a quarter, and the corn-markets of England were as low as those of the continent, a premium of five shillings a quarter upon exportation must have occasioned an increase of real price, and given encouragement to the cultivation of grain. But the changes produced in the direction of capital to or from the land will always be slow. Those who have been in the habit of employing their stock in mercantile concerns do not readily turn it into the channel of agriculture; and it is a still more difficult and slower operation to withdraw capital from the soil, to employ it in commerce. For the first 25 years after the establishment of the bounty in this country the price of corn rose 2 or 3 shillings in the quarter; but owing probably to the wars of William and Anne, to bad seasons, and a scarcity of money, capital seems to have accumulated slowly on the land, and no great surplus growth was effected. It was not till after the peace of Utrecht[8] that the capital of the country began in a marked manner to increase; and it is impossible that the bounty should not gradually have directed a larger portion of this accumulation to the land than would otherwise have gone to it. A surplus growth, and a fall of price for thirty or forty years, followed.

It will be said that this period of low prices was too long to be occasioned by a bounty, even according to the theory just laid down. This is perhaps true, and in all probability the period would have been shorter if the bounty alone had operated; but in this case other causes powerfully combined with it.

The fall in the price of British corn was accompanied by a fall of prices on the continent. Whatever were the general causes which produced this effect in foreign countries, it is probable that they were not wholly inoperative in England. At all events nothing could be so powerfully calculated to produce cheapness, and to occasion a slow return to high prices, as a considerable surplus growth, which was unwillingly received, and only at low prices, by other nations. When such a surplus growth had been obtained, some time would necessarily be required to destroy it by cheapness, particularly as the moral stimulus of the bounty would probably continue to act long after the fall of prices had commenced. If to these causes we add that a marked fall in the rate of interest, about the same time, evinced an abundance of capital, and a consequent difficulty of finding a profitable employment for it; and consider further the natural obstacles to the moving of capital from the land; we shall see sufficient reason why even a long period might elapse without any essential alteration in the comparative abundance and cheapness of corn.

Adam Smith attributes this cheapness to a rise in the value of silver. The fall in the price of corn which took place in France and some other countries about the same time might give some countenance to the conjecture. But the accounts we have lately had of the produce of the mines during the period in question does not sufficiently support it; and it is much more probable that it arose from the comparative state of peace in which Europe was placed after the termination of the wars of Louis

---

[8] [The Peace of Utrecht, in the spring of 1713, ended the War of the Spanish Succession, and virtually established a balance of power (as far as Europe was concerned) which lasted until the revolutionary wars at the end of the eighteenth century.]

XIV, which facilitated the accumulation of capital on the land, and encouraged agricultural improvements.

With regard to this country, indeed, it is observed by Adam Smith himself, that labour[9] and other articles were rising; a fact very unfavourable to the supposition of an increased value of the precious metals. Not only the money price of corn fell, but its value relative to other articles was lowered, and this fall of relative value, together with great exportations, clearly pointed to a relative abundance of corn, in whatever way it might be occasioned, as the main course of the facts observed, rather than a scarcity of silver. This great fall in the British corn-market, particularly during the ten years from 1740 to 1750, accompanied by a great fall in the continental markets, owing in some degree perhaps to the great exportations of British corn, especially during the years 1748, 1749, and 1750, must necessarily have given some check to its cultivation, while the increase of the real price of labour must at the same time have given a stimulus to the increase of population. The united operation of these two causes is exactly calculated first to diminish and ultimately to destroy a surplus of corn; and as, after 1764,[10] the wealth and manufacturing population of Great Britain increased more rapidly than those of her neighbours, the returning stimulus to agriculture, considerable as it was, arising almost exclusively from a home demand, was incapable of producing a surplus; and not being confined, as before, to British cultivation, owing to the alteration in the corn-laws, was inadequate even to effect an independent supply. Had the old corn-laws remained in full force, we should still probably have lost our surplus growth, owing to the causes above mentioned, although, from their restrictive clauses, we should certainly have been nearer the growth of an independent supply immediately previous to the scarcity of 1800.

It is not therefore necessary, in order to object to the bounty, to say

---

[9] [In 1826 Malthus added a footnote here:

It is certainly a very remarkable fact, that although Adam Smith repeatedly states, in the most distinct manner, that labour alone is the true measure of the value of silver and of all other commodities, he should suppose that silver was rising at the very time when he says the money price of labour was rising. There cannot be a more decided contradiction.

[10] [This date is the last given in Adam Smith's table of the prices of wheat (per quarter measure) from 1202 to 1764, twelve years before the publication of the *Wealth of Nations* in 1776; he did not trouble to bring the figures up to date in subsequent editions. The table may be easily found at the very end of Book I of the *Wealth of Nations*; the most important references to it are in the 'Digression concerning the Variations in the Value of Silver during the Course of the Four last Centuries'.]

with Adam Smith that the fall in the price of corn which took place during the first half of the last century must have happened in spite of the bounty, and could not possibly have happened in consequence of it. We may allow, on the contrary, what I think we ought to allow according to all general principles, that the bounty, when granted under favourable circumstances, is really calculated, after going through a period of dearness, to produce the surplus and the cheapness which its advocates promise,[11] but according to the same general principles we must allow that this surplus and cheapness, from their operating at once as a check to produce and an encouragement to population, cannot be for any great length of time maintained.

The objection then to a bounty on corn, independently of the objections to bounties in general, is that, when imposed under the most favourable circumstances, it cannot produce permanent cheapness: and if it be imposed under unfavourable circumstances; that is, if an attempt be made to force exportation by an adequate bounty at a time when the country does not fully grow its own consumption; it is obvious not only that the tax necessary for the purpose must be a very heavy one, but that the effect will be absolutely prejudicial to the population, and the surplus growth will be purchased by a sacrifice very far beyond its worth.

But notwithstanding the strong objections to bounties on general grounds, and their inapplicability in cases which are not unfrequent, it must be acknowledged that while they are operative (that is, while they produce an exportation which would not otherwise have taken place) they unquestionably encourage an increased growth of corn in the countries in which they are established, or maintain it at a point to which it would not otherwise have attained.

Under peculiar and favourable circumstances a country might maintain a considerable surplus growth for a great length of time, with an inconsiderable increase of the growing price of corn; and perhaps little or no increase of the average price, including years of scarcity.[12] If from any

---

[11] As far as the bounty might tend to force the cultivation of poorer land, so far no doubt it would have a tendency to raise the price of corn; but we know from experience that the rise of price naturally occasioned in this way is continually counteracted by improvements in agriculture. As a matter of fact it must be allowed that, during the period of the last century when corn was falling, more land must have been taken into cultivation.

[12] The average price is different from the growing price. Years of scarcity, which must occasionally occur, essentially affect the average price; and the growth of a surplus quantity of corn, which tends to prevent scarcity, will tend to lower this average, and make it approach nearer to the growing price.

period during the last century, when an average excess of growth for exportation had been obtained by the stimulus of a bounty, the foreign demand for our corn had increased at the same rate as the domestic demand, our surplus growth might have become permanent. After the bounty had ceased to stimulate to fresh exertions, its influence would by no means be lost. For some years it would have given the British grower an absolute advantage over the foreign grower. This advantage would of course gradually diminish; because it is the nature of all effectual demand to be ultimately supplied, and oblige the producers to sell at the lowest price they can afford consistently with the general rate of profits. But, after having experienced a period of decided encouragement, the British grower would find himself in the habit of supplying a larger market than his own upon equal terms with his competitors. And if the foreign and British markets continued to extend themselves equally, he would continue to proportion his supplies to both; because, unless a particular increase of demand were to take place at home, he could never withdraw his foreign supply without lowering the price of his whole crop; and the nation would thus be in possession of a constant store for years of scarcity.

But even supposing that by a bounty, combined with the most favourable state of prices in other countries, a particular state could maintain permanently an average excess of growth for exportation, it must not of course be imagined that its population would not still be checked by the difficulty of procuring subsistence. It would indeed be less exposed to the particular pressure arising from years of scarcity; but in other respects it would be subject to the same checks as those already described in the preceding chapters; and whether there was an habitual exportation or not, the population would be regulated by the real wages of labour, and would come to a stand when the necessaries which these wages could command were not sufficient, under the actual habits of the people, to encourage an increase of numbers.

CHAPTER XII

Of Corn-Laws. Restrictions upon Importation

The laws which prohibit the importation of foreign grain, though by no means unobjectionable, are not open to the same objections as bounties, and must be allowed to be adequate to the object they have in view – the maintenance of an independent supply. A country with landed resources, which determines never to import corn but when the price indicates an approach towards a scarcity, will necessarily, in average years, supply its own wants. Though we may reasonably therefore object to restrictions upon the importation of foreign corn, on the grounds of their tending to prevent the most profitable employment of the national capital and industry, to check population, and to discourage the export of our manufactures; yet we cannot deny their tendency to encourage the growth of corn at home, and to procure and maintain an independent supply. A bounty, it has appeared, sufficient to make it answer its purpose in forcing a surplus growth, would, in many cases, require so very heavy a direct tax, and would bear so large a proportion to the whole price of the corn, as to make it in some countries next to impracticable. Restrictions upon importation impose no direct tax upon the people. On the contrary, they might be made, if it were thought advisable, sources of revenue to the government, and they can always, without difficulty, be put in execution, and be made infallibly to answer their express purpose of securing, in average years, a sufficient growth of corn for the actual population.

We have considered, in the preceding chapters, the peculiar disadvantages which attend a system either almost exclusively agricultural or exclusively commercial, and the peculiar advantages which attend a system in which they are united and flourish together. It has further appeared that, in a country with great landed resources, the commercial population may, from particular causes, so far predominate as to subject it to some of the evils which belong to a state purely commercial and manufacturing, and to a degree of fluctuation in the price of corn greater than is found to take place in such a state. It is obviously possible, by restrictions upon the importation of foreign corn, to maintain a balance between the agricultural and commercial classes. The question is not a question of the efficiency or inefficiency of the measure proposed, but of its policy or impolicy. The object can certainly be accomplished, but it may be purchased too dear; and to those who do not at once reject all inquiries on points of this kind, as impeaching a principle which they hold sacred, the question whether a balance between the agricultural and commercial classes of society, which would not take place naturally, ought, under certain circumstances, to be maintained artificially, must appear to be the most important practical question in the whole compass of political economy.[1]

One of the objections to the admission of the doctrine, that restrictions upon importation are advantageous, is that it cannot possibly be laid down as a general rule that every state ought to raise its own corn. There are some states so circumstanced that the rule is clearly and obviously inapplicable to them.

In the first place there are many states which have made some figure in history, the territories of which have been perfectly inconsiderable compared with their main town or towns, and utterly incompetent to supply the actual population with food. In such communities, what is called the principal internal trade of a large state, the trade which is carried on between the towns and the country, must necessarily be a foreign trade, and the importation of foreign corn is absolutely necessary to their existence. They may be said to be born without the advantage of land, and to whatever risks and disadvantages a system merely commercial and manufacturing may be exposed, they have no power of choosing any other. All that they can do is to make the most of their own situation, compared with the situation of their neighbours, and to endeavour by superior industry, skill, and capital, to make up for so important a deficiency. In these efforts, some states of which we have accounts have been wonderfully successful; but the reverses to which they have been subject have been almost as conspicuous as the degree of their prosperity compared with the scantiness of their natural resources.

Secondly, restrictions upon the importation of foreign corn are evidently not applicable to a country which, from its soil and climate, is subject to very great and sudden variations in its home supplies, from the variations of the seasons. A country so circumstanced will unquestionably increase its chance of a steady supply of grain by opening as many

---

[1] [In 1826 this was altered to:
 ... must appear to be a most important practical question.

markets for importation and exportation as possible, and this will probably be true, even though other countries occasionally prohibit or tax the exports of their grain. The peculiar evil to which such a country is subject can only be mitigated by encouraging the freest possible foreign trade in corn.

Thirdly, restrictions upon importation are not applicable to a country which has a very barren territory, although it may be of some extent. An attempt fully to cultivate and improve such a territory by forcibly directing capital to it would probably, under any circumstances, fail; and the actual produce obtained in this way might be purchased by sacrifices which the capital and industry of the nation could not possibly continue to support. Whatever advantages those countries may enjoy, which possess the means of supporting a considerable population from their own soil, such advantages are not within the reach of a state so circumstanced. It must either consent to be a poor and inconsiderable community, or it must place its chief dependence on other resources than those of land. It resembles in many respects those states which have a very small territory; and its policy, with regard to the importation of corn, must of course be nearly the same.

In all these cases there can be no doubt of the impolicy of attempting to maintain a balance between the agricultural and commercial classes of society which would not take place naturally.

Under other and opposite circumstances, however, this impolicy is by no means so clear.

If a nation possesses a large territory consisting of land of an average quality, it may without difficulty support from its own soil a population fully sufficient to maintain its rank in wealth and power among the countries with which it has relations either of commerce or of war. Territories of a certain extent must ultimately in the main support their own population. As each exporting country approaches towards that complement of wealth and population to which it is naturally tending, it will gradually withdraw the corn which for a time it had spared to its more manufacturing and commercial neighbours, and leave them to subsist on their own resources. The peculiar products of each soil and climate are objects of foreign trade which can never, under any circumstances, fail. But food is not a peculiar product; and the country which produces it in the greatest abundance may, according to the laws which govern the progress of population, have nothing to spare for others. An extensive foreign trade in corn beyond what arises from the variableness of the seasons in different countries is rather a temporary and incidental trade, depending chiefly upon the different stages of improvement which different countries may have reached, and on other accidental circumstances, than a trade which is in its nature permanent, and the stimulus to which will remain in the progress of society unabated. In the wildness of speculation it has been suggested (of course more in jest than in earnest) that Europe ought to grow its corn in America, and devote itself solely to manufactures and commerce, as the best sort of division of the labour of the globe. But even on the extravagant supposition that the natural course of things might lead to such a division of labour for a time, and that by such means Europe could raise a population greater than its lands could possibly support, the consequences ought justly to be dreaded. It is an unquestionable truth that it must answer to every territorial state, in its natural progress to wealth, to manufacture for itself, unless the countries from which it had purchased its manufactures possess some advantages peculiar to them besides capital and skill. But when upon this principle America began to withdraw its corn from Europe, and the agricultural exertions of Europe were inadequate to make up for the deficiency, it would certainly be felt that the temporary advantages of a greater degree of wealth and population (supposing them to have been really attained) had been very dearly purchased by a long period of retrograde movements and misery.

If then a country be of such a size that it may fairly be expected finally to supply its own population with food; if the population which it can thus support from its own resources in land be such as to enable it to maintain its rank and power among other nations; and further, if there be reason to fear not only the final withdrawing of foreign corn used for a certain time, which might be a distant event, but the immediate effects that attend a great predominance of a manufacturing population, such as increased unhealthiness, increased turbulence, increased fluctuations in the price of corn, and increased variableness in the wages of labour; it may not appear impolitic artificially to maintain a more equal balance between the agricultural and commercial classes by restricting the importation of foreign corn, and making agriculture keep pace with manufactures.

Thirdly, if a country be possessed of such a soil and climate, that the variations in its annual growth of corn are less than in most other countries, this may be an additional reason for admitting the policy of restricting the importation of foreign corn. Countries are very different in the degree of variableness to which their annual supplies are subject; and though it is unquestionably true that if all were nearly equal in this respect, and the trade in corn *really* free, the steadiness of price in a particular state would increase with an increase in the number of the nations connected with it by the commerce of grain; yet it by no means follows that the same conclusion will hold good when the premises are essentially different; that is, when some of the countries taken into the circle of trade are subject to very great comparative variations in their supplies of grain, and when this defect is aggravated by the acknowledged want of real freedom in the foreign trade of corn.

Suppose, for instance, that the extreme variations above and below the average quantity of corn grown, were in England $\frac{1}{4}$ and in France $\frac{1}{3}$, a free intercourse between the two countries would probably increase the variableness of the English markets. And if, in addition to England and France, such a country as Bengal could be brought near, and admitted into the circle – a country in which, according to Sir George Colebrook, rice is sometimes sold four times as cheap in one year as in the succeeding without famine or scarcity;[2] and where, notwithstanding the frequency of abundant harvests, deficiencies sometimes occur of such extent as necessarily to destroy a considerable portion of the population; it is quite certain that the supplies both of England and France would become very much more variable than before the accession.

In point of fact, there is reason to believe that the British isles, owing to the nature of their soil and climate, are peculiarly free from great variations in their annual produce of grain. If we compare the prices of corn in England and France from the period of the commencement of the Eton tables to the beginning of the revolutionary war, we shall find that in England the highest price of the quarter of wheat of 8 bushels during the whole of that time was 3*l*. 15*s*. 6$\frac{3}{4}$*d*. (in 1648), and the lowest price 1*l*. 2*s*. 1*d*. (in 1743), while in France the highest price of the septier was 62 francs 78 centimes (in 1662), and the lowest price 8 francs 89 centimes (in 1718).[3] In the one case the difference is a little above 3$\frac{1}{4}$ times, and in

---

[2] Husbandry of Bengal, p. 108. Note. He observes in the text of the same page that the price of corn fluctuates much more than in Europe.

[3] Garnier's Edition of the Wealth of Nations vol. ii. Table, p. 188.

[The Eton tables are taken from the accounts of Eton College, originally a religious foundation, but later an expensive boarding-school for boys: their provisions included what Adam Smith called 'the best wheat at Windsor market'. It was not necessary for Malthus to give a reference here to the *Wealth of Nations* for the English figures, but obviously his readers would have been less familiar with the

the other very nearly 7 times. In the English tables, during periods of ten or twelve years, only two instances occur of a variation amounting to as much as 3 times; in the French tables, during periods of the same length, one instance occurs of a variation of above 6 times, and three instances besides of a variation of 4 times or above.[4]

These variations may, perhaps, have been aggravated by a want of freedom in the internal trade of corn, but they are strongly confirmed by the calculations of Turgot, which relate solely to variations of produce, without reference to any difficulties or obstructions in its free transport from one part of the country to another.

On land of an average quality he estimates the produce at seven septiers the arpent in years of great abundance, and three septiers the arpent in years of great scarcity; while the medium produce he values at five septiers the arpent.[5] These calculations he conceives are not far removed from the truth; and proceeding on these grounds he observes that, in a very abundant year, the produce will be five months above its ordinary consumption, and in a very scarce year as much below. These variations are, I should think, much greater than those which take place in this country, at least if we may judge from prices, particularly as in a given degree of scarcity in the two countries there is little doubt that, from the superior riches of England, and the extensive parish relief which it affords to the poorer classes in times of dearth, its prices would rise more above the usual average than those of France.

If we look to the prices of wheat in Spain during the same period, we shall find, in like manner, much greater variations than in England. In a table of the prices of the fanega of wheat in the market of Seville from 1675 to 1764 inclusive, published in the Appendix to the Bullion Report,[6] the highest price is 48 reals vellon (in 1677), and the lowest

prices in France, included by Garnier in his copious addenda to Smith's original work.]

[4] [In 1826 this was corrected to:
    . . . in the French tables, during periods of the same length, one instance occurs of a variation of 4 times or above.

[5] Oeuvres de Turgot, tom. vi, p. 143. Edit. 1808.
    [An *arpent*, before the French adopted the metric system in 1791, was a portion of land roughly equal to one and a quarter English acres, or 0.5 hectares; the word still survives in *arpentage*, which means land-surveying. *Septier* is no longer used as a measure of capacity; it equalled about four English bushels, half a 'quarter' of corn. A quarter equalled 2.9 hectolitres, but the comparison is irrelevant today, since grain is now sold by weight and not capacity. With the passing of the Weights and Measures Act of 1963, it became illegal to use the old bushel for trading purposes.]

[6] Appendix, p. 182.

price 7 reals vellon (in 1720), a difference of nearly seven times; and in periods of ten or twelve years the difference is, in two or three instances, as much as four times. In another table, from 1788 to 1792 inclusive, relating to the towns of Old Castille, the highest price in 1790 was 109 reals vellon the fanega, and in 1792 the lowest price was only 16 reals vellon the fanega. In the market of Medina del Rio Seco, a town of the kingdom of Leon, surrounded by a very fine corn country, the price of the load of four fanegas of wheat was, in May, 1800, 100 reals vellon, and in May, 1804, 600 reals vellon, and these were both what are called *low prices*, as compared with the highest prices of the year. The difference would be greater if the high prices were compared with the low prices. Thus, in 1799, the low price of the four fanegas was 88 reals vellon, and in 1804 the high price of the four fanegas was 640 reals vellon – a difference of above seven times in so short a period as six years.[7]

In Spain, foreign corn is freely admitted; yet the variation of price, in the towns of Andalusia, a province adjoining the sea, and penetrated by the river Guadalquiver, though not so great as those just mentioned, seem to show that the coasts of the Mediterranean by no means furnish very steady supplies. It is known, indeed, that Spain is the principal competitor of England in the purchase of grain in the Baltic; and as it is quite certain that what may be called the growing or usual price of corn in Spain is much lower than in England, it follows that the difference between the prices of plentiful and scarce years must be very considerable.

I have not the means of ascertaining the variations in the supplies and prices of the northern nations. They are, however, occasionally great, as it is well known that some of these countries are at times subject to very severe scarcities. But the instances already produced are sufficient to show, that a country which is advantageously circumstanced with regard to the steadiness of its home supplies may rather diminish than increase this steadiness by uniting its interests with a country less favourably circumstanced in this respect; and this steadiness will unquestionably be still further diminished, if the country which is the most variable in its supplies is allowed to inundate the other with its crops when they are abundant, while it reserves to itself the privilege of retaining them in a

---

[7] Bullion Report. Appendix, p. 185.

period of slight scarcity, when its commercial neighbour happens to be in the greatest want.[8]

Thirdly, if a nation be possessed of a territory, not only of sufficient extent to maintain under its actual cultivation a population adequate to a state of the first rank, but of sufficient unexhausted fertility to allow of a very great increase of population, such a circumstance would of course make the measure of restricting the importation of foreign corn more applicable to it.

A country which, though fertile and populous, had been cultivated nearly to the utmost, would have no other means of increasing its population than by the admission of foreign corn. But the British isles show at present no symptoms whatever of this species of exhaustion. The necessary accompaniments of a territory worked to the utmost are very low profits and interest, a very slack demand for labour, low wages, and a stationary population. Some of these symptoms may indeed take place without an exhausted territory; but an exhausted territory cannot take place without all these symptoms. Instead, however, of such symptoms, we have seen in this country, during the twenty years previous to 1814, a high rate of profits and interest, a very great demand for labour, good wages, and an increase of population more rapid, perhaps, than during any period of our history. The capitals which have been laid out in bringing new land into cultivation, or improving the old, must necessarily have yielded good returns, or, under the actual rate of general profits, they would not have been so employed; and although it is strictly true that, as capital accumulates upon the land, its profits must ultimately diminish; yet owing to the increase of agricultural skill, and other causes noticed in a former chapter, these two effects of progressive cultivation do not by any means always keep pace with each other.[9] Though they must finally unite and terminate the career of their progress together, they are often, during the course of their progress, separated for a considerable time and at a considerable distance. In some countries, and some soils, the quantity of capital which can be absorbed before any essential diminution of profits necessarily takes place is so great that its limit is not easily calculated; and certainly, when we consider what has actually been done in some districts of England and Scotland, and

---

[8] These two circumstances essentially change the premises on which the question of a free importation, as applicable to a particular state, must rest.

[9] [In 1826 this was altered to:

. . . these two events do not by any means always keep pace with each other.

compare it with what remains to be done in other districts, we must allow that no near approach to this limit has yet been made. On account of the high money price of labour, and of the materials of agricultural capital, occasioned partly by direct and indirect taxation, and partly, or perhaps chiefly, by the great prosperity of our foreign commerce,[10] new lands cannot be brought into cultivation, nor great improvements made on the old, without a high money price of grain; but these lands, when they have been so brought into cultivation, or improved, have by no means turned out unproductive. The quantity and value of their produce have borne a full and fair proportion to the quantity of capital and labour employed upon them; and they were cultivated with great advantage both to individuals and the state, as long as the same, or nearly the same, relations between the value of produce and the cost of production, which prompted this cultivation, continued to exist.

In such a state of the soil, the British empire[11] might unquestionably be able, not only to support from its own agricultural resources its present population, but double, and in time, perhaps, even treble the number; and consequently a restriction upon the importation of foreign corn, which might be thought greatly objectionable in a country which had reached nearly the end of its resources, might appear in a very different light in a country capable of supporting from its own lands a very great increase of population.

But it will be said that, although a country may be allowed to be capable of maintaining from its own soil not only a great, but an increasing population; yet if it be acknowledged that, by opening its ports for the free admission of foreign corn, it may be made to support a greater and more rapidly increasing population, it is unjustifiable to go

[10] [In 1826 Malthus added a footnote here:
No restrictions upon the importation of grain, however absurdly severe, could permanently maintain our corn and labour at a much higher price than in the rest of Europe, if such restrictions were essentially to interfere with the prosperity of our foreign commerce. When the money price of labour is high in any country, or, what is the same thing, when the value of money is low, nothing can prevent it from going out to find its level, but some comparative advantages, either natural or acquired, which enable such country to maintain the abundance of its exports, notwithstanding the high money price of its labour.

[11] [It is important to remember in this connection that for Malthus 'the British empire' meant England and Wales, Scotland and Ireland. Overseas settlements and possessions were not included in the term *British Empire* until about the middle of the nineteenth century, to be replaced roughly a hundred years later by 'the British Commonwealth of Nations', now simply 'the Commonwealth'.]

out of our way to check this tendency, and to prevent that degree of wealth and population which would naturally take place.

This is unquestionably a powerful argument; and granting fully the premises, (which however may admit of some doubt)[12] it cannot be answered upon the principles of political economy solely. I should say, however, that if it could be clearly ascertained that the addition of wealth and population so acquired would subject the society to a greater degree of uncertainty in its supplies of corn, greater fluctuations in the wages of labour, greater unhealthiness and immorality owing to a larger proportion of the population being employed in manufactories, and a greater chance of long and depressing retrograde movements occasioned by the natural progress of those countries from which corn had been imported; I should have no hesitation in considering such wealth and population as much too dearly purchased. The happiness of a society is, after all, the legitimate end even of its wealth, power, and population. It is certainly true that with a view to the structure of society most favourable to this happiness, and an adequate stimulus to the production of wealth from the soil, a very considerable admixture of commercial and manufacturing population with the agricultural is absolutely necessary; but there is no argument so frequently and obviously fallacious as that which infers that what is good to a certain extent is good to any extent; and though it will be most readily admitted that, in a large landed nation, the evils which belong to the manufacturing and commercial system are much more than counterbalanced by its advantages, as long as it is supported by agriculture; yet, in reference to the effect of the excess which is not so supported, it may fairly be doubted whether the evils do not decidedly predominate.

It is observed by Adam Smith, that the 'capital which is acquired to any country by commerce and manufactures is all a very uncertain and precarious possession, till some part of it has been secured and realized in the cultivation and improvement of its lands'.[13]

It is remarked in another place, that the monopoly of the colony trade, by raising the rate of mercantile profit, discourages the improvement of the soil, and retards the natural increase of that great original source of revenue – the rent of land.[14]

Now it is certain that, at no period, have the manufactures, commerce

[12] [In 1826 this significant parenthesis was omitted.]
[13] Vol. ii. b. iii. c. 4. p. 137.
[14] Id. b. iv. c. 8. p. 495.

and colony trade of the country been in a state to absorb so much capital as during the twenty years ending with 1814. From the year 1764 to the peace of Amiens, it is generally allowed that the commerce and manufactures of the country increased faster than its agriculture, and that it became gradually more and more dependent on foreign corn for its support. Since the peace of Amiens the state of its colonial monopoly and of its manufactures has been such as to demand an unusual quantity of capital; and if the peculiar circumstances of the subsequent war, the high freights and insurance, and the decrees of Buonaparte, had not rendered the importation of foreign corn extremely difficult and expensive, we should at this moment, according to all general principles, have been in the habit of supporting a much larger portion of our population upon it, than at any former period of our history. The cultivation of the country would be in a very different state from what it is at present. Very few or none of those great improvements would have taken place which may be said to have purchased fresh land for the state that no fall of price can destroy. And the peace, or accidents of different kinds, might have curtailed essentially both our colonial and manufacturing advantages, and destroyed or driven away our capital before it had spread itself on the soil, and become national property.

As it is, the practical restrictions thrown in the way of importing foreign corn during the war have forced our steam-engines and our colonial monopoly to cultivate our lands; and those very causes which, according to Adam Smith, tend to draw capital from agriculture, and would certainly have so drawn it if we could have continued to purchase foreign corn at the market prices of France and Holland, have been the means of giving such a spur to our agriculture, that it has not only kept pace with a very rapid increase of commerce and manufactures, but has recovered the distance at which it had for many years been left behind, and now marches with them abreast.

But restrictions upon the importation of foreign corn, in a country which has great landed resources, not only tend to spread every commercial and manufacturing advantage possessed, whether permanent or temporary, on the soil, and thus, in the language of Adam Smith, secure and realize it; but also tend to prevent those great oscillations in the progress of agriculture and commerce which are seldom unattended with evil.

It is to be recollected, and it is a point of great importance to keep constantly in our minds, that the distress which has been experienced among almost all classes of society from the sudden fall of prices, except as far as it has been aggravated by the state of the currency, has been occasioned by *natural*, not *artificial*, causes.

There is a tendency to an alternation in the rate of the progress of agriculture and manufactures in the same manner as there is a tendency to an alternation in the rate of the progress of food and population. In periods of peace and uninterrupted trade, these alternations, though not favourable to the happiness and quiet of society, may take place without producing material evil; but the intervention of war is always liable to give them a force and rapidity that must unavoidably produce a convulsion in the state of property.

The war that succeeded to the peace of Amiens found us dependent upon foreign countries for a very considerable portion of our supplies of corn; and we now grow our own consumption, notwithstanding an unusual increase of population in the interval. This great and sudden change in the state of our agriculture could only have been effected by very high prices occasioned by an inadequate home supply and the great expense and difficulty of importing foreign corn. But the rapidity with which this change has been effected must necessarily create a glut in the market as soon as the home growth of corn became fully equal or a little in excess above the home consumption; and, aided only by a small foreign importation, must inevitably occasion a very sudden fall of prices. If the ports had continued open for the free importation of foreign corn, there can be little doubt that the price of corn in 1815 would have been still considerably lower. This low price of corn, even if by means of lowered rents our present state of cultivation could be in a great degree preserved, must give such a check to future improvement that, if the ports were to continue open, we should certainly not grow a sufficiency at home to keep pace with our increasing population; and at the end of ten or twelve years we might be found by a new war in the same state that we were at the commencement of the present. We should then have the same career of high prices to pass through, the same excessive stimulus to agriculture[15] followed by the same sudden and depressing check to it, and the same enormous loans borrowed with the price of wheat at 90 or 100 shillings a quarter, and the monied incomes of

[15] According to the evidence before the House of Lords (Reports, p. 49), the freight and insurance alone on a quarter of corn were greater by 48 shillings in 1811 than in 1814. Without any artificial interference then, it appears that war alone may occasion unavoidably a prodigious increase of price.

the landholders and industrious classes of society nearly in proportion, to be paid when wheat is at 50 or 60 shillings a quarter, and the incomes of the landlords and industrious classes of society greatly reduced – a state of things which cannot take place without an excessive aggravation of the difficulty of paying taxes, and particularly that invariable monied amount which pays the interest of the national debt.

On the other hand a country which so restricts the importations of foreign corn as on an average to grow its own supplies, and to import merely in periods of scarcity, is not only certain of spreading every invention in manufactures and every peculiar advantage it may possess from its colonies or general commerce on the land, and thus of fixing them to the spot and rescuing them from accidents; but is necessarily exempt from those violent and distressing convulsions of property which almost unavoidably arise from the coincidence of a general war and an insufficient home supply of corn.

If the late war had found us independent of foreigners for our average consumption, not even our paper currency could have made the prices of our corn approach to the prices which were at one time experienced.[16] And if we had continued, during the course of the contest, independent of foreign supplies, except in an occasional scarcity, it is impossible that the growth of our own consumption, or a little above it, should have produced at the end of the war so universal a feeling of distress.

The chief practical objection to which restrictions on the importation of corn are exposed is a glut from an abundant harvest, which cannot be relieved by exportation. And in the consideration of that part of the question which relates to the fluctuations of prices this objection ought to have its full and fair weight. But the fluctuation of prices arising from this cause has sometimes been very greatly exaggerated. A glut which might essentially distress the farmers of a poor country, might be comparatively little felt by the farmers of a rich one; and it is difficult to conceive that a nation with an ample capital, and not under the influence

---

[16] It will be found upon examination, that the prices of our corn led the way to the excess and diminution of our paper currency, rather than followed, although the prices of corn could never have been either so high or so low if this excess and diminution had not taken place.

[In 1826 Malthus added a sentence at the beginning of this footnote:

According to Mr. Tooke (High and Low Prices, p. 215), if the last war had found us with a growth beyond our consumption, we should have witnessed a totally different set of phenomena connected with prices. It will be found upon examination ...

of a great shock to commercial confidence, as this country was in 1815, would find much difficulty in reserving the surplus of one year to supply the wants of the next or some future year. It may fairly indeed be doubted whether, in such a country as our own, the fall of price arising from this cause would be so great as that which would be occasioned by the sudden pouring in of the supplies from an abundant crop in Europe, particularly from those states which do not regularly export corn. If our ports were always open, the existing laws of France would still prevent such a supply as would equalize prices; and French corn would only come in to us in considerable quantities in years of great abundance, when we were the least likely to want it, and when it was most likely to occasion a glut.[17]

But if the fall of price occasioned in these two ways would not be essentially different, as it is quite certain that the rise of price in years of general scarcity would be less in those countries which habitually grow their own supplies; it must be allowed that the range of variation will be the least under such a system of restrictions as, without preventing importation when prices are high, will secure in ordinary years a growth equal to the consumption.[18]

[17] Almost all the corn merchants who gave their evidence before the committees of the two houses in 1814 seemed fully aware of the low prices likely to be occasioned by an abundant crop in Europe, if our ports were open to receive it.

[18] [In 1826 a long footnote was added here:

[1825.] In the sixth number of the Westminster Review, in which prodigious stress is laid upon the necessary effect of the corn laws in occasioning great fluctuations in the price of corn, a table, said to be from the very highest mercantile authority, is given of the average prices of wheat at Rotterdam for each of the ten years ending with 1824. The purpose for which the table is produced is to show the average price of wheat in Holland during these ten years; but it incidentally shows that, even in Holland, which in many respects must be peculiarly favourable to steady prices, a free trade in corn can by no means secure them.

In the year 1817, the price per last of 86 Winchester bushels was 574 guilders; and in 1824, it was only 147 guilders; a difference of nearly four times. During the same period of ten years the greatest variation in the average price of each year in England was between 94s. 9d., which was the price in 1817, and 43s. 9d., which was the price in 1822 (Appendix to Mr. Tooke's work on High and Low Prices. Table xii. p. 31) – a difference short of $2\frac{1}{5}$!!

It is repeated over and over again, apparently without the slightest reference to facts, that the freedom of the trade in corn would infallibly secure us from the possibility of a scarcity. The writer of the article *Corn Laws* in the supplement to the Encyclopædia Britannica goes so far as to say, 'it is constantly found that when the crops of one country fail, plenty reigns in some other quarter ... There is always abundance of food in the world. To enjoy a constant plenty, we have only to lay aside our prohibitions and restrictions, and cease to counteract the benevolent wisdom of Providence.' The same kind of language is repeated in the Review above

One objection, however, to systems of restriction, must always remain. They are essentially unsocial. I certainly think that, in reference to the interests of a particular state, a restriction upon the importation of foreign corn may sometimes be advantageous; but I feel still more certain that in reference to the interests of Europe in general the most perfect freedom of trade in corn, as well as in every other commodity, would be the most advantageous. Such a perfect freedom, however, could hardly fail to be followed by a more free and equal distribution of capital, which, though it would greatly advance the riches and happiness of Europe, would unquestionably render some parts of it poorer and less populous than they are at present; and there is little reason to expect that individual states will ever consent to sacrifice the wealth within their own confines to the wealth of the world.

It is further to be observed that, independently of more direct regulations, taxation alone produces a system of discouragements and encouragements which essentially interferes with the natural relations of commodities to each other; and as there is no hope of abolishing taxation, it may sometimes be only by a further interference that these natural relations can be restored.

A perfect freedom of trade therefore is a vision which it is to be feared can never be realized. But still it should be our object to make as near approaches to it as we can. It should always be considered as the great general rule. And when any deviations from it are proposed, those who propose them are bound clearly to make out the exception.

adverted to: 'If there be a bad harvest', it is said, 'in one country, there is a good one in another, and the surplus produce of the latter supplies the deficiency of the former', etc., etc. Now there are the best reasons for believing that these statements are decidedly contradicted by the most enlarged experience. In the first place, if they were true, and if the general plenty alluded to were only prevented by the want of a free trade in corn, we should necessarily see a great rise in prices in one country contemporaneous with a great fall in others; but a slight glance at the prices of corn in the countries of the commercial world for the last one or two centuries will be sufficient to convince any impartial person that, on the contrary, there is a very remarkable sympathy of prices at the same periods, which is absolutely inconsistent with the truth of the above statements. Secondly, all travellers who have paid any attention to the seasons, agree in stating that the same sort of weather often prevails in different countries at the same time. The peculiar and excessive heats of the very last summer not only prevailed generally over the greatest part of Europe, but extended even to America. Mr. Tooke, On High and Low Prices (p. 247, 2nd edit.), quotes a passage from Mr. Lowe's work on the Present State of England, in which he observes that 'The Public, particularly the untravelled part of the public, are hardly aware of the similarity of temperature prevailing throughout what may be called the corn-country of Europe, we mean Great Britain, Ireland, the north of

France, the Netherlands, Denmark, the north-west of Germany, and in some measure Poland and the north-east of Germany.' He then goes on to state instances of scarcity in different countries of Europe at the same time. And in the justness of these remarks, on the prevalence of a general similarity of seasons in Europe within certain latitudes, Mr. Tooke says he perfectly concurs. Many of the corn-merchants examined before the Committees of the two Houses, both in 1814 and 1821, expressed similar opinions; and I do not recollect a single instance of the opinion that good and bad harvests generally balance each other in different countries being stated by any person who had been in a situation to observe the facts. Such statements, therefore, must be considered as mere assertions quite unsupported by the least shadow of proof.

I am very far, however, from meaning to say that the circumstance of different countries having often an abundance or deficiency of corn at the same time, though it must prevent the possibility of steady prices, is a decisive reason against the abolition or alteration of the corn-laws. The most powerful of all the arguments against restrictions is their unsocial tendency, and the acknowledged injury which they must do to the interests of the commercial world in general. The weight of this argument is increased rather than diminished by the numbers which may suffer from scarcity at the same time. And at a period when our ministers are most laudably setting an example of a more liberal system of commercial policy, it would be greatly desirable that foreign nations should not have so marked an exception as our present corn-laws to cast in our teeth. A duty on importation not too high, and a bounty nearly such as was recommended by Mr. Ricardo, would probably be best suited to our present situation, and best secure steady prices. A duty on foreign corn would resemble the duties laid by other countries on our manufactures as objects of taxation, and would not in the same manner impeach the principles of free trade.

But whatever system we may adopt, it is essential to a sound determination, and highly useful in preventing disappointments, that all the arguments both for and against corn-laws should be thoroughly and impartially considered; and it is because on a calm, and, as far as I can judge, an impartial review of the arguments of this chapter, they still appear to me of weight sufficient to deserve such consideration, and not as a kind of protest against the abolition or change of the corn-laws, that I republish them in another edition.

CHAPTER XIII

Of increasing Wealth, as it affects the Condition of the Poor

The professed object of Adam Smith's *Inquiry* is *the Nature and Causes of the Wealth of Nations*. There is another, however, still more interesting, which he occasionally mixes with it – the causes which affect the happiness and comfort of the lower orders of society, which in every nation form the most numerous class. These two subjects are, no doubt, nearly connected; but the nature and extent of this connexion, and the mode in which increasing wealth operates on the condition of the poor, have not been stated with sufficient correctness and precision.

Adam Smith, in his chapter on the wages of labour, considers every increase in the stock or revenue of the society as an increase in the funds for the maintenance of labour; and having before laid down the position that the demand for those who live by wages can only increase in proportion to the increase of the funds for the payment of wages, the conclusion naturally follows that every increase of wealth tends to increase the demand for labour, and to improve the condition of the lower classes of society.[1]

Upon a nearer examination, however, it will be found that the funds for the maintenance of labour do not necessarily increase with the increase of wealth, and very rarely increase in *proportion* to it; and that the condition of the lower classes of society does not depend exclusively upon the increase of the funds for the maintenance of labour, or the power of supporting a greater number of labourers.

Adam Smith defines the wealth of a state to be the annual produce of its land and labour. This definition evidently includes manufactured produce as well as the produce of the land. Now, upon the supposition that a nation, from peculiar situation and circumstances, was unable to procure an additional quantity of food, it is obvious that the produce of its labour would not necessarily come to a stand, although the produce of its land or its power of importing corn were incapable of further increase.

---

[1] Vol. i. book i. c. 8.

If the materials of manufactures could be obtained either at home or from abroad, improved skill and machinery might work them up to a greatly increased amount with the same number of hands, and even the number of hands might be considerably increased by an increased taste for manufactures, compared with war and menial service, and by the employment consequently of a greater proportion of the whole population in manufacturing and commercial labour.

That such a case does not frequently occur will be most readily allowed. It is not only however possible, but forms the specific limit to the increase of population in the natural progress of cultivation, with which limit, the limit to the further progress of wealth is obviously not contemporary. But though cases of this kind do not often occur, because these limits are seldom reached; yet approximations to them are constantly taking place, and in the usual progress of improvement the increase of wealth and capital is rarely accompanied with a proportionately increased power of supporting an additional number of labourers.

Some ancient nations which, according to the accounts we have received of them, possessed but an inconsiderable quantity of manufacturing and commercial capital, appear to have cultivated their lands highly by means of an agrarian division of property, and were unquestionably very populous. In such countries, though full of people already, there would evidently be room for a very great increase of capital and riches; but, allowing all the weight that is in any degree probable to the increased production or importation of food occasioned by the stimulus of additional capital, there would evidently not be room for a proportionate increase of the means of subsistence.

If we compare the early state of our most flourishing European kingdoms with their present state, we shall find this conclusion confirmed almost universally by experience.

Adam Smith, in treating of the different progress of opulence in different nations, says that England, since the time of Elizabeth, has been continually advancing in commerce and manufactures. He then adds: 'The cultivation and improvement of the country has no doubt been gradually advancing. But it seems to have followed slowly and at a distance the more rapid progress of commerce and manufactures. The greater part of the country must probably have been cultivated before the reign of Elizabeth, and a very great part of it still remains uncultivated, and the cultivation of the far greater part is much inferior to what it might be.'[2] The same observation is applicable to most of the other countries of Europe. The best land would naturally be the first occupied. This land, even with that sort of indolent cultivation and great waste of labour which particularly marked the feudal times, would be capable of supporting a considerable population; and on the increase of capital, the increasing taste for conveniences and luxuries, combined with the decreasing power of production in the new land to be taken into cultivation, would naturally and necessarily direct the greatest part of this new capital to commerce and manufactures, and occasion a more rapid increase of wealth than of population.

The population of England accordingly in the reign of Elizabeth appears to have been nearly five millions, which would not be very far short of the half of what it is at present;[3] but when we consider the very great proportion which the products of commercial and manufacturing industry now bear to the quantity of food raised for human consumption, it is probably a very low estimate to say that the mass of wealth or the stock and revenue of the country must, independently of any change in the value of the circulating medium, have increased above four times. Few of the other countries in Europe have increased to the same extent in commercial and manufacturing wealth as England; but as far as they have proceeded in this career, all appearances clearly indicate that the progress of their general wealth has been greater than the progress of their means of supporting an additional population.

That every increase of the stock or revenue of a nation cannot be considered as an increase of the real funds for the maintenance of labour will appear in a striking light in the case of China.

Adam Smith observes, that China has probably long been as rich as the nature of her laws and institutions will admit; but intimates that, with other laws and institutions, and if foreign commerce were held in honour, she might still be much richer.

If trade and foreign commerce were held in great honour in China, it is evident that, from the great number of her labourers and the cheapness of her labour, she might work up manufactures for foreign sale to a great amount. It is equally evident that, from the great bulk of provisions and

---

[2] Vol. ii. book iv. c. 4, p. 133.
[3] [In 1826 Malthus inserted '(1811)' here, to show that he had not taken into account the census returns of 1821. He had already added a note about this census to chapter xi of Book II. 'Of the checks to population in England (continued)' – not included in this edition.]

the prodigious extent of her inland territory, she could not in return import such a quantity as would be any sensible addition to her means of subsistence. Her immense amount of manufactures, therefore, she would either consume at home, or exchange for luxuries collected from all parts of the world. At present the country appears to be overpeopled compared with what its stock can employ, and no labour is spared in the production of food. An immense capital could not be employed in China in preparing manufactures for foreign trade, without altering this state of things, and taking off some labourers from agriculture, which might have a tendency to diminish the produce of the country. Allowing, however, that this would be made up, and indeed more than made up, by the beneficial effects of improved skill and economy of labour in the cultivation of the poorest lands, yet, as the quantity of subsistence could be but little increased, the demand for manufactures, which would raise the price of labour, would necessarily be followed by a proportionate rise in the price of provisions, and the labourer would be able to command but little more food than before. The country would, however, obviously be advancing in wealth; the exchangeable value of the annual produce of its land and labour would be annually augmented; yet the real funds for the maintenance of labour would be nearly stationary. The argument perhaps appears clearer when applied to China, because it is generally allowed that its wealth has been long stationary, and its soil cultivated nearly to the utmost.[4]

In all these cases, it is not on account of any undue preference given to commerce and manufactures, compared with agriculture, that the effect just described takes place, but merely because the powers of the earth in the production of food have narrower limits than the skill and tastes of mankind in giving value to raw materials, and consequently in the approach towards the limits of subsistence there is naturally more room, and consequently more encouragement, for the increase of the one species of wealth than of the other.

It must be allowed then, that the funds for the maintenance of labour do not *necessarily* increase with the increase of wealth, and very *rarely* increase in *proportion* to it.

---

[4] How far this latter opinion is to be depended upon it is not very easy to say. Improved skill and a saving of labour would certainly enable the Chinese to cultivate some lands with advantage which they cannot cultivate now, but the more general use of horses instead of men might prevent this extended cultivation from giving any encouragement to an increase of people.

But the condition of the lower classes of society certainly does not depend exclusively upon the increase of the funds for the maintenance of labour, or the means of supporting more labourers. That these means form always a very powerful ingredient in the condition of the poor, and the main ingredient in the increase of population, is unquestionable. But, in the first place, the comforts of the lower classes of society do not depend solely upon food, nor even upon strict necessaries; and they cannot be considered as in a good state unless they have the command of some conveniences and even luxuries. Secondly, the tendency in population fully to keep pace with the means of subsistence must in general prevent the increase of these means from having a great and permanent effect in improving the condition of the poor. And, thirdly, the cause which has the most lasting effect in improving the situation of the lower classes of society depends chiefly upon the conduct and prudence of the individuals themselves, and is therefore not immediately and necessarily connected with an increase in the means of subsistence.

With a view, therefore, to the other causes which affect the condition of the labouring classes, as well as the increase of the means of subsistence, it may be desirable to trace more particularly the mode in which increasing wealth operates, and to state both the disadvantages as well as the advantages with which it is accompanied.

In the natural and regular progress of a country to a state of great wealth and population, there are two disadvantages to which the lower classes of society seem necessarily to be subjected. The first is, a diminished power of supporting children under the existing habits of the society with respect to the necessaries of life. And the second – the employment of a larger proportion of the population in occupations less favourable to health, and more exposed to fluctuations of demand and unsteadiness of wages.

A diminished power of supporting children is an absolutely unavoidable consequence of the progress of a country towards the utmost limits of its population. If we allow that the power of a given quantity of territory to produce food has some limit, we must allow that as this limit is approached, and the increase of population becomes slower and slower, the power of supporting children will be less and less, till finally, when the increase of produce stops, it becomes only sufficient to maintain, on an average, families of such a size as will not allow of a further addition of numbers. This state of things is generally accompanied by a fall in the *corn* price of labour; but should this effect be prevented by the prevalence of prudential habits among the lower classes of society, still the result just described must take place; and though, from the powerful operation of the preventive check to increase, the wages of labour estimated even in corn might not be low, yet it is obvious that in this case the power of supporting children would rather be nominal than real; and the moment this power began to be exercised to its apparent extent, it would cease to exist.

The second disadvantage to which the lower classes of society are subjected in the progressive increase of wealth is, that a larger portion of them is engaged in unhealthy occupations, and in employments in which the wages of labour are exposed to much greater fluctuations than in agriculture, and the simpler kinds of domestic trade.

On the state of the poor employed in manufactories with respect to health, and the fluctuations of wages, I will beg leave to quote a passage from Dr. Aikin's Description of the Country round Manchester:

'The invention and improvements of machines to shorten labour have had a surprising influence to extend our trade, and also to call in hands from all parts, particularly children for the cotton-mills. It is the wise plan of Providence, that in this life there shall be no good without its attendant inconvenience. There are many which are too obvious in these cotton-mills, and similar factories, which counteract that increase of population usually consequent on the improved facility of labour. In these, children of a very tender age are employed, many of them collected from the work-houses in London and Westminster, and transported in crowds as apprentices to masters resident many hundred miles distant, where they serve unknown, unprotected and forgotten by those to whose care nature or the laws had consigned them. These children are usually too long confined to work in close rooms, often during the whole night. The air they breathe from the oil, &c., employed in the machinery, and other circumstances, is injurious; little attention is paid to their cleanliness; and frequent changes from a warm and dense to a cold and thin atmosphere are predisposing causes to sickness and debility, and particularly to the epidemic fever which is so generally to be met with in these factories. It is also much to be questioned if society does not receive detriment from the manner in which children are thus employed during their early years. They are not generally strong to labour, or capable of pursuing any other branch of business when the term of their apprenticeship expires. The females are wholly uninstructed in sewing, knitting, and other domestic affairs requisite to make them notable and frugal wives and mothers. This is a very great misfortune to them and to the public, as is sadly proved by a comparison of the families of labourers in husbandry and those of manufacturers in general. In the former we meet with neatness, cleanliness and comfort; in the latter with filth, rags and poverty, although their wages may be nearly double to those of the husbandman. It must be added that the want of early religious instruction and example, and the numerous and indiscriminate association in these buildings, are very unfavourable to their future conduct in life.'[5]

In the same work it appears that the register for the collegiate church of Manchester, from Christmas, 1793, to Christmas, 1794, showed a decrease of 168 marriages, 538 christenings, and 250 burials. In the parish of Rochdale, in the neighbourhood, a still more melancholy reduction in proportion to the number of people took place. In 1792 the births were 746, the burials 646, and the marriages 389. In 1794 the births were 373, the burials 671, and the marriages 199. The cause of this sudden check to population was the failure of demand and of commercial credit which occurred at the commencement of the war, and such a check could not have taken place in so sudden a manner without the most severe distress, occasioned by the sudden reduction of wages.

In addition to the fluctuations arising from the changes from peace to war and from war to peace, it is well known how subject particular manufactures are to fail from the caprices of taste. The weavers of Spitalfields were plunged into the most severe distress by the fashion of muslins instead of silks; and great numbers of workmen in Sheffield and Birmingham were for a time thrown out of employment owing to the adoption of shoe strings and covered buttons, instead of buckles and metal buttons. Our manufactures, taken in the mass, have increased with prodigious rapidity, but in particular places they have failed; and the parishes where this has happened are invariably loaded with a crowd of poor in the most distressed and miserable condition.

In the evidence brought before the House of Lords during the inquiries which preceded the Corn-Bill of 1815, various accounts are produced from different manufactories, intended to show that the high price of corn has rather the effect of lowering than of raising the price of

---

[5] P. 219. Dr. Aikin says that endeavours have been made to remedy these evils, which in some factories have been attended with success. And it is very satisfactory to be able to add that, since this account was written, the situation of the children employed in the cotton-mills has been further very essentially improved, partly by the interference of the legislature, and partly by the humane and liberal exertions of individuals.

manufacturing labour.[6] Adam Smith has clearly and correctly stated that the money price of labour depends upon the money price of provisions, and the state of the demand and the supply of labour. And he shows how much he thinks it is occasionally affected by the latter cause, by explaining in what manner it may vary in an opposite direction from the price of provisions during the pressure of a scarcity. The accounts brought before the House of Lords are a striking illustration of this part of his proposition; but they certainly do not prove the incorrectness of the other part of it, as it is quite obvious that, whatever may take place for a few years, the supply of manufacturing labour cannot possibly be continued in the market unless the natural or necessary price, that is, the price necessary to continue it in the market be paid, and this of course is not done unless the money price be so proportioned to the price of provisions, that labourers are enabled to bring up families of such a size as will supply the number of hands required.

But though these accounts do not in any degree invalidate the usual doctrines respecting labour, or the statements of Adam Smith, they show very clearly the great fluctuations to which the condition of the manufacturing labourer is subjected.

In looking over these accounts, it will be found that in some cases the price of weaving has fallen a third, or nearly one-half, at the same time that the price of wheat has risen a third, or nearly one half; and yet these proportions do not always express the full amount of the fluctuations, as it sometimes happens that when the price is low, the state of the demand will not allow of the usual number of hours of working; and when the price is high, it will admit of extra hours.

That from the same causes there are sometimes variations of a similar kind in the price of task-work in agriculture will be readily admitted; but, in the first place, they do not appear to be nearly so considerable; and secondly, the great mass of agricultural labourers is employed by the day, and a sudden and general fall in the money price of agricultural day-labour is an event of extremely rare occurrence.[7]

It must be allowed then, that in the natural and usual progress of wealth, the means of marrying early and supporting a family are dim-

---

[6] Reports, p. 51.

[7] Almost the only instance on record in this country is that which has lately taken place (1815 and 1816), occasioned by an unparalleled fall in the exchangeable value of the raw produce, which has necessarily disabled the holders of it from employing the same quantity of labour at the same price.

inished, and a greater proportion of the population is engaged in employments less favourable to health and morals, and more subject to fluctuations in the price of labour, than the population employed in agriculture.

These are no doubt considerable disadvantages, and they would be sufficient to render the progress of riches decidedly unfavourable to the condition of the poor, if they were not counteracted by advantages which nearly, if not fully, counterbalance them.

And first, it is obvious that the profits of stock are that source of revenue from which the middle classes are chiefly maintained; and the increase of capital, which is both the cause and effect of increasing riches, may be said to be the efficient cause of the emancipation of the great body of society from a dependence on the landlords. In a country of limited extent, consisting of fertile land divided into large properties, as long as the capital remains inconsiderable, the structure of society is most unfavourable to liberty and good government. This was exactly the state of Europe in the feudal times. The landlords could in no other way spend their incomes than by maintaining a great number of idle followers; and it was by the growth of capital in all the employments to which it is directed that the pernicious power of the landlords was destroyed, and their dependent followers were turned into merchants, manufacturers, tradesmen, farmers, and independent labourers – a change of prodigious advantage to the great body of society, including the labouring classes.

Secondly; in the natural progress of cultivation and wealth, the production of an additional quantity of corn will require more labour, while, at the same time, from the accumulation and better distribution of capital, the continual improvements made in machinery, and the facilities opened to foreign commerce, manufactures and foreign commodities will be produced or purchased with less labour; and consequently a given quantity of corn will command a much greater quantity of manufactures and foreign commodities than while the country was poor. Although, therefore, the labourer may earn less corn than before, the superior value which every portion which he does not consume in kind will have in the purchase of conveniences may more than counterbalance this diminution. He will not indeed have the same power of maintaining a large family; but with a small family he may be better lodged and clothed, and better able to command the decencies and comforts of life.

Thirdly; it seems to be proved by experience, that the lower classes of society seldom acquire a decided taste for conveniences and comforts till they become plentiful compared with food, which they never do till food has become in some degree scarce. If the labourer can obtain the full support of himself and family by two or three days' labour; and if, to furnish himself with conveniences and comforts, he must work three or four days more, he will generally think the sacrifice too great compared with the objects to be obtained, which are not strictly necessary to him, and will therefore often prefer the luxury of idleness to the luxury of improved lodging and clothing. This is said by Humboldt to be particularly the case in some parts of South America, and to a certain extent prevails in Ireland, India, and all countries where food is plentiful compared with capital and manufactured commodities. On the other hand, if the main part of the labourer's time be occupied in procuring food, habits of industry are necessarily generated, and the remaining time, which is but inconsiderable compared with the commodities it will purchase, is seldom grudged. It is under these circumstances, particularly when combined with a good government, that the lower classes of society are most likely to acquire a decided taste for the conveniences and comforts of life; and this taste may be such as even to prevent, after a certain period, a further fall in the corn price of labour. But if the corn price of labour continues tolerably high while the relative value of commodities compared with corn falls very considerably, the labourer is placed in a most favourable situation. Owing to his decided taste for conveniences and comforts, the good corn wages of labour will not generally lead to early marriages; yet in individual cases, where large families occur, there will be the means of supporting them independently, by the sacrifice of the accustomed conveniences and comforts; and thus the poorest of the lower classes will rarely be stinted in food, while the great mass of them will not only have sufficient means of subsistence, but be able to command no inconsiderable quantity of those conveniences and comforts, which, at the same time that they gratify a natural or acquired want, tend unquestionably to improve the mind and elevate the character.

On an attentive review then of the effects of increasing wealth on the condition of the poor, it appears that, although such an increase does not imply a proportionate increase of the funds for the maintenance of mere labour,[8] yet it brings with it advantages to the lower classes of society which may fully counterbalance the disadvantages with which it is

---

[8] [In 1826 the word *mere* was excised.]

attended; and, strictly speaking, the good or bad condition of the poor is not *necessarily* connected with any particular stage in the progress of society to its full complement of wealth. A rapid increase of wealth indeed, whether it consists principally in additions to the means of subsistence or to the stock of conveniences and comforts, will always, *cæteris paribus*, have a favourable effect on the poor; but the influence even of this cause is greatly modified and altered by other circumstances, and nothing but the union of individual prudence with the skill and industry which produce wealth can permanently secure to the lower classes of society that share of it which it is on every account so desirable that they should possess.

Of the principal Sources of the prevailing Errors on the Subject of Population[1]

It has been observed, that many countries at the period of their greatest degree of populousness, have lived in the greatest plenty, and have been able to export corn; but at other periods, when their population was very low, have lived in continual poverty and want, and have been obliged to import corn. Egypt, Palestine, Rome, Sicily, and Spain are cited as particular exemplifications of this fact: and it has been inferred that an increase of population in any state, not cultivated to the utmost, will tend rather to augment than diminish the relative plenty of the whole society; and that, as Lord Kaimes observes, a country cannot easily become too populous for agriculture; because agriculture has the signal property of producing food in proportion to the number of consumers.[2]

The general facts, from which these inferences are drawn, there is no reason to doubt; but the inferences by no means follow from the premises. It is the nature of agriculture,[3] particularly when well conducted, to produce support for a considerable number above that which it employs; and consequently if these members of the society, or as Sir James Steuart calls them, the free hands, do not increase so as to reach the limit of the number which can be supported by the surplus produce, the whole population of the country may continue for ages increasing with the improving state of agriculture, and yet always be able to export corn. But this increase, after a certain period, will be very different from the natural and unrestricted increase of population; it will merely follow the slow augmentation of produce from the gradual improvement of agriculture; and population will still be checked by the difficulty of

---

[1] [In 1806 this chapter was entitled 'Of the prevailing Errors respecting Population and Plenty'. In 1817 (when this had become chapter xiv) the heading was changed to 'General Observations'.]

[2] Sketches of the History of Man, b. i. sketch i. p. 106, 107. 8vo. 1788.

[3] [In 1817 Malthus added a parenthesis here:
   ... the nature of agriculture (as it has before been observed) particularly when well conducted ...

procuring subsistence. [4]● It is very justly observed by Sir James Steuart that the population of England in the middle of the last century, when the exports of corn were considerable, was still checked for want of food. ●[4] The precise measure of the population in a country thus circumstanced will not, indeed, be the quantity of food, because part of it is exported, but the quantity of employment. The state of this employment, however, will necessarily regulate the wages of labour, on which depends the power of the lower classes of people to procure food; and according as the employment in the country is increasing, whether slowly or rapidly, these wages will be such as either to check or to encourage early marriages; such as to enable a labourer to support only two or three, or as many as five or six children.

[In 1817 (Vol. III, pp. 29–34) nine paragraphs were inserted here:

In stating that in this, and all the other cases and systems which have been considered, the progress of population will be mainly regulated and limited by the real wages of labour, it is necessary to remark that, practically, the current wages of labour estimated in the necessaries of life do not always correctly represent the quantity of these necessaries which it is in the power of the lower classes to consume; and that sometimes the error is in excess and sometimes in defect.

In a state of things when the prices of corn and of all sorts of commodities are rising, the money wages of labour do not always rise in proportion; but this apparent disadvantage to the labouring classes is sometimes more than counterbalanced by the plenty of employment, the quantity of task-work[5] that can be obtained, and the opportunity given to women and children to add considerably to the earnings of the family. In this case, the power of the labouring classes to command the necessaries of life is much greater than is implied by the current rate of their wages, and will of course have a proportionably greater effect on the population.

On the other hand, when prices are generally falling, it often happens that the current rate of wages does not fall in proportion; but this apparent advantage is in the same manner often more than counterbalanced by the scarcity of work, and the impossibility of finding employment for all the members of a labourer's family who are able and willing to be industrious. In this case, the powers of the labouring classes to command the necessaries of life will evidently be less than is implied by the current rate of their wages.

In the same manner parish allowances distributed to families, the habitual practice of task-work, and the frequent employment of women and children, will

---

[4] Polit. Econ. vol. i. b. i. c. xv. p. 100. [This sentence was omitted in 1817.]
[5] [This is now called piece-work.]

affect population like a rise in the real wages of labour. And, on the other hand, the paying of every sort of labour by the day, the absence of employment for women and children, and the practice among labourers of not working more than three or four days in the week, either from inveterate indolence, or any other cause, will affect population like a low price of labour.

In all these cases the real earnings of the labouring classes throughout the year, estimated in food, are different from the apparent wages; but it will evidently be the average earnings of the families of the labouring classes throughout the year on which the encouragement to marriage, and the power of supporting children, will depend, and not merely the wages of day-labour estimated in food.

An attention to this very essential point will explain the reason why, in many instances, the progress of population does not appear to be regulated by what are usually called the real wages of labour; and why this progress may occasionally be greater, when the price of a day's labour will purchase rather less than the medium quantity of corn, than when it will purchase rather more.

In our own country, for instance, about the middle of the last century, the price of corn was very low; and for twenty years together, from 1735 to 1755, a day's labour would, on an average, purchase a peck of wheat. During this period, population increased at a moderate rate; but not by any means with the same rapidity as from 1790 to 1811, when the average wages of day-labour would not in general purchase quite[6] so much as a peck of wheat. In the latter case, however, there was a more rapid accumulation of capital, and a greater demand for labour; and though the continued rise of provisions still kept them rather ahead of wages, yet the fuller employment for every body that would work, the greater quantity of task-work done, the higher relative value of corn compared with manufactures, the increased use of potatoes, and the greater sums distributed in parish allowances, unquestionably gave to the lower classes of society the power of commanding a greater quantity of food, and will account for the more rapid increase of population in the latter period, in perfect consistency with the general principle.

On similar grounds if, in some warm climates and rich soils, where corn is cheap, the quantity of food earned by a day's labour be such as to promise a more rapid progress in population than is really known to take place, the fact will be fully accounted for, if it be found that inveterate habits of indolence, fostered by a vicious government, and a slack demand for labour, prevent anything like constant employment.[7] It would of course require high corn wages of day-labour even to keep up the supply of a stationary population, where the days of working would only amount to half of the year.

In the case also of the prevalence of prudential habits, and a decided taste for the conveniences and comforts of life, as, according to the supposition, these

---

[6] [In 1826 the word *quite* was deleted.]

[7] This observation is exemplified in the slow progress of population in some parts of the Spanish dominions in America, compared with its progress in the United States.

habits and tastes do not operate as an encouragement to early marriages, and are not in fact spent almost entirely in the purchase of corn, it is quite consistent with the general principles laid down, that the population should not proceed at the same rate as is usual, *cæteris paribus*, in other countries, where the corn wages of labour are equally high.

The quantity of employment in any country will not of course vary from year to year, in the same manner as the quantity of produce must necessarily do, from the variation of the seasons; and consequently the check from want of employment will be much more steady in its operation, and be much more favourable to the lower classes of people, than the check from the immediate want of food. The first will be the preventive check; the second the positive check. When the demand for labour is either stationary, or increasing very slowly, people, not seeing any employment open by which they can support a family, or the wages of common labour being inadequate to this purpose, will of course be deterred from marrying. But if a demand for labour continue increasing with some rapidity, although the supply of food be uncertain, on account of variable seasons and a dependence on other countries, the population will evidently go on, till it is positively checked by famine or the diseases arising from severe want.

Scarcity and extreme poverty, therefore, may or may not accompany an increasing population, according to circumstances. But they must necessarily accompany a permanently declining population; because there never has been, nor probably ever will be, any other cause than want of food which makes the population of a country permanently decline. In the numerous instances of depopulation which occur in history, the causes of it may always be traced to the want of industry, or the ill direction of that industry arising from violence, bad government, ignorance, &c., which first occasion a want of food, and of course depopulation follows. When Rome adopted the custom of importing all her corn, and laying all Italy into pasture, she soon declined in population. The causes of the depopulation of Egypt and Turkey have already been alluded to;[8] and, in the case of Spain, it was certainly not the numerical loss of people, occasioned by the expulsion of the Moors, but the industry and capital thus expelled, which permanently injured her population. When a country has been depopulated by violent causes, if a bad government, with its usual concomitant, insecurity of property,

---

[8] [In 1817 *alluded to* was replaced by 'adverted to'.]

ensue, which has generally been the case in all those countries which are now less peopled than formerly; neither the food nor the population can recover themselves,[9] and the inhabitants will probably live in severe want. But when an accidental depopulation takes place, in a country which was before populous and industrious, and in the habit of exporting corn, if the remaining inhabitants be left at liberty to exert, and do exert, their industry in the same direction as before, it is a strange idea to entertain, that they would then be unable to supply themselves with corn in the same plenty; particularly as the diminished numbers would, of course, cultivate principally the more fertile parts of their territory, and not be obliged, as in their more populous state, to apply to ungrateful soils. Countries in this situation would evidently have the same chance of recovering their former number, as they had originally of reaching this number; and indeed if absolute populousness were necessary to relative plenty, as some agriculturists have supposed,[10] it would be impossible for new colonies to increase with the same rapidity as old states.

[9] [In 1807 *themselves* was changed to 'itself'.

[10] Among others, I allude more particularly to Mr. Anderson, who, in a *Calm Investigation of the Circumstances which have led to the present Scarcity of Grain in Britain,* (published in 1801,) has laboured, with extraordinary earnestness, and I believe with the best intentions possible,[a] to impress this curious truth on the minds of his countrymen. The particular position which he attempts to prove is, *that an increase of population in any state whose fields have not been made to attain their highest possible degree of productiveness, (a thing that probably has never yet been seen on this globe,) will necessarily have its means of subsistence rather augmented, than diminished, by that augmentation of its population; and the reverse.* The proposition is, to be sure, expressed rather obscurely; but, from the context, his meaning evidently is, that every increase of population tends to increase relative plenty, and vice versa. He concludes his proofs by observing, that, if the facts which he has thus brought forward and connected, do not serve to remove the fears of those who doubt the possibility of this country producing abundance to sustain its increasing population, were it to augment in a ratio greatly more progressive than it has yet done, he should doubt, whether they could be convinced of it, were one even to rise from the dead to tell them so. [b]●Mr. A. is, perhaps, justified in this doubt, from the known incredulity of the age, which might cause people to remain unconvinced in both cases.●[b] I agree with Mr. A. however, entirely, respecting the importance of directing a greater part of the national industry to agriculture; but from the circumstance of its being possible for a country with a certain direction of its industry, always to export corn,[c] although it may be very populous, he has been led into the strange error of supposing, that an agricultural country could support an unchecked population.

[a] [In 1817 the word *possible* was deleted.]

[b] [In 1817 this sentence was omitted.]

[c] [In 1817 this was altered to:
    ... direction of its industry, always to grow corn sufficient for its own supplies, although it may be very populous ...

The prejudices on the subject of population bear a very striking resemblance to the old prejudices about specie, and we know how slowly, and with what difficulty, these last have yielded to juster conceptions. Politicians, observing that states which were powerful and prosperous were almost invariably populous, have mistaken an effect for a cause, and concluded that their population was the cause of their prosperity, instead of their prosperity being the cause of their population; as the old political economists concluded that the abundance of specie was the cause of national wealth, instead of being the effect of it. The annual produce of the land and labour, in both these instances, became in consequence a secondary consideration; and its increase, it was conceived, would naturally follow the increase of specie in the one case, or of population in the other. The folly of endeavouring by forcible means to increase the quantity of specie in any country, and the absolute impossibility of accumulating it beyond a certain level by any human laws that can be devised, are now fully established, and have been completely exemplified in the instances of Spain and Portugal; but the illusion still remains respecting population; and under this impression, almost every political treatise has abounded in proposals to encourage population, with little or no comparative reference to the means of its support. Yet surely the folly of endeavouring to increase the quantity of specie in any country, without an increase of the commodities which it is to circulate, is not greater than that of endeavouring to increase the number of people, without an increase of the food which is to maintain them; and it will be found that the level above which no human laws can raise the population of a country, is a limit more fixed and impassable than the limit to the accumulation of specie. However improbable in fact, it is possible to conceive that means might be invented of retaining a quantity of specie in a state, greatly beyond what was demanded by the produce of its land and labour;[11] but when, by great encouragements, population has been raised to such a height that this produce is meted out to each individual in the smallest portions that can support life, no stretch of ingenuity can even conceive the possibility of going further.

It has appeared, I think, clearly, in the review of different societies given in the former part of this work, that those countries, the inhabitants of which were sunk in the most barbarous ignorance, or oppressed

---

[11] [In 1817 there was an insertion here:
  ... the produce of its land and labour, and the relative state of other countries. But when ...

by the most cruel tyranny, however low they might be in actual population, were very populous in proportion to their means of subsistence; and upon the slightest failure of the seasons generally suffered the severities of want. Ignorance and despotism seem to have no tendency to destroy the passion which prompts to increase; but they effectually destroy the checks to it from reason and foresight. The improvident barbarian who thinks only of his present wants, or the miserable peasant who, from his political situation, feels little security of reaping what he has sown, will seldom be deterred from gratifying his passions by the prospect of inconveniences which cannot be expected to press on him under three or four years. But though this want of foresight, which is fostered by ignorance and despotism, tend thus rather to encourage the procreation of children, it is absolutely fatal to the industry which is to support them. Industry cannot exist without foresight and security. The indolence of the savage is well known; and the poor Egyptian or Abyssinian farmer without capital, who rents land which is let out yearly to the highest bidder, and who is constantly subject to the demands of his tyrannical masters, to the casual plunder of an enemy, and not unfrequently to the violation of his miserable contract, can have no heart to be industrious, and if he had, could not exercise that industry with success. Even poverty itself, which appears to be the great spur to industry, when it has once passed certain limits, almost ceases to operate. The indigence which is hopeless destroys all vigorous exertion, and confines the efforts to what is sufficient for bare existence. It is the hope of bettering our condition, and the fear of want, rather than want itself, that is the best stimulus to industry, and its most constant and best directed efforts will almost invariably be found among a class of people above the class of the wretchedly poor.

The effect of ignorance and oppression will therefore always be to destroy the springs of industry, and consequently to diminish the annual produce of the land and labour in any country; and this diminution will inevitably be followed by a decrease of the population, in spite of the birth of any number of children whatever annually. The desire of immediate gratification, and the removal of the restraints to it from prudence, may perhaps, in such countries, prompt universally to early marriages; but when these habits have once reduced the people to the lowest possible state of poverty, they can evidently have no further effect upon the population. Their only effect must be on the degree of mortality; and there is no doubt that, if we could obtain accurate bills of mortality in those southern countries, where very few women remain unmarried, and all marry young, the proportion of the annual deaths would be 1 in 17, 18, or 20, instead of 1 in 34, 36, or 40, as in European states, where the preventive check operates.

That an increase of population, when it follows in its natural order, is both a positive good in itself,[12] and absolutely necessary to a further increase in the annual produce of the land and labour of any country, I should be the last to deny. The only question is, what is the natural[13] order of its progress? In this point Sir James Steuart, who has in general explained this subject so well, appears to me to have fallen into an error. He determines that multiplication is the efficient cause of agriculture, and not agriculture of multiplication.[14] But though it may be allowed that the increase of people, beyond what could easily subsist on the natural fruits of the earth, first prompted man to till the ground; and that the view of maintaining a family, or of obtaining some valuable consideration in exchange for the products of agriculture, still operates as the principal stimulus to cultivation; yet it is clear that these products, in their actual state, must be beyond the lowest wants of the existing population, before any permanent increase can possibly be supported. And we know that multiplication has in numberless instances taken place,[15] which has produced no effect upon agriculture, and has merely been followed by an increase of diseases; but perhaps there is no instance where a permanent increase of agriculture has not effected a permanent increase of population somewhere or other. Consequently, agriculture may with more propriety be termed the efficient cause of population, than population of agriculture,[16] though they certainly re-act upon each other, and are mutually necessary to each other's support. This indeed seems to be the hinge on which the subject turns, and all the prejudices respecting population have, perhaps, arisen from a mistake about the order of precedence.

The author of *L'Ami des Hommes*, in a chapter on the effects of a decay

[12] [In 1806 this was changed to:
   ... a great positive good in itself, ...
[13] [In 1817 the word *natural* was deleted.]
[14] Polit. Econ. vol. i. b. i. c. xviii. p. 114.
[15] [In 1806 this was corrected to:
   ... a multiplication of births has in numberless instances ...
[16] Sir James Steuart explains himself afterwards, by saying that he means principally the multiplication of those persons who have some valuable consideration to give for the products of agriculture; but this is evidently not mere increase of population, and such an explanation seems to admit the incorrectness of the general proposition.

of agriculture upon population, acknowledges that he had fallen into a fundamental error in considering population as the source of revenue; and that he was afterwards fully convinced that revenue was the source of population.[17] From a want of attention to this most important distinction, statesmen, in pursuit of the desireable object of population, have been led to encourage early marriages, to reward the fathers of families, and to disgrace celibacy; but this, as the same author justly observes, is to dress and water a piece of land without sowing it,[18] and yet to expect a crop.

[In 1817 Malthus inserted five paragraphs here:

What is here said of the order of precedence with respect to agriculture and population, does not invalidate what was said in an earlier part of this work on the tendency to an oscillation or alternation in the increase of population and food in the natural course of their progress. In this progress nothing is more usual than for the population to increase at certain periods faster than food; indeed it is a part of the general principle that it should do so; and when the money wages of labour are prevented from falling by the employment of the increasing population in manufactures, the rise in the price of corn which the increased competition for it occasions is practically the most natural and frequent stimulus to agriculture. But then it must be recollected that the greater relative increase of population absolutely implies a previous increase of food at some time or other greater than the lowest wants of the people. Without this, the population could not possibly have gone forward.[19]

Universally, when the population of a country is for a longer or shorter time stationary, owing to the low corn wages of labour, a case which is not unfrequent, it is obvious that nothing but a previous increase of food, or at least an increase of the portion awarded to the labourer, can enable the population again to proceed forwards.

And, in the same manner, with a view to any essential improvement in the condition of the labourer, which is to give him a greater effective command over the means of comfortable subsistence, it is absolutely necessary that, setting out from the lowest point, the increase of food must precede and be greater than the increase of population.

[17] Tom. viii. p. 84. 12mo. 9 vols. 1762.
[18] [To 'dress' a piece of land meant to spread manure over it.]
[19] According to the principle of population, the human race has a tendency to increase faster than food. It has therefore a constant tendency to people a country fully up to the limits of subsistence; but by the laws of nature it can never go beyond them; meaning, of course, by these limits, the lowest quantity of food which will maintain a stationary population. Population, therefore, can never, strictly speaking, precede food.

Strictly speaking then, as man cannot live without food, there can be no doubt that in the order of precedence food must take the lead; although when, from the state of cultivation and other causes, the average quantity of food awarded to the labourer is considerably more than sufficient to maintain a stationary population, it is quite natural that the diminution of this quantity, from the tendency of population to increase, should be one of the most powerful and constant stimulants to agriculture.

It is worthy also of remark that on this account a stimulus to the increase of agriculture is much more easy when, from the prevalence of prudential restraint, or any other cause, the labourer is well paid; as in this case a rise in the price of corn, occasioned either by the increase of population or a foreign demand, will increase for a time the profits of the farmer, and often enable him to make permanent improvements; whereas, when the labourer is paid so scantily that his wages will not allow even of any temporary diminution without a diminution of population, the increase of cultivation and population must from the first be accompanied with a fall of profits. The prevalence of the preventive check to population and the good average wages of the labourer will rather promote than prevent that occasional increase and decrease of them, which as a stimulus seems to be favourable to the increase both of food and population.

Among the other prejudices which have prevailed on the subject of population, it has been generally thought that, while there is either waste among the rich, or land remaining uncultivated in any country, the complaints for want of food cannot be justly founded or, at least, that the pressure of distress upon the poor is to be attributed to the ill-conduct of the higher classes of society and the bad management of the land. The real effect, however, of these two circumstances, is merely to narrow the limit of the actual population; but they have little or no influence on what may be called the average pressure of distress on the poorer members of society. If our ancestors had been so frugal and industrious, and had transmitted such habits to their posterity, that nothing superfluous was now consumed by the higher classes, no horses were used for pleasure, and no land was left uncultivated, a striking difference would appear in the state of the actual population; but probably none whatever in the state of the lower classes of people, with respect to the price of labour, and the facility of supporting a family. The waste among the rich, and the horses kept for pleasure, have indeed a little the effect of the consumption of grain in distilleries, noticed before with regard to China. On the supposition that the food consumed in this manner may be withdrawn on the occasion of a scarcity, and be applied to the relief of the poor, they operate, certainly, as far as they go, like granaries, which are only opened at the time that they are most wanted, and must therefore tend rather to benefit than to injure the lower classes of society.

With regard to uncultivated land, it is evident that its effect upon the poor is neither to injure nor to benefit them. The sudden cultivation of it will indeed tend to improve their condition for a time, and the neglect of lands before cultivated will certainly make their situation worse for a certain period; but when no changes of this kind are going forward, the effect of uncultivated land on the lower classes operates merely like the possession of a smaller territory. It is, indeed, a point of very great importance to the poor,[20] whether a country be in the habit of exporting or importing corn; but this point is not necessarily connected with the complete or incomplete cultivation of the whole territory, but depends upon the proportion of the surplus produce to those who are supported by it; and in fact this proportion is generally the greatest in countries which have not yet completed the cultivation of all their territory. If every inch of land in this country were well cultivated, there would be no reason to expect, merely from this circumstance, that we should be able to export corn. Our power in this respect would depend entirely on the proportion of the surplus produce to the commercial population; and this, of course, would in its turn depend on the direction of capital to agriculture or commerce.

It is not probable that any country with a large territory should ever be completely cultivated; and I am inclined to think that we often draw very inconsiderate conclusions against the industry and government of states from the appearance of uncultivated lands in them. It seems to be the clear and express duty of every government to remove all obstacles and give every facility to the inclosure and cultivation of land; but when this has been done, the rest must be left to the operation of individual interest; and, upon this principle, it cannot be expected that any new land should be brought into cultivation, the manure and the labour necessary for which might be employed to greater advantage on the improvement of land already in cultivation; and this is a case which will very frequently occur. In countries possessed of a large territory, there will always be a great quantity of land of a middling quality, which requires constant dressing to prevent it from growing worse; but which would admit of very great improvement if a greater quantity of manure

---

[20] [In 1817 this sentence began:
   It may indeed be a point of some importance to the poor, whether a country be in the habit of importing or exporting corn . . .

and labour could be employed upon it. The great obstacle to the amelioration of land is the difficulty, the expense, and sometimes the impossibility, of procuring a sufficient quantity of dressing. As this instrument of improvement, therefore, is in practice limited, whatever it may be in theory, the question will always be, how it may be most profitably employed; and in any instance where a certain quantity of dressing and labour employed to bring new land into cultivation, would have yielded a permanently greater produce if employed upon old land, both the individual and the nation are losers. Upon this principle, it is not uncommon for farmers in some situations never to dress their poorest land, but to get from it merely a scanty crop every three or four years, and to employ the whole of their manure, which they practically feel is limited, on those parts of their farms where it will produce a greater proportional effect.

The case will be different, of course, in a small territory with a great population, supported on funds not derived from their own soil. In this case there will be little or no choice of land, and a comparative super-abundance of manure; and under such circumstances the poorest soils may be brought under cultivation. But for this purpose, it is not mere population that is wanted, but a population which can obtain the produce of other countries, while it is gradually improving its own; otherwise it would be immediately reduced in proportion to the limited produce of this small and barren territory; and the amelioration of the land might perhaps never take place; or if it did, it would take place very slowly indeed, and the population would always be exactly measured by this tardy rate, and could not possibly increase beyond it.

This subject is illustrated in the cultivation of the Campine in Brabant, which, according to the Abbé Mann,[21] consisted originally of the most barren and arid sand. Many attempts were made by private individuals to bring it under cultivation, but without success; which prove that, as a farming project, and considered as a sole dependence, the cultivation of it would not answer. Some religious houses, however, at last settled there, and being supported by other funds, and improving the land merely as a secondary object, they by degrees, in the course of some centuries, brought nearly the whole under cultivation, letting it out to farmers as soon as it was sufficiently improved.

There is no spot, however barren, which might not be made rich this

---

[21] Memoir on the Agriculture of the Netherlands, published in vol. i. of Communications to the Board of Agriculture, p. 225.

way, or by the concentrated population of a manufacturing town; but this is no proof whatever that with respect to population and food, population has the precedence; because this concentrated population could not possibly exist without the preceding existence of an adequate quantity of food in the surplus produce of some other district.

In a country like Brabant or Holland, where territory is the principal want, and not manure, such a district as the Campine is described to be, may perhaps be cultivated with advantage. But in countries, possessed of a large territory, and with a considerable quantity of land of a middling quality, the attempt to cultivate such a spot would be a palpable misdirection and waste, both of individual and national resources.

The French have already found their error in bringing under cultivation too great a quantity of poor land. They are now sensible that they have employed in this way a portion of labour and dressing, which would have produced a permanently better effect, if it had been applied to the further improvement of better land. Even in China, which is so fully cultivated and so fully peopled, barren heaths have been noticed in some districts; which proves that, distressed as the people appear to be for subsistence, it does not answer to them to employ any of their manure on such spots. These remarks will be still further confirmed, if we recollect that, in the cultivation of a large surface of bad land, there must necessarily be a very great waste of seed corn.[22]

We should not, therefore, be too ready to make inferences against the internal economy of a country, from the appearance of uncultivated heaths, without other evidence. But the fact is, that as no country has ever reached, or probably ever will reach, its highest possible acme of produce, it appears always as if the want of industry, or the ill-direction of that industry, was the actual limit to a further increase of produce and population, and not the absolute refusal of nature to yield any more; but a man who is locked up in a room may be fairly said to be confined by the walls of it, though he may never touch them; and with regard to the principle of population, it is never the question whether a country will produce *any more*, but whether it may be made to produce a sufficiency to keep pace with an unchecked increase of people.[23] In China, the question is not whether a certain additional quantity of rice might be raised by improved culture, but whether such an addition could be expected

22 [In 1817 the word *very* was deleted.]
23 [In 1817 this was changed to:
     ... to keep pace with a nearly unchecked increase of people.

during the next twenty-five years, as would be sufficient to support an additional three hundred millions of people. And in this country, it is not the question, whether by cultivating all our commons, we could raise considerably more corn than at present; but whether we could raise sufficient for a population of twenty millions in the next twenty-five years, and forty millions, in the next fifty years.

The allowing of the produce of the earth to be absolutely unlimited, scarcely removes the weight of a hair from the argument, which depends entirely upon the differently increasing ratios of population and food: and all that the most enlightened governments, and the most persevering and best guided efforts of industry can do, is to make the necessary checks to population operate more equably, and in a direction to produce the least evil; but to remove them, is a task absolutely hopeless.

[In 1817 Malthus added a footnote here, which was printed in the volume of *Additions* as a continuation of the main text:

It may be thought that the effects here referred to as resulting from greatly increased resources could not take place in a country where there were towns and manufactories; and that they are not quite consistent with what was said in a former part of this work, namely, that the ultimate check to population (the want of food) is never the immediate check, except in cases of actual famine.

If the expressions are unguardedly strong, they will certainly allow of considerable mitigation, without any sensible diminution in the practical force and application of the argument. But I am inclined to think that, although they are unquestionably strong, they are not very far from the truth. The great cause which fills towns and manufactories is an insufficiency of employment, and consequently of the means of support in the country; and if each labourer, in the parish where he was born, could command food, clothing, and lodging for ten children, the population of the towns would soon bear but a small proportion to the population in the country. And if to this consideration we add that, in the case supposed, the proportion of births and marriages in towns would be greatly increased, and all the mortality arising from poverty almost entirely removed, I should by no means be surprised (after a short interval for the change of habits) at an increase of population, even in China, equal to that which is referred to in the text.

With regard to this country, as it is positively known that the rate of increase has changed from that which would double the population in 120 years, or more, to that which would double it in 55 years, under a great increase of towns and manufactures, I feel very little doubt that, if the resources of the country were so augmented and distributed, as that every man could marry at 18 or 20, with a certainty of being able to support the largest family, the population of the British

Isles would go on increasing at a rate which would double the population in 25 years. It appears, from our registers, that England is a healthier country than America. At the time that America was increasing with extraordinary rapidity, in some of her towns the deaths exceeded the births. In the English towns, with their present improvements, I do not think this would ever be the case, if all the lower classes could marry as soon as they pleased, and there was little or no premature mortality from the consequences of poverty.

But whether the habits and customs of an old state could be so changed by an abundance of food, as to make it increase nearly like a new colony, is a question of mere curiosity. The argument only requires that a change from scanty to abundant means of supporting a family should occasion, in old states, a marked increase of population; and this, it is conceived, cannot possibly be denied.

ESSAY, &c

OF OUR FUTURE PROSPECTS RESPECTING THE REMOVAL OR MITIGATION OF THE EVILS ARISING FROM THE PRINCIPLE OF POPULATION

CHAPTER I

Of moral restraint, and the foundations of our obligation to practise this virtue[1]

As it appears that, in the actual state of every society which has come within our review, the natural progress of population has been constantly and powerfully checked; and as it seems evident, that no improved form of government, no plans of emigration, no benevolent institutions, and no degree or direction of national industry, can prevent the continued action of a great check to population in some form or other; it follows that we must submit to it as an inevitable law of nature; and the only inquiry that remains is how it may take place with the least possible prejudice to the virtue and happiness of human society. The various[2] checks to population, which have been observed to prevail in the same and different countries, seem all to be resolvable into moral restraint, vice, and misery; and if our choice be confined to these three, we cannot long hesitate in our decision respecting which it would be most eligible to encourage.

In the former edition of this essay,[3] I observed that as, from the laws of nature, it appeared that some check to population must exist, it was better that this check should arise from a foresight of the difficulties

---

[1] [In 1806 this was altered to:
'Of moral restraint, and our obligation to practise this virtue'.

[2] [In 1806 this was changed to:
All the immediate checks to population ...

[3] [In 1806 this was altered to:
In the first edition of this essay ... [See the 1798 *Essay*, pp. 89–90.]

attending a family, and the fear of dependent poverty, than from the actual presence of want and sickness. This idea will admit of being pursued further; and I am inclined to think that, from the prevailing opinions respecting population, which undoubtedly originated in barbarous ages, and have been continued and circulated by that part of every community which may be supposed to be interested in their support, we have been prevented from attending to the clear dictates of reason and nature on this subject.

Natural and moral evil seem to be the instruments employed by the Deity in admonishing us to avoid any mode of conduct which is not suited to our being, and will consequently injure our happiness. If we be intemperate in eating and drinking, we are disordered;[4] if we indulge the transports of anger, we seldom fail to commit acts of which we afterwards repent; if we multiply too fast, we die miserably of poverty and contagious diseases. The laws of nature in all these cases are similar and uniform. They indicate to us that we have followed these impulses too far, so as to trench upon some other law which equally demands attention. The uneasiness we feel from repletion, the injuries that we inflict on ourselves or others in anger, and the inconveniences we suffer on the approach of poverty, are all admonitions to us to regulate these impulses better; and if we heed not this admonition, we justly incur the penalty of our disobedience, and our sufferings operate as a warning to others.

From the inattention of mankind, hitherto, to the consequences of increasing too fast, it must be presumed that these consequences are not so immediately and powerfully connected with the conduct which leads to them, as in the other instances; but the delayed knowledge of particular effects does not alter their nature, nor our obligation to regulate our conduct accordingly, as soon as we are satisfied of what this conduct ought to be. In many other instances, it has not been till after long and painful experience that the conduct most favourable to the happiness of man has been forced upon his attention. The kind of food, and the mode of preparing it, best suited to the purposes of nutrition and the gratification of the palate; the treatment and remedies of different disorders; the bad effects on the human frame of low and marshy situations; the invention of the most convenient and comfortable clothing; the construction of good houses; and all the advantages and

---

[4] [In 1817 this was amended to:
   If we be intemperate in eating and drinking, our health is disordered.

extended enjoyments, which distinguish civilized life, were not pointed out to the attention of man at once; but were the slow and late result of experience, and of the admonitions received by repeated failures.

Diseases have been generally considered as the inevitable inflictions of Providence; but, perhaps, a great part of them may more justly be considered as indications that we have offended against some of the laws of nature. The plague at Constantinople, and in other towns of the East, is a constant admonition of this kind to the inhabitants. The human constitution cannot support such a state of filth and torpor; and as dirt, squalid poverty, and indolence are in the highest degree unfavourable to happiness and virtue, it seems a benevolent dispensation that such a state should, by the laws of nature, produce disease and death, as a beacon to others to avoid splitting on the same rock.

The prevalence of the plague in London till the year 1666 operated in a proper manner on the conduct of our ancestors; and the removal of nuisances, the construction of drains, the widening of the streets, and the giving more room and air to their houses, had the effect of eradicating completely this dreadful disorder, and of adding greatly to the health and happiness of the inhabitants.[5]

In the history of every epidemic it has almost invariably been observed that the lower classes of people, whose food was poor and insufficient, and who lived crowded together in small and dirty houses, were the principal victims. In what other manner can nature point out to us, that if we increase too fast for the means of subsistence, so as to render it necessary for a considerable part of the society to live in this miserable manner, we have offended against one of her laws? This law she has declared exactly in the same manner as she declares that intemperance in eating and drinking will be followed by ill health; and that, however grateful it may be to us at the moment to indulge these passions to excess,[6] this indulgence will ultimately produce unhappiness. It is as much a law of nature that repletion is bad for the human frame, as that eating and drinking, unattended with this consequence, are good for it.

An implicit obedience to the impulses of our natural passions would lead us into the wildest and most fatal extravagancies; and yet we have the strongest reasons for believing that all these passions are so necessary

---

[5] [It should be remembered that all Malthus's own editions of the *Essay* appeared before the first outbreak of cholera in nineteenth-century Britain, in 1831–2; two more occurred after Malthus's death, in 1848 and 1865–6.]

[6] [In 1826 *these passions* were changed to 'this propensity'.

to our being, that they could not be generally weakened or diminished, without injuring our happiness. The most powerful and universal of all our desires is the desire of food, and of those things, such as clothing, houses, &c. which are immediately necessary to relieve us from the pains of hunger and cold. It is acknowledged by all, that these desires put in motion the greatest part of that activity from which spring the multiplied improvements and advantages of civilized life;[7] and that the pursuit of these objects and the gratification of these desires form the principal happiness of the larger half of mankind, civilized or uncivilized, and are indispensably necessary to the more refined enjoyments of the other half. We are all conscious of the inestimable benefits that we derive from these desires when directed in a certain manner; but we are equally conscious of the evils resulting from them when not directed in this manner; so much so, that society has taken upon itself to punish most severely what it considers as an irregular gratification of them. And yet the desires in both cases are equally natural and, abstractedly considered, equally virtuous. The act of the hungry man, who satisfies his appetite by taking a loaf from the shelf of another, is in no respect to be distinguished from the act of him who does the same thing with a loaf of his own, but by its consequences. From the consideration of these consequences, we feel the most perfect conviction that, if people were not prevented from gratifying their natural desires with the loaves in the possession of others, the number of loaves would universally diminish. This experience is the foundation of the laws relating to property, and of the distinctions of virtue and vice, in the gratification of desires otherwise perfectly the same.

If the pleasure arising from the gratification of these propensities were universally diminished in vividness, violations of property would become less frequent; but this advantage would be greatly overbalanced by the narrowing of the sources of enjoyment. The diminution in the quantity of all those productions, which contribute to human gratification, would be much greater in proportion than the diminution of thefts; and the loss of general happiness on the one side would be beyond comparison greater than the gain to happiness on the other. When we contemplate the constant and severe toils of the greatest part of mankind, it is impossible not to be forcibly impressed with the reflection, that the

---

[7] [In 1806 this sentence was altered to:
    ... from which the multiplied improvements and advantages of civilized life are derived; ...

sources of human happiness would be most cruelly diminished, if the prospect of a good meal, a warm house, and a comfortable fireside in the evening, were not incitements sufficiently vivid to give interest and cheerfulness to the labours and privations of the day.

After the desire of food, the most powerful and general of our desires is the passion between the sexes, taken in an enlarged sense. Of the happiness spread over human life by this passion, very few are unconscious. Virtuous love, exalted by friendship, seems to be that sort of mixture of sensual and intellectual enjoyment, particularly suited to the nature of man, and most powerfully calculated to awaken the sympathies of the soul, and produce the most exquisite gratifications. Perhaps there is scarcely a man who has once experienced the genuine delight of virtuous love, however great his intellectual pleasures may have been, who does not look back to that period, as the sunny spot in his whole life, where his imagination loves most to bask, which he recollects and contemplates with the fondest regret, and which he would most wish to live over again.

It has been said by Mr. Godwin, in order to show the evident inferiority of the pleasures of sense: 'Strip the commerce of the sexes of all its attendant circumstances, and it would be generally despised.' He might as well say to a man who admired trees, strip them of their spreading branches and lovely foliage, and what beauty can you see in a bare pole? But it was the tree with the branches and foliage, and not without them, that excited admiration. It is 'the symmetry of person, the vivacity, the voluptuous softness of temper, the affectionate kindness of feeling, the imagination and the wit'[8] of a woman, which excite the passion of love, and not the mere distinction of her being a female.[9]

It is a very great mistake to suppose that the passion between the sexes only operates and influences human conduct when the immediate gratification of it is in contemplation. The formation and steady pursuit of some particular plan of life has been justly considered as one of the most permanent sources of happiness; but I am inclined to believe that there are not many of these plans formed which are not connected, in a considerable degree, with the prospect of the gratification of this passion, and with the support of children arising from it. The evening meal, the warm house, and the comfortable fireside, would lose half of their

[8] Political Justice, vol. i. b. i. c. v. p. 72. 8vo. [Third edition.]
[9] [This paragraph, and the one preceding it, are taken from pp. 211–15 of the 1798 *Essay.*]

interest, if we were to exclude the idea of some object of affection with whom they were to be shared.

We have also great reason to believe that the passion between the sexes has the most powerful tendency to soften and meliorate the human character, and keep it more alive to all the kindlier emotions of benevolence and pity. Observations on savage life have generally tended to prove, that nations in which this passion appeared to be less vivid, were distinguished by a ferocious and malignant spirit; and particularly by tyranny and cruelty to the sex. If, indeed, this bond of conjugal affection were considerably weakened, it seems probable, either that the man would make use of his superior physical strength, and turn his wife into a slave, as among the generality of savages; or at best, that every little inequality of temper, which must necessarily occur between two persons, would produce a total alienation of affection; and this could hardly take place without a diminution of parental fondness and care, which would have the most fatal effect on the happiness of society.

It may be further remarked, that observations on the human character in different countries warrant us in the conclusion, that the passion is stronger, and its general effects in producing gentleness, kindness, and suavity of manners, much more powerful, where obstacles are thrown in the way of very early and universal gratification. In some of the southern countries where every impulse may be almost immediately indulged, the passion sinks into mere animal desire, is soon weakened and almost extinguished by excess; and its influence on the character is extremely confined. But in European countries where, though the women are not secluded, yet manners have imposed considerable restraints on this gratification, the passion not only rises in force, but in the universality and beneficial tendency of its effects, and has often the greatest influence in the formation and improvement of the character, where it is the least gratified.

Considering then the passion between the sexes in all its bearings and relations, and including the endearing engagement of parent and child resulting from it, few will be disposed to deny that it is one of the principal ingredients of human happiness. Yet experience teaches us that much evil flows from the irregular gratification of it; and though the evil be of little weight in the scale, when compared with the good; yet its absolute quantity cannot be inconsiderable, on account of the strength and universality of the passion. It is evident, however, from the general conduct of all governments in their distribution of punishments, that the evil resulting from this cause is not so great, and so immediately dangerous to society, as the irregular gratification of the desire of property; but placing this evil in the most formidable point of view, we should evidently purchase a diminution of it at a very high price, by the extinction or diminution of the passion which causes it; a change which would probably convert human life either into a cold and cheerless blank, or a scene of savage and merciless ferocity.

A careful attention to the remote as well as immediate effect of all the human passions, and all the general laws of nature, leads us strongly to the conclusion that, under the present constitution of things, few or none of them would admit of being greatly diminished without narrowing the sources of good more powerfully than the sources of evil. And the reason seems to be obvious. They are, in fact, the materials of all our pleasures, as well as of all our pains; of all our happiness, as well as of all our misery; of all our virtues, as well as of all our vices. It must therefore be regulation and direction that are wanted, not diminution or extinction.

It is justly observed by Dr. Paley that: 'Human passions are either necessary to human welfare, or capable of being made, and in a great majority of instances in fact made, conducive to its happiness. These passions are strong and general; and perhaps would not answer their purpose unless they were so. But strength and generality, when it is expedient that particular circumstances should be respected, become, if left to themselves, excess and misdirection. From which excess and misdirection the vices of mankind (the causes no doubt of much misery) appear to spring. This account, while it shows us the principle of vice, shows us at the same time, the province of reason and self-government.'[10]

Our virtue, therefore, as reasonable beings, evidently consists in educing, from the general materials which the Creator has placed under our guidance, the greatest sum of human happiness; and as all our[11] natural impulses are abstractedly considered good, and only to be distinguished by their consequences, a strict attention to these consequences, and the regulation of our conduct conformably to them, must be considered as our principal duty.

The fecundity of the human species is, in some respects, a distinct consideration from the passion between the sexes, as it evidently depends

---

[10] Natural Theology, c. xxvi. p. 547.

[11] [In 1806 the word *all* was excised; in 1807 *our natural impulses* was changed to 'natural impulses', *our* being excised.]

more upon the power of women in bearing children, than upon the strength or weakness of this passion. It is, however, a law, exactly similar in its great features to all the other laws of nature. It is strong and general, and apparently would not admit of any very considerable diminution, without being inadequate to its object; the evils arising from it are incidental to these necessary qualities of strength and generality; and these evils are capable of being very greatly mitigated and rendered comparatively light by human energy and virtue. We cannot but conceive, that it is an object of the Creator, that the earth should be replenished, at least to a considerable degree;[12] and it appears to me clear, that this could not be effected without a tendency in population to increase faster than food; and as, with the present law of increase, the peopling of the earth does not proceed very rapidly, we have undoubtedly some reason to believe that this law is not too powerful for its apparent object. The desire of the means of subsistence would be comparatively confined in its effects, and would fail of producing that general activity so necessary to the improvement of the human faculties, were it not for the strong and universal effort of population to increase with greater rapidity than its supplies. If these two tendencies were exactly balanced, I do not see what motive there would be sufficiently strong to overcome the acknowledged indolence of man, and make him proceed in the cultivation of the soil. The population of any large territory, however fertile, would be as likely to stop at five hundred, or five thousand, as at five millions, or fifty millions. Such a balance, therefore, would clearly defeat one great purpose of creation; and if the question be merely a question of degree, a question of a little more or a little less strength, we may fairly distrust our competence to judge of the precise quantity necessary to answer the object with the smallest sum of incidental evil. In the present state of things we appear to have under our guidance a great power, capable of peopling a desert region in a small number of years; and yet, under other circumstances, capable of being confined by human energy and virtue to any limits, however narrow, at the expense of a small comparative quantity of evil. The analogy of all the other laws of nature would be completely violated, if in this instance alone there were no provision for accidental failures, no resources against the vices of mankind, or the partial mischiefs resulting from other general laws. To effect the apparent object without any attendant evil, it is evident that a perpetual change in the law of increase would be

12 [In 1806 this qualification, *at least to a considerable degree*, was omitted.]

necessary, varying with the varying circumstances of each country. But instead of this, it is not only more consonant to the analogy of the other parts of nature, but we have reason to think that it is more conducive to the formation and improvement of the human mind, that the law should be uniform, and the evils, incidental to it under certain circumstances, be left to be mitigated or removed by man himself. His duties in this case vary with his situation; he is thus kept more alive to the consequences of his actions; and his faculties have evidently greater play, and opportunity of improvement, than if the evil were removed by a perpetual change of the law according to circumstances.

Even if from passions too easily subdued, or the facility of illicit intercourse, a state of celibacy were a matter of indifference, and not a state of some privation, the end of nature in the peopling of the earth would be apparently liable to be defeated. It is of the very utmost importance to the happiness of mankind, that they[13] should not increase too fast; but it does not appear that the object to be accomplished would admit of any very considerable diminution in the desire of marriage. It is clearly the duty of each individual not to marry till he has a prospect of supporting his children; but it is at the same time to be wished that he should retain undiminished his desire of marriage, in order that he may exert himself to realize this prospect, and be stimulated to make provision for the support of greater numbers.

It is evidently, therefore, regulation and direction which are required with regard to the principle of population, not diminution or alteration. And if moral restraint be the only virtuous mode of avoiding the incidental evils arising from this principle, our obligation to practise it will evidently rest exactly upon the same foundation as our obligation to practise any of the other virtues, the foundation of utility.[14]

[15]●Whatever indulgence we may be disposed to allow to occasional

---

[13] [In 1817 this was altered to:
    ... that population should not increase too fast; ...]
[14] [In 1817 *the foundation of utility* was excised.]
[15] [This paragraph was revised twice. In 1806 it read:
    ... difficulty; yet of the strict line of duty we cannot doubt. Our obligation not to marry till we have a fair prospect of being able to support our children will appear to deserve the attention of the moralist, if it can be proved that an attention to this obligation ...
[In 1807 Malthus altered the original passage again:
    ... an attention to this obligation is of most powerful effect in the prevention of misery; and that if it were the general custom to follow the first impulse of nature
    . . .

failures in the discharge of a duty of acknowledged difficulty; yet of the strict line of duty, during the period of celibacy, whatever that may be, we cannot doubt. And with regard to the necessity of this celibacy in countries that have been long peopled, or our obligation not to marry till we have a fair prospect of being able to support our children, it will appear to deserve the attention of the moralist, if it can be proved that an attention to this obligation is of more effect in the prevention of misery than all the other virtues combined; and that if, in violation of this duty, it were the general custom to follow the first impulse of nature, and marry at the age of puberty, the universal prevalence of every known virtue in the greatest conceivable degree would fail of rescuing society from the most wretched and desperate state of want, and all the diseases and famines which usually accompany it.●[15]

[The excision of the *period of celibacy* in 1806 may have been a concession to reviewers, who declared that it was an impossibility; the affirmation that delayed marriage might prevent misery more effectively than all the other virtues combined was possibly expunged in 1807 after theological discussions with friends, at the East India College and elsewhere.]

Of the Effects which would result to Society from the general practice of this virtue[1]

One of the principal reasons which has prevented an assent to the doctrine, of the constant tendency of population to increase beyond the means of subsistence, is a great unwillingness to believe that the Deity would, by the laws of nature, bring beings into existence which, by the laws of nature, could not be supported in that existence. But if, in addition to that general activity and direction of our industry put in motion by these laws, we further consider that the incidental evils arising from them are constantly directing our attention to the proper check to population, moral restraint; and if it appear that by a strict obedience to those duties which are pointed out to us by the light of nature and reason, and are confirmed and sanctioned by revelation, these evils may be avoided, the objection will, I trust, be removed, and all apparent imputation on the goodness of the Deity be done away.

The heathen moralists never represented happiness as attainable on earth, but through the medium of virtue; and among their virtues, prudence ranked in the first class, and by some was even considered as including every other. The Christian religion places our present as well as future happiness in the exercise of those virtues which tend to fit us for a state of superior enjoyment; and the subjection of the passions to the guidance of reason, which, if not the whole, is a principal branch of prudence, is in consequence most particularly inculcated.

If, for the sake of illustration, we might be permitted to draw a picture of society, in which each individual endeavoured to attain happiness by the strict fulfilment of those duties, which the most enlightened of the ancient philosophers deduced from the laws of nature, and which have been directly taught, and received such powerful sanctions in the moral code of Christianity, it would present a very different scene from that which we now contemplate. Every act which was prompted by the desire

---

[1] [In 1806 this chapter was headed 'Of the Effects which would result to Society from the Prevalence of this Virtue'. In 1817 it was changed again to 'Of the Effects which would result to Society from the Prevalence of Moral Restraint'.]

of immediate gratification, but which threatened an ultimate overbalance of pain, would be considered as a breach of duty; and, consequently no man, whose earnings were only sufficient to maintain two children, would put himself in a situation in which he might have to maintain four or five, however he might be prompted to it by the passion of love. This prudential restraint, if it were generally adopted, by narrowing the supply of labour in the market, would, in the natural course of things soon raise its price. The period of delayed gratification would be passed in saving the earnings which were above the wants of a single man, and in acquiring habits of sobriety, industry, and economy, which would enable him, in a few years, to enter into the matrimonial contract without fear of its consequences. The operation of the preventive check in this way, by constantly keeping the population within the limits of the food, though constantly following its increase, would give a real value to the rise of wages and the sums saved by labourers before marriage, very different from those forced advances in the price of labour, or arbitrary parochial donations which, in proportion to their magnitude and extensiveness, must of necessity be followed by a proportional advance in the price of provisions. As the wages of labour would thus be sufficient to maintain with decency a large family, and as every married couple would set out with a sum for contingencies, all squalid[2] poverty would be removed from society; or would at least be confined to a very few, who had fallen into misfortunes against which no prudence or foresight could provide.

The interval between the age of puberty and the period at which each individual might venture on marriage must, according to the supposition, be passed in strict chastity; because the law of chastity cannot be violated without producing evil. The effect of anything like a promiscuous intercourse, which prevents the birth of children, is evidently to weaken the best affections of the heart, and in a very marked manner to degrade the female character. And any other intercourse would, without improper arts, bring as many children into the society as marriage, with a much greater probability of their becoming a burden to it.

These considerations show that the virtue of chastity is not, as some have supposed, a forced produce of artificial society; but that it has the most real and solid foundation in nature and reason; being apparently

---

[2] [In 1817 *squalid* was changed to 'abject'.

the only virtuous means of avoiding the vice and misery which result[3] from the principle of population.

In such a society as we have been supposing, it might be necessary for both sexes[4] to pass many of the early years of life in the single state; and if this were general, there would certainly be room for a much greater number to marry afterwards, so that fewer, upon the whole, would be condemned to pass their lives in celibacy. If the custom of not marrying early prevailed generally, and if violations of chastity were equally dishonourable in both sexes, a more familiar and friendly intercourse between them might take place without danger. Two young people might converse together intimately, without its being immediately supposed that they either intended marriage or intrigue; and a much better opportunity would thus be given to both sexes of finding out kindred dispositions, and of forming those strong and lasting attachments, without which the married state is generally more productive of misery than of happiness. The earlier years of life would not be spent without love, though without the full gratification of it. The passion, instead of being extinguished, as it now too frequently is by early sensuality, would only be repressed for a time, that it might afterwards burn with a brighter, purer, and steadier flame; and the happiness of the married state, instead of an opportunity of immediate indulgence,[5] would be looked forward to as the prize of industry and virtue, and the reward of a genuine and constant attachment.[6]

The passion of love is a powerful stimulus in the formation of character, and often prompts to the most noble and generous exertions;

[3] [In 1806 this was amended to:
    ... which result so often from the principle of population.
[4] [In 1817 Malthus altered this to:
    ... for some of both sexes ...
[5] [In 1817 this was altered to:
    ... instead of only affording the means of immediate indulgence, would be ...
[6] Dr. Currie, in his interesting observations on the character and condition of the Scotch Peasantry, which he has prefixed to his life of Burns, remarks, with a just knowledge of human nature, that 'in appreciating the happiness and virtue of a community, there is perhaps no single criterion on which so much dependence may be placed, as the state of the intercourse between the sexes. Where this displays ardour of attachment, accompanied by purity of conduct, the character and the influence of women rise, our imperfect nature mounts in the scale of moral excellence; and, from the source of this single affection, a stream of felicity descends, which branches into a thousand rivulets, that enrich and adorn the field of life. Where the attachment between the sexes sinks into an appetite, the heritage of our species is comparatively poor, and man approaches to the condition of the brutes that perish.' Vol. i. p. 18.

but this is only when the affections are centred in one object; and generally, when full gratification is delayed by difficulties.[7] The heart is perhaps never so much disposed to virtuous conduct, and certainly at no time is the virtue of chastity so little difficult to men, as when under the influence of such a passion. Late marriages taking place in this way would be very different from those of the same name at present, where the union is too frequently prompted solely by interested views, and the parties meet, not unfrequently, with exhausted constitutions, and generally with exhausted affections. The late marriages at present are indeed principally confined to the men; and there are few, however advanced in life they may be, who, if they determine to marry, do not fix their choice on a very young wife.[8] A young woman without fortune, when she has passed her twenty-fifth year, begins to fear, and with reason, that she may lead a life of celibacy; and with a heart capable of forming a strong attachment, feels, as each year creeps on, her hopes of finding an object on which to rest her affections gradually diminishing, and the uneasiness of her situation aggravated by the silly and unjust prejudices of the world. If the general age of marriage among women were later, the period of youth and hope would be prolonged, and fewer would be ultimately disappointed.

That a change of this kind would be a most decided advantage to the more virtuous half of society, we cannot for a moment doubt. However impatiently the privation might be borne by the men, it would be supported by the women readily and cheerfully; and if they could look forwards with just confidence to marriage at twenty-eight or thirty,[9] I fully believe that, if the matter were left to their free choice, they would clearly prefer waiting till this period, to the being involved in all the cares of a large family at twenty-five. The most eligible age of marriage, however, could not be fixed; but must depend on circumstances and

[7] Dr. Currie observes, that the Scottish peasant, in the course of his passion, often exerts a spirit of adventure, of which a Spanish cavalier need not be ashamed. Burns' Works, vol. i. p. 16. It is not to be doubted, that this kind of romantic passion, which, Dr. C. says, characterizes the attachments of the humblest of the people of Scotland, and which has been greatly fostered by the elevation of mind given to them by a superior education, has had a most powerful and most beneficial influence on the national character.

[8] [In 1817 this was changed:
    ... men; of whom there are few, however advanced in life, who, if they determine to marry, do not fix their choice on a young wife.

[9] [In 1817 Malthus lowered the ages to
    ... twenty-seven or twenty-eight, ...

situation, and must be determined entirely by experience.[10] There is no period of human life at which nature more strongly prompts to an union of the sexes, than from seventeen or eighteen, to twenty. In every society above that state of depression which almost excludes reason and foresight, these early tendencies must necessarily be restrained; and if, in the actual state of things, such a restraint on the impulses of nature be found unavoidable, at what time can we be consistently released from it, but at that period, whatever it may be, when in the existing circumstances of the society a fair prospect presents itself of maintaining a family?

The difficulty of moral restraint, will perhaps be objected to this doctrine. To him who does not acknowledge the authority of the Christian religion, I have only to say that, after the most careful investigation, this virtue appears to be absolutely necessary, in order to avoid certain evils which would otherwise result from the general laws of nature. According to his own principles, it is his duty to pursue the greatest good consistent with these laws; and not to fail in this important end, and produce an overbalance of misery, by a partial obedience to some of the dictates of nature while he neglects others. The path of virtue, though it be the only path which leads to permanent happiness, has always been represented by the heathen moralists as of difficult ascent.

To the Christian I would say that the scriptures most clearly and precisely point it out to us as our duty, to restrain our passions within the bounds of reason; and it is a palpable disobedience of this law to indulge our desires in such a manner, as reason tells us, will unavoidably end in misery. The Christian cannot consider the difficulty of moral restraint as any argument against its being his duty; since in almost every page of the sacred writings, man is described as encompassed on all sides by temptations which it is extremely difficult to resist; and though no duties are enjoined which do not contribute to his happiness on earth as well as in a future state, yet an undeviating obedience is never represented as an easy task.

There is in general so strong a tendency to love in early youth, that it is extremely difficult, at this period, to distinguish a genuine from a transient passion. If the earlier years of life were passed by both sexes in moral restraint, from the greater facility that this would give to the meeting of kindred dispositions, it might even admit of a doubt whether

[10] [In 1806 this was altered to:
　　... but must depend entirely on circumstance and situation.

more happy marriages would not take place, and consequently more pleasure from the passion of love, than in a state such as that of America, the circumstances of which allow of a very early union of the sexes. But if we compare the intercourse of the sexes in such a society as I have been supposing, with that which now exists in Europe, taken under all its circumstances, it may safely be asserted that, independently of the load of misery which would be removed by the prevalence of moral restraint,[11] the sum of pleasurable sensations from the passion of love would be increased in a very great degree.

If we could suppose such a system general, the accession of happiness to society in its internal economy would scarcely be greater than in its external relations. It might fairly be expected that war, that great pest of the human race, would, under such circumstances, soon cease to extend its ravages so widely and so frequently, as it does at present,[12] and might ultimately perhaps cease entirely.

One of its first causes and most powerful impulses was undoubtedly an insufficiency of room and food; and, greatly as the circumstances of mankind have changed since it first began, the same cause still continues to operate and to produce, though in a smaller degree, the same effects. The ambition of princes would want instruments of destruction, if the distresses of the lower classes of people did not drive them under their standards. A recruiting serjeant always prays for a bad harvest and a want of employment, or, in other words, a redundant population.

In the earlier ages of the world, when war was the great business of mankind, and the drains of population from this cause were, beyond comparison, greater than in modern times, the legislators and statesmen of each country, adverting principally to the means of offence and defence, encouraged an increase of people in every possible way, fixed a stigma on barrenness and celibacy, and honoured marriage. The popular religions followed these prevailing opinions. In many countries the prolific power of nature was the object of solemn worship. In the religion of Mahomet, which was established by the sword, and the promulgation of which, in consequence, could not be unaccompanied by an extraordinary destruction of its followers, the procreation of children to glorify the Creator was laid down as one of the principal duties of man; and he who had the most numerous offspring was considered as having

---

[11] [In 1806 *by the prevalence of moral restraint* was excised.]

[12] [In 1806 this paragraph concluded with the words 'at present', the optimistic attitude being impossible to maintain while Napoleon was supreme in Europe.]

best answered the end of his creation. The prevalence of such moral sentiments had naturally a great effect in encouraging marriage; and the rapid procreation which followed, was partly the effect and partly the cause of incessant war. The vacancies occasioned by former desolations made room for the rearing of fresh supplies; and the overflowing rapidity, with which these supplies followed, constantly furnished fresh incitements and fresh instruments for renewed hostilities. Under the influence of such moral sentiments, it is difficult to conceive how the fury of incessant war should ever abate.

It is a pleasing confirmation of the truth and divinity of the Christian religion, and of its being adapted to a more improved state of human society, that it places our duties respecting marriage and the procreation of children in a different light from that in which they were before beheld.

Without entering minutely into the subject, which would evidently lead too far, I think it will be admitted, that if we apply the spirit of St. Paul's declarations respecting marriage to the present state of society, and the known constitution of our nature, the natural inference seems to be that, when marriage does not interfere with higher duties, it is right; when it does, it is wrong. According to the genuine principles of moral science: 'The method of coming at the will of God from the light of nature is to inquire into the tendency of the action to promote or diminish the general happiness.'[13] There are perhaps few actions that tend so directly to diminish the general happiness as to marry without the means of supporting children. He who commits this act, therefore, clearly offends against the will of God; and having become a burden on the society in which he lives, and plunged himself and family into a situation in which virtuous habits are preserved with more difficulty than in any other, he appears to have violated his duty to his neighbours and to himself, and thus to have listened to the voice of passion in opposition to his higher obligations.

In a society such as I have supposed, all the members of which endeavour to attain happiness by obedience to the moral code, derived from the light of nature, and enforced by strong sanctions in revealed religion, it is evident that no such marriages could take place; and the prevention of a redundant population, in this way, would remove one of the principal causes, and certainly the principal means of offensive

[13] Paley's Moral Philosophy, vol. i. b. ii. c. iv. p. 65.

war;[14] and at the same time tend powerfully to eradicate those two fatal political disorders, internal tyranny and internal tumult, which mutually produce each other.

Weak in offensive war,[15] in a war of defence such a society would be strong as a rock of adamant. Where every family possessed the necessaries of life in plenty, and a decent portion of its comforts and conveniences, there could not exist that hope of change, or at best that melancholy and disheartening indifference to it, which sometimes prompts the lower classes of people to say, 'let what will come, we cannot be worse off than we are now'.[16] Every heart and hand would be united to repel an invader, when each individual felt the value of the solid advantages which he enjoyed, and a prospect of change presented only a prospect of being deprived of them.

As it appears, therefore, that it is in the power of each individual to avoid all the evil consequences to himself and society resulting from the principle of population, by the practice of a virtue clearly dictated to him by the light of nature, and expressly enjoined in revealed religion; and as we have reason to think that the exercise of this virtue to a certain degree would rather tend to increase than diminish individual happiness; we can have no reason to impeach the justice of the Deity because his general laws make this virtue necessary, and punish our offences against it by the evils attendant upon vice, and the pains that accompany the various forms of premature death. A really virtuous society, such as I have supposed, would avoid these evils. It is the apparent object of the Creator to deter us from vice by the pains which accompany it, and to lead us to virtue by the happiness that it produces. This object appears to our conceptions to be worthy of a benevolent Creator. The laws of nature respecting population tend to promote this object. No imputation, therefore, on the benevolence of the Deity can be founded on these laws, which is not equally applicable to any of the evils necessarily incidental to an imperfect state of existence.

[14] [In 1806 this was changed to:
    ... remove one of the principal encouragements to offensive war; ...
[15] [In 1806 this was amended to:
    Indisposed to a war of offence, ...
[16] [This echoes a pamphlet of Malthus's tutor Gilbert Wakefield (1756–1801) who died of typhus after two years' imprisonment for writing it: *A Reply to some parts of the Bishop of Llandaff's Address to the People of Great Britain*. Wakefield affirmed that 'the lower orders of the community' would not fight a French invading army, because 'they cannot well be poorer, or made to work harder than they did before' (second edition, London, 1798, p. 33).]

CHAPTER III

Of the only effectual mode of improving the condition of the Poor

He who publishes a moral code, or system of duties, however firmly he may be convinced of the strong obligation on each individual strictly to conform to it, has never the folly to imagine that it will be universally or even generally practised. But this is no valid objection against the publication of the code. If it were, the same objection would always have applied; we should be totally without general rules; and to the vices of mankind arising from temptation would be added a much longer list, than we have at present, of vices from ignorance.

Judging merely from the light of nature, if we feel convinced of the misery arising from a redundant population on the one hand, and of the evils and unhappiness, particularly to the female sex, arising from promiscuous intercourse, on the other, I do not see how it is possible for any person, who acknowledges the principle of utility as the great foundation of morals,[1] to escape the conclusion that moral restraint, till we are in a condition to support a family, is the strict line of duty;[2] and when revelation is taken into the question, this duty undoubtedly receives very powerful confirmation. At the same time, I believe that few of my readers can be less sanguine in their expectations of any great change in the general conduct of men on this subject than I am;[3] and the chief reason why, in the last chapter, I allowed myself to suppose the universal prevalence of this virtue, was that I might endeavour to remove any imputation on the goodness of the Deity, by showing that the evils arising from the principle of population were exactly of the same nature

---

[1] [In 1817 this was altered to:
   ... utility as the great criterion of moral rules, ...

[2] [In 1806 Malthus changed this to:
   ... moral restraint, or the abstaining from marriage till we are in a condition to support a family, with a perfectly moral conduct during that period, is the strict line of duty; ...

[3] [In 1817 this sentence began:
   At the same time I believe that few of my readers can be less sanguine than I am in their expectations of any sudden and great change in the general conduct of men on this subject; and the chief reason ...

as the generality of other evils which excite fewer complaints, that they were increased by human ignorance and indolence, and diminished by human knowledge and virtue; and on the supposition, that each individual strictly fulfilled his duty, would be almost totally removed; and this without any general diminution of those sources of pleasure, arising from the regulated indulgence of the passions, which have been justly considered as the principal ingredients of human happiness.

If it will answer any purpose of illustration, I see no harm in drawing the picture of a society in which each individual is supposed strictly to fulfil his duties; nor does a writer appear to be justly liable to the imputation of being visionary, unless he make such universal or general obedience necessary to the practical utility of his system, and to that degree of moderate and partial improvement, which is all that can rationally be expected from the most complete knowledge of our duties.

But in this respect there is an essential difference between that improved state of society, which I have supposed in the last chapter, and most of the other speculations on this subject. The improvement there supposed, if we ever should make approaches towards it, is to be effected in the way in which we have been in the habit of seeing all the greatest improvements effected, by a direct application to the interest and happiness of each individual. It is not required of us to act from motives to which we are unaccustomed; to pursue a general good, which we may not distinctly comprehend, or the effect of which may be weakened by distance and diffusion. The happiness of the whole is to be the result of the happiness of individuals, and to begin first with them. No co-operation is required. Every step tells. He who performs his duty faithfully will reap the full fruits of it, whatever may be the number of others who fail. This duty is express, and intelligible to the humblest capacity.[4] It is merely that he is not to bring beings into the world for whom he cannot find the means of support. When once this subject is cleared from the obscurity thrown over it by parochial laws and private benevolence, every man must feel the strongest conviction of such an obligation. If he cannot support his children, they must starve; and if he marry in the face of a fair probability that he shall not be able to support his children, he is guilty of all the evils which he thus brings upon himself, his wife, and his offspring. It is clearly his interest, and will tend greatly to promote his happiness, to defer marrying till, by industry and

[4] [In 1807 this was altered to:
    This duty is intelligible to the humblest capacity.

economy, he is in a capacity to support the children that he may reasonably expect from his marriage; and as he cannot in the meantime gratify his passions without violating an express command of God, and running a great risk of injuring himself, or some of his fellow creatures, considerations of his own interest and happiness will dictate to him the strong obligation to moral restraint.[5]

However powerful may be the impulses of passion, they are generally in some degree modified by reason. And it does not seem entirely visionary to suppose that, if the true and permanent cause of poverty were clearly explained, and forcibly brought home to each man's bosom, it would have some, and perhaps not an inconsiderable, influence on his conduct; at least the experiment has never yet been fairly tried. Almost everything that has been hitherto done for the poor has tended, as if with solicitous care, to throw a veil of obscurity over this subject, and to hide from them the true cause of their poverty. When the wages of labour are hardly sufficient to maintain two children, a man marries and has five or six. He of course finds himself miserably distressed. He accuses the insufficiency of the price of labour to maintain a family. He accuses his parish for their tardy and sparing fulfilment of their obligation to assist him. He accuses the avarice of the rich, who suffer him to want what they can so well spare. He accuses the partial and unjust institutions of society, which have awarded him an inadequate share of the produce of the earth. He accuses perhaps the dispensations of Providence, which have assigned to him a place in society so beset with unavoidable distress and dependence. In searching for objects of accusation, he never adverts to the quarter from which all his misfortunes originate. The last person that he would think of accusing is himself, on whom, in fact, the whole of the blame lies,[6] except in as far as he has been deceived by the higher classes of society. He may perhaps wish that he had not married, because he now feels the inconveniences of it; but it never enters into his head that he can have done any thing wrong. He has always been told that to raise up subjects for his king and country is a very meritorious act. [7]●He has done this act, and yet is suffering for it. He naturally thinks that he is suffering for righteousness sake;●[7] and it cannot but strike him as most

[5] [In 1806 Malthus changed this to:
    ... strong obligation to a moral conduct while he remains unmarried.
[6] [In 1806 this was modified:
    ... on whom, in fact, the principal blame lies, ...
[7] [In 1817 this passage was altered:
    He has done this, and yet is suffering for it; and it cannot but strike him ...

extremely unjust and cruel in his king and country, to allow him thus to suffer, in return, for giving them what they are continually declaring that they particularly want.

Till these erroneous ideas have been corrected, and the language of nature and reason has been generally heard on the subject of population, instead of the language of error and prejudice, it cannot be said that any fair experiment has been made with the understandings of the common people; and we cannot justly accuse them of improvidence and want of industry, till they act as they do now, after it has been brought home to their comprehensions, that they are themselves the cause of their own poverty; that the means of redress are in their own hands, and in the hands of no other persons whatever; that the society in which they live, and the government which presides over it, are totally without power in this respect;[8] and that however ardently they may desire to relieve them, and whatever attempts they may make to do so, they are really and truly unable to execute what they benevolently wish, but unjustly promise; that when the wages of labour will not maintain a family, it is an incontrovertible sign that their king and country do not want more subjects, or at least that they cannot support them; that if they marry in this case, so far from fulfilling a duty to society, they are throwing a useless burden on it, at the same time that they are plunging themselves into distress; and that they are acting directly contrary to the will of God, and bringing down upon themselves various diseases, which might all, or in a great part,[9] have been avoided, if they had attended to the repeated admonitions which he gives, by the general laws of nature, to every being capable of reason.

Dr. Paley, in his Moral Philosophy, observes, that 'in countries in which subsistence is become scarce, it behoves the state to watch over the public morals with increased solicitude; for nothing but the instinct of nature, under the restraint of chastity, will induce men to undertake the labour, or consent to the sacrifice of personal liberty and indulgence, which the support of a family in such circumstances requires'.[10] That it is always the duty of a state to use every exertion, likely to be effectual, in discouraging vice and promoting virtue, and that no temporary circum-

---

[8] [In 1806 this was changed to:
    ... over it, are without any direct power in this respect; ...
[In 1817 the word *direct* was italicised.]
[9] [In 1806 this was changed to:
    ... which might all, or the greater part, have been avoided, ...
[10] Vol. ii. c. xi. p. 352.

stances ought to cause any relaxation in these exertions, is certainly true. The means therefore proposed are always good; but the particular end in view, in this case, appears to be absolutely criminal. We wish to force people into marriage when, from the acknowledged scarcity of subsistence, they will have little chance of being able to support their children. We might as well force people into the water who are unable to swim. In both cases we rashly tempt Providence. Nor have we more reason to believe that a miracle will be worked to save us from the misery and mortality resulting from our conduct, in the one case, than in the other.

The object of those who really wish to better the condition of the lower classes of society must be to raise the relative proportion between the price of labour and the price of provisions; so as to enable the labourer to command a larger share of the necessaries and comforts of life. We have hitherto principally attempted to attain this end by encouraging the married poor, and consequently increasing the number of labourers, and overstocking the market with a commodity which we still say that we wish to be dear. It would seem to have required no great spirit of divination to foretell the certain failure of such a plan of proceeding. There is nothing, however, like experience. It has been tried in many different countries, and for many hundred years, and the success has always been answerable to the nature of the scheme. It is really time now to try something else.

When it was found that oxygen, or pure vital air, would not cure consumptions, as was expected, but rather aggravated their symptoms, a trial was made of an air of the most opposite kind. I wish we had acted with the same philosophical[11] spirit in our attempts to cure the disease of poverty; and having found that the pouring in of fresh supplies of labour only tended to aggravate the symptoms, had tried what would be the effect of withholding a little these supplies.

In all old and fully-peopled states it is from this method, and this alone, that we can rationally expect any essential and permanent amelioration in the condition of the lower classes of people.[12]

In an endeavour to raise the proportion of the quantity of provisions to the number of consumers, in any country, our attention would naturally be first directed to the increasing of the absolute quantity of provisions; but finding that as fast as we did this, the number of consumers more

[11] [*Philosophical* at this period corresponded to the modern word 'scientific'.]
[12] [In 1826 this was altered to:
    . . . the condition of the labouring classes of the people.

than kept pace with it, and that, with all our exertions, we were still as far as ever behind, we should be convinced that our efforts, directed only in this way, would never succeed. It would appear to be setting the tortoise to catch the hare. Finding therefore that, from the laws of nature, we could not proportion the food to the population, our next attempt should naturally be to proportion the population to the food. If we can persuade the hare to go to sleep, the tortoise may have some chance of overtaking her.

We are not, however, to relax our efforts in increasing the quantity of provisions, but to combine another effort with it; that of keeping the population, when once it has been overtaken, at such a distance behind as to effect the relative proportion which we desire; and thus unite the two grand *desiderata*, a great actual population, and a state of society in which squalid poverty[13] and dependence are comparatively but little known; two objects which are far from being incompatible.

If we be really serious in what appears to be the object of such general research, the mode of essentially and permanently bettering the condition of the poor, we must explain to them the true nature of their situation, and show them that the withholding of the supplies of labour is the only possible way of really raising its price; and that they themselves, being the possessors of this commodity, have alone the power to do this.

I cannot but consider this mode of diminishing poverty as so perfectly clear in theory, and so invariably confirmed by the analogy of every other commodity which is brought to market, that nothing but its being shown to be calculated to produce greater evils than it proposes to remedy can justify us in not making the attempt to put it into execution.

13 [In 1817 *squalid* was changed to 'abject'.

CHAPTER IV

Objections to this mode considered

One objection, which perhaps will be made to this plan, is that from which alone it derives its value – a market rather understocked with labour. This must undoubtedly take place in a certain degree; but by no means in such a degree as to affect the wealth and prosperity of the country. [1]●The way in which we are going on at present, and the enormous increase in the price of provisions which seems to threaten us, will tend much more effectually to enable foreigners to undersell us in the markets of Europe, than the plan now proposed. If the population of this country were better proportioned to its food, the nominal price of labour might be lower than it is now, and yet be sufficient to maintain a wife and six children.●[1] But putting this subject of a market understocked with labour in the most unfavourable point of view, if the rich will not submit to a slight inconvenience necessarily attendant on the attainment of what they profess to desire, they cannot really be in earnest in their professions. Their benevolence to the poor must be either childish play or hypocrisy; it must be either to amuse themselves, or to pacify the minds of the common people with a mere show of attention to their wants. To wish to better the condition of the poor, by enabling them to command a greater quantity of the necessaries and comforts of life, and then to complain of high wages, is the act of a silly boy who gives away his cake and then cries for it. A market overstocked with labour, and an ample remuneration to each labourer, are objects perfectly incompatible with each other. In the annals of the world they never existed together; and to couple them, even in imagination, betrays a gross ignorance of the simplest principles of political economy.

A second objection that may be made to this plan is the diminution of population that it would cause. It is to be considered, however, that this diminution is merely relative; and when once this relative diminution had been effected, by keeping the population stationary, while the supply of food had increased, it might then start afresh, and continue increasing for ages, with the increase of food, maintaining always the same relative

[1] [In 1817 these two sentences were omitted.]

proportion to it.[2] I can easily conceive that this country, with a proper direction of the national industry, might, in the course of some centuries, contain two or three times its present population, and yet every man in the kingdom be much better fed and clothed than he is at present. While the springs of industry continue in vigour, and a sufficient part of that industry is directed to agriculture, we need be under no apprehensions of a deficient population; and nothing perhaps would tend so strongly to excite a spirit of industry and economy among the poor, as a thorough knowledge that their happiness must always depend principally upon themselves; and that, if they obey their passions in opposition to their reason, or be not industrious and frugal while they are single men,[3] to save a sum for the common contingencies of the married state, they must expect to suffer the natural evils which Providence has prepared for those who disobey its repeated admonitions.

A third objection which may be started to this plan, and the only one which appears to me to have any kind of plausibility, is that, by endeavouring to urge the duty of moral restraint on the poor, we may increase the quantity of vice relating to the sex.

I should be most extremely sorry to say anything which could either directly or remotely be construed unfavourably to the cause of virtue: but I certainly cannot think that the vices which relate to the sex, are the only vices which are to be considered in a moral question; or that they are even the greatest and most degrading to the human character. They can rarely or never be committed without producing unhappiness some-where or other, and therefore ought always to be strongly reprobated; but there are other vices, the effects of which are still more pernicious; and there are other situations which lead more certainly to moral offences than the refraining from marriage. Powerful as may be the temptations to a breach of chastity, I am inclined to think that they are impotent in comparison of the temptations arising from continued distress. A large class of women, and many men, I have no doubt, pass a considerable part of their lives in moral restraint;[4] but I believe there will be found very few, who pass through the ordeal of squalid and hopeless

---

[2] [In 1817 this read:
    ... always nearly the same relative proportion to it.
[3] [In 1817 the word *men* was excised.]
[4] [In 1806 *in moral restraint* was changed to:
    ... in chastity; ...
    [In 1807 this was altered again to:
    ... pass a considerable part of their lives consistently with the laws of chastity; ...

poverty, or even of long continued embarrassed circumstances, without a considerable[5] moral degradation of character.

In the higher and middle classes of society it is a melancholy and distressing sight to observe, not unfrequently, a man of a noble and ingenuous disposition, once feelingly alive to a sense of honour and integrity, gradually sinking under the pressure of circumstances, making his excuses at first with a blush of conscious shame, afraid of seeing the faces of his friends from whom he may have borrowed money, reduced to the meanest tricks and subterfuges to delay or avoid the payment of his just debts; till ultimately grown familiar with falsehood, and at enmity with the world, he loses all the grace and dignity of man.

To the general prevalence of indigence, and the extraordinary encouragements which we afford in this country to a total want of foresight and prudence among the common people,[6] is to be attributed the principal part of those continual depredations on property, and other more atrocious crimes, which drives us to the painful resource of such a number of executions.[7] According to Mr. Colquhoun, above twenty thousand miserable individuals of various classes rise up every morning without knowing how, or by what means, they are to be supported during the passing day, or where, in many instances, they are to lodge on the succeeding night.[8] It is by these unhappy persons that the principal depredations on the public are committed; and supposing but few of them to be married, and driven to these acts from the necessity of supporting their children; yet still it will not cease to be true[9] that the too great frequency of marriage among the poorest classes is one of the

---

[5] [In 1807 *considerable* was changed to 'great'.

[6] Mr. Colquhoun, speaking of the poor laws, observes that 'in spite of all the ingenious arguments which have been used in favour of a system, admitted to be wisely conceived in its origin, the effects it has produced incontestably prove that, with respect to the mass of the poor, there is something radically wrong in the execution. If it were not so, it is impossible that there could exist in the metropolis such an inconceivable portion of human misery amidst examples of munificence and benevolence unparalleled in any age or country.' Police of Metropolis, c. xiii. p. 359.

[7] In the effects of the poor laws, I fully agree with Mr. Colquhoun; but I cannot agree with him in admitting that the system was well conceived in its origin. I attribute still more evil to the original ill conception than to the subsequent ill execution.

Mr. Colquhoun observes, that: 'Indigence, in the present state of society, may be considered as a principal cause of the increase of crimes.' Police of Metropolis, c. xiii. p. 352.

[8] Id. c. xi. p. 313.

[9] [In 1817 this was changed to:

... yet still it is probably true that the too great frequency of marriage ...

principal causes of the temptations to these crimes. A considerable part
of these unhappy wretches will probably be found to be the offspring of
such marriages, educated in workhouses where every vice is propagated,
or bred up at home in filth and rags, and with an utter ignorance of every
moral obligation.[10] A still greater part perhaps consists of persons who,
being unable for some time to get employment, owing to the full supply
of labour, have been urged to these extremities by their temporary wants,
and having thus lost their characters, are rejected even when their labour
may be wanted by the well-founded caution of civil society.[11]

When indigence does not produce overt acts of vice, it palsies every
virtue. Under the continued temptations to a breach of chastity, occasional failures may take place, and the moral sensibility, in other
respects, not be very strikingly impaired; but the continued temptations
which beset hopeless poverty, and the strong sense of injustice that
generally accompanies it from an ignorance of its true cause, tend so
powerfully to sour the disposition, to harden the heart, and deaden the

[10] Police of Metropolis, c. xi. p. 313 and c. xii. p. 355, 370.

[11] Police of the Metropolis, c. xiii. p. 353. et seq. In so large a town as London, which
must necessarily encourage a prodigious influx of strangers from the country, there
must be always a great many persons out of work; and it is possible that some public
institution for the relief of the casual poor, upon a plan similar to that proposed by
Mr. Colquhoun (c. xiii. p. 371.) might, under very judicious management, produce
more good than evil. But for this purpose it would be absolutely necessary that, if
work were provided by the institution, the sum that a man could earn by it should
be less than the worst paid common labour; otherwise the claimants would rapidly
increase, and the funds would soon be inadequate to their object. In the institution
at Hamburgh, which appears to have been the most successful of any yet established, the nature of the work was such that, though paid above the usual price, a
person could not easily earn by it more than eighteen pence a week. It was the
determined principle of the managers of the institution to reduce the support which
they gave lower than what any industrious man or woman in such circumstances
could earn. (Account of the management of the poor in Hamburgh, by C. Voght,
p. 18.) And it is to this principle that they attribute their success. It should be
observed, however, that neither the institution at Hamburgh, nor that planned by
Count Rumford in Bavaria, has subsisted long enough for us to be able to
pronounce on their permanent good effects. It will not admit of a doubt that
institutions for the relief of the poor, on their first establishment, remove a great
quantity of distress. The only question is whether, as succeeding generations arise,
the increasing funds necessary for their support, and the increasing numbers that
become dependent, are not greater evils than that which was to be remedied; and
whether the country will not ultimately be left with as much mendicity as before,
besides all the poverty and dependence accumulated in the public institutions. This
seems to be nearly the case in England at present. I do not believe[(a)] that we should
have more beggars if we had no poor laws.

[(a)] [In 1817 *I do not believe* was changed to:
    It may be doubted ...

moral sense that, generally speaking, virtue takes her flight clear away from the tainted spot, and does not often return.

Even with respect to the vices which relate to the sex, marriage has been found to be by no means a complete remedy. Among the higher classes, our Doctors Commons,[12] and the lives that many married men are known to lead, sufficiently prove this; and the same kind of vice, though not so much heard of among the lower classes of people, owing to their indifference and want of delicacy on these subjects,[13] is probably not very much less frequent.

Add to this, that squalid poverty,[14] particularly when joined with idleness, is a state the most unfavourable to chastity that can well be conceived. The passion is as strong, or nearly so, as in other situations, and every restraint on it, from personal respect, or a sense of morality, is generally removed. There is a degree of squalid poverty, in which, if a girl was brought up, I should say that her being really modest at twenty was an absolute miracle. Those persons must have extraordinary minds indeed, and such as are not usually formed under similar circumstances, who can continue to respect themselves when no other person whatever respects them. If the children thus brought up were even to marry at twenty, it is probable that they would have passed some years in vicious habits before that period.

If after all, however, these arguments should appear insufficient; if we reprobate the idea of endeavouring to encourage the virtues of moral restraint and prudence among the poor,[15] from a fear of producing vice; and if we think that to facilitate marriage by all possible means is a point of the first consequence to the morality and happiness of the people; let us act consistently and, before we proceed, endeavour to make ourselves acquainted with the mode by which alone we can effect our object.

[12] [*Doctors' Commons* originally meant the 'common table' (where simple set meals were provided) of the Association or College of Doctors of Civil Law in London, founded in 1509 and incorporated in 1768. In the buildings which became known as Doctors' Commons there were five 'courts'; they dealt with ecclesiastical law, including prosecution for heresy, Admiralty cases – frequently relating to prize money – and family matters such as the probate of wills, licences for marriage, and divorce suits.]

[13] [In 1817 these words were excised, and the passage read:
    ... lower classes of people, is probably in all our great towns not much less frequent.

[14] [In 1817 *squalid* was again changed to 'abject', as in ch. ii, n.2, and ch. iii, n.13.]

[15] [In 1806 this was altered:
    ... to encourage the virtue of moral restraint among the poor, ...

CHAPTER V

Of the consequences of pursuing the opposite mode

It is an evident truth that, whatever may be the rate of increase in the means of subsistence, the increase of population must be limited by it, at least after the food has once been divided into the smallest shares that will support life. All the children born, beyond what would be required to keep up the population to this level, must necessarily perish, unless room be made for them by the deaths of grown persons. It has appeared indeed clearly, in the course of this work, that in all old states the marriages and births depend principally upon the deaths, and that there is no encouragement to early unions so powerful as a great mortality. To act consistently, therefore, we should facilitate, instead of foolishly and vainly endeavouring to impede the operations of nature, in producing this mortality; and if we dread the too frequent visitation of the horrid form of famine, we should sedulously encourage the other forms of destruction which we compel nature to use. Instead of recommending cleanliness to the poor, we should encourage contrary habits. In our towns we should make the streets narrower, crowd more people into the houses, and court the return of the plague. In the country we should build our villages near stagnant pools, and particularly encourage settlements in all marshy and unwholesome situations.[1] But above all, we should reprobate specific remedies for ravaging diseases, and those benevolent, but much mistaken men, who have thought they were doing

---

[1] Necker, speaking of the proportion of the births in France, makes use of a new and instructive expression on this subject, though he hardly seems to be sufficiently aware of it himself. He says: 'Le nombre des naissances est a celui des habitans de un a vingt-trois et vingt-quatre dans le lieux *contrariés par la nature, ou par des circonstances morales*: ce meme rapport dans la plus grande partie de la France, est de un a 25, 25½, & 26.' Administ. des Finances, tom. i. c. ix. p. 254. 12mo. It would appear, therefore, that we had nothing more to do,[(a)] than to settle people in marshy situations, and oppress them by a bad government, in order to attain what politicians have hitherto considered as so desirable – a great proportion of marriages, and a great proportion of births. ['The proportion of births to the number of inhabitants is one to twenty-three or twenty-four in situations that are naturally unhealthy or socially unfavourable; the same ratio in the greater part of France is one to 25, 25½ or 26.']
[(a)] [In 1826 this sentence began:
    It appears, therefore, that we have nothing more to do ...

a service to mankind by projecting schemes for the total extirpation of particular disorders. If by these, and similar means, the annual mortality were increased from 1 in 36 or 40, to 1 in 18 or 20, we might probably every one of us marry at the age of puberty, and yet few be absolutely starved.

If, however, we all marry at this age, and yet still continue our exertions to impede the operations of nature, we may rest assured that all our efforts will be vain. Nature will not, nor cannot, be defeated in her purposes. The necessary mortality must come in some form or other; and the extirpation of one disease will only be the signal for the birth of another, perhaps more fatal. We cannot lower the waters of misery by pressing them down in different places which must necessarily make them rise somewhere else: the only way in which we can hope to effect our purpose is by drawing them off. To this course nature is constantly directing our attention by the chastisements which await a contrary conduct. These chastisements are more or less severe, in proportion to the degree in which her admonitions produce their intended effect. In this country, at present, these admonitions are by no means entirely neglected. The preventive check to population prevails to a considerable degree, and her chastisements are in consequence moderate: but if we were all to marry at the age of puberty, they would be severe indeed. Political evils would probably be added to physical. A people goaded by constant distress, and visited by frequent returns of famine, could not be kept down but by a cruel despotism. We should approach to the state of the people in Egypt or Abyssinia; and I would ask whether, in that case, it is probable that we should be more virtuous?

Physicians have long remarked the great changes which take place in diseases; and that, while some appear to yield to the efforts of human care and skill, others seem to become in proportion more malignant and fatal. Dr. William Heberden published, not long since, some valuable observations on this subject deduced from the London bills of mortality. In his preface, speaking of these bills, he says: 'the gradual changes they exhibit in particular diseases correspond to the alterations which in time are known to take place in the channels through which the great stream of mortality is constantly flowing'.[2] In the body of his work afterwards, speaking of some particular diseases, he observes with that candour which always distinguishes true science: 'It is not easy to give a satisfac-

---

[2] Observations on the Increase and Decrease of different Diseases. Preface, p. v. 4to. 1801.

tory reason for all the changes which may be observed to take place in the history of diseases. Nor is it any disgrace to physicians, if their causes are often so gradual in their operation, or so subtle, as to elude investigation.'[3]

I hope I shall not be accused of presumption, in venturing to suggest that, under certain circumstances, such changes must take place; and perhaps without any alteration in those proximate causes which are usually looked to on these occasions. If this should appear to be true, it will not seem extraordinary that the most skilful and scientific physicians, whose business it is principally to investigate proximate causes, should sometimes search for these causes in vain.

In a country which keeps its population at a certain standard, if the average number of marriages and births be given, it is evident, that the average number of deaths will also be given; and, to use Dr. Heberden's metaphor, the channels through which the great stream of mortality is constantly flowing will always convey off a given quantity. Now if we stop up any of these channels, it is perfectly clear that the stream of mortality must run with greater force through some of the other channels; that is, if we eradicate some diseases, others will become proportionally more fatal. In this case the only distinguishable cause is the damming up a necessary outlet of mortality.[4] Nature, in the attainment of her great purposes, seems always to seize upon the weakest part. If this part be made strong by human skill, she seizes upon the next weakest part, and so on in succession; not like a capricious deity, with an intention to sport with our suffering and constantly to defeat our labours; but like a kind though sometimes severe instructor, with the intention of teaching us to make all parts strong, and to chase vice and misery from the earth. In avoiding one fault we are too apt to run into some other; but we always find Nature faithful to her great object, at every false step we commit ready to admonish us of our errors, by the infliction of some physical or moral evil. If the prevalence of the preventive check to population, in a sufficient degree, were to remove many of those diseases which now afflict us, yet be accompanied by a considerable increase of the vice of promiscuous intercourse; it is probable that the disorders and unhappiness, the physical and moral evils arising from this vice, would increase in strength and degree; and,

---

[3] Id. p. 43.

[4] The way in which it operates is probably by increasing poverty, in consequence of a supply of labour too rapid for the demand.

admonishing us severely of our error, would point to the only line of conduct approved by nature, reason, and religion: abstinence from marriage till we can support our children, and chastity till that period arrives.

In the case just stated, in which the population and the number of marriages are supposed to be fixed, the necessity of a change in the mortality of some diseases, from the diminution or extinction of others, is capable of mathematical demonstration. The only obscurity which can possibly involve this subject arises from taking into consideration the effect that might be produced by a diminution of mortality in increasing the population, or in decreasing the number of marriages. That the removal of any of the particular causes of mortality can have no further effect upon population than the means of subsistence will allow; and that it has little or no influence on these means of subsistence is a fact of which, I hope, the reader is already convinced.[5] Of its operation in tending to prevent marriage, by diminishing the demand for fresh supplies of children, I have no doubt; and there is reason to think that it had this effect, in no inconsiderable degree, on the extinction of the plague, which had so long and so dreadfully ravaged this country. Dr. Heberden draws a striking picture of the favourable change observed in the health of the people of England since this period; and justly attributes it to the improvements which have gradually taken place, not only in London, but in all great towns; and in the manner of living throughout the kingdom, particularly with respect to cleanliness and ventilation.[6] But these causes would not have been adequate to the effect observed,[7] if they had not been accompanied by an increase of the preventive check; and probably the spirit of cleanliness, and better mode of living, which then began to prevail, by spreading more generally a decent and useful pride, principally contributed to this increase. The diminution in the number of marriages, however, was not sufficient to make up for the great decrease of mortality from the extinction of the plague, and the striking reduction of the deaths in the dysentery.[8] While these and some other disorders

---

[5] [In 1817 (Vol. III, pp. 133–4) this sentence was altered:
  ... than the means of subsistence will allow, and that it has no certain and necessary influence on these means of subsistence, are facts of which the reader must be already convinced.

[6] Observ. on Inc. and Dec. of Diseases, p. 35.

[7] [In 1806 this sentence began:
  But these causes would not have produced the effect observed, if they had not been accompanied ...

[8] Observ. on Inc. and Dec. of Diseases, p. 34.

became almost evanescent, consumption, palsy, apoplexy, gout, lunacy, and the small-pox, became more mortal.[9] The widening of these drains was necessary to carry off the population which still remained redundant, notwithstanding the increased operation of the preventive check, and the part which was annually disposed of and enabled to exist[10] by the increase of agriculture.

Dr. Haygarth, in the sketch of his benevolent plan for the extermination of the casual small-pox, draws a frightful picture of the mortality which has been occasioned by this distemper; attributes to it the slow progress of population; and makes some curious calculations on the favourable effects which would be produced, in this respect, by its extermination.[11] His conclusions, however, I fear, would not follow from his premises. I am far from doubting that millions and millions of human beings have been destroyed by the small-pox. But were its devastations, as Dr. Haygarth supposes, many thousand degrees greater than the plague,[12] I should still doubt whether the average population of the earth had been diminished by them a single unit.[13] The small-pox is certainly one of the channels, and a very broad one, which nature has opened for the last thousand years, to keep down the population to the level of the means of subsistence; but had this been closed, others would have become wider, or new ones would have been formed. In ancient times the mortality from war and the plague was incomparably greater than in modern. On the gradual diminution of this stream of mortality, the generation and almost universal prevalence of the small-pox is a great and striking instance of one of those changes in the channels of mortality, which ought to awaken our attention, and animate us to patient and persevering investigation. For my own part, I feel not the slightest doubt that, if the introduction of the cow-pox should extirpate the small-pox, and yet the number of marriages continue the same, we shall find a very perceptible difference in the increased mortality of some other diseases. Nothing could prevent this effect but a sudden start in our agriculture; and should this take place, which I fear we have not much reason to expect, it will not be owing[14] to the number of children saved from death by the cow-pox inoculation, but to the alarms occasioned among the

---

[9] Id. p. 36 et seq.   [10] [In 1806 *exist* was changed to 'subsist'.
[11] Vol. i. part ii. sect. v. and vi.
[12] Vol. i. part ii. s. viii p 164.   [13] [In 1806 *a single unit* was excised.]
[14] [In 1817 this sentence was altered:
    ... agriculture; and if this should take place, it will not be so much owing ...

people of property by the late scarcities,[15] and to the increased gains of farmers, which have been so absurdly reprobated. I am strongly, however, inclined to believe that the number of marriages will not, in this case, remain the same; but that the gradual light which may be expected to be thrown on this interesting topic of human inquiry will teach us how to make the extinction of a mortal disorder a real blessing to us, a real improvement in the general health and happiness of the society.

If, on contemplating the increase of vice which might contingently follow an attempt to inculcate the duty of moral restraint, and the increase of misery that must necessarily follow the attempts to encourage marriage and population, we come to the conclusion not to interfere in any respect, but to leave every man to his own free choice, and responsible only to God for the evil which he does in either way; this is all I contend for; I would on no account do more; but I contend that at present we are very far from doing this.

Among the lower classes,[16] where the point is of the greatest importance, the poor laws afford a direct, constant, and systematical encouragement to marriage, by removing from each individual that heavy responsibility, which he would incur by the laws of nature, for bringing beings into the world which he could not support. Our private benevolence has the same direction as the poor laws, and almost invariably tends to facilitate the rearing of families,[17] and to equalize, as much as possible, the circumstances of married and single men.

Among the higher classes of people, the superior distinctions which married women receive, and the marked inattentions to which single women of advanced age are exposed, enable many men, who are agreeable neither in mind or person, and are besides in the wane of life, to choose a partner among the young and fair instead of being confined, as nature seems to dictate, to persons of nearly their own age and accomplishments. It is scarcely to be doubted that the fear of being an old maid, and of that silly and unjust ridicule, which folly sometimes

---

[15] [In 1817 a footnote was added here:

The scarce harvests of 1799 and 1800. The start here alluded to, certainly took place from 1801 to 1814, and provision was really made for the diminished mortality.

[16] [In 1817 this was altered to:

Among the lower classes of society, . . .

[17] [In 1817 this was changed to:

. . . and almost invariably tends to encourage marriage, and to equalize, as much as possible, . . .

attaches to this name, drives many women into the marriage union with men whom they dislike or, at best to whom they are perfectly indifferent. Such marriages must to every delicate mind appear little better than legal prostitutions; and they often burden the earth with unnecessary children, without compensating for it by an accession of happiness and virtue to the parties themselves.

Throughout all the ranks of society, the prevailing opinions respecting the duty and obligation of marriage cannot but have a very powerful influence. The man who thinks that, in going out of the world without leaving representatives behind him, he shall have failed in an important duty to society, will be disposed to force rather than to repress his inclinations on this subject; and when his reason represents to him the difficulties attending a family, he will endeavour not to attend to these suggestions, will still determine to venture, and will hope that, in the discharge of what he conceives to be his duty, he shall not be deserted by Providence.

In a civilized country, such as England, where a taste for the decencies and comforts of life prevails among a very large class of people, it is not possible that the encouragements to marriage from positive institutions and prevailing opinions should entirely obscure the light of nature and reason on this subject; but still they contribute to make it comparatively weak and indistinct. And till this obscurity is entirely removed, and the poor are undeceived with respect to the principal cause of their past poverty, and taught to know that their future happiness or misery must depend chiefly upon themselves, it cannot be said that, with regard to the great question of marriage or celibacy, we leave every man to his own free and fair choice.[18]

---

[18] [This sentence was amended three times. In 1806 Malthus omitted *or celibacy*, so that the final words were:

 ... with regard to the great question of marriage, we leave every man ...

[In 1817 the sentence began:

 And till this obscurity is removed, and the poor are undeceived with respect to the principal cause of their poverty, and taught to know ...

[In 1826 the word *future* was expunged, like the word *past* in 1817:

 ... taught to know that their happiness or misery must depend chiefly upon themselves, ...

CHAPTER VI

Effect of the knowledge of the principal cause of poverty on Civil Liberty[1]

It may appear, perhaps, that a doctrine, which attributes the greatest part of the sufferings of the lower classes of society exclusively to themselves, is unfavourable to the cause of liberty; as affording a tempting opportunity to governments of oppressing their subjects at pleasure, and laying the whole blame on the laws of nature and the imprudence of the poor. We are not, however, to trust to first appearances; and I am strongly disposed to believe that those who will be at the pains to consider this subject deeply, will be convinced that nothing would so powerfully contribute to the advancement of rational freedom as a thorough knowledge, generally circulated, of the principal cause of poverty; and that the ignorance of this cause, and the natural consequences of this ignorance, form, at present, one of the chief obstacles to its progress.

The pressure of distress on the lower classes of people, together with the habit of attributing this distress to their rulers, appears to me to be the rock of defence, the castle, the guardian spirit of despotism. It affords to the tyrant the fatal and unanswerable plea of necessity. It is the reason why every free government tends constantly to destruction; and that its

[1] [The cherished British ideal of civil liberty was at this period a subject of violent debate. Civil liberty included free speech (which involved freedom of the press, freedom of association and assembly, and freedom to correspond overseas) as well as the equality of all classes before the law, and the old right of *Habeas Corpus*, which was interpreted as meaning no imprisonment without a public trial. The Act of Parliament embodying the principle of *Habeas Corpus* was passed in 1679; in times of emergency, such as the Jacobite rebellion of 1745, the Habeas Corpus Act was suspended.

British liberty was sustained by a hereditary House of Lords and a House of Commons elected by a very limited number of voters; their franchise was determined by the chances of local history even more than by a property qualification. Inevitably there was agitation for reform, and William Pitt, as Prime Minister, had tried in vain to effect a small re-distribution of seats in the Commons in 1785. The whole situation was transformed by the French Revolution of 1789; fears of invasion, and of insurrection at home, led to repressive measures by the government, and Pitt suspended the Habeas Corpus Act in 1794, for the first time since 1745. At the turn of the century a serious shortage of food intensified the general unrest, and bread riots were widespread.

appointed guardians become daily less jealous of the encroachments of power. It is the reason why so many noble efforts in the cause of freedom have failed, and why almost every revolution, after long and painful sacrifices, has terminated in a military despotism. While any dissatisfied man of talents has power to persuade the lower classes of people that all their poverty and distress arise solely from the iniquity of the government, though perhaps the greatest part of what they suffer is totally unconnected with this cause, it is evident that the seeds of fresh discontent and fresh revolutions are continually sowing. When an established government has been destroyed, finding that their poverty is not removed, their resentment naturally falls upon the successors to power; and when these have been immolated without producing the desired effect, other sacrifices are called for, and so on without end. Are we to be surprised that, under such circumstances, the majority of well-disposed people, finding that a government with proper restrictions is unable to support itself against the revolutionary spirit, and weary and exhausted with perpetual change, to which they can see no end, should give up the struggle in despair, and throw themselves into the arms of the first power which can afford them protection against the horrors of anarchy?

A mob, which is generally the growth of a redundant population, goaded by resentment for real sufferings, but totally ignorant of the quarter from which they originate, is of all monsters the most fatal to freedom. It fosters a prevailing tyranny, and engenders one where it was not; and though, in its dreadful fits of resentment, it appears occasionally to devour its unsightly offspring; yet no sooner is the horrid deed committed, than, however unwilling it may be to propagate such a breed, it immediately groans with the pangs of[2] a new birth.

Of the tendency of mobs to produce tyranny, we may not be long[3] without an example in this country. As a friend to freedom, and an enemy to large standing armies, it is with extreme reluctance that I am compelled to acknowledge that, had it not been for the organized force in the country,[4] the distresses of the people during the late scarcities,[5]

---

[2] [In 1806 *the pangs of* were excised.]
[3] [In 1817 this was changed to:
      ... we may not, perhaps, be long without an example in this country.
[4] [In 1806 Malthus made two alterations to this sentence:
      As a friend to freedom, and naturally an enemy to large standing armies ... I am compelled to acknowledge that, had it not been for the great organized force in the country, ...
[5] [In 1817 a footnote was added here:
      1800 and 1801.

encouraged by the extreme ignorance and folly of many among the higher classes, might have driven them to commit the most dreadful outrages, and ultimately to involve the country in all the horrors of famine. Should such periods often recur (a recurrence which we have too much reason to apprehend from the present state of the country) the prospect which opens to our view is melancholy in the extreme. The English constitution will be seen hastening with rapid strides to the *Euthanasia* foretold by Hume, unless its progress be interrupted by some popular commotion; and this alternative presents a picture still more appalling to the imagination. If political discontents were blended with the cries of hunger, and a revolution were to take place by the instrumentality of a mob clamouring for want of food, the consequences would be unceasing change and unceasing carnage, the bloody career of which nothing but the establishment of some complete despotism could arrest.

We can scarcely believe that the appointed guardians of British liberty should quietly have acquiesced in those gradual encroachments of power, which have taken place of late years, but from the apprehension of these still more dreadful evils. Great as has been the influence of corruption, I cannot yet think so meanly of the country gentlemen of England as to believe that they would thus have given up a part of their birthright of liberty, if they had not been actuated by a real and genuine fear that it was then in greater danger from the people than from the crown. They appeared to surrender themselves to government on condition of being protected from the mob; but they never would have made this melancholy and disheartening surrender, if such a mob had not existed either in reality or in imagination. That the fears on this subject were artfully exaggerated, and increased beyond the limits of just apprehension, is undeniable; but I think it is also undeniable that the frequent declamation which was heard against the unjust institutions of society, and the delusive arguments on equality which were circulated among the lower classes, gave us just reason to suppose that, if the *vox populi* had been allowed to speak, it would have appeared to be the voice of error and absurdity instead of the *vox Dei*.[6]

---

[6] [*Vox populi, vox Dei*, the voice of the people is the voice of God, was a Latin maxim cited in England from the fifteenth century onwards.

The whole of the above paragraph is reminiscent of a pamphlet Malthus wrote in 1796 but never published, and of which only fragmentary quotations survive: it was called *The Crisis, a View of the Present Interesting State of Great Britain, by a Friend to the Constitution*. Malthus's younger colleague at the East India College, William Empson, referred to this pamphlet in his article on the 'Life, Writings and Character

To say that our conduct is not to be regulated by circumstances is to betray an ignorance of the most solid and incontrovertible principles of morality. Though the admission of this principle may sometimes afford a cloak to changes of opinion that do not result from the purest motives; yet the admission of a contrary principle would be productive of infinitely worse consequences. The phrase of 'existing circumstances' has, I believe, not unfrequently created a smile in the English House of Commons; but the smile should have been reserved for the application of the phrase, and not have been excited by the phrase itself. A very frequent repetition of it has indeed, of itself, rather a suspicious air; and its application should always be watched with the most jealous and anxious attention; but no man ought to be judged *in limine*[7] for saying that existing circumstances had obliged him to alter his opinions and conduct. The country gentlemen were perhaps too easily convinced that existing circumstances called upon them to give up some of the most valuable privileges of Englishmen; but, as far as they were really convinced of this obligation, they acted consistently with the clearest rule of morality.

The degree of power to be given to the civil government, and the measure of our submission to it, must be determined by general expediency; and in judging of this expediency, every circumstance is to be taken into consideration; particularly the state of public opinion, and the degree of ignorance and delusion prevailing among the common people. The patriot, who might be called upon by the love of his country to join with heart and hand in a rising of the people for some specific attainable object of reform, if he knew that they were enlightened respecting their

of Mr. Malthus' in the *Edinburgh Review* for January 1837, Vol. LXIV, p. 479. According to Empson, Malthus wrote that: 'In the country gentleman of 1796, it is impossible to recognize that old and noble character, the jealous guardian of British freedom.' Malthus went on:

> It appears to me that nothing can save the Constitution but the revival of the true Whig principles in a body of the community sufficiently numerous and powerful to snatch the object of contention from the opposing factions. In the Portland party, it is in vain to look for a revival, fettered with blue ribbands, secretaryships and military commands: freedom of action may be as soon expected from prisoners in chains. ... The only hope that Great Britain has, is in the returning sense and reason of the country gentleman, and middle classes of society, which may influence the legislature to adopt the safe and enlightened policy of removing the weight of the objections to our constitution by diminishing the truth of them.

7 [*In limine* means literally 'on the threshold', but it was used in Latin for 'at the outset' or 'initially'.]

own situation, and would stop short when they had attained their demand, would be called upon by the same motive to submit to very great oppression, rather than give the slightest countenance to a popular tumult, the members of which (at least the greater number of them) were persuaded that the destruction of the Parliament, the Lord Mayor, and the monopolizers, would make bread cheap, and that a revolution would enable them all to support their families. In this case, it is more the ignorance and delusion of the lower classes of people that occasions the oppression, than the actual disposition of the government to tyranny.

That there is, however, in all power a constant tendency to encroach is an incontrovertible truth, and cannot be too strongly inculcated. The checks which are necessary to secure the liberty of the subject will always, in some degree, embarrass and delay the operations of the executive government. The members of this government feeling these inconveniences, while they are exerting themselves, as they conceive, in the service of their country, and conscious, perhaps, of no ill intention towards the people, will naturally be disposed on every occasion to demand the suspension or abolition of these checks; but if once the convenience of ministers be put into competition with the liberties of the people, and we get into a habit of relying on fair assurances and personal character, instead of examining, with the most scrupulous and jealous care, the merits of each particular case, there is an end of British freedom. If we once admit the principle that the government must know better with regard to the quantity of power which it wants, than we can possibly do with our limited means of information, and that therefore it is our duty to surrender up our private judgments, we may just as well, at the same time, surrender up the whole of our constitution. Government is a quarter in which liberty is not, nor cannot be, very faithfully preserved. If we are wanting to ourselves, and inattentive to our great interests in this respect, it is the height of folly and unreasonableness, to expect that government will attend to them for us. Should the British constitution ultimately lapse into a despotism, as has been prophesied, I shall think that the country gentlemen of England will have really[8] much more to answer for than the ministers.

To do the country gentlemen justice, however, I should readily acknowledge that, in the partial desertion of their posts as guardians of British freedom, which has already taken place, they have been actuated

---

[8] [In 1817 the word *really* was excised.]

more by fear than treachery.[9] And the principal reason of this fear was, I conceive, the ignorance and delusions of the common people, and the prospective horrors which were contemplated if, in such a state of mind, they should by any revolutionary movement obtain an ascendant.

The circulation of Paine's Rights of Man, it is supposed, has done great mischief among the lower and middling classes of people in this country. This is probably true; but not because man is without rights, or that these rights ought not to be known; but because Mr. Paine has fallen into some fundamental errors respecting the principles of government, and in many important points has shown himself totally unacquainted with the structure of society, and the different moral effects to be expected from the physical difference between this country and America. Mobs, of the same description as those collections of people known by this name in Europe, could not exist in America. The number of people without property is there, from the physical state of the country, comparatively small; and therefore the civil power which is to protect property cannot require the same degree of strength. Mr. Paine very justly observes that whatever the apparent cause of any riots may be, the real one is always want of happiness; but when he goes on to say it shows that something is wrong in the system of government, that injures the felicity by which society is to be preserved, he falls into the common error of attributing all want of happiness to government. It is evident that this want of happiness might have existed, and from ignorance might have been the principal cause of the riots, and yet be almost wholly unconnected with any of the proceedings of government. The redundant population of an old state furnishes materials of unhappiness unknown to such a state as that of America; and if an attempt were to be made to remedy this unhappiness, by distributing the produce of the taxes to the poorer classes of society, according to the plan proposed by Mr. Paine, the evil would be aggravated a hundred fold, and in a very short time no sum that the society could possibly raise would be adequate to the proposed object.

Nothing would so effectually counteract the mischiefs occasioned by Mr. Paine's Rights of Man as a general knowledge of the real rights of man. What these rights are, it is not my business at present to explain; but there is one right which man has generally been thought to possess, which I am confident he neither does, nor can possess – a right to

[9] [In 1806 *treachery* was replaced by 'corruption'.

subsistence when his labour will not fairly purchase it. Our laws indeed say that he has this right, and bind the society to furnish employment and food to those who cannot get them in the regular market; but in so doing, they attempt to reverse the laws of nature; and it is in consequence to be expected, not only that they should fail in their object, but that the poor who were intended to be benefited, should suffer most cruelly from this inhuman deceit which is practised upon them.

[10]●A man who is born into a world already possessed, if he cannot get subsistence from his parents on whom he has a just demand, and if the society do not want his labour, has no claim of *right* to the smallest portion of food, and, in fact, has no business to be where he is. At nature's mighty feast there is no vacant cover for him. She tells him to be gone, and will quickly execute her own orders, if he do not work upon the compassion of some of her guests. If these guests get up and make room for him, other intruders immediately appear demanding the same favour. The report of a provision for all that come fills the hall with numerous claimants. The order and harmony of the feast is disturbed, the plenty that before reigned is changed into scarcity; and the happiness of the guests is destroyed by the spectacle of misery and dependence in every part of the hall, and by the clamorous importunity of those who are justly enraged at not finding the provision which they had been taught to expect. The guests learn too late their error, in counteracting those strict orders to all intruders, issued by the great mistress of the feast, who, wishing that all her guests should have plenty, and knowing that she could not provide for unlimited numbers, humanely refused to admit fresh comers when her table was already full.●[10]

The Abbé Raynal has said, that: 'Avant toutes les loix sociales l'homme avoit le droit de subsister!'[11] He might with just as much propriety have said that, before the institution of social laws, every man had a right to live a hundred years. Undoubtedly he had then, and has still, a good right to live a hundred years, nay, a thousand *if he can*, without interfering with the right of others to live; but the affair in both cases is principally an affair of power, not of right. Social laws very greatly increase this power, by enabling a much greater number to subsist than could subsist without them, and so far very greatly enlarge *le droit de subsister*; but neither before nor after the institution of social laws

[10] [In 1806 this famous paragraph was omitted.]

[11] Raynal, Hist. des Indes, vol. x. s. x. p. 322. 8vo. 'Before any laws were made, man had the right to eat, to keep himself alive.'

could an unlimited number subsist; and before, as well as since, he who ceased to have the power ceased to have the right.

If the great truths on these subjects were more generally circulated, and the lower classes of people could be convinced that, by the laws of nature, independently of any particular institutions, except the great one of property, which is absolutely necessary in order to attain any considerable produce, no person has any claim of right[12] on society for subsistence, if his labour will not purchase it, the greatest part of the mischievous declamation on the unjust institutions of society would fall powerless to the ground. The poor are by no means inclined to be visionary. Their distresses are always real, though they are not attributed to the real causes. If these real causes were properly explained to them, and they were taught to know how small a part of their present distress was attributable to government, and how great a part to causes totally unconnected with it,[13] discontent and irritation among the lower classes of people would show themselves much less frequently than at present; and when they did show themselves, would be much less to be dreaded. The efforts of turbulent and discontented men in the middle classes of society might safely be disregarded, if the poor were so far enlightened respecting the real nature of their situation, as to be aware that, by aiding them in their schemes of renovation, they would probably be promoting the ambitious views of others without in any respect benefiting themselves. And the country gentlemen and men of property in England might securely return to a wholesome jealousy of the encroachments of power; and instead of daily sacrificing the liberties of the subject on the altar of public safety, might, without any just apprehension from the people, not only tread back their late steps, but firmly insist upon those gradual reforms which the lapse of time, and the storms of circumstances,[14] have rendered necessary, to prevent the gradual destruction of the British constitution.

All improvements in government must necessarily originate with persons of some education, and these will of course be found among the people of property. Whatever may be said of a few, it is impossible to

[12] [In 1806 the word *right* was italicised.]

[13] [In 1817 this sentence began:

If these causes were properly explained to them, and they were taught to know what part of their present distress was attributable to government, and what part to causes totally unconnected with it, discontent and irritation ...

[14] [In 1806 this was altered to:

... and the storms of the political world, ...

suppose that the great mass of the people of property should be really interested in the abuses of government. They merely submit to them, from the fear that an endeavour to remove them might be productive of greater evils. Could we but take away this fear, reform and improvement would proceed with as much facility as the removal of nuisances,[15] or the paving and lighting of the streets. In human life we are continually called upon to submit to a lesser evil in order to avoid a greater; and it is the part of a wise man to do this readily and cheerfully; but no wise man will submit to any evil if he can get rid of it without danger. Remove all apprehension from the tyranny or folly of the people, and the tyranny of government could not stand a moment. It would then appear in its proper deformity, without palliation, without pretext, without protector. Naturally feeble in itself, when it was once stripped naked, and deprived of the support of public opinion, and of the great plea of necessity, it would fall without a struggle. Its few interested defenders would hide their heads abashed, and would be ashamed any longer to advocate a cause for which no human ingenuity could invent a plausible argument.

The most successful supporters of tyranny are without doubt those general declaimers, who attribute the distresses of the poor, and almost all the evils to which society is subject, to human institutions and the iniquity of governments. The falsity of these accusations, and the dreadful consequences that would result from their being generally admitted and acted upon, make it absolutely necessary that they should at all events be resisted; not only on account of the immediate revolutionary horrors to be expected from a movement of the people acting under such impressions (a consideration which must at all times have very great weight); but also on account of the extreme probability that such a revolution would terminate in a much worse despotism than that which it had destroyed. On these grounds, a genuine friend of freedom, a zealous advocate for the real rights of man, might be found among the defenders of a considerable degree of tyranny. A cause bad in itself, might be supported by the good and the virtuous, merely because that which was opposed to it was much worse; and because it was absolutely necessary at the moment to make a choice between the two. Whatever therefore may be the intention of those indiscriminate and wholesale accusations against governments,[16] their real effect undoubtedly is to add

---

[15] [According to Dr Johnson's Dictionary, nuisances could consist of rotting vegetables and offal, as well as ordure.]

[16] [In 1806 the words *and wholesale* were excised.]

a weight of talents and principles to the prevailing power, which it never would have received otherwise.

It is a truth, which I trust has been sufficiently proved in the course of this work, that under a government constructed upon the best and purest principles, and executed by men of the highest talents and integrity, the most squalid poverty and wretchedness might universally prevail from the principle of population alone.[17] And as this cause of unhappiness has hitherto been so little understood, that the efforts of society have always tended rather to aggravate than to lessen it, we have the strongest reasons for supposing that, in all the governments with which we are acquainted, a very great part of the misery[18] to be observed among the lower classes of the people arises from this cause.

The inference therefore, which Mr. Paine and others have drawn against governments from the unhappiness of the people, is palpably unfair; and before we give a sanction to such accusations, it is a debt we owe to truth and justice, to ascertain how much of this unhappiness arises from the principle of population, and how much is fairly to be attributed to government. When this distinction has been properly made, and all the vague, indefinite, and false accusations removed, government would remain, as it ought to be, clearly responsible for the rest. ●A tenfold weight would be immediately given to the cause of the people, and every man of principle would join in asserting and enforcing, if necessary, their rights.●

[In 1806 Malthus excised this last sentence and continued thus:

... clearly responsible for the rest; and the amount of this would still be such as to make the responsibility very considerable. Though government has but little power in the direct and immediate relief of poverty, yet its indirect influence on the prosperity of its subjects is striking and incontestable. And the reason is, that though it is comparatively impotent in its efforts to make the food of a country keep pace with an unrestricted increase of population, yet its influence is great in giving the best direction to those checks, which in some form or other must necessarily take place. It has clearly appeared in the former part of this work, that the most despotic and worst-governed countries, however low they might be in actual population, were uniformly the most populous in proportion to their means of subsistence; and the necessary effect of this state of things must of

---

[17] [In 1806 this was altered:
    ... squalid poverty and wretchedness might universally prevail from an in-attention to the prudential check to population.
[18] [In 1806 the word *very* was excised.]

course be very low wages. In such countries the checks to population arise more from the sickness and mortality consequent on poverty, than from the prudence and foresight which restrain the frequency and universality of early marriages. The checks are more of the positive and less of the preventive kind.

The first grand requisite to the growth of prudential habits is the perfect security of property; and the next perhaps is that respectability and importance which are given to the lower classes by equal laws, and the possession of some influence in the framing of them. The more excellent therefore is the government, the more does it tend to generate that prudence and elevation of sentiment by which alone, in the present state of our being, poverty can be avoided.

It has been sometimes asserted that the only reason why it is advantageous that the people should have some share in the government is that a representation of the people tends best to secure the framing of good and equal laws; but that, if the same object could be attained under a despotism, the same advantage would accrue to the community. If however the representative system, by securing to the lower classes of society a more equal and liberal mode of treatment from their superiors, gives to each individual a greater personal respectability, and a greater fear of personal degradation; it is evident that it will powerfully co-operate with the security of property in animating the exertions of industry and in generating habits of prudence; and thus more powerfully tend to increase the riches and prosperity of the lower classes of the community than if the same laws had existed under a despotism.

But though the tendency of a free constitution and a good government to diminish poverty be certain; yet their effect in this way must necessarily be indirect and slow, and very different from the direct and immediate relief which the lower classes of people are too frequently in the habit of looking forward to as the consequence of a revolution. This habit of expecting too much, and the irritation occasioned by disappointment, continually give a wrong direction to their efforts in favour of liberty, and constantly tend to defeat the accomplishment of those gradual reforms in government, and that slow melioration of the condition of the lower classes of society, which are really attainable. It is of the very highest importance therefore, to know distinctly what government cannot do, as well as what it can. If I were called upon to name the cause, which, in my conception, . . .

I may be deceived; but I confess that if I were called upon to name the cause which, in my conception, had more than any other contributed to the very slow progress of freedom, so disheartening to every liberal mind, I should say that it was the confusion that had existed respecting the causes of the unhappiness and discontents which prevail in society; and the advantage which governments had been able to take, and indeed had been compelled to take, of this confusion, to confirm and strengthen their power. I cannot help thinking, therefore, that a knowledge generally circulated, that the principal cause of want and unhappiness is unconnected[19] with government, and totally beyond its power to remove, and that it depends upon the conduct of the poor themselves, would, instead of giving any advantage to governments, give a great additional weight to the popular side of the question, by removing the dangers with which from ignorance it is at present accompanied; and thus tend, in a very powerful manner, to promote the cause of rational freedom.

[19] [In 1806 this was changed to:
    ... is only indirectly connected with government, ...

CHAPTER VII

Continuation of the same Subject[1]

The reasonings of the foregoing chapter have been strikingly confirmed by the events of the last two or three years. Perhaps there never was a period when more erroneous views were formed by the lower classes of society of the effects to be expected from reforms in the government, when these erroneous views were more immediately founded on a total misapprehension of the principal cause of poverty, and when they more directly led to results unfavourable to liberty.

One of the main causes of complaint against the government has been, that a considerable number of labourers, who are both able and willing to work, are wholly out of employment, and unable consequently to command the necessaries of life.

That this state of things is one of the most afflicting events that can occur in civilized life, that it is a natural and pardonable cause of discontent among the lower classes of society, and that every effort should be made by the higher classes to mitigate it, consistently with a proper care not to render it permanent, no man of humanity can doubt. But that such a state of things may occur in the best-conducted and most economical government that ever existed is as certain as that governments have not the power of commanding, with effect, the resources of a country to be progressive, when they are naturally stationary or declining.

It will be allowed that periods of prosperity may occur in any well-governed state, during which an extraordinary stimulus may be given to its wealth and population which cannot in its nature be permanent. If, for instance, new channels of trade are opened, new

---

[1] Written in 1817.

[Malthus added this brief footnote in 1826. His additional chapter was inspired by widespread disturbances, caused partly by long-term industrial changes, which gave rise to outbursts of machine-breaking; there was also an exceptionally wet summer and bad harvest in 1816. These factors increased the distress which resulted from the cessation of the war-time demand for men and commodities, and led to renewed popular agitation for parliamentary reform; the government retaliated with strong repressive measures, in the name of law and order, and the Habeas Corpus Act was suspended again in 1817.]

colonies are possessed, new inventions take place in machinery, and new and great improvements are made in agriculture, it is quite obvious that while the markets at home and abroad will readily take off at advantageous prices the increasing produce, there must be a rapid increase of capital, and an unusual stimulus given to the population. On the other hand, if subsequently these channels of trade are either closed by accident or contracted by foreign competition; if colonies are lost, or the same produce is supplied from other quarters; if the markets, either from glut or competition, cease to extend with the extension of the new machinery; and if the improvements in agriculture from any cause whatever cease to be progressive, it is as obvious that, just at the time when the stimulus to population has produced its greatest effect, the means of employing and supporting this population may, in the natural course of things, and without any fault whatever in the government, become deficient. This failure must unavoidably produce great distress among the labouring classes of society; but it is quite clear that no inference can be drawn from this distress that a radical change is required in the government; and the attempt to accomplish such a change might only aggravate the evil.

It has been supposed in this case that the government has in no respect, by its conduct, contributed to the pressure in question, a supposition which in practice perhaps will rarely be borne out by the fact. It is unquestionably in the power of a government to produce great distress by war and taxation, and it requires some skill to distinguish the distress which is the natural result of these causes from that which is occasioned in the way just described. In our own case unquestionably both descriptions of causes have combined, but the former in a greater degree than the latter. War and taxation, as far as they operate directly and simply, tend to destroy or retard the progress of capital, produce and population; but during the late war these checks to prosperity have been much more than overbalanced by a combination of circumstances which has given an extraordinary stimulus to production. That for this overbalance of advantages the country cannot be considered as much indebted to the government, is most certain. The government during the last twenty-five years has shown no very great love either of peace or liberty; and no particular economy in the use of the national resources. It has proceeded in a very straight-forward manner to spend great sums in war, and to raise them by very heavy taxes. It has no doubt done its part towards the dilapidation of the national resources. But still the broad fact must stare every impartial observer in the face, that at the end of the war in 1814 the national resources were not dilapidated; and that not only were the wealth and population of the country considerably greater than they were at the commencement of the war, but that they had increased in the interval at a more rapid rate than was ever experienced before.

Perhaps this may justly be considered as one of the most extraordinary facts in history; and it certainly follows from it, that the sufferings of the country since the peace have not been occasioned so much by the usual and most natural effects to be expected from war and taxation, as by the sudden ceasing of an extraordinary stimulus to production, the distresses consequent upon which, though increased no doubt by the weight of taxation, do not essentially arise from it, and are not directly therefore, and immediately, to be relieved by its removal.

That the labouring classes of society should not be fully aware that the main causes of their distress are to a certain extent and for a certain time, irremediable, is natural enough; and that they should listen much more readily and willingly to those who confidently promise immediate relief, rather than to those who can only tell them unpalatable truths, is by no means surprising. But it must be allowed that full advantage has been taken by the popular orators and writers of a crisis which has given them so much power.[2] Partly from ignorance, and partly from design, everything that could tend to enlighten the labouring classes as to the real nature of their situation, and encourage them to bear an unavoidable pressure with patience, has been either sedulously kept out of their view, or clamorously reprobated; and every thing that could tend to deceive them, to aggravate and encourage their discontents, and to raise unreasonable and extravagant expectations as to the relief to be expected from reform, has been as sedulously brought forward. If under these circumstances the reforms proposed had been accomplished, it is impossible that the people should not have been most cruelly disappointed; and under a system of universal suffrage and annual parliaments,[3] a general

[2] [The 'popular orators and writers' would have included Henry Hunt (1773–1835) known as 'Orator Hunt', who tried to organise nationwide petitions to the Prince Regent; at a great meeting in Spa Fields, on the outskirts of London, on 15 November 1816, Hunt appeared with an escort carrying a tricolour flag and a cap of liberty on a pike. William Cobbett (1763–1835) was an old enemy of Malthus, and constantly attacked him in his *Weekly Register*; he could well have been one of the 'popular' writers whom Malthus had in mind.]

[3] [Universal suffrage, at this period, meant manhood suffrage; annual general elections were intended to keep members of parliament properly subservient to their constituents. These suggestions for reform were particularly associated with Sir

disappointment of the people would probably lead to every sort of experiment in government, till the career of change was stopped by a military despotism. The warmest friends of genuine liberty might justly feel alarmed at such a prospect. To a cause conducted upon such principles, and likely to be attended with such results, they could not of course, consistently with their duty, lend any assistance. And if with great difficulty, and against the sense of the great mass of petitioners, they were to effect a more moderate and more really useful reform, they could not but feel certain that the unavoidable disappointment of the people would be attributed to the half-measures which had been pursued; and that they would be either forced to proceed to more radical changes, or submit to a total loss of their influence and popularity by stopping short while the distresses of the people were unrelieved, their discontents unallayed, and the great *panacea* on which they had built their sanguine expectations untried.

These considerations have naturally paralyzed the exertions of the best friends of liberty; and those salutary reforms which are acknowledged to be necessary in order to repair the breaches of time, and improve the fabric of our constitution, are thus rendered much more difficult, and consequently much less probable.

But not only have the false expectations and extravagant demands suggested by the leaders of the people given an easy victory to government over every proposition for reform, whether violent or moderate, but they have furnished the most fatal instruments of offensive attack against the constitution itself. They are naturally calculated to excite some alarm, and to check moderate reform; but alarm, when once excited, seldom knows where to stop, and the causes of it are particularly liable to be exaggerated. There is reason to believe that it has been under the influence of exaggerated statements, and of inferences drawn by exaggerated fears from these statements, that acts unfavourable to liberty have been passed without an adequate necessity. But the power of creating these exaggerated fears, and of passing these acts, has been unquestionably furnished by the extravagant expectations of the people. And it must be allowed that the present times furnish a very striking illustration of the doctrine that an ignorance of the principal cause of poverty is peculiarly unfavourable, and that a knowledge of it must be peculiarly favourable, to the cause of civil liberty.

Francis Burdett (1770–1844); as M.P. for Westminster he unsuccessfully introduced in 1817 a motion for a committee to enquire into parliamentary representation.]

CHAPTER VIII

Plan of the gradual abolition of the Poor Laws proposed

If the principles in the preceding chapters should stand the test of examination, and we should ever feel the obligation of endeavouring to act upon them, the next inquiry would be in what way we ought practically to proceed. The first grand obstacle which presents itself in this country is the system of the poor laws, which has been justly stated to be an evil in comparison of which the national debt, with all its magnitude of terror, is of little moment.[1] [2]●The extraordinary rapidity with which the poor's rates have increased of late years, presents us, indeed, with the prospect of a monstrous deformity in society, which, if it did not really exist to a great degree at present, and were not daily advancing in growth, would be considered as perfectly incredible. It presents us with the prospect of a great nation, flourishing in arts and arms and commerce, and with a government, which has generally been allowed to be the best, which has hitherto stood the test of experience, in any country, and yet the larger half of the people reduced to the condition of paupers.●[2]

Greatly as we may be shocked at such a prospect, and ardently as we may wish to remove it, the evil is now so deeply seated, and the relief given by the poor laws so widely extended, that no man of humanity could venture to propose their immediate abolition. To mitigate their effects, however, and stop their future increase, to which, if left to

[1] Reports of the Society for bettering the condition of the poor, vol. iii. p. 21.
[2] [In 1806 this passage was altered:
   The rapidity with which the poor's rates have increased of late years presents us indeed with the prospect of such an extraordinary proportion of paupers in the society as would seem to be incredible in a nation flourishing in arts, agriculture, and commerce, and with a government which has generally been allowed to be the best that has hitherto stood the test of experience.[(a)]
[(a)] It has been said, that, during the late scarcities, half of the population of the country received relief. If the poor's rates continue increasing as rapidly as they have done on the average of the last ten years, how melancholy are our future prospects! The system of the poor laws has been justly stated by the French to be *la plaie politique de l'Angleterre la plus dévorante*. (Comité de Mendicité.)
   [This footnote was retained in all the editions, but in 1817 the first sentence was omitted.]

continue upon their present plan, we can see no probable termination, it has been proposed to fix the whole sum to be raised at its present rate, or any other that might be determined upon; and to make a law that on no account this sum should be exceeded. The objection to this plan is that a very large sum would be still to be raised, and a great number of people to be supported; the consequence of which would be, that the poor would not be easily able to distinguish the alteration that had been made. Each individual would think that he had as good a right to be supported when he was in want as any other person; and those who unfortunately chanced to be in distress when the fixed sum had been collected, would think themselves particularly ill-used on being excluded from all assistance, while so many others were enjoying this advantage. If the sum collected were divided among all that were in want, however their numbers might increase, though such a plan would be perfectly fair, with regard to those who became dependent after the sum had been fixed,[3] it would undoubtedly be rather hard upon those who had been in the habit of receiving a more liberal supply, and had done nothing to justify its being taken from them.

[In 1806 Malthus added to this paragraph:
 ... justify its being taken from them: and in both cases it would certainly be unjust in the society to undertake the support of the poor, and yet, if their numbers increased, to feed them so sparingly that they must necessarily die of hunger and disease.

I have reflected much on the subject of the poor laws and hope, therefore, that I shall be excused in venturing to suggest a mode of their gradual abolition, to which I confess that at present I can see no material objection. Of this, indeed, I feel nearly convinced: that should we ever become sufficiently sensible[4] of the wide-spreading tyranny, dependence, indolence, and unhappiness which they create, as seriously to make an effort to abolish them, we shall be compelled[5] to adopt the principle, if not the plan, which I shall mention. It seems impossible to get rid of so extensive a system of support, consistently with humanity, without

---

[3] [In 1806 this was altered to:
 ... though such a plan would not be so unfair with regard to those who became dependent after the sum had been fixed ...
[4] [In 1826 *sufficiently sensible* was replaced by 'so fully sensible.'
[5] [In 1806 Malthus wrote:
 ... we shall be compelled by a sense of justice to adopt the principle, if not the plan ...

applying ourselves directly to its vital principle, and endeavouring to counteract that deeply-seated cause, which occasions the rapid growth of all such establishments, and invariably renders them inadequate to their object.

[In 1806 a short paragraph was inserted here:

As a previous step even to any considerable alteration in the present system, which would contract or stop the increase of the relief to be given, it appears to me that we are bound in justice and honour formally to disclaim the *right* of the poor to support.

To this end, I should propose a regulation to be made, declaring that no child born from any marriage taking place after the expiration of a year from the date of the law, and no illegitimate child born two years from the same date, should ever be entitled to parish assistance. And to give a more general knowledge of this law, and to enforce it more strongly on the minds of the lower classes of people, the clergyman of each parish should, previously to the solemnization of a marriage, read a short address to the parties,[6] stating the strong obligation on every man to support his own children; the impropriety, and even immorality, of marrying without a fair prospect[7] of being able to do this; the evils which had resulted to the poor themselves, from the attempt which had been made to assist, by public institutions, in a duty which ought to be exclusively appropriated to parents; and the absolute necessity which had at length appeared, of abandoning all such institutions, on account of their producing effects totally opposite to those which were intended.

This would operate as a fair, distinct, and precise notice, which no man could well mistake; and, without pressing hard on any particular individuals, would at once throw off the rising generation from that miserable and helpless dependence upon the government and the rich, the moral as well as physical consequences of which are almost incalculable. [8]●When the poor are in the habit of constantly looking to these sources, for all the good or evil they enjoy or suffer, their minds must almost necessarily be under a continual state of irritation against the higher classes of society whenever they feel distressed from the pressure of circumstances.

[6] [In 1806 this was altered to:
... should, after the publication of banns, read a short address, stating ...
[7] [In 1807 the word *fair* was excised.]
[8] [In 1806 this sentence and the whole of the following paragraph were expunged.]

I have often heard great surprise expressed that the poor in this country should be with such difficulty persuaded to take to any substitutes during a period of scarcity; but I confess that this fact never surprised me in the least. The poor are told that the parish is obliged to provide for them. This, they naturally conceive, is a rich source of supply; and when they are offered any kind of food to which they are not accustomed, they consider it as a breach of obligation in the parish, and as proceeding not from the hard law of necessity, from which there is no appeal; but from the injustice and hardheartedness of the higher classes of society, against which they would wish to appeal to the right of the strongest. The language which they generally make use of upon these occasions is: 'See what stuff *they* want to make us eat, I wonder how *they* would like it *themselves*. I should like to see some of *them* do a day's work upon it.' The words *they* and *them* generally refer to Parliament, the Lord Mayor, the Justices, the Parish, and in general to all the higher classes of society. Both the irritation of mind and the helplessness in expedients, during the pressure of want, arise in this instance from the wretched system of governing too much. When the poor were once taught, by the abolition of the poor laws, and a proper knowledge of their real situation, to depend more upon themselves, we might rest secure that they would be fruitful enough in resources, and that the evils which were absolutely irremediable they would bear with the fortitude of men and the resignation of Christians. ●[8]

After the public notice which I have proposed had been given, and the system of poor laws had ceased with regard to the rising generation, if any man chose to marry, without a prospect of being able to support a family, he should have the most perfect liberty so to do. Though to marry, in this case, is in my opinion clearly an immoral act, yet it is not one which society can justly take upon itself to prevent or punish; because the punishment provided for it by the laws of nature falls directly and most severely upon the individual who commits the act, and, through him, only more remotely and feebly on the society. When nature will govern and punish for us, it is a very miserable ambition to wish to snatch the rod from her hands, and draw upon ourselves the odium of executioner. To the punishment, therefore, of nature he should be left, the punishment of severe want.[9] He has erred in the face of a most clear and precise warning, and can have no just reason to complain of any

[9] [In 1806 the word *severe* was omitted.]

person but himself when he feels the consequences of his error. All parish assistance should be most rigidly denied him: and if the hand of private charity be stretched forth in his relief, the interests of humanity imperiously require that it should be administered very sparingly.[10] He should be taught to know that the laws of nature, which are the laws of God, had doomed him and his family to starve[11] for disobeying their repeated admonitions; that he had no claim of right on society for the smallest portion of food, beyond that which his labour would fairly purchase; and that if he and his family were saved from suffering the utmost extremities of hunger,[12] he would owe it to the pity of some kind benefactor, to whom, therefore, he ought to be bound by the strongest ties of gratitude.

If this system were pursued, we need be under no apprehensions whatever[13] that the number of persons in extreme want would be beyond the power and the will of the benevolent to supply. The sphere for the exercise of private charity would, I am confident, be less than it is at present; and the only difficulty would be, to restrain the hand of benevolence from assisting those in distress in so liberal[14] a manner as to encourage indolence and want of foresight in others.

With regard to illegitimate children, after the proper notice had been given, they should on no account whatever be allowed to have any claim to parish assistance.[15] If the parents desert their child, they ought to be

---

[10] [In 1806 this read:
  All parish assistance should be denied him: ... private charity ... should be administered sparingly.
  [In 1817 this sentence was altered again:
  All parish assistance should be denied him, and he should be left to the uncertain support of private charity.
[11] [In 1806 *starve* was changed to 'suffer'.
[12] [This sentence was altered twice. In 1806 the word *utmost* was excised.]
  [In 1817 it read:
  ... if he and his family were saved from feeling the natural consequences of his imprudence, he would owe it to the pity of some kind benefactor ...
[13] [In 1806 the word *whatever* was excised.]
[14] [In 1806 *liberal* was changed to 'indiscriminate'.
  [In 1817 the sentence was altered:
  The sphere for the exercise of private charity would, probably, not be greater than it is at present; and the principal difficulty would be to restrain the hand of benevolence from assisting those in distress in so indiscriminate a manner as to encourage ...
[15] [In 1806 this sentence was altered:
  ... had been given, they should not be allowed to have any claim to parish assistance, but be left entirely to the support of private charity.

made answerable for the crime. The infant is, comparatively speaking, of no value[16] to the society, as others will immediately supply its place. Its principal value is on account of its being the object of one of the most delightful passions in human nature – parental affection. But if this value be disregarded by those who are alone in a capacity to feel it, the society cannot be called upon to put itself in their place; and has no further business in its protection than, in the case of its murder or intentional ill-treatment, to follow the general rules in punishing such crimes; which rules, for the interests of morality, it is bound to pursue, whether the object, in the particular instance, be of value to the state or not.[17]

At present the child is taken under the protection of the parish,[18] and generally dies, at least in London, within the first year. The loss to the society, if it be one, is the same;[19] but the crime is diluted by the number of people concerned, and the death passes as a visitation of Providence, instead of being considered as the necessary consequence of the conduct of its parents, for which they ought to be held responsible to God and to society.

The desertion of both parents, however, is not so common as the desertion of one. When a servant or labouring man has an illegitimate child, his running away is perfectly a matter of course; and it is by no means uncommon for a man with a wife and large family to withdraw into a distant county, and leave them to the parish; indeed, I once heard a hard-working good sort of man propose to do this, as the best mode of providing for a wife and six children.[20] If the simple fact of these frequent desertions were related in some countries, a strange inference would be drawn against the English character; but the wonder would cease when our public institutions were explained.

By the laws of nature, a child is confided directly and exclusively to the

[16] [In 1806 *no value* was amended to 'little value'.]
[17] [In 1806 this was changed:
 . . . in their place; and has no further business in its protection than to punish the crime of desertion or intentional ill-treatment in the persons whose duty it is to provide for it.
[18] I fully agree with Sir F. M. Eden, in thinking that the constant public support which deserted children receive is the cause of their very great numbers in the two most opulent countries of Europe, France and England. State of the Poor, vol. i. p. 339.
[19] [In 1806 the words *if it be one* were omitted.]
[20] 'That many of the poorer classes of the community avail themselves of the liberality of the law, and leave their wives and children on the parish, the reader will find abundant proof in the subsequent part of this work.' Sir F. M. Eden on the State of the Poor, vol. i. p. 339.

protection of its parents. By the laws of nature, the mother of a child is confided almost as strongly and exclusively to the man who is the father of it. If these ties were suffered to remain in the state in which nature has left them, and the man were convinced that the woman and the child depended solely upon him for support, I scarcely believe that there are ten men breathing so atrocious as to desert them. But our laws, in opposition to the laws of nature, say that if the parents forsake their child, other persons will undertake to support it; or, if the man forsake the woman, that she shall still meet with protection elsewhere; that is, we take all possible pains to weaken and render null the ties of nature, and then say that men are unnatural. But the fact is, that the society itself, in its body politic, is the unnatural character, for framing laws that thus counteract the laws of nature and give premiums to the violation of the best and most honourable feelings of the human heart.

It is a common thing in most parishes, when the father of an illegitimate child can be seized, to endeavour to frighten him into marriage by the terrors of a jail; but such a proceeding cannot surely be too strongly reprobated. In the first place, it is almost shallow policy in the parish officers; for if they succeed the effect, upon the present system, will generally be that of having three or four children to provide for, instead of one. And, in the next place, it is difficult to conceive a more gross and scandalous profanation of a religious ceremony. Those who believe that the character of the woman is salved by such a forced engagement,[21] or that the moral worth of the man is enhanced by affirming a lie before God, have, I confess, very different ideas of delicacy and morality from those which I have been taught to consider as just. If a man deceive a woman into a connexion with him under a promise of marriage, he has undoubtedly been guilty of a most atrocious act; and there are few crimes which merit a more severe punishment: but the last that I should choose is that which will oblige him to affirm another falsehood, which will probably render the woman that he is to be joined to miserable, and will burden the society with a family of paupers.

The obligation on every man to support his children, whether legitimate or illegitimate, is so clear and strong, that it would be just to arm society with any power to enforce it which would be likely to answer the purpose. But I am inclined to believe that no exercise of the civil power, however rigorous, would be half so effectual as a knowledge generally

---

[21] [In 1817 *salved* was replaced by 'restored'.

circulated, that children were in future to depend solely for support upon their parents, and would perhaps starve if they were deserted.[22]

It may appear to be hard that a mother and her children, who had been guilty of no particular crime themselves, should suffer for the ill-conduct of the father; but this is one of the invariable laws of nature; and knowing this, we should think twice upon the subject, and be very sure of the ground on which we go, before we presume *systematically* to counteract it.

I have often heard the goodness of the Deity impeached on account of that part of the decalogue, in which he declares that he will visit the sins of the father upon the children; but the objection has not perhaps been sufficiently considered. Without a most complete and fundamental change in the whole constitution of human nature; without making man an angel, or at least something totally different from what he is at present; it seems absolutely necessary that such a law should prevail. Would it not require a perpetual miracle, which is perhaps a contradiction in terms, to prevent children from being affected in their moral and civil condition by the conduct of their parents? What man is there, that has been brought up by his parents, who is not at the present moment enjoying something from their virtues, or suffering something from their vices; who, in his moral character, has not been elevated in some degree by their prudence, their justice, their benevolence, their temperance, or depressed by the contraries; who, in his civil condition, has not been raised by their reputation, their foresight, their industry, their good fortune; or lowered by their want of character, their imprudence, their indolence, and their adversity? And how much does a knowledge of this transmission of blessings contribute to excite and invigorate virtuous exertion? Proceeding upon this certainty, how ardent and incessant are the efforts of parents to give their children a good education, and to provide for their future situation in the world! If a man could neglect or desert his wife and children without their suffering any injury, how many individuals there are who, not being very fond of their wives, or being tired of the shackles of matrimony, would withdraw from household cares and difficulties, and resume their liberty and independence as single men! But the consideration that children may suffer for the faults of their parents has a strong hold even upon vice, and many

---

[22] [In 1806 this was altered:
   ... upon their parents, and would be left only to casual charity if they were deserted.

who are in such a state of mind as to disregard the consequences of their habitual course of life, as far as relates to themselves, are yet greatly anxious that their children should not suffer from their vices and follies. In the moral government of the world, it seems evidently necessary that the sins of the fathers should be visited upon the children; and if in our overweening vanity we imagine that we can govern a private society better by endeavouring *systematically* to counteract this law, I am inclined to believe that we shall find ourselves very greatly mistaken.

If the plan which I have proposed were adopted, the poor's rates in a few years would begin very rapidly to decrease, and in no great length of time would be completely extinguished; and yet, as far as it appears to me at present, no individual would be either deceived or injured, and consequently no person could have a just right to complain.

The abolition of the poor-laws, however, is not of itself sufficient; and the obvious answer to those who lay too much stress upon this system is to desire them to look at the state of the poor in some other countries, where such laws do not prevail, and to compare it with their condition in England. But this comparison, it must be acknowledged, is in many respects unfair; and would by no means decide the question of the utility or inutility of such a system. England possesses very great natural and political advantages in which, perhaps, the countries that we should in this case compare with her would be found to be palpably deficient. The nature of her soil and climate is such, that those almost universal failures in the crops of grain, which are known in some countries, never occur in England. Her insular situation and extended commerce are peculiarly favourable for importation. Her numerous manufactures employ all the hands that are not engaged in agriculture,[23] and afford the means of a regular distribution of the annual produce of the land and labour to the whole of her inhabitants. But above all, throughout a very large class of the people, a decided taste for the conveniences and comforts of life, a strong desire of bettering their condition (that master-spring of public prosperity) and, in consequence, a most laudable spirit of industry and foresight, are observed to prevail. These dispositions, so contrary to the hopeless indolence remarked in despotic countries, are probably generated, in great measure, by the

---

[23] [In 1806 Malthus altered this to:
    ... manufactures employ nearly all the hands that are not engaged in agriculture,
    ...

constitution of the English government,[24] and the excellence of its laws, which secure to every individual the produce of his industry. When, therefore, on a comparison with other countries, England appears to have the advantage in the state of her poor, the superiority is entirely to be attributed to these favourable circumstances, and not to the poor laws. A woman with one bad feature may greatly excel in beauty some other who may have this individual feature tolerably good; but it would be rather strange to assert, in consequence, that the superior beauty of the former was occasioned by this particular deformity. [25]●The poor laws have constantly tended, in the most powerful manner, to counteract the natural and acquired advantages of this country. Fortunately these advantages have been so considerable that, though greatly weakened, they could not be entirely overcome; and to these advantages, and these alone, it is owing, that England has been able to bear up so long against this pernicious system. I am so strongly of this opinion, that I do not think that any other country in the world, except perhaps Holland before the revolution, could have acted upon it so completely, for the same period of time, without utter ruin.●[25]

It has been proposed by some, to establish poor laws in Ireland; but, from the wretched and degraded state of the common people, and the total want of that decent pride, which in England prevents so many from having recourse to parish assistance,[26] there is little reason to doubt that, on the establishment of such laws, the whole of the landed property would very soon be absorbed, or the system be given up in despair.

In Sweden, from the dearths which are not unfrequent, owing to the general failure of crops in an unpropitious climate, and the impossibility of great importations in a poor country, an attempt to establish a system of parochial relief such as that in England (if it were not speedily

[24] [In 1806 this was changed to:
   These dispositions ... are generated by the constitution of the English government, ...
[25] [In 1806 this passage was modified:
   The poor-laws have constantly tended to counteract the natural and acquired advantages of this country. Fortunately these advantages have been so considerable that, though weakened, they could not be overcome; and to these advantages, together with the checks to marriage which the laws themselves create, it is owing that England has been able to bear up so long against this pernicious system. Probably there is not any other country in the world, except perhaps Holland before the revolution, which could have acted upon it ...
[26] [In 1817 this was amended to:
   ... but, from the depressed state of the common people, there is little reason to doubt ...

abandoned from the physical impossibility of executing it) would level the property of the kingdom from one end to the other, and convulse the social system in such a manner, as absolutely to prevent it from recovering its former state on the return of plenty.

Even in France, with all her advantages of situation and climate, the tendency to population is so great, and the want of foresight among the lower classes of the people so conspicuous,[27] that if poor laws were established, the landed property would soon sink under the burden, and the wretchedness of the people at the same time be increased. On these considerations the committee *de Mendicité*, at the beginning of the revolution, very properly and judiciously rejected the establishment of such a system which had been proposed.

The exception of Holland, if it were an exception, would arise from very particular circumstances – her extensive foreign trade, and her numerous colonial emigrations, compared with the smallness of her territory, together with the extreme unhealthiness of a great part of the country, which occasions a much greater average mortality than is common in other states. These, I conceive, were the unobserved causes which principally contributed to render Holland so famous for the management of her poor, and able to employ and support all who applied for relief.

No part of Germany is sufficiently rich to support an extensive system of parochial relief; but I am inclined to think that, from the absence of it, the lower classes of the people in some parts of Germany are in a better situation than those of the same class in England. In Switzerland for the same reason their condition, before the late troubles, was perhaps universally superior. And in a journey through the dutchies of Holstein and Sleswick belonging to Denmark, the houses of the lower classes of people appeared to me to be neater and better, and in general there were fewer indications of poverty and wretchedness among them, than among the same ranks in this country.[28]

Even in Norway, notwithstanding the disadvantage of a severe and uncertain climate, from the little that I saw in a few weeks residence in the country, and the information that I could collect from others, I am inclined to think that the poor were, on the average, better off than in England. Their houses and clothing were superior and, though they had

---

[27] [In 1817 *conspicuous* was changed to 'remarkable'.]
[28] [See *The Travel Diaries of T. R. Malthus* (Cambridge University Press, 1966) pp. 40–7.]

no white bread, they had much more meat, fish, and milk than our labourers; and I particularly remarked that the farmers' boys were much stouter and healthier looking lads than those of the same description in England. This degree of happiness, superior to what could be expected from the soil and climate, arises almost exclusively from the degree in which the preventive check to population operates;[29] and the establishment of a system of poor-laws, which would destroy this check, would at once sink the lower classes of the people into a state of the most miserable poverty and wretchedness; would diminish their industry, and consequently the produce of the land and labour of the country; would weaken the resources of ingenuity in times of scarcity; and ultimately involve the country in all the horrors of continual famines.

If, as in Ireland, and in Spain, and many of the southern countries, the people be in so degraded a state as to propagate their species like brutes, totally regardless of consequences,[30] it matters little whether they have poor-laws or not. Misery in all its various forms must be the predominant check to their increase. Poor-laws, indeed, will always tend to aggravate the evil, by diminishing the general resources of the country, and in such a state of things could [31]●exist only for a very short time; but with or without them, no stretch of human ingenuity and exertion could●[31] rescue the people from the most extreme poverty and wretchedness.

[29] [See *The Travel Diaries of T. R. Malthus*, pp. 117–18, 124, 133–4, 139–40, 142, 145, 175, 202.

In 1817 Malthus rather surprisingly changed the past to the present tense:

. . . the poor are, on the average, better off . . . Their houses and clothing are often superior; and though they have no white bread, they have much more meat, fish and milk . . .

[30] [In 1817 this was altered:

If, as in Ireland, Spain, and many countries of the more southern climates, the people are in so degraded a state as to propagate their species without regard to consequences, it matters little . . .

[31] [In 1817 *could* was replaced by 'can':

. . . can exist only for a very short time . . . no stretch of human ingenuity and exertion can rescue the people . . .

Of the modes of correcting the prevailing opinions on the subject of[1] Population

It is not enough to abolish all the positive institutions which encourage population; but we must endeavour, at the same time, to correct the prevailing opinions which have the same or perhaps even a more powerful effect. This must necessarily be a work of time; and can only be done by circulating juster notions on these subjects in writings and conversation; and by endeavouring to impress as strongly as possible on the public mind that it is not the duty of man simply to propagate his species, but to propagate virtue and happiness; and that, if he has not a tolerably fair prospect of doing this, he is by no means called upon to leave descendants.

[2]● The merits of the childless, and of those who have brought up large families, should be compared without prejudice, and their different influence on the general happiness of society justly appreciated.

The matron who has reared a family of ten or twelve children, and whose sons, perhaps, may be fighting the battles of their country, is apt to think that society owes her much; and this imaginary debt society is, in general, fully inclined to acknowledge. But if the subject be fairly considered, and the respected matron weighed in the scales of justice against the neglected old maid, it is possible that the matron might kick the beam. She will appear rather in the character of a monopolist than of a great benefactor to the state. If she had not married and had so many children, other members of the society might have enjoyed this satisfaction; and there is no particular reason for supposing that her sons would fight better for their country than the sons of other women. She has therefore rather subtracted from, than added to, the happiness of the other parts of society. The old maid, on the contrary, has exalted others by depressing herself. Her self-denial has made room for another marriage, without any additional distress; and she has not, like the generality

---

[1] [In 1806 the words *the subject of* were omitted.]
[2] [In 1806 the following six paragraphs were expunged, possibly in consequence of Malthus's own marriage in 1804.]

of men, in avoiding one error, fallen into its opposite. She has really and truly contributed more to the happiness of the rest of the society arising from the pleasures of marriage, than if she had entered in this union herself, and had besides portioned twenty maidens with a hundred pounds each; whose particular happiness would have been balanced either by an increase in the general difficulties of rearing children and getting employment, or by the necessity of celibacy in twenty other maidens somewhere else. Like the truly benevolent man in an irremediable scarcity, she has diminished her own consumption, instead of raising up a few particular people by pressing down the rest. On a fair comparison, therefore, she seems to have a better founded claim to the gratitude of society than the matron. Whether we could always completely sympathize with the motives of her conduct has not much to do with the question. The particular motive which influenced the matron to marry was certainly not the good of her country. To refuse a proper tribute of respect to the old maid, because she was not directly influenced in her conduct by the desire of conferring on society a certain benefit which, though it must undoubtedly exist, must necessarily be so diffused as to be invisible to her, is in the highest degree impolitic and unjust. It is expecting a strain of virtue beyond humanity. If we never reward any persons with our approbation but those who are exclusively influenced by motives of general benevolence, this powerful encouragement to good actions will not be very often called into exercise.

There are very few women who might not have married in some way or other. The old maid, who has either never formed an attachment, or has been disappointed in the object of it, has, under the circumstances in which she has been placed, conducted herself with the most perfect propriety; and has acted a much more virtuous and honourable part in society than those women who marry without a proper degree of love, or at least of esteem, for their husbands; a species of immorality which is not reprobated as it deserves.

If, in comparisons of this kind, we should be compelled to acknowledge that, in considering the general tendency of population to increase beyond the means of subsistence, the conduct of the old maid had contributed more to the happiness of the society than that of the matron; it will surely appear not only unjust, but strikingly impolitic, not to proportion our tribute of honour and estimation more fairly according to their respective merits. Though we should not go so far as to reward single women with particular distinctions; yet the plainest principles of equity and policy require that the respect which they might claim from their personal character should, in no way whatever, be impeded by their particular situation; and that, with regard to rank, precedence, and the ceremonial attentions of society, they should be completely on a level with married women.

It is still however true that the life of a married person with a family is of more consequence to society than that of a single person; because, when there is a family of children already born, it is of the utmost importance that they should be well taken care of and well educated; and of this there is very seldom so fair a probability when they have lost their parents. Our object should be merely to correct the prevailing opinions with regard to the duty of marriage; and, without positively discouraging it, to prevent any persons from being attracted or driven into this state by the respect and honour which await the married dame, and the neglect and inconveniences attendant on the single woman.

It is perfectly absurd, as well as unjust, that a giddy girl of sixteen should, because she is married, be considered by the forms of society as the protector of women of thirty, should come first into the room, should be assigned the highest place at table, and be the prominent figure to whom the attentions of the company are more particularly addressed. Those who believe that these distinctions (added to the very long confinement of single women to the parental roof, and their being compelled on all occasions to occupy the background of the picture) have not an influence in impelling many young women into the married state against their natural inclinations, and without a proper degree of regard for their intended husbands, do not as I conceive reason with much knowledge of human nature. And till these customs are changed, as far as circumstances will admit, and the respect and liberty which women enjoy are made to depend more upon personal character and propriety of conduct, than upon their situation as married or single; it must be acknowledged that among the higher ranks of life we encourage marriage by considerable premiums.●[2]

It is not, however, among the higher ranks of society, that we have most reason to apprehend the too great frequency of marriage.[3] Though the circulation of juster notions on this subject might, even in this part of the community, do much good, and prevent many unhappy marriages;

[3] [In 1806 this sentence was altered to take account of the previous long excision:
    Among the higher ranks of society we have not much reason to apprehend the too great frequency of marriage.

yet whether we make particular exertions for this purpose or not, we may rest assured that the degree of proper pride and spirit of independence, almost invariably connected with education and a certain rank in life, will secure the operation of the preventive check[4] to a considerable extent. All that the society can reasonably require of its members is that they should not have families without being able to support them. [5]●This may be fairly enjoined as a solemn duty. Every restraint beyond this, though in many points of view highly desirable, must be considered as a matter of choice and taste;●[5] but from what we already know of the habits which prevail among the higher ranks of life, we have reason to think that little more is wanted to attain the object required than to award a greater degree of respect and of personal liberty to single women, and to remove the distinctions in favour of married women, so as to place them exactly upon a level;[6] a change which, independently of any particular purpose in view, the plainest principles of equity seem to demand.

If, among the higher classes of society, the object of securing the operation of the preventive check to population[7] to a sufficient degree appear to be attainable without much difficulty, the obvious mode of proceeding with the lower classes of society, where the point is of the principal importance, is, to endeavour to infuse into them a portion of that knowledge and foresight which so much facilitates the attainment of this object in the educated part of the community.

The fairest chance of accomplishing this end would probably be by the establishment of a system of parochial education upon a plan similar to that proposed by Dr. Smith.[8] In addition to the usual subjects of instruction, and those which he has mentioned, I should be disposed to lay considerable stress on the frequent explanation of the real state of the lower classes of society, as affected by the principle of population, and their consequent dependence on themselves, for the chief part of their happiness or misery.

[4] [In 1806 this was changed to:
　　... the operation of the prudential check to marriage ...
[5] [In 1806 Malthus made two more alterations here:
　　This may be fairly enjoined as a positive duty. Every restraint beyond this must be considered as a matter of choice and taste; but from what we already know ...
[6] [In 1806 this was altered:
　　... single women, and place them nearer upon a level with married women; – a change which, ...
[7] [In 1806 this was changed to:
　　... the operation of the prudential check to marriage ...
[8] Wealth of Nations, vol. iii. b. v. c. i. p. 187.

[In 1806 Malthus added the following passage here, to conclude the paragraph:

... happiness or misery. It would be by no means necessary or proper in these explanations to underrate, in the smallest degree, the desirableness of marriage. It should always be represented as, what it really is, a state peculiarly suited to the nature of man, and calculated greatly to advance his happiness and remove the temptations to vice; but, like property or any other desirable object, its advantages should be shown to be unattainable except under certain conditions. And a strong conviction in a young man of the great desirableness of marriage, with a conviction at the same time, that the power of supporting a family was the only condition which would enable him really to enjoy its blessings, would be the most effectual motive imaginable to industry and sobriety before marriage, and would powerfully urge him to save that superfluity of income which single labourers necessarily possess for the accomplishment of a rational and desirable object, instead of dissipating it, as is now usually done, in idleness and vice.

If, in the course of time, a few of the simplest principles of political economy could be added to these instructions,[9] the benefit to society would be almost incalculable.[10] In some conversations with labouring

---

[9] [In 1806 this was altered to:

... added to the instruction given in these schools, the benefit to society ...

[10] Dr. Smith proposes that the elementary parts of geometry and mechanics should be taught in these parish schools; and I cannot help thinking that the common principles by which markets are regulated might be made sufficiently clear to be of considerable use. It is certainly a subject that, as it interests the lower classes of people nearly, would be likely to attract their attention. At the same time it must be confessed that it is impossible to be in any degree sanguine on this point, recollecting how very ignorant in general the educated part of the community is of these principles. If, however, political economy cannot be taught to the common people, I really think that it ought to form a branch of a university education. Scotland has set us an example in this respect, which we ought not to be so slow to imitate. It is of the utmost importance that the gentlemen of the country, and particularly the clergy, should not from ignorance aggravate the evils of scarcity every time that it unfortunately occurs. During the late dearths, half of the gentlemen and clergymen in the kingdom richly deserved to have been prosecuted for sedition. After inflaming the minds of the common people against the farmers and corn-dealers, by the manner in which they talked of them or preached about them, it was but a feeble antidote to the poison which they had infused coldly to observe that, however the poor might be oppressed or cheated, it was their duty to keep the peace. It was little better than Anthony's repeated declaration that the conspirators were all honourable men, which did not save either their houses or their persons from the attacks of the mob. Political economy is perhaps the only science of which it may be said that the ignorance of it is not merely a deprivation of good, but produces great evil.

[In 1826 Malthus added to this note:

[1825.] This note was written in 1803; and it is particularly gratifying to me, at the end of the year 1825, to see that what I stated as so desirable twenty-two years

men, during the late scarcities,[11] I confess that I was to the last degree disheartened at observing their inveterate prejudices on the subject of grain; and I felt very strongly the almost absolute incompatibility of a government really free with such a degree of ignorance. The delusions are of such a nature that, if acted upon, they must at all events be repressed by force; and it is extremely difficult to give such a power to the government as will be sufficient at all times for this purpose, without the risk of its being employed improperly and endangering the liberty of the subject. [12]●And this reflection cannot but be disheartening to every friend to freedom.●[12]

We have lavished immense sums on the poor, which we have every reason to think have constantly tended to aggravate their misery. But in their education, and in the circulation of those important political truths that most nearly concern them, which are perhaps the only means in our power of really raising their condition, and of making them happier men and more peaceable subjects, we have been miserably deficient. It is surely a great national disgrace, that the education of the lower classes of people in England should be left merely to a few Sunday schools, supported by a subscription from individuals, who of course[13] can give to the course of instruction in them any kind of bias which they please. And even the improvement of Sunday schools, for objectionable as they are in some points of view, and imperfect in all, I cannot but consider them as an improvement, is of very late date.[14]

The arguments which have been urged against instructing the people appear to me to be not only illiberal, but to the last degree, feeble; and they ought, on the contrary, to be extremely forcible, and to be supported by the most obvious and striking necessity, to warrant us in

ago, seems to be now on the eve of its accomplishment. The increasing attention which in the interval has been paid generally to the science of political economy; the lectures which have been given at Cambridge, London, and Liverpool; the chair which has lately been established at Oxford; the projected University in the Metropolis; and, above all, the Mechanic's Institution, open the fairest prospect that, within a moderate period of time, the fundamental principles of political economy will, to a very useful extent, be known to the higher, middle, and a most important portion of the working classes of society in England.

[11] [In 1817 a note was added here:
    1800 and 1801.
[12] [In 1806 this sentence was omitted, the paragraph concluding with the words:
    ... liberty of the subject.
[13] [In 1817 the words *of course* were excised.]
[14] [In 1817 there was a footnote here:
    Written in 1803.

withholding the means of raising the condition of the lower classes of people, when they are in our power. Those who will not listen to any answer to these arguments drawn from theory cannot, I think, refuse the testimony of experience; and I would ask whether the advantage of superior instruction, which the lower classes of people in Scotland are known to possess, has appeared to have any tendency towards creating a spirit of tumult and discontent amongst them. And yet from the natural inferiority of its soil and climate, the pressure of want is more constant, and the dearths are not only more frequent but more dreadful than in England. In the case of Scotland, the knowledge circulated among the common people, though not sufficient essentially to better their condition by increasing, in an adequate degree, their habits of prudence and foresight, has yet the effect of making them bear with patience the evils they suffer, from being aware of the folly and inefficacy of turbulence. The quiet and peaceable habits of the instructed Scotch peasant, compared with the turbulent disposition of the ignorant Irishman, ought not to be without effect upon every impartial reasoner.

The principal argument which I have heard advanced against a system of national education in England is, that the common people would be put in a capacity to read such works as those of Paine, and that the consequences would probably be fatal to government. But, on this subject, I agree most cordially with Dr. Smith[15] in thinking that an instructed and well-informed people would be much less likely to be led away by inflammatory writings, and much better able to detect the false declamation of interested and ambitious demagogues, than an ignorant people. One or two readers in a parish are sufficient to circulate any quantity of sedition; and if these be gained to the democratic side, they will probably have the power of doing much more mischief, by selecting the passages best suited to their hearers, and choosing the moments when their oratory is likely to have the most effect, than if each individual in the parish had been in a capacity to read and judge of the whole work himself; and, at the same time, to read and judge of the opposing arguments, which we may suppose would also reach him.

But in addition to this, a double weight would undoubtedly be added to the observation of Dr. Smith, if these schools were made the means of instructing the people in the real nature of their situation; if they were taught, what is really true, that without an increase of their own industry

[15] Wealth of Nations, vol. iii. b. v. c. i. p. 192.

and prudence, no change of government could essentially better their condition; that, though they might get rid of some particular grievance, yet in the great point of supporting their families they would be but little or perhaps not at all benefited; that a revolution would not alter in their favour the proportion of the supply of labour to the demand, or the quantity of food to the number of the consumers; and that, if the supply of labour were greater than the demand, and the demand for food greater than the supply, they might suffer the utmost severity of want under the freest, the most perfect, and best executed government that the human imagination could conceive.

A knowledge of these truths so obviously tends to promote peace and quietness, to weaken the effect of inflammatory writings, and to prevent all unreasonable and ill-directed opposition to the constituted authorities, that those who would still object to the instruction of the people may fairly be suspected of a wish to encourage their ignorance, as a pretext for tyranny, and an opportunity of increasing the power and the influence of the executive government.

Besides correcting the prevailing opinions respecting marriage, and explaining the real situation of the lower classes of society, as depending almost entirely upon themselves for their happiness or misery,[16] the parochial schools would, by early instruction and the judicious distribution of rewards, have the fairest chance of training up the rising generation in habits of sobriety, industry, independence, and prudence, and in a proper discharge of their religious duties; which would raise them from their present degraded state, and approximate them in some degree to the middle classes of society, whose habits, generally speaking, are certainly superior.

In most countries, among the lower classes of people, there appears to be something like a standard of wretchedness, a point below which they will not continue to marry and propagate their species. This standard is different in different countries, and is formed by various concurring circumstances of soil, climate, government, degree of knowledge, and civilization, &c. The principal circumstances which contribute to raise it are liberty, security of property, the spread of knowledge,[17] and a taste

---

[16] [In 1806 this was altered to:

Besides explaining the real situation of the lower classes of society, as depending principally upon themselves for their happiness or misery, the parochial schools would ...

[17] [In 1817 *spread* was changed to 'diffusion'.

for the conveniences and the comforts of life. Those which contribute principally to lower it are despotism and ignorance.

In an attempt to better the condition of the lower classes of society,[18] our object should be to raise this standard as high as possible, by cultivating a spirit of independence, a decent pride, and a taste for cleanliness and comfort [19]●among the poor. These habits would be best inculcated by a system of general education and, when strongly fixed, would be the most powerful means of preventing their marrying with the prospect of being obliged to forfeit such advantages; and would consequently raise them nearer to the middle classes of society.●[19]

---

[18] [In 1826 *lower classes* was changed to 'labouring classes'.

[19] [In 1806 the words *among the poor* were omitted, and the chapter concluded thus:
     ... and a taste for cleanliness and comfort. The effect of a good government in increasing the prudential habits and personal respectability of the lower classes of society has already been insisted on; but certainly this effect will always be incomplete without a good system of education; and, indeed, it may be said that no government can approach to perfection that does not provide for the instruction of the people. The benefits derived from education are among those which may be enjoyed without restriction of numbers; and, as it is in the power of governments to confer these benefits, it is undoubtedly their duty to do it.

CHAPTER X

Of the direction of our charity

An important and interesting inquiry yet remains, relating to the mode of directing our private charity so as not to interfere with the great object in view, of ameliorating the condition of the lower classes of people[1] by preventing the population from pressing too hard against the limits of the means of subsistence.

The emotion which prompts us to relieve our fellow creatures in distress is, like all our other natural passions, general, and in some degree indiscriminate and blind. Our feelings of compassion may be worked up to a higher pitch by a well-wrought scene in a play, or a fictitious tale in a novel, than by almost any events in real life; and if, among ten petitioners, we were to listen only to the first impulses of our feelings, without making further inquiries, we should undoubtedly give our assistance to the best actor of the party. It is evident, therefore, that the impulse of benevolence, like the impulses of love, of anger, of ambition, of eating and drinking,[2] or any other of our natural propensities, must be regulated by experience, and frequently brought to the test of utility, or it will defeat its intended purpose.

The apparent object of the passion between the sexes is the continuation of the species, and the formation of such an intimate union of views and interests between two persons as will best promote their happiness, and at the same time secure the proper degree of attention to the helplessness of infancy and the education of the rising generation; but if every man were to obey at all times the impulses of nature in the gratification of this passion, without regard to consequences, the principal part of these important objects would not be attained, and even the continuation of the species might be defeated by a promiscuous intercourse.

The apparent end of the impulse of benevolence is to draw the whole

---

[1] [In 1826 *lower classes of people* was changed to:
    ... labouring classes of people ...
[2] [In 1806 this was altered to:
    ... of ambition, the desire of eating and drinking, or any other ...

human race together, but more particularly that part of it which is of our own nation and kindred, in the bonds of brotherly love; and by giving men an interest in the happiness and misery of their fellow creatures, to prompt them, as they have power, to mitigate some of the partial evils arising from general laws, and thus to increase the sum of human happiness; but if our benevolence be indiscriminate, and the degree of apparent distress be made the sole measure of our liberality, it is evident that it will be exercised almost exclusively upon common beggars, while modest unobtrusive merit, struggling with unavoidable difficulties, yet still maintaining some slight appearances of decency and cleanliness, will be totally neglected. We shall raise the worthless above the worthy; we shall encourage indolence and check industry; and, in the most marked manner subtract from the sum of human happiness.

Our experience has, indeed, informed us that the impulse of benevolence is not so strong as the passion between the sexes, and that, generally speaking, there is much less danger to be apprehended from the indulgence of the former than of the latter; but, independently of this experience, and of the moral codes founded upon it, [3]•a youth of eighteen would be as completely justified in indulging the sexual passion with every object capable of exciting it, as in following indiscriminately every impulse of his benevolence.•[3] They are both natural passions, excited by their appropriate objects, and to the gratification of which we are prompted by the pleasurable sensations which accompany them. As animals, or till we know their consequences, our only business is to follow these dictates of nature; but, as reasonable beings, we are under the strongest obligations to attend to their consequences; and if they be evil to ourselves or others, we may justly consider it as an indication that such a mode of indulging these passions is not suited to our state or conformable to the will of God. As moral agents, therefore, it is clearly our duty to restrain their indulgence in these particular directions: and by thus carefully examining the consequences of our natural passions, and frequently bringing them to the test of utility, gradually to acquire a habit of gratifying them only in that way which, being unattended with evil, will clearly add to the sum of human happiness and fulfil the apparent purpose of the Creator.

Though utility, therefore, can never be the immediate excitement to

[3] [In 1817 this was altered:
  ... founded upon it, we should be as much justified in a general indulgence of the former passion as in following indiscriminately every impulse of our benevolence.

the gratification of any passion, it is the test by which alone we can know whether it ought or ought not to be indulged;[4] and is, therefore, the surest foundation of all morality[5] which can be collected from the light of nature. All the moral codes which have inculcated the subjection of the passions to reason have been, as I conceive, really built upon this foundation, whether the promulgators of them were aware of it or not.

I remind the reader of these truths in order to apply them to the habitual direction of our charity; and, if we keep the criterion of utility constantly in view, we may find ample room for the exercise of our benevolence without interfering with the great purpose which we have to accomplish.

One of the most valuable parts of charity is its effect upon the giver. It is more blessed to give than to receive. Supposing it to be allowed that the exercise of our benevolence in acts of charity is not, upon the whole, really beneficial to the poor, yet we could never sanction any endeavour to extinguish an impulse, the proper gratification of which has so evident a tendency to purify and exalt the human mind. But it is particularly satisfactory and pleasing to find that the mode of exercising our charity which, when brought to the test of utility, will appear to be most beneficial to the poor, is precisely that which will have the best and most improving effect on the mind of the donor.

The quality of charity like that of mercy,

> is not strained;
> It droppeth as the gentle rain from heaven
> Upon the earth beneath.

The immense sums distributed to the poor in this country, by the parochial laws, are improperly called charity. They want its most distinguishing attribute; and, as might be expected, from an attempt to force that which loses its essence the moment that it ceases to be voluntary, their effects upon those from whom they are collected are as prejudicial as on those to whom they are distributed. On the side of the receivers of this miscalled charity, instead of real relief, we find accumulated distress and more extended poverty; on the side of the givers, instead of pleasurable sensations, unceasing discontent and irritation.

---

[4] [In 1817 Malthus made an important insertion here:
   ... by which alone we can know, independently of the revealed will of God, whether it ought or ought not ...
[5] [In 1817 *the surest foundation of all morality* was changed to 'the surest criterion of moral rules'.

In the great charitable institutions supported by voluntary contributions, many[6] of which are certainly of a prejudicial tendency, the subscriptions, I am inclined to fear, are sometimes given grudgingly, and rather because they are expected by the world from certain stations, and certain fortunes, than because they are prompted by motives of genuine benevolence; and as the greater part of the subscribers do not interest themselves in the management of the funds, or in the fate of the particular objects relieved, it is not to be expected that this kind of charity should have any strikingly beneficial influence on the minds of the majority who exercise it.

Even in the relief of common beggars, we shall find that we are more frequently influenced by the desire of getting rid of the importunities of a disgusting object than by the pleasure of relieving it.[7] We wish that it had not fallen in our way, rather than rejoice in the opportunity given us of assisting a fellow-creature. We feel a painful emotion at the sight of so much apparent misery; but the pittance we give does not relieve it. We know that it is totally inadequate to produce any essential effect. We know, besides, that we shall be addressed in the same manner at the corner of the next street; and we know that we are liable to the grossest impositions. We hurry therefore sometimes by them,[8] and shut our ears to their importunate demands. We give no more than we can help giving without doing actual violence to our feelings. Our charity is in some degree forced and, like forced charity, it leaves no satisfactory impression on the mind, and cannot therefore have any very beneficial and improving effect on the heart and affections.

But it is far otherwise with that voluntary and active charity, which makes itself acquainted with the objects which it relieves; which seems to feel, and to be proud of, the bond which unites the rich with the poor; which enters into their houses; informs itself not only of their wants, but of their habits and dispositions; checks the hopes of clamorous and obstrusive poverty, with no other recommendation but rags; and encourages with adequate relief the silent and retiring sufferer, labouring under unmerited difficulties. This mode of exercising our charity presents a very different picture from that of any other; and its contrast with the

[6] [In 1806 Malthus changed *many* to 'some'.
[7] [In 1806 this was altered:
  ... we shall find that we are often as much influenced by the desire of getting rid
  ... of a disgusting object as by the pleasure of relieving it.
[8] [In 1826 *them* was changed to 'such objects'.

common mode of parish relief cannot be better described than in the words of Mr. Townsend, in the conclusion of his admirable dissertation on the Poor Laws: 'Nothing in nature can be more disgusting than a parish pay-table, attendant upon which, in the same objects of misery, are too often found combined snuff, gin, rags, vermin, insolence, and abusive language; nor in nature can any thing be more beautiful than the mild complacency of benevolence hastening to the humble cottage to relieve the wants of industry and virtue, to feed the hungry, to clothe the naked, and to soothe the sorrows of the widow with her tender orphans; nothing can be more pleasing, unless it be their sparkling eyes, their bursting tears, and their uplifted hands, the artless expressions of unfeigned gratitude for unexpected favours. Such scenes will frequently occur whenever men shall have power to dispose of their own property.'

I conceive it to be almost impossible, that any person could be much engaged in such scenes without daily making advances in virtue. No exercise of our affections can have a more evident tendency to purify and exalt the human mind. It is almost exclusively this species of charity that blesseth him that gives; and, in a general view, it is almost exclusively this species of charity which blesseth him that takes; at least it may be asserted that there is no other mode of exercising our charity[9] in which large sums can be distributed without a greater chance of producing evil than good.

The discretionary power of giving or withholding relief, which is, to a certain extent, vested in parish officers and justices, is of a very different nature, and will have a very different effect from the discrimination which may be exercised by voluntary charity. Every man in this country, under certain circumstances, is entitled by law to parish assistance; and unless his disqualification is clearly proved, has a right to complain if it be withheld. The inquiries necessary to settle this point, and the extent of the relief to be granted, too often produce evasion and lying on the part of the petitioner, and afford an opening to partiality and oppression in the overseer. If the proposed relief be given, it is of course received with unthankfulness; and if it be denied, the party generally thinks himself severely aggrieved, and feels resentment and indignation at his treatment.

[9] [This was modified twice. In 1806 it was changed to:
 ... that there is hardly any other mode of exercising our charity ...
[In 1817 Malthus wrote:
 ... that there are but few other modes of exercising our charity ...

In the distribution of voluntary charity, nothing of this kind can take place. The person who receives it is made the proper subject of the pleasurable sensation of gratitude; and those who do not receive it cannot possibly conceive themselves in the slightest degree injured. Every man has a right to do what he will with his own; and cannot, in justice, be called upon to render a reason why he gives in the one case and abstains from it in the other. This kind of despotic power, essential to voluntary charity, gives the greatest facility to the selection of worthy objects of relief, without being accompanied by any ill consequences; and has further a most beneficial effect from the degree of uncertainty which must necessarily be attached to it. It is, in the highest degree, important to the general happiness of the poor that no man should look to charity as a fund on which he may confidently depend. He should be taught that his own exertions, his own industry and foresight, are his only just ground of dependence; that if these fail, assistance in his distresses could only be the subject of rational hope; and that even the foundation of this hope must be in his own good conduct,[10] and the consciousness that he had not involved himself in these difficulties by his indolence or imprudence.

That, in the distribution of our charity, we are under a strong moral obligation to inculcate this lesson on the poor, by a proper discrimination, is a truth of which I cannot feel a doubt. If all could be completely relieved, and poverty banished from the country, even at the expense of three-fourths of the fortunes of the rich, I would be the last person to say a single syllable against relieving all, and making the degree of distress alone the measure of our bounty. But as experience has proved, I believe without a single exception, that poverty and misery have always increased in proportion to the quantity of indiscriminate charity; are we not bound to infer, reasoning as we usually do from the laws of nature, that it is an intimation that such a mode of distribution is not the proper office of benevolence?

The laws of nature say, with St. Paul: 'If a man will not work, neither shall he eat.' They also say that he is not rashly to trust to Providence. They appear indeed to be constant and uniform for the express purpose of telling him what he is to trust to, and that if he marry, without being

[10] [In 1817 this was altered:
    ... and that even the foundation of this hope will depend in a considerable degree on his own good conduct, ...

able to support a family, he must expect severe want.[11] These inti-
mations appear from the constitution of human nature to be absolutely
necessary, and to have a strikingly beneficial tendency. If in the direction
either of our public or our private charity we say that though a man will
not work, yet he shall eat; and though he marry, without being able to
support a family, yet his family shall be supported; it is evident that we
do not merely endeavour to mitigate some of the partial evils arising from
general laws, but regularly and systematically to counteract the obviously
beneficial effects of these general laws themselves.[12] And we cannot
easily conceive that the Deity should implant any passion in the human
breast for such a purpose.

In the great course of human events, the best-founded expectations
will sometimes be disappointed; and industry, prudence, and virtue, not
only fail of their just reward, but be involved in unmerited calamities.
Those who are thus suffering in spite of the best-directed endeavours to
avoid it, and from causes which they could not be expected to foresee, are
the genuine objects of charity. In relieving these, we exercise the
appropriate office of benevolence, that of mitigating some of[13] the partial
evils arising from general laws; and in this direction of our charity,
therefore, we need not apprehend any ill consequences. Such objects
ought to be relieved according to our means liberally and adequately,
even though the worthless were starving.[14]

When indeed this first claim on our benevolence was satisfied, we
might then turn our attention to the idle and improvident: but the
interests of human happiness most clearly require, that the relief which
we afford them should be very scanty.[15] We may perhaps take upon
ourselves, with great caution, to mitigate in some degree[16] the punishments which they are suffering from the laws of nature; but on no
account to remove them entirely. They are deservedly at the bottom in
the scale of society; and if we raise them from this situation, we not only

[11] [In 1817 this was modified:
    ... if he marry without a reasonable prospect of supporting a family, he must
    expect to suffer want.
[12] [In 1817 Malthus italicised *regularly* and *systematically*.]
[13] [In 1806 the words *some of* were omitted.]
[14] [In 1817 this was changed to:
    ... even though the worthless were in much more severe distress.
[15] [In 1806 the word *very* was excised.]
    [In 1817 this was altered again to:
    ... the relief which we afford them should not be abundant.
[16] [In 1806 the words *in some degree* were omitted.]

palpably defeat the end of benevolence, but commit a most glaring injustice to those who are above them. They should on no account be enabled to command so much of the necessaries of life as can be obtained by the worst-paid common labour.[17] [18]●The brownest bread, with the coarsest and scantiest apparel, is the utmost which they should have the means of purchasing.●[18]

It is evident that these reasonings do not apply to those cases of urgent distress arising from disastrous accidents, unconnected with habits of indolence and improvidence. If a man break a leg or an arm, we are not to stop to inquire into his moral character before we lend him our assistance; but in this case we are perfectly consistent, and the touchstone of utility completely justifies our conduct. By affording the most indiscriminate assistance in this way, we are in little danger of encouraging people to break their arms and legs. According to the touchstone of utility, the high approbation which Christ gave to the conduct of the good Samaritan, who followed the immediate impulse of his benevolence in relieving a stranger, in the urgent distress of an accident, does not in the smallest degree contradict the expression of St. Paul, 'If a man will not work, neither shall he eat.'[19]

We are not, however, in any case, to lose a present opportunity of doing good from the mere supposition that we may possibly meet with a worthier object. In all doubtful cases, it may safely be laid down as our duty to follow the natural impulse of our benevolence; but when in fulfilling our obligation, as reasonable beings, to attend to the consequences of our actions, we have from our own experience and that of others drawn the conclusion that the exercise of our benevolence in one

[17] [In 1817 this was altered to:
   ... can be obtained by the wages of common labour.
[18] [In 1817 this sentence was omitted.]
[19] [Jesus Christ's parable of the good man of Samaria may be found in the tenth chapter of St Luke's Gospel (vv.25–37). It was to illustrate the commandment that, after loving God, a man should love his neighbour as himself. In reply to the question: 'Who is my neighbour?' Christ told the story of a traveller who was attacked by robbers and left half dead on the road. Two later travellers saw him lying there, and each in turn passed by on the other side; a third traveller, a Samaritan, had pity on the injured man, bound up his wounds, and took him to an inn, where he paid the landlord to care for him. The good Samaritan was obviously 'neighbour unto him that fell among thieves', and Christ concluded with the words, 'Go and do thou likewise' (Bible of 1611). In his pamphlet on *Dr Parr's Spital Sermon*, Godwin pointed out (p. 43) that Christ had not merely justified, but applauded, the good Samaritan; presumably Malthus had Godwin in mind when he wrote this paragraph.]

mode is prejudicial, and in another is beneficial in its effects; we are certainly bound, as moral agents, to check our natural propensities in the one direction, and to encourage them and acquire the habits of exercising them in the other.

Of the errors in different plans which have been proposed, to improve the condition of the Poor[1]

In the distribution of our charity, or in any efforts which we may make to better the condition of the lower classes of society, there is another point relating to the main argument of this work to which we must be particularly attentive. We must on no account do anything which tends directly to encourage marriage; or to remove, in any regular and systematic manner, that inequality of circumstances which ought always to exist between the single man and the man with a family. The writers who have best understood the principle of population appear to me all to have fallen into very important errors on this point.

Sir James Steuart, who is fully aware of what he calls vicious procreation, and of the misery that attends a redundant population, recommends, notwithstanding, the general establishment of foundling hospitals; the taking of children, under certain circumstances, from their parents, and supporting them at the expense of the state; and particularly laments the inequality of condition between the married and single man, so ill-proportioned to their respective wants.[2] He forgets, in these instances, that if, without the encouragement to multiplication of foundling hospitals, or of public support for the children of some married persons, and under the discouragement of great pecuniary disadvantages on the side of the married man, population be still redundant; which is evinced by the inability of the poor to maintain all their children; it is a clear proof that the funds destined for the maintenance of labour cannot properly support a greater population; and that, if further encouragements to multiplication be given, and discouragements removed, the result must be an increase, somewhere or other, of that vicious procreation which he so justly reprobates.

Mr. Townsend, who in his Dissertation on the Poor Laws has treated this subject with great skill and perspicuity, appears to me to conclude

---

[1] [In 1806 this heading was changed to:
Different plans of improving the condition of the Poor considered.
[2] Political Occonomy, vol. i. b. i. c. xii.

with a proposal which violates the principles on which he had reasoned so well. He wishes to make the benefit clubs or friendly societies, which are now voluntarily established in many parishes, compulsory and universal; and proposes, as a regulation, that an unmarried man should pay a fourth part of his wages, and a married man with four children not more than a thirtieth part.[3]

I must first remark that the moment these subscriptions are made compulsory, they will necessarily operate exactly like a direct tax upon labour, which, as Dr. Smith justly states, will always be paid, and in a more expensive manner, by the consumer. The landed interest, therefore, would receive no[4] relief from this plan, but would pay the same sum as at present, only in the advanced price of labour and of commodities, instead of in the parish rates. A compulsory subscription of this kind would have almost all the ill effects[5] of the present system of relief and, though altered in name, would still possess the essential spirit of the poor laws.

Dean Tucker, in some remarks on a plan of the same kind, proposed by Mr. Pew, observed that, after much talk and reflection on the subject, he had come to the conclusion that they must be voluntary associations and not compulsory assemblies. A voluntary subscription is like a tax upon a luxury, and does not necessarily raise the price of labour.

It should be recollected, also, that in a voluntary association of a small extent, over which each individual member can exercise a superintendence, it is highly probable that the original agreements will all be strictly fulfilled, or if they be not, every man may at least have the redress of withdrawing himself from the club. But in an universal compulsory subscription, which must necessarily become a natural concern, there would be no security whatever for the fulfilment of the original agreements; and when the funds failed, which they certainly would do, when all the idle and dissolute were included, instead of some of the most industrious and provident, as at present, a larger subscription would probably be demanded, and no man would have the right to refuse it. The evil would thus go on increasing as the poor rates do now. If, indeed, the assistance given were always specific, and on no account to be increased, as in the present voluntary associations, this would certainly

[3] Dissertation on the Poor Laws, p. 89. 2d edit. 1787.
[4] [In 1826 *no* was changed to 'little'.
[5] [In 1817 *ill effects* was changed to 'bad effects'.

be a striking advantage; but the same advantage might be completely attained by a similar distribution of the sums collected by the parish rates. On the whole, therefore, it appears to me that, if the friendly societies were made universal and compulsory, it would be merely a different mode of collecting parish rates; and any particular mode of distribution might be as well adopted upon one system as upon the other.

With regard to the proposal of making single men pay a fourth part of their earnings weekly, and married men with families only a thirtieth part, it would evidently operate as a heavy fine upon bachelors and a high bounty upon children; and is therefore directly adverse to the general spirit in which Mr. Townsend's excellent dissertation is written. Before he introduces this proposal, he lays it down as a general principle that no system for the relief of the poor can be good, which does not regulate population by the demand for labour;[6] but this proposal clearly tends to encourage population without any reference to the demand for labour, and punishes a young man for his prudence in refraining from marriage at a time, perhaps, when this demand is so small[7] that the wages of labour are totally inadequate to the support of a family. I should be averse to any compulsory system whatever for the poor; but certainly if single men were compelled to pay a contribution for the future contingencies of the married state, they ought in justice to receive a benefit proportioned to the period of their privation; and the man who had contributed a fourth of his earnings for merely one year ought not to be put upon a level with him who has contributed this proportion for ten years.

Arthur Young, in most of his works, appears clearly to understand the principle of population, and is fully aware of the evils which must necessarily result from an increase of people beyond the demand for labour and the means of comfortable subsistence. In his Tour through France he has particularly laboured this point, and shown most forcibly the misery which results, in that country, from the excess of population occasioned by the too great division of property. Such an increase he justly calls merely a multiplication of wretchedness. 'Couples marry and procreate on the idea, not the reality, of a maintenance; they increase beyond the demand of towns and manufactures; and the consequence is distress, and numbers dying of diseases arising from insufficient nourishment.'[8]

[6] P. 84.   [7] [In 1817 *is so small* was changed to 'may be so small'.
[8] Travels in France, vol. i. c. xii. p. 408.

In another place he quotes a very sensible passage from the report of the Committee on Mendicity which, alluding to the evils of over-population, concludes thus: 'Il faudroit enfin necessairement que le prix de travail baissat par la plus grand concurrence de travailleurs, d'ou resulteroit un indigence complette pour ceux qui ne trouveroient pas de travail, et une subsistence incomplette pour ceux mêmes aux quels il ne seroit pas refusé.'[9] And in remarking upon this passage, he observes: 'France itself affords an irrefragable proof of the truth of these senti-ments; for I am clearly of opinion, from the observations I made in every province of the kingdom, that her population is so much beyond the proportion of her industry and labour, that she would be much more powerful and infinitely more flourishing if she had five or six millions less of inhabitants. From her too great population she presents, in every quarter, such spectacles of wretchedness as are absolutely inconsistent with that degree of national felicity which she was capable of attaining, even under the old government. A traveller much less attentive than I was to objects of this kind must see at every turn most unequivocal signs of distress. That these should exist, no one can wonder, who considers the price of labour and provisions, and the misery into which a small rise in the price of wheat throws the lower classes.'[10]

'If you would see', he says, 'a district with as little distress in it as is consistent with the political system of the old government of France, you must assuredly go where there are no little properties at all. You must visit the great farms in Beauce, Picardy, part of Normandy, and Artois, and there you will find no more population than what is regularly employed and regularly paid; and if in such districts you should, contrary to this rule, meet with much distress, it is twenty to one but that it is in a parish which has some commons, which tempt the poor to have cattle – to have property – and in consequence misery. When you are engaged in this political tour, finish it by seeing England, and I will shew you a set of peasants well clothed, well nourished, tolerably drunken from superfluity, well lodged, and at their ease; and yet, amongst them not one in a thousand has either land or cattle.'[11] A little further on, alluding to encouragements to marriage, he says of France: 'the predomi-nant evil of the kingdom is the having so great a population that she can

[9] ['Excessive competition among labourers must in the end necessarily lower the wages of labour, which will result in utter poverty for those who cannot find work, and an inadequate subsistence for those who can.']

[10] Travels in France, vol. i. c. xvii. p. 469.   [11] Id. p. 471.

neither employ nor feed it; why then encourage marriage? Would you breed more people, because you have more already than you know what to do with? You have so great a competition for food, that your people are starving or in misery; and you would encourage the production of more to encrease that competition. It may almost be questioned whether the contrary policy ought not to be embraced; whether difficulties should not be laid on the marriage of those who cannot make it appear that they have the prospect of maintaining the children that shall be the fruit of it? But why encourage marriages, which are sure to take place in all situations in which they ought to take place? There is no instance to be found of plenty of regular employment being first established where marriages have not followed in a proportionate degree. The policy therefore, at best, is useless, and may be pernicious.'

After having once so clearly understood the principle of population as to express these and many other sentiments on the subject, equally just and important, it is not a little surprising to find Mr. Young in a pamphlet, intitled, *The Question of Scarcity plainly stated, and Remedies considered, (published in* 1800), observing that 'the means which would of all others perhaps tend most surely to prevent future scarcities so oppressive to the poor as the present, would be to secure to every country labourer in the kingdom, that has three children and upwards, half an acre of land for potatoes, and grass enough to feed one or two cows[12] ... If each had his ample potatoe ground and a cow, the price of wheat would be of little more consequence to them than it is to their brethren in Ireland.

Every one admits the system to be good, but the question is, how to enforce it.'

I was by no means aware that the excellence of the system had been so generally admitted. For myself I strongly protest against being included in the general term of *every one*, as I should consider the adoption of this system as the most cruel and fatal blow to the happiness of the lower classes of people in this country, that they had ever received.

Mr. Young, however, goes on to say that: 'The magnitude of the object should make us disregard any difficulties, but such as are insuperable: none such would probably occur if something like the following means were resorted to:

1 Where there are common pastures, to give to a labouring man

[12] P. 77.

having children, a right to demand an allotment proportioned to the family, to be set out by the parish officers, &c. ... and a cow bought. Such labourer to have both for life, paying 40s. a year till the price of the cow, &c. was reimbursed: at his death to go to the labourer having the most numerous family, for life, paying [oo] shillings a week to the widow of his predecessor.

II Labourers thus demanding allotments by reason of their families to have land assigned, and cows bought, till the proportion so allotted amounts to one [o^th] of the extent of the common.

III In parishes where there are no commons, and the quality of the land adequate, every cottager having [oo] children, to whose cottage there is not within a given time land sufficient for a cow, and half an acre of potatoes, assigned at a fair average rent, subject to appeal to the sessions, to have a right to demand [oo] shillings per week of the parish for every child, till such land be assigned; leaving to landlords and tenants the means of doing it. Cows to be found by the parish, under an annual reimbursement.'[13]

'The great object is, by means of milk and potatoes, to take the mass of the country poor from the consumption of wheat, and to give them substitutes equally wholesome and nourishing, and as independent of scarcities, natural and artificial, as the providence of the Almighty will admit.'[14]

Would not this plan operate, in the most direct manner, as an encouragement to marriage and a bounty on children, which Mr. Young has with so much justice reprobated in his travels in France? and does he seriously think that it would be an eligible thing, to feed the mass of the people in this country on milk and potatoes, and make them as independent of the price of corn, and of the demand for labour, as their brethren in Ireland?

The specific cause of the poverty and misery of the lower classes of people in France and Ireland is that, from the extreme subdivision of property in the one country, and the facility of obtaining a potatoe ground in the other,[15] a population is brought into existence, which is not demanded by the quantity of capital and employment in the country; and the consequence of which must therefore necessarily be, as is very justly expressed in the report of the Committee on Mendicity before

[13] P. 78.   [14] P. 79.
[15] [In 1806 this was altered to:
    ... and the facility of obtaining a cabin and potatoes in the other ...

mentioned, to lower in general the price of labour by too great competition; from which must result complete indigence to those who cannot find employment, and an incomplete subsistence even to those who can.

The obvious tendency of Mr. Young's plan is, by encouraging marriage and furnishing a cheap food, independent of the price of corn, and of course of the demand for labour, to place the lower classes of people exactly in this situation.

It may perhaps be said that our poor laws, at present, regularly encourage marriage and children by distributing relief in proportion to the size of families; and that this plan, which is proposed as a substitute, would merely do the same thing in a less objectionable manner. But surely, in endeavouring to get rid of the evil of the poor laws, we ought not to retain their most pernicious quality: and Mr. Young must know as well as I do that the principal reason why poor laws have invariably been found ineffectual in the relief of the poor is, that they tend to encourage a population which is not regulated by the demand for labour. Mr. Young himself, indeed, expressly takes notice of this effect in England, and observes that, notwithstanding the unrivalled prosperity of her manufactures, 'population is sometimes too active, as we see clearly by the dangerous increase of poor's rates in country villages'.[16]

But the fact is, that Mr. Young's plan would be incomparably more powerful in encouraging a population beyond the demand for labour than our present poor laws. A laudable repugnance to the receiving of parish relief, arising partly from a spirit of independence not yet extinct, and partly from the disagreeable mode in which the relief is given, undoubtedly deters many from marrying with a certainty of falling on the parish; and the proportion of marriages to the whole population, which has before been noticed, clearly proves that the poor laws, though they have undoubtedly a considerable influence in this respect, do not encourage marriage so much as might be expected from theory.[17] But the case would be very different if, when a labourer had an early marriage in contemplation, the terrific forms of workhouses and parish officers, which might disturb his resolution, were to be exchanged for the fascinating visions of land and cows. If the love of property, as Mr.

[16] Travels in France, vol. i. c. xvii. p. 470.
[17] [In 1806 this was amended:
   ... falling on the parish; and the proportion of births and marriages to the whole population, which has before been noticed, clearly proves that the poor-laws do not encourage marriage so much as might be expected from theory.

Young has repeatedly said, will make a man do much, it would be rather strange if it would not make him marry; an action to which, it appears from experience that he is by no means disinclined.

The population which would be thus called into being would be supported by the extended cultivation of potatoes, and would of course go on without any reference to the demand for labour. In the present state of things, notwithstanding the flourishing condition of our manufactures and the numerous checks to our population, there is no practical problem so difficult as to find employment for the poor; but this difficulty would evidently be aggravated a hundred fold under the circumstances here supposed.

In Ireland, or in any other country where the common food is potatoes, and every man who wishes to marry may obtain a piece of ground sufficient, when planted with this root, to support a family, prizes may be given till the treasury is exhausted for essays on the best means of employing the poor; but till some stop to the progress of population naturally arising from this state of things take place, the object in view is really a physical impossibility.[18]

Mr. Young has intimated that if the people were fed upon milk and potatoes, they would be more independent of scarcities than at present; but why this should be the case I really cannot comprehend. Undoubtedly people who live upon potatoes will not be much affected by a scarcity of wheat; but is there any contradiction in the supposition of a failure in the crops of potatoes? I believe it is generally understood that they are more liable to suffer damage during the winter than grain. From the much greater quantity of food yielded by a given piece of land, when planted with potatoes, than under any other kind of cultivation, it would naturally happen that, for some time after the introduction of this root as the general food of the lower classes of people,[19] a greater quantity would be grown than was demanded, and they would live in plenty. Mr. Young,

---

[18] Dr. Crumpe's prize essay on the best means of finding employment for the people is an excellent treatise, and contains much valuable information;[(a)] but, till the capital of the country is better proportioned to its population, it is perfectly chimerical to expect success in any project of the kind. I am also strongly disposed to believe that the indolent and turbulent habits of the lower Irish can never be corrected while the potatoe system enables them to increase so much beyond the regular demand for labour.

[(a)] [In 1807 Malthus subtly altered this to:
    most valuable information.

[19] [In 1826 this was changed to:
    ... labouring classes of people. ...

in his travels through France, observes, that: 'In districts which contain immense quantities of waste land of a certain degree of fertility, as in the roots of the Pyrenees, belonging to communities ready to sell them, economy and industry, animated with the views of settling and marrying, flourish greatly; in such neighbourhoods something like an American increase takes place and, if the land be cheap, little distress is found. But as procreation goes on rapidly under such circumstances, the least check to subsistence is attended with great misery; as wastes becoming dearer, or the best portions being sold, or difficulties arising in the acquisition; all which circumstances I met with in those mountains. The moment that any impediment happens, the distress of such people will be proportioned to the activity and vigour which had animated population.'[20]

This description will apply exactly to what would take place in this country, on the distribution of small portions of land to the common people, and the introduction of potatoes as their general food. For a time the change might appear beneficial, and of course the idea of property would make it, at first, highly acceptable to the poor; but, as Mr. Young in another place says: 'You presently arrive at the limit beyond which the earth, cultivate it as you please, will feed no more mouths; yet those simple manners which instigate to marriage still continue; what then is the consequence but the most dreadful misery imaginable?'[21]

When the commons were all divided and difficulties began to occur in procuring potato-grounds, the habit of early marriages, which had been introduced, would occasion the most complicated distress; and when, from the increasing population and diminishing sources of subsistence, the average growth of potatoes was not more than the average consumption, a scarcity of potatoes would be, in every respect, as probable as a scarcity of wheat at present, and when it did arrive it would be, beyond all comparison, more dreadful.

When the common people of a country live principally upon the dearest grain, as they do in England on wheat, they have great resources in a scarcity; and barley, oats, rice, cheap soups, and potatoes, all present themselves as less expensive yet at the same time wholesome means of nourishment; but when their habitual food is the lowest in this scale, they appear to be absolutely without resource, except in the bark of trees, like the poor Swedes; and a great portion of them must necessarily be

---

[20] Travels in France, vol. i. c. xvii. p. 470.   [21] Ibid, c. xii. p. 409.

starved. [22]●Wheaten bread, roast beef, and turbot, which might not fail at the same time, are indeed in themselves unexceptionable substitutes for potatoes, and would probably be accepted as such, without murmuring, by the common people; but the misfortune is that a large population, which had been habitually supported by milk and potatoes, would find it difficult to obtain these substitutes in sufficient quantities, even if the whole benevolence of the kingdom were called into action for the purpose.●[22]

The wages of labour will always be regulated by the proportion of the supply to the demand.[23] And as, upon the potato system, a supply more than adequate to the demand would very soon take place, and this supply might be continued at a very cheap rate, on account of the cheapness of the food which would furnish it, the common price of labour would soon be regulated principally by the price of potatoes, instead of the price of wheat, as at present; and the rags and wretched cabins of Ireland would follow of course.

When the demand for labour occasionally exceeds the supply, and wages are regulated by the price of the dearest grain, they will generally be such as to yield something besides mere food, and the common people may be able to obtain decent houses and decent clothing. If the contrast between the state of the French and English labourers, which Mr. Young has drawn, be in any degree near the truth, the advantage on the side of England has been occasioned precisely and exclusively by these two circumstances; and if, by the adoption of milk and potatoes as the general food of the common people, these circumstances were totally altered, so as to make the supply of labour constantly in a great excess above the demand for it, and regulate wages by the price of the cheapest food, the advantage would be immediately lost, and no efforts of benevolence could prevent the most general and abject poverty.

Upon the same principle, it would by no means be eligible that the cheap soups of Count Rumford should be adopted as the general food of the common people. They are excellent inventions for public institutions, and as occasional resources; but if they were once universally adopted by the poor, it would be impossible to prevent the price of labour from being regulated by them; and the labourer, though at first he

[22] [In 1817 this passage was expunged.]
[23] [In 1826 this sentence read:

The wages of labour will always be regulated mainly by the proportion of the supply of labour to the demand.

might have more to spare for other expenses besides food, would ultimately have much less to spare than before.

The desirable thing, with a view to the happiness of the common people, seems to be that their habitual food should be dear, and their wages regulated by it; but that, in a scarcity, or other occasional distress, the cheaper food should be readily and cheerfully adopted.[24] With a view of rendering this transition easier, and at the same time of making a useful distinction between these who are dependent on parish relief, and those who are not, I should think that one plan which Mr. Young proposes would be extremely eligible. This is 'to pass an act prohibiting relief, so far as subsistence is concerned, in any other manner than by potatoes, rice, and soup, not merely as a measure of the moment, but permanently'.[25] I do not think that this plan would necessarily introduce these articles as the common food of the lower classes; and if it merely made the transition to them in periods of distress easier, and at the same time drew a more marked line than at present between dependence and independence, it would have a very beneficial effect.

As it is acknowledged that the introduction of milk and potatoes, or of cheap soups, as the general food of the lower classes of people, would lower the price of labour, perhaps some cold politician might propose to adopt the system, with a view of underselling foreigners in the markets of Europe. I should not envy the feelings which could suggest such a proposal. I really cannot conceive anything much more detestable than the idea of knowingly condemning the labourers of this country to the rags and wretched cabins of Ireland, for the purpose of selling a few more broadcloths and calicoes.[26] The wealth and power of nations are,

---

[24] It is certainly to be wished that every cottage in England should have a garden to it, well stocked with vegetables. A little variety of food is in every point of view highly useful. Potatoes are undoubtedly a most valuable subsidiary, though I should be very sorry ever to see them the principal dependence of our labourers.

[25] Question of Scarcity, &c. p. 80. This might be done, at least, with regard to workhouses. In assisting the poor at their own homes, it might be subject to some practical difficulties.

[26] In this observation, I have not the least idea of alluding to Mr. Young who, I firmly believe, ardently wishes to ameliorate the condition of the lower classes of people, though I do not think that his plan would effect the object in view. He either did not see those consequences which I apprehend from it; or he has a better opinion of the happiness of the common people in Ireland than I have. In his Irish tour he seemed much struck with the plenty of potatoes which they possessed, and the absence of all apprehension of want. Had he travelled in 1800 and 1801, his impressions would by all accounts have been very different. From the facility which has hitherto prevailed in Ireland of procuring potatoe grounds, scarcities have certainly been rare, and all

after all, only desirable as they contribute to happiness. In this point of view, I should be very far from undervaluing them, considering them, in general, as absolutely necessary means to attain the end; but if any particular case should occur, in which they appeared to be in direct opposition to each other, we cannot rationally doubt which ought to be postponed.[27]

Fortunately, however, even on the narrowest political principles, the adoption of such a system would not answer. It has always been observed that those who work chiefly on their own property, work very indolently and unwillingly when employed for others; and it must necessarily happen when, from the general adoption of a very cheap food, the population of a country increases considerably beyond the demand for labour, that habits of idleness and turbulence will be generated, most peculiarly unfavourable to a flourishing state of manufactures. In spite of the cheapness of labour in Ireland, there are few manufactures which can be prepared in that country for foreign sale so cheap as in England: and this is evidently owing[28] to the want of those industrious habits which can only be produced by regular employment.

the effects of the system have not yet been felt, though certainly enough to make it appear very far from desirable.

Mr. Young has since pursued his idea more in detail, in a pamphlet entitled *An Inquiry into the Propriety of applying Wastes to the better Maintenance and Support of the Poor*. But the impression on my mind is still the same; and it appears to me calculated to assimilate the condition of the labourers of this country to that of the lower classes of the Irish. Mr. Young seems, in a most unaccountable manner, to have forgotten all his general principles on this subject. He has treated the question of a provision for the poor as if it was merely, How to provide in the cheapest and best manner for a *given number* of people? If this had been the sole question, it would never have taken so many hundred years to resolve. But the real question is, How to provide for those who are in want in such a manner as to prevent a continual accumulation of their numbers? and it will readily occur to the reader, that a plan of giving them land and cows cannot promise much success in this respect. If, after all the commons had been divided, the poor laws were still to continue in force, no good reason can be assigned why the rates should not in a few years be as high as they are at present, independently of all that had been expended in the purchase of land and stock.

[27] [In 1817 this was changed:
... but if any particular case should occur, where they appear to be in direct opposition to each other, we cannot rationally doubt which ought to be preferred.

[28] [In 1806 this was altered to:
... and this is in a great measure owing ...

CHAPTER XII

Continuation of the same Subject[1]

The increasing portion of the society which has of late years become either wholly or partially dependent upon parish assistance, together with the increasing burden of the poor's rates on the landed property, has for some time been working a gradual change in the public opinion respecting the benefits resulting to the labouring classes of society, and to society in general, from a legal provision for the poor. But the distress which has followed the peace of 1814, and the great and sudden pressure which it has occasioned on the parish rates, have accelerated this change in a very marked manner. More just and enlightened views on the subject are daily gaining ground; the difficulties attending a legal provision for the poor are better understood, and more generally acknowledged; and opinions are now seen in print, and heard in conversation, which twenty years ago would almost have been considered as treason to the interests of the state.

This change of public opinion, stimulated by the severe pressure of the moment, has directed an unusual portion of attention to the subject of the poor-laws; and as it is acknowledged that the present system has essentially failed, various plans have been proposed either as substitutes or improvements. It may be useful to inquire shortly how far the plans which have already been published are calculated to accomplish the ends which they propose. It is generally thought that some measure of importance will be the result of the present state of public opinion. To the permanent success of any such measure, it is absolutely necessary that it should apply itself in some degree to the real source of the difficulty. Yet there is reason to fear, that notwithstanding the present improved knowledge on the subject, this point may be too much overlooked.

Among the plans which appear to have excited a considerable degree of the public attention, is one of Mr. Owen. I have already adverted to some views of Mr. Owen in a chapter on Systems of Equality, and

---

[1] [This chapter was added in 1817 and in the edition of 1826 there was a footnote: Written in 1817.

spoken of his experience with the respect which is justly due to it. If the question were merely how to accommodate, support and train, in the best manner, societies of 1200 people, there are perhaps few persons more entitled to attention than Mr. Owen: but in the plan which he has proposed, he seems totally to have overlooked the nature of the problem to be solved. This problem is, *How to provide for those who are in want, in such a manner as to prevent a continual increase of their numbers, and of the proportion which they bear to the whole society.* And it must be allowed that Mr. Owen's plan not only does not make the slightest approach towards accomplishing this object, but seems to be peculiarly calculated to effect an object exactly the reverse of it, that is, to increase and multiply the number of paupers.

If the establishments which he recommends could really be conducted according to his apparent intentions, the order of nature and the lessons of providence would indeed be in the most marked manner reversed; and the idle and profligate would be placed in a situation which might justly be the envy of the industrious and virtuous. The labourer or manufacturer who is now ill lodged and ill clothed, and obliged to work twelve hours a day to maintain his family, could have no motive to continue his exertions, if the reward for slackening them, and seeking parish assistance, was good lodging, good clothing, the maintenance and education of all his children, and the exchange of twelve hours hard work in an unwholesome manufactory for four or five hours of easy agricultural labour on a pleasant farm. Under these temptations, the numbers yearly falling into the new establishments from the labouring and manufacturing classes, together with the rapid increase by procreation of the societies themselves, would very soon render the first purchases of land utterly incompetent to their support. More land must then be purchased, and fresh settlements made; and if the higher classes of society were bound to proceed in the system according to its apparent spirit and intention, there cannot be a doubt that the whole nation would shortly become a nation of paupers with a community of goods.

Such a result might not perhaps be alarming to Mr. Owen. It is just possible indeed that he may have had this result in contemplation when he proposed his plan, and have thought that it was the best mode of quietly introducing that community of goods which he believes is necessary to complete the virtue and happiness of society. But to those who totally dissent from him as to the effects to be expected from a community of goods; to those who are convinced that even his favourite doctrine, that a man can be trained to produce more than he consumes, which is no doubt true at present, may easily cease to be true, when cultivation is pushed beyond the bounds prescribed to it by private property,[2] the approaches towards a system of this kind will be considered as approaches towards a system of universal indolence, poverty and wretchedness.

Upon the supposition, then, that Mr. Owen's plan could be effectively executed, and that the various pauper societies scattered over the country could at first be made to realize his most sanguine wishes, such might be expected to be their termination in a moderately short time, from the natural and necessary action of the principle of population.

But it is probable that the other grand objection to all systems of common property would even at the very outset confound the experience of Mr. Owen, and destroy the happiness to which he looks forward. In the society at the Lanerk Mills, two powerful stimulants to industry and good conduct are in action, which would be totally wanting in the societies proposed. At Lanerk, the whole of every man's earnings is his own; and his power of maintaining himself, his wife and children, in decency and comfort, will be in exact proportion to his industry, sobriety and economy. At Lanerk, also, if any workman be perseveringly indolent and negligent, if he get drunk and spoil his work, or if in any way he conduct himself essentially ill, he not only naturally suffers by the diminution of his earnings, but may at any time be turned off, and the society be relieved from the influence and example of a profligate and dangerous member. On the other hand, in the pauper establishments proposed in the present plan, the industry, sobriety and good conduct of each individual would be very feebly indeed connected with his power of maintaining himself and family comfortably; and in the case of persevering idleness and misconduct, instead of the simple and effective remedy of dismission, recourse must be had to a system of direct punishment of some kind or other, determined, and enforced by authority, which is always painful and distressing, and generally inefficient.

I confess it appears to me that the most successful experience, in such an establishment as that of Lanerk, furnishes no ground whatever to say what could be done towards the improvement of society in an establishment where the produce of all the labour employed would go to a common stock, and dismissal, from the very nature and object of the

[2] See vol. ii b. iii. ch. x.

institution, would be impossible. If under such disadvantages the proper management of these establishments were within the limits of possibility, what judgment, what firmness, what patience, would be required for the purpose! But where are such qualities to be found in sufficient abundance to manage one or two millions of people?

On the whole, then, it may be concluded that Mr. Owen's plan would have to encounter obstacles that really appear to be insuperable, even at its first outset; and that if these could by any possible means be overcome, and the most complete success attained, the system would, without some most unnatural and unjust laws to prevent the progress of population, lead to a state of universal poverty and distress, in which, though all the rich might be made poor, none of the poor could be made rich – not even so rich as a common labourer at present.

The plan for bettering the condition of the labouring classes of the community, published by Mr. Curwen, is professedly a slight sketch; but principles, not details, are what it is our present object to consider; and the principles on which he would proceed are declared with sufficient distinctness, when he states the great objects of his design to be,

1. Meliorating the present wretched condition of the lower orders of the people.

2. Equalizing by a new tax the present poor's rates, which *must* be raised for their relief.

3. And giving to all those, who may think proper to place themselves under its protection, a voice in the local management and distribution of the fund destined for their support.

The first proposition is, of course, or ought to be, the object of every plan proposed. And the two last may be considered as the modes by which it is intended to accomplish it.

But it is obvious that these two propositions, though they may be both desirable on other accounts, not only do not really touch, but do not even propose to touch, the great problem. We wish to check the increase and diminish the proportion of paupers, in order to give greater wealth, happiness and independence to the mass of the labouring classes. But the equalization of the poor's rates, simply considered, would have a very strong tendency to increase rather than to diminish the number of the dependent poor. At present the parochial rates fall so very heavily upon one particular species of property, that the persons whose business it is to allow them have in general a very strong interest indeed to keep them low; but if they fell equally on all sorts of property, and particularly if they were collected from large districts, or from counties, the local distributors would have comparatively but very feeble motives to reduce them, and they might be expected to increase with great rapidity.

It may be readily allowed, however, that the peculiar weight with which the poor's rates press upon land is essentially unfair. It is particularly hard upon some country parishes, where the births greatly exceed the deaths, owing to the constant emigrations which are taking place to towns and manufactories, that, under any circumstances, a great portion of these emigrants should be returned upon them, when old, disabled, or out of work. Such parishes may be totally without the power of furnishing either work or support for all the persons born within their precincts. In fact, the same number would not have been born in them unless these emigrations had taken place. And it is certainly hard, therefore, that parishes so circumstanced should be obliged to receive and maintain all who may return to them in distress. Yet, in the present state of the country, the most pressing evil is not the weight upon the land, but the increasing proportion of paupers. And, as the equalization of the rates would certainly have a tendency to increase this proportion, I should be sorry to see such a measure introduced, even if it were easily practicable, unless accompanied by some very strong and decisive limitations to the continued increase of the rates so equalized.

The other proposition of Mr. Curwen will, in like manner, be found to afford no security against the increase of pauperism. We know perfectly well that the funds of the friendly societies, as they are at present constituted, though managed by the contributors themselves, are seldom distributed with the economy necessary to their permanent efficiency; and in the national societies proposed, as a considerable part of the fund would be derived from the poor's rates, there is certainly reason to expect that every question which could be influenced by the contributors would be determined on principles still more indulgent and less economical.

On this account it may well be doubted whether it would ever be advisable to mix any public money, derived from assessments, with the subscriptions of the labouring classes. The probable result would be, that in the case of any failure in the funds of such societies, arising from erroneous calculations and too liberal allowances, it would be expected that the whole of the deficiency should be made up by the assessments. And any rules which might have been made to limit the amount applied in this way would probably be but a feeble barrier against claims founded on a plan brought forward by the higher classes of society.

Another strong objection to this sort of union of parochial and private contributions is, that from the first the members of such societies could not justly feel themselves independent. If one half or one third of the fund were to be subscribed from the parish, they would stand upon a very different footing from the members of the present benefit-clubs. While so considerable a part of the allowances to which they might be entitled in sickness or in age would really come from the poor's rates, they would be apt to consider the plan as what, in many respects, it really would be – only a different mode of raising the rates. If the system were to become general, the contributions of the labouring classes would have nearly the effects of a tax on labour, and such a tax has been generally considered as more unfavourable to industry and production than most other taxes.

The best part of Mr. Curwen's plan is that which proposes to give a credit to each contributor in proportion to the amount of his contributions, and to make his allowance in sickness, and his annuity in old age, dependent upon this amount; but this object could easily be accomplished without the objectionable accompaniments. It is also very properly observed, that 'want of employment must furnish no claims on the society; for, if this excuse were to be admitted, it would most probably be attended with the most pernicious consequences'. Yet it is at the same time rather rashly intimated, that employment must be found for all who are able to work; and, in another place, it is observed that timely assistance would be afforded by these societies, without degradation, on all temporary occasions of suspended labour.

On the whole, when it is considered that a large and probably increasing amount of poor's rates would be subscribed to these societies; that on this account their members could hardly be considered as independent of parish assistance; and that the usual poor's rates would still remain to be applied as they are now, without any proposed limitations, there is little hope that Mr. Curwen's plan would be successful in diminishing the whole amount of the rates and the proportion of dependent poor.

There are two errors respecting the management of the poor, into which the public seem inclined to fall at the present moment. The first is a disposition to attach too much importance to the effects of subscriptions from the poor themselves, without sufficient attention to the mode in which they are distributed. But the mode of distribution is much the more important point of the two; and if this be radically bad, it is of little consequence in what manner the subscriptions are raised, whether from the poor themselves or from any other quarter. If the labouring classes were universally to contribute what might at first appear a very ample proportion of their earnings, for their own support in sickness and in old age, when out of work, and when the family consisted of more than two children, it is quite certain that the funds would become deficient. Such a mode of distribution implies a power of supporting a rapidly increasing and unlimited population on a limited territory, and must therefore terminate in aggravated poverty. Our present friendly societies or benefit-clubs aim at only limited objects, which are susceptible of calculation; yet many have failed, and many more it is understood are likely to fail from the insufficiency of their funds. If any society were to attempt to give much more extensive assistance to its members; if it were to endeavour to imitate what is partially effected by the poor-laws, or to accomplish those objects which Condorcet thought were within the power of proper calculations; the failure of its funds, however large at first, and from whatever sources derived, would be absolutely inevitable. In short, it cannot be too often or too strongly impressed upon the public, especially when any question for the improvement of the condition of the poor is in agitation, that no application of knowledge and ingenuity to this subject, no efforts either of the poor or of the rich, or both, in the form of contributions, or in any other way, can possibly place the labouring classes of society in such a state as to enable them to marry generally at the same age in an old and fully-peopled country as they may do with perfect safety and advantage in a new one.

The other error towards which the public seems to incline at present is that of laying too much stress upon the *employment* of the poor. It seems to be thought that one of the principal causes of the failure of our present system is the not having properly executed that part of the 43d of Elizabeth which enjoins the purchase of materials to set the poor to work. It is certainly desirable, on many accounts, to employ the poor when it is practicable, though it will always be extremely difficult to make people work actively who are without the usual and most natural motives to such exertions; and a system of coercion involves the necessity of placing great power in the hands of persons very likely to abuse it. Still, however, it is probable that the poor might be employed more than they have hitherto been, in a way to be advantageous to their habits and morals, without being prejudicial in other respects. But we should fall into the grossest error if we were to imagine that any essential part of the evils of the poor-laws, or of the difficulties under which we are at present labouring, has arisen from not employing the poor; or if we were to suppose that any possible scheme for giving work to all who are out of employment can ever in any degree apply to the source of these evils and difficulties, so as to prevent their recurrence. In no conceivable case can the forced employment of the poor, though managed in the most judicious manner, have any direct tendency to proportion more accurately the supply of labour to the natural demand for it. And without great care and caution it is obvious that it may have a pernicious effect of an opposite kind. When, for instance, from deficient demand or deficient capital, labour has a strong tendency to fall, if we keep it up to its usual price by creating an artificial demand by public subscriptions or advances from the government, we evidently prevent the population of the country from adjusting itself gradually to its diminished resources, and act much in the same manner as those who would prevent the price of corn from rising in a scarcity, which must necessarily terminate in increased distress.

Without then meaning to object to all plans for employing the poor, some of which, at certain times and with proper restrictions, may be useful as temporary measures, it is of great importance, in order to prevent ineffectual efforts and continued disappointments, to be fully aware that the permanent remedy which we are seeking cannot possibly come from this quarter.

It may indeed be affirmed with the most perfect confidence that there is only one class of causes from which any approaches towards a remedy can be rationally expected; and that consists of whatever has a tendency to increase the prudence and foresight of the labouring classes. This is the touchstone to which every plan proposed for the improvement of the condition of the poor should be applied. If the plan be such as to co-operate with the lessons of Nature and Providence, and to encourage and promote habits of prudence and foresight, essential and permanent benefit may be expected from it: if it has no tendency of this kind, it may possibly still be good as a temporary measure, and on other accounts, but we may be quite certain that it does not apply to the source of the specific evil for which we are seeking a remedy.

Of all the plans which have yet been proposed for the assistance of the labouring classes, the saving-banks, as far as they go, appear to me much the best, and the most likely, if they should become general, to effect a permanent improvement in the condition of the lower classes of society.[3] By giving to each individual the full and entire benefit of his own industry and prudence, they are calculated greatly to strengthen the lessons of Nature and Providence; and a young man, who had been saving from fourteen or fifteen, with a view to marriage at four or five and twenty, or perhaps much earlier, would probably be induced to wait two or three years longer if the times were unfavourable; if corn were high; if wages were low; or if the sum he had saved had been found by experience not to be sufficient to furnish a tolerable security against want. A habit of saving a portion of present earnings for future contingencies can scarcely be supposed to exist without general habits of prudence and foresight; and if the opportunity furnished by provident banks to individuals, of reaping the full benefit of saving, should render the practice general, it might rationally be expected that, under the varying resources of the country, the population would be adjusted to the actual demand for labour, at the expense of less pain and less poverty; and the remedy thus appears, so far as it goes, to apply to the very root of the evil.

The great object of saving-banks, however, is to prevent want and dependence by enabling the poor to provide against contingencies themselves. And in a natural state of society, such institutions, with the aid of private charity well directed, would probably be all the means necessary to produce the best practicable effects. In the present state of things in this country the case is essentially different. With so very large a body of poor habitually dependent upon public funds, the institutions of saving-banks cannot be considered in the light of substitutes for the poor's rates.

---

[3] [Savings Banks (or Parish Banks, as they were sometimes called) date only from the beginning of the nineteenth century. They must not be confused with the old Friendly Societies or Provident Associations, whose members subscribed their weekly pennies specifically for sickness, unemployment, or funeral benefits, and whose funds were often spent on what was politely termed 'entertainment', since they usually met in ale-houses. Savings Banks, in the words of the *Edinburgh Review* for June 1815, were organised by 'benevolent persons who take an interest in their humble neighbours'; their object was 'to open to the lower orders a place of deposit for their small savings, with the allowance of a reasonable monthly interest, and with full liberty of withdrawing their money at any time, either in whole or in part – an accommodation which it is impracticable for the ordinary banks to furnish'. There were two fundamental principles: the managers or trustees (often clergymen) were not to be paid for their services, and all funds were to be invested in government stock. Malthus himself is listed as a 'manager' of one such bank in London in 1816: see Patricia James, *Population Malthus* (Routledge and Kegan Paul, 1979), pp. 222 3.]

The problem how to support those who are in want in such a manner as not continually to increase the proportion which they bear to the whole society will still remain to be solved. But if any plan should be adopted either of gradually abolishing or gradually reducing and fixing the amount of the poor's rates, saving-banks would essentially assist it; at the same time that they would receive a most powerful aid in return.

In the actual state of things, they have been established at a period likely to be particularly unfavourable to them – a period of very general distress, and of the most extensive parochial assistance; and the success which has attended them, even under these disadvantages, seems clearly to show, that in a period of prosperity and good wages, combined with a prospect of diminished parochial assistance, they might spread very extensively, and have a considerable effect on the general habits of the people.[4]

With a view to give them greater encouragement at the present moment, an act has been passed allowing persons to receive parish assistance at the discretion of the justices, although they may have funds of their own under a certain amount in a saving-bank. But this is probably a short-sighted policy. It is sacrificing the principle for which saving-banks are established, to obtain an advantage which, on this very account, will be comparatively of little value. We wish to teach the labouring classes to rely more upon their own exertions and resources, as the only way of really improving their condition; yet we reward their saving by making them still dependent upon that very species of assistance which it is our object that they should avoid. The progress of saving-banks under such a regulation will be but an equivocal and uncertain symptom of good; whereas without such a regulation every step would tell, every fresh deposition would prove the growth of a desire to become independent of parish assistance; and both the great extension of the friendly societies, and the success of the saving-banks in proportion to the time they have been established, clearly show that much progress might be expected in these institutions under favourable circumstances, without resorting to a measure which is evidently calculated to sacrifice the end to the means.

With regard to the plans which have been talked of for reducing and limiting the poor's rates, they are certainly of a kind to apply to the root of the evil; but they would be obviously unjust without a formal

---

[4] [In 1826 this was altered to:
    ... the general habits of a people.

retraction of the *right* of the poor to support; and for many years they would unquestionably be much more harsh in their operation than the plan of abolition which I have ventured to propose in a preceding chapter. At the same time, if it be thought that this country cannot entirely get rid of a system which has been so long interwoven in its frame, a limitation of the amount of the poor's rates, or rather of their proportion to the wealth and population of the country, which would be more rational and just, accompanied with a very full and fair notice of the nature of the change to be made, might be productive of essential benefit, and do much towards improving the habits and happiness of the poor.

CHAPTER XIII

Of the necessity of general principles on this subject

It has been observed by Hume that, of all sciences, there is none where first appearances are more deceitful than in politics.[1] The remark is undoubtedly very just, and is most peculiarly applicable to that department of the science which relates to the modes of improving the condition of the lower classes of society.

We are continually hearing declamations against theory and theorists, by men who pride themselves upon the distinction of being practical. It must be acknowledged that bad theories are very bad things, and the authors of them useless and sometimes pernicious members of society. But these advocates of practice do not seem to be aware that they themselves very often come under this description, and that a great part of them may be classed among the most mischievous theorists of their time. When a man faithfully relates any facts which have come within the scope of his own observation, however confined it may have been, he undoubtedly adds to the sum of general knowledge, and confers a benefit on society. But when, from this confined experience, from the management of his own little farm, or the details of the workhouse in his neighbourhood, he draws a general inference, as is very frequently the case,[2] he then at once erects himself into a theorist; and is the more dangerous because, experience being the only just foundation for theory, people are often caught merely by the sound of the word, and do not stop to make the distinction between that partial experience which, on such subjects, is no foundation whatever for a just theory, and that general experience on which alone a just theory can be founded.

There are perhaps few subjects on which human ingenuity has been more exerted than the endeavour to ameliorate the condition of the poor; and there is certainly no subject in which it has so completely failed. The question between the theorist who calls himself practical, and the genuine theorist, is, whether this should prompt us to look into all the holes and corners of workhouses, and content ourselves with mulcting the parish officers for their waste of cheese-parings and candle-ends, and

---

[1] Essay xi. vol. i. p. 431. 8vo.   [2] [In 1817 the word *very* was excised.]

with distributing more soups and potatoes; or to recur to general principles, which show us at once the cause of the failure, and prove that the system has been from the beginning radically erroneous. There is no subject to which general principles have been so seldom applied; and yet, in the whole compass of human knowledge, I doubt if there be one in which it is so dangerous to lose sight of them; because the partial and immediate effects of a particular mode of giving assistance are so often directly opposite to the general and permanent effects.

It has been observed in particular districts, where cottagers are possessed of small pieces of land, and are in the habit of keeping cows, that, during the late scarcities some of them were able to support themselves without parish assistance, and others with comparatively little.[3]

According to the partial view in which this subject has been always contemplated, a general inference has been drawn from such instances that, if we could place all our labourers in a similar situation, they would all be equally comfortable, and equally independent of the parish. This is an inference, however, that by no means follows. The advantage which cottagers who at present keep cows enjoy, arises in a great measure from its being peculiar, and would be destroyed if it were made general.[4]

A farmer or gentleman living in a grazing country[5] has, we will suppose, a certain number of cottages on his farm. Being a liberal man, and liking to see all the people about him comfortable, he may join a piece of land to his cottages[6] sufficient to keep one or two cows, and give, besides, high wages. His labourers will of course live in plenty, and be able to rear up large families; but a grazing farm requires few hands; and though the master may choose to pay those that he employs well, he will not probably wish to have more labourers on his farm than his work requires.[7] He does not therefore build more houses; and the children of the labourers whom he employs must evidently emigrate and settle in other countries. While such a system continues peculiar to certain

---

[3] See an Inquiry into the State of Cottagers in the Counties of Lincoln and Rutland by Robert Gourlay. Annals of Agriculture, vol. xxxvii. p. 514.

[4] [In 1806 *destroyed* was modified to 'considerably diminished'.

[5] [In 1806 the words *living in a grazing country* were omitted.]

[6] [In 1817 this was altered to:
   ... he may join a piece of land to each cottage sufficient to keep one or two cows ...

[7] [In 1806 this was changed:
   ... large families; but his farm may not require many hands; and though he may choose to pay those which he employs well, he will not probably wish to have more labourers on his land than his work requires.

families, or certain districts, no great inconveniences arise from it to the community in general;[8] and it cannot be doubted that the individual labourers employed on these farms are in an enviable situation, and such as we might naturally wish was the lot of all our labourers. But it is perfectly clear that such a system could not, in the nature of things, possess the same advantages if it were made general, because there would then be no countries to which the children could emigrate with any prospect of finding work. Population would evidently increase beyond the demand of towns and manufactories, and universal poverty must necessarily ensue.[9]

It should be observed also, that one of the reasons why the labourers who at present keep cows are so comfortable is that they are able to make a considerable profit of the milk which they do not use themselves; an advantage which would evidently be very much diminished if the system were universal. And though they were certainly able to struggle through the late scarcities with less assistance than their neighbours, as might naturally be expected, from their having other resources besides the article which in those individual years was scarce; yet if the system were universal, there can be no reason assigned why they would not be subject to suffer as much from a scarcity of grass and a mortality among cows,[10] as our common labourers do now from a scarcity of wheat. We should be extremely cautious therefore of trusting to such appearances, and of drawing a general inference from this kind of partial experience.

The main principle, on which the Society for Increasing the Comforts and Bettering the Condition of the Poor, professes to proceed, is excellent. To give effect to that masterspring of industry, the desire of bettering our condition,[11] is the true mode of improving the state of the

---

[8] [In 1806 this sentence was altered:
    ... or certain districts, the emigrants would easily be able to find work in other places; and it cannot be doubted ...

[9] [In 1806 these two sentences were modified:
    ... no countries to which the children could emigrate with the same prospect of finding work. Population would evidently increase ... and the price of labour would universally fall.

[10] [In 1806 Malthus added a footnote here:
    At present the loss of a cow, which must now and then happen, is generally remedied by a petition and subscription; and as the event is considered as a most serious misfortune to a labourer, these petitions are for the most part attended to; but if the cow system were universal, losses would occur so frequently that they could not possibly be repaired in the same way, and families would be continually dropping from comparative plenty into want.

[11] Preface to vol. ii of the Reports.

lower classes; and we may safely agree with Mr. Bernard, in one of his able prefaces, that whatever encourages and promotes habits of industry, prudence, foresight, virtue, and cleanliness, among the poor, is beneficial to them and to the country; and whatever removes or diminishes the incitements to any of these qualities, is detrimental to the state and pernicious to the individual.[12]

Mr. Bernard indeed, himself, seems in general to be fully aware of the difficulties which the Society has to contend with in the accomplishment of its object. But still it appears to be in some danger of falling into the error before alluded to, of drawing general inferences from insufficient experience. Without adverting to the plans respecting cheaper foods and parish shops, recommended by individuals, the beneficial effects of which depend entirely upon their being peculiar to certain families or certain parishes, and would be lost if they were general, by lowering the wages of labour; I shall only notice one observation of a more comprehensive nature, which occurs in the preface to the second volume of the Reports. It is there remarked, that the experience of the Society seemed to warrant the conclusion that the best mode of relieving the poor was by assisting them at their own homes, and placing out their children as soon as possible in different employments, apprenticeships, &c. I really believe that this is the best, and it is certainly the most agreeable mode in which occasional and discriminate assistance can be given. But it is evident that it must be done with caution, and cannot be adopted as a general principle and made the foundation of universal practice. It is open exactly to the same objection as the cow system, in pasture countries,[13] which has just been noticed, and that part of the act of the 43d of Elizabeth which directs the overseers to employ and provide for the children of the poor. A particular parish where all the children, as soon as they were of a proper age, were taken from their parents and placed out in proper situations, might be very comfortable; but if the system were general, and the poor saw that all their children would be thus provided for, every employment would presently be overstocked with hands, and the consequence need not be again repeated.

Nothing can be more clear than that it is within the power of money,

---

[12] Preface to vol. iii of the Reports.
[Mr Bernard became Sir Thomas Bernard on the death of his brother in 1810, and Malthus refers to him by his title in the editions of 1817 and 1826.]

[13] [In 1806 the words *in pasture countries* were omitted.]

and of the exertions of the rich, adequately to relieve a particular family, a particular parish, and even a particular district. But it will be equally clear, if we reflect a moment on the subject, that it is totally out of their power to relieve the whole country in the same way; at least without providing a regular vent for the overflowing numbers in emigration, or without the prevalence of a particular virtue among the poor, which the distribution of this assistance tends obviously to discourage.

Even industry itself is, in this respect, not very different from money. A man who possesses a certain portion of it, above what is usually possessed by his neighbours, will, in the actual state of things, be almost sure of a competent livelihood; but if all his neighbours were to become at once as industrious as himself, the absolute portion of industry which he before possessed would no longer be a security against want. Hume fell into a very great error[14] when he asserted that 'almost all the moral, as well as natural evils of human life, arise from idleness'; and for the cure of these ills required only that the whole species should possess naturally an equal diligence with that which many individuals are able to attain by habit and reflection.[15] It is evident that this given degree of industry possessed by the whole species, if not combined with another virtue of which he takes no notice, would totally fail of rescuing society from want and misery, and would scarcely remove a single moral or physical evil of all those to which he alludes.

I am aware of an objection which will, with great appearance of justice, be urged against the general tenour[16] of these reasonings. It will be said that to argue thus is at once to object to every mode of assisting the poor, as it is impossible, in the nature of things, to assist people individually without altering their relative situation in society, and proportionally depressing others; and that as those who have families are the persons naturally most subject to distress, and as we are certainly not called upon to assist those who do not want our aid, we must necessarily, if we act at all, relieve those who have children, and thus encourage marriage and population.

I have already observed, however, and I here repeat it again, that the general principles on these subjects ought not to be pushed too far, though they should always be kept in view; and that many cases may occur in which the good resulting from the relief of the present distress

---

[14] [In 1817 the word *very* was excised.]
[15] Dialogues on Natural Religion, Part xi. p. 212.
[16] [In 1807 *tenour* was replaced by 'scope'.]

may more than overbalance the evil to be apprehended from the remote consequence.

All relief in instances of distress, not arising from idle and improvident habits, clearly comes under this description; and in general it may be observed, that it is only that kind of systematic and certain relief,[17] on which the poor can confidently depend, whatever may be their conduct, that violates general principles, in such a manner as to make it clear that the general consequence is worse than the particular evil.

Independently of this discriminate and occasional assistance, the beneficial effects of which I have fully allowed in a preceding chapter, I have before endeavoured to show that much might be expected from a better and more general system of education. Everything that can be done in this way has indeed a very peculiar value; because education is one of those advantages which not only all may share without interfering with each other, but the raising of one person may actually contribute to the raising of others. If, for instance, a man by education acquires that decent kind of pride, and those juster habits of thinking, which will prevent him from burdening society with a family of children which he cannot support, his conduct, as far as an individual instance can go, tends evidently to improve the condition of his fellow labourers; and a contrary conduct from ignorance would tend as evidently to depress it.

I cannot help thinking also, that something might be done towards bettering the situation of the poor by a general improvement of their cottages, if care were taken, at the same time, not to make them so large as to allow of two families settling in them; and not to increase their number faster than the demand for labour required. Perhaps[18] one of the most salutary and least pernicious checks to the frequency of early marriages in this country is the difficulty of procuring a cottage, and the laudable habits which prompt a labourer rather to defer his marriage some years, in the expectation of a vacancy, than to content himself with a wretched mud cabin, like those in Ireland.[19]

---

[17] [In 1806 Malthus italicised the words *systematic* and *certain*.]

[18] [In 1806 the word *Perhaps* was excised.]

[19] Perhaps, however, this is not often left to his choice, on account of the fear which every parish has of increasing its poor. There are many ways by which our poor laws operate in counteracting their first obvious tendency to increase population, and this is one of them. I have little doubt that it is almost exclusively owing to these counteracting causes that we have been able to persevere in this system so long, and

Even the cow system, upon a more confined plan, might not be open to objection. With any view of making it a substitute for the Poor Laws, and of giving labourers a right to demand land and cows in proportion to their families; or of taking the common people from the consumption of wheat, and feeding them on milk and potatoes; it appears to me, I confess, truly preposterous: but if it were so ordered as merely to provide a comfortable situation for the better and more industrious class of labourers,[20] and to supply, at the same time, a very important want among the poor in general, that of milk for their children, I think that it would be extremely beneficial, and might be made a very powerful incitement to habits of industry, economy, and prudence. With this view, however, it is evident that only a certain portion of the labourers in each parish could be embraced in the plan; that good conduct, and not mere distress, should have the most valid claim to preference; that too much attention should not be paid to the number of children; and that, universally, those who had saved money enough for the purchase of a cow should be preferred to those who required to be furnished with one by the parish.[21]

[22]•To facilitate the saving of small sums of money for this purpose, and encourage young labourers to economize their earnings with a view to a provision for marriage, it might be extremely useful to have country banks, where the smallest sums would be received, and a fair interest paid for them. At present the few labourers who save a little money are often greatly at a loss to know what to do with it; and under such circumstances we cannot be much surprised that it should sometimes be ill employed, and last but a short time. It would probably be essential to the success of any plan of this kind that the labourer should be able to draw out his money whenever he wanted it, and have the most perfect liberty of disposing of it in every respect as he pleased. Though we may regret that money so hardly earned should sometimes be spent to little

---

that the condition of the poor has not been so much injured by it as might have been expected.

[20] [In 1817 the words *class of* were omitted.]

[21] The act of Elizabeth which prohibited the building of cottages, unless four acres of land were annexed to them, is probably impracticable in a manufacturing country like England; but upon this principle, certainly the greatest part of the poor might possess land; because the difficulty of procuring such cottages would always operate as a powerful check to their increase. The effect of such a plan would be very different from that of Mr. Young.

[22] [This paragraph was omitted in 1817 because the subject had been dealt with in the previous chapter, which was added in that year.]

purpose; yet it seems to be a case in which we have no right to interfere; nor if we had, would it, in a general view, be advantageous; because the knowledge of possessing this liberty would be of more use in encouraging the practice of saving than any restriction of it in preventing the misuse of money so saved.●[22]

One should undoubtedly be extremely unwilling not to make as much use as possible of that known stimulus to industry and economy, the desire of, and the attachment to, property: but it should be recollected that the good effects of this stimulus show themselves principally when this property is to be procured or preserved by personal exertions; and that they are by no means so general under other circumstances. If any idle man with a family could demand and obtain a cow and some land, I should expect to see both very often neglected.

It has been observed that those cottagers who keep cows are more industrious and more regular in their conduct than those who do not. This is probably true, and what might naturally be expected; but the inference that the way to make all people industrious is to give them cows, may by no means be quite so certain. Most of those who keep cows at present have purchased them with the fruits of their own industry. It is therefore more just to say that their industry has given them a cow, than that a cow has given them their industry; though I would by no means be understood to imply that the sudden possession of property never generates industrious habits.

The practical good effects which have been already experienced, from cottagers keeping cows,[23] arise in fact from the system being nearly such as the confined plan which I have mentioned. In the districts where cottagers of this description most abound, they do not bear a very large proportion to the population of the whole parish: they consist in general of the better sort of labourers, who have been able to purchase their own cows; and the peculiar comforts of their situation arise more from the relative than the positive advantages which they possess.[24]

From observing, therefore, their industry and comforts, we should be very cautious of inferring that we could give the same industry and comforts to all the lower classes of people by giving them the same

---

[23] Inquiry into the State of Cottagers in the Counties of Lincoln and Rutland, by Robert Gourlay. Annals of Agriculture, vol. xxxvii. p. 514.

[24] [In 1826 this was altered to:
    ... the peculiar comforts of their situation arise as much from the relative as the positive advantages which they possess.

possessions. There is nothing that has given rise to such a cloud of errors as a confusion between relative and positive, and between cause and effect.

It may be said, however, that any plan of generally improving the cottages of the poor, or of enabling more of them to keep cows, would evidently give them the power of rearing a greater number of children, and, by thus encouraging population, violate the principles which I have endeavoured to establish. But if I have been successful in making the reader comprehend the principal bent of this work, he will be aware that the precise reason why I think that more children ought not to be born than the country can support, is, that the greatest possible number of those that are born may be supported. We cannot, in the nature of things, assist the poor, in any way, without enabling them to rear up to manhood a greater number of their children. But this is, of all other things, the most desirable, both with regard to individuals and the public. Every loss of a child from the consequences of poverty must evidently be preceded and accompanied by great misery to individuals; and in a public view, every child that dies under ten years of age is a loss to the nation of all that had been expended in its subsistence till that period. Consequently, in every point of view, a decrease of mortality at all ages is what we ought to aim at. We cannot however effect this object without first crowding the population, in some degree, by making more children grow up to manhood; but we shall do no harm in this respect if, at the same time, we can impress these children with the idea that, to possess the same advantages as their parents, they must defer marriage till they have a fair prospect of being able to maintain a family. And it must be candidly confessed that if we cannot do this all our former efforts will have been thrown away. It is not in the nature of things that any permanent and general improvement in the condition of the poor can be effected without an increase in the preventive check: and unless this take place, either with or without our efforts, everything that is done for the poor must be temporary and partial: a diminution of mortality at present will be balanced by an increased mortality in future; and the improvement of their condition in one place will proportionally depress it in another. This is a truth so important, and so little understood, that it can scarcely be too often insisted on. [25]●The generality of charitable people, and of the encouragers of marriage, are not in the smallest degree aware of the real effects of what they do.●[25]

[25] [In 1807 this sentence was excised.]

Dr. Paley, in a chapter on population, provision, &c. in his Moral Philosophy, observes that the condition most favourable to the population of a country, and at the same time to its general happiness, is 'that of a laborious frugal people ministering to the demands of an opulent, luxurious nation'.[26] Such a form of society has not, it must be confessed, an inviting aspect. Nothing but the conviction of its being absolutely necessary could reconcile us to the idea of ten millions of people condemned to incessant toil, and to the privation of everything but absolute necessaries, in order to minister to the excessive luxuries of the other million. But the fact is, that such a form of society is by no means necessary. It is by no means necessary that the rich should be excessively luxurious, in order to support the manufactures of a country, or that the poor should be deprived of all luxuries in order to make them sufficiently numerous. The best, and in every point of view the most advantageous manufactures in this country, are those which are consumed by the great body of the people. The manufactures which are confined exclusively to the rich are not only trivial on account of the comparative smallness of their quantity; but are further liable to the great disadvantage of producing much occasional misery among those employed in them, from changes of fashion. It is the spread[27] of luxury, therefore, among the mass of the people, and not an excess of it in a few, that seems to be the most advantageous, both with regard to national wealth and national happiness; and what Dr. Paley considers as the true evil and proper danger of luxury, I should be disposed to consider as its true good and peculiar advantage. If, indeed, it be allowed that in every society, not in the state of a new colony some powerful check to population must prevail; and if it be observed that a taste for the comforts and conveniences of life will prevent people from marrying under the certainty of being deprived of these advantages; it must be allowed that we can hardly expect to find any check to marriage so little prejudicial to the happiness and virtue of society as the general prevalence of such a taste;

[26] Vol. ii. c. xi. p. 359. From a passage in Dr. Paley's late work on Natural Theology, I am inclined to think that subsequent reflection has induced him to modify some of his former ideas on the subject of population. He has stated most justly, (chap. xxv. p. 539) that mankind will in every country breed up to a certain point of distress. If this be allowed, that country will evidently be the happiest where the degree of distress at this point is the least, and consequently, if the spread[(a)] of luxury, by producing the check sooner, tend to diminish this degree of distress, it is certainly desirable.

[(a)] [In 1817 *spread* was changed to 'diffusion'.

[27] [In 1817 *spread* was changed to 'diffusion'.

and consequently that the spread of luxury[28] in this sense of the term is particularly desirable; and one of the best means of raising that standard of wretchedness, alluded to in the eighth chapter[29] of this book.

It has been generally found that the middle parts of society are most favourable to virtuous and industrious habits, and to the growth of all kinds of talents. But it is evident that all cannot be in the middle. Superior and inferior parts are, in the nature of things, absolutely necessary; and not only necessary, but strikingly beneficial. If no man could hope to rise or fear to fall in society; if industry did not bring with it its reward, and indolence its punishment; we could not expect to see that animated activity in bettering our condition which now forms the master-spring of public prosperity. But in contemplating the different states of Europe, we observe a very considerable difference in the relative proportions of the superior, the middle, and the inferior parts; and from the effect of these differences, it seems probable that our best-grounded expectations of an increase in the happiness of the mass of human society are founded in the prospect of an increase in the relative proportions of the middle parts. And if the lower classes of people had acquired the habit of proportioning the supplies of labour to a stationary or even decreasing demand, without an increase of misery and mortality, as at present; we might even venture to indulge a hope that at some future period the processes for abridging human labour, the progress of which has of late years been so rapid, might ultimately supply all the wants of the most wealthy society with less personal labour than at present; and if they did not diminish the severity of individual exertion, might, at least, diminish the number of those employed in severe toil. If the lowest classes of society were thus diminished, and the middle classes increased, each labourer might indulge a more rational hope of rising by diligence and exertion into a better station; the rewards of industry and virtue

---

[28] In a note to the tenth chapter of the last book, I have mentioned the point at which, alone, it is probable that luxury becomes really prejudicial to a country. But this point does not depend upon the spread of luxury, as diminishing the frequency of marriage among the poor, but upon the proportion which those employed in preparing or procuring luxuries bears to the funds which are to support them.
[In 1817 *the spread of luxury* was altered to 'the extension of luxury', and the footnote was omitted.]

[29] [In 1817 this was changed to 'alluded to in a former chapter'. It is chapter ix of Book IV in this edition, 'Of the modes of correcting the prevailing opinions on the subject of Population'. In the last two paragraphs of this chapter Malthus stressed the desirability of an increased demand for the conveniences and comforts of life.]

would be increased in number; human society[30] would appear to consist of fewer blanks and more prizes; and the sum of social happiness would be evidently augmented.

To indulge, however, in any distant views of this kind, unaccompanied by the evils usually attendant on a stationary or decreasing demand for labour, we must suppose the general prevalence of such prudential habits among the poor as would prevent them from marrying when the actual price of labour, joined to what they might have saved in their single state, would not give them the prospect of being able to support a wife and six children[31] without assistance. And in every point of view[32] such a degree of prudential restraint would be extremely beneficial; and would produce a very striking amelioration in the condition of the lower classes of people.

It may be said, perhaps, that even this degree of prudence might not always avail, as when a man marries he cannot tell what number of children he shall have, and many have more than six. This is certainly true; and in this case I do not think that any evil would result from making a certain allowance to every child above this number; not with a view of rewarding a man for his large family, but merely of relieving him from a species of distress which it would be unreasonable in us to expect that he should calculate upon. And with this view, the relief should be merely such as to place him exactly in the same situation as if he had had six children. Montesquieu disapproves of an edict of Lewis the fourteenth, which gave certain pensions to those who had ten and twelve children, as being of no use in encouraging population.[33] For the very reason that he disapproves of it, I should think that some law of the kind might be adopted without danger, and might relieve particular individuals from a very pressing and unlooked-for distress, without operating in any respect as an encouragement to marriage.

If, at some future period, any approach should be made towards the more general prevalence of prudential habits with respect to marriage among the poor, from which alone any permanent and general improvement of their condition can arise, I do not think that the narrowest politician need be alarmed at it, from the fear of its occasioning such an advance in the price of labour as will enable our commercial competitors

---

[30] [In 1806 this was amended to 'the lottery of human society'.

[31] [In 1807 this was changed to 'five or six children'.

[32] [In 1807 *in every point of view* was changed to 'undoubtedly'.

[33] Esprit des Loix, liv. xxiii. c. xxvii.

to undersell us in foreign markets. There are four circumstances that might be expected to accompany it, which would probably either prevent, or fully counterbalance, any effect of this kind. These are, 1st, The more equable and lower price of provisions, from the demand being less frequently above the supply. 2dly, The removal of that heavy burden on agriculture, and that great addition to the present wages of labour, the poor's rates. 3dly, The national saving of a great part of that sum which is expended without return, in the support of those children who die prematurely from the consequences of poverty. And, lastly, The more general prevalence of economical and industrious habits, particularly among unmarried men, which prevent that indolence, drunkenness, and waste of labour, which at present are too frequently a consequence of high wages.

CHAPTER XIV

Of our rational expectations respecting the future improvement of Society

In taking a general and concluding view of our rational expectations respecting the mitigations of the evils arising from the principle of population, it may be observed that though the increase of population in a geometrical ratio be incontrovertible, and the period of doubling, when unchecked, has been uniformly stated in this work rather below than above the truth; yet there are some natural consequences of the progress of society and civilization which necessarily repress its full effects. There are, more particularly, great towns and manufactures, in which we can scarcely hope, and certainly not expect, to see any very material change. It is undoubtedly our duty, and in every point of view highly desirable, to make towns and manufacturing employments as little injurious as possible to the duration of human life; but, after all our efforts, it is probable that they will always remain less healthy than country situations and country employments; and consequently, operating as positive checks, will diminish in some degree the necessity of the preventive check.

In every old state it is observed that a considerable number of grown-up people remain for a time unmarried. The duty of practising the common and acknowledged rules of morality during this period has never been controverted in theory, however it may have been opposed in practice. This branch of the duty of moral restraint has scarcely been touched by the reasonings of this work. It rests on the same foundation as before, neither stronger nor weaker. And knowing how incompletely this duty has hitherto been fulfilled, it would certainly be visionary to expect any very material change for the better in future.[1]

The part which has been affected by the reasonings of this work is not, therefore, that which relates to our conduct during the period of celibacy, but to the duty of extending this period till we have a prospect of being able to maintain our children. And it is by no means visionary to

---

[1] [In 1817 this was changed to:
... visionary to expect that in future it would be completely fulfilled.

indulge a hope of some favourable change in this respect; because it is found by experience that the prevalence of this kind of prudential restraint is extremely different in different countries, and in the same countries at different periods.

It cannot be doubted that throughout Europe in general, and most particularly in the northern states, a decided change has taken place in the operation of prudential restraint since the prevalence of those warlike and enterprising habits which destroyed so many people. In later times the gradual diminution and almost total extinction of the plagues which so frequently visited Europe, in the seventeenth and the beginning of the eighteenth centuries, produced a change of the same kind. And in this country it is not to be doubted that the proportion of marriages has become smaller since the improvement of our towns, the less frequent returns of epidemics, and the adoption of habits of greater cleanliness. During the late scarcities, it appears that the number of marriages diminished;[2] and the same motives which prevented many people from marrying during such a period would operate precisely in the same way if, in future, the additional number of children reared to manhood from the introduction of the cow-pox were to be such as to crowd all employments, lower the price of labour, and make it more difficult to support a family.

Universally, the practice of mankind on the subject of marriage has been much superior to their theories; and however frequent may have been the declamations on the duty of entering into this state, and the advantage of early unions to prevent vice, each individual has practically found it necessary to consider of the means of supporting a family before he ventured to take so important a step. That great *vis medicatrix reipublicæ*,[3] the desire of bettering our condition, and the fear of making it worse, has been constantly in action, and has been constantly directing people into the right road in spite of all the declamations which tended to lead them aside. Owing to this powerful spring of health in every state, which is nothing more than an inference from the general course of the laws of nature, irresistibly forced on each man's attention, the prudential check to marriage has increased in Europe; and it cannot be unreasonable to conclude that it will still make further advances. If this take place,

---

[2] [In 1817 Malthus added his usual footnote:
   1800 and 1801.

[3] [This might be freely translated as: 'That great and wholesome force in the life of a nation, the desire of bettering our condition ...']

without any marked and decided increase of a vicious intercourse with the sex, the happiness of society will evidently be promoted by it; and with regard to the danger of such increase, it is consolatory to remark that those countries in Europe where marriages are the least frequent[4] are by no means particularly distinguished by vices of this kind. It has appeared that Norway, Switzerland, England, and Scotland, are above all the rest in the prevalence of the preventive check; and though I do not mean to insist particularly on the virtuous habits of these countries, yet I think that no person would select them as the countries most marked for profligacy of manners. Indeed, from the little that I know of the continent, I should have been inclined to select them as most distinguished for contrary habits, and as rather above than below their neighbours in the chastity of their women, and consequently in the virtuous habits of their men. Experience therefore seems to teach us that it is possible for moral and physical causes to counteract the effects that might at first be expected from an increase of the preventive check;[5] but allowing all the weight to these effects which is in any degree probable, it may be safely asserted that the diminution of the vices arising from indigence would fully counterbalance them; and that all the advantages of diminished mortality and superior comforts, which would certainly result from an increase of the preventive check, may be placed entirely on the side of the gains to the cause of happiness and virtue.

It is less the object of the present work to propose new plans of improving society, than to inculcate the necessity of resting contented with that mode of improvement which is dictated by the course of nature,[6] and of not obstructing the advances which would otherwise be made in this way.

It would be undoubtedly highly advantageous that all our positive institutions, and the whole tenour of our conduct to the poor, should be such as actively to co-operate with that lesson of prudence inculcated by the common course of human events; and if we take upon ourselves, sometimes, to mitigate the natural punishments of imprudence, that we could balance it by increasing the rewards of an opposite conduct. But

[4] [In 1817 this was amended to:
      ... where marriages are the latest or least frequent are by no means ...
[5] [In 1806 Malthus changed this to:
      ... an increase of the check to marriage; ...
[6] [In 1826 this was altered to:
      ... that mode of improvement, which already has in part been acted upon, as dictated by the course of nature ...

much would be done, if merely the institutions which directly tend to encourage marriage were gradually changed, and we ceased to circulate opinions and inculcate doctrines which positively counteract the lessons of nature.

The limited good, which it is sometimes in our power to effect, is often lost by attempting too much, and by making the adoption of some particular plan essentially necessary even to a partial degree of success. In the practical application of the reasonings of this work, I hope that I have avoided this error. I wish to press on the recollection of the reader that, though I may have given some new views of old facts, and may have indulged in the contemplation of a considerable degree of *possible* improvement, that I might not absolutely shut out that prime cheerer, hope;[7] yet in my expectations of probable improvement, and in suggesting the means of accomplishing it, I have been very cautious. The gradual abolition of the poor laws has already often been proposed, in consequence of the practical evils which have been found to flow from them, and the danger of their becoming a weight absolutely intolerable on the landed property of the kingdom. The establishment of a more extensive system of national education, has neither the advantage of novelty with some, nor its disadvantage with others, to recommend it. The practical good effects of education have long been experienced in Scotland; and almost every person, who has been placed in a situation to judge, has given his testimony, that education appears to have a considerable effect in the prevention of crimes,[8] and the promotion of industry, morality, and regular conduct. Yet these are the only plans which have been offered; and though the adoption of them in the modes suggested, would very powerfully contribute to forward the object of this work, and better the condition of the poor; yet if nothing be done in this way, I shall not absolutely despair of some partial good effects from the general tenour of the reasoning.[9]

If the principles which I have endeavoured to establish be false, I most

---

[7] [In 1817 the word *absolutely* was omitted.]

[8] Mr. Howard found fewer prisoners in Switzerland and Scotland, than in other countries, which he attributed to a more regular education among the lower classes of the Swiss and the Scotch. During the number of years which the late Mr. Fielding presided at Bow-street, only six Scotchmen were brought before him. He used to say that of the persons committed, the greater part were Irish. Preface to vol. iii of the Reports of the Society for Bettering the Condition of the Poor, p. 32.

[9] [In 1817 this was changed to:

...not absolutely despair of some partial good resulting from the general effects of the reasoning.

sincerely hope to see them completely refuted; but if they be true, the subject is so important, and interests the question of human happiness so nearly, that it is impossible that they should not in time be more fully known and more generally circulated, whether any particular efforts be made for the purpose or not.

Among the higher and middle classes of society, the effect of this knowledge would,[10] I hope, be to direct without relaxing their efforts in bettering the condition of the poor; to show them what they can and what they cannot do; and that, although much may be done by advice and instruction, by encouraging habits of prudence and cleanliness, by occasional and discriminate charity,[11] and by any mode of bettering the present condition of the poor which is followed by an increase of the preventive check; yet that, without this last effect, all the former efforts would be futile; and that, in any old and well-peopled state, to assist the poor in such a manner as to enable them to marry as early as they please, and rear up large families, is a physical impossibility. This knowledge, by tending to prevent the rich from destroying the good effects of their own exertions, and wasting their efforts in a direction where success is unattainable, would confine their attention to the proper objects, and thus enable them to do more good.

Among the poor themselves, its effects would be still more important. That the principal and most permanent cause of poverty has little or no relation[12] to forms of government, or the unequal division of property; and that, as the rich do not in reality possess the power of finding employment and maintenance for the poor, the poor cannot, in the nature of things, possess the right to demand them,[13] are important truths flowing from the principle of population, which, when properly explained, would by no means be above the most ordinary comprehensions. And it is evident that every man in the lower classes of society, who became acquainted with these truths, would be disposed to bear the distresses in which he might be involved with more patience; would feel less discontent and irritation at the government and the higher classes of society on account of his poverty; would be on all occasions less disposed to insubordination and turbulence; and if he received assistance, either

---

[10] [In 1817 the word *would* was replaced by 'will'.
[11] [In 1807 the words *occasional and* were expunged.]
[12] [In 1806 this was altered to:

   ... little or no direct relation to forms of government, ...
[13] [In 1817 the words *direct, power,* and *right* in this passage were all italicised.]

from any public institution or from the hand of private charity, he would receive it with more thankfulness, and more justly appreciate its value.

If these truths were by degrees more generally known (which in the course of time does not seem to be improbable, from the natural effects of the mutual interchange of opinions) the lower classes of people, as a body, would become more peaceable and orderly; would be less inclined to tumultuous proceedings in seasons of scarcity, and would at all times be less influenced by inflammatory and seditious publications, from knowing how little the price of labour, and the means of supporting a family, depend upon a revolution. The mere knowledge of these truths, even if they did not operate sufficiently to produce any marked change in the prudential habits of the poor, with regard to marriage, would still have a most beneficial effect on their conduct in a political light; and undoubtedly, one of the most valuable of these effects would be the power that would result to the higher and middle classes of society of gradually improving their governments[14] without the apprehension of those revolutionary excesses, the fear of which, at present, threatens to deprive Europe even of that degree of liberty which she had before experienced to be practicable, and the salutary effects of which she had long enjoyed.

From a review of the state of society in former periods, compared with the present, I should certainly say that the evils resulting from the principle of population have rather diminished than increased, even under the disadvantage of an almost total ignorance of the real cause. And if we can indulge the hope that this ignorance will be gradually dissipated, it does not seem unreasonable to expect that they will be still further diminished. The increase of absolute population, which will of course take place, will evidently tend but little to weaken this expectation, as everything depends upon the relative proportion between population and food, and not on the absolute number of people. In the former part of this work, it appeared that the countries which possessed the fewest people often suffered the most from the effects of the principle of population; and it can scarcely be doubted that, taking Europe

---

[14] I cannot believe that the removal of all unjust grounds of discontent against constituted authorities would render the people torpid and indifferent to advantages which are really attainable. The blessings of civil liberty are so great that they surely cannot need the aid of false colouring to make them desirable. I should be sorry to think that the lower classes of people could never be animated to assert their rights but by means of such illusory promises as will generally make the remedy of resistance much worse than the disease that it was intended to cure.

throughout, fewer famines, and fewer diseases arising from want have prevailed in the last century than in those which preceded it.

On the whole, therefore, though our future prospects respecting the mitigation of the evils arising from the principle of population may not be so bright as we could wish, yet they are far from being entirely disheartening, and by no means preclude that gradual and progressive improvement in human society, which, before the late wild speculations on this subject, was the object of rational expectation. To the laws of property and marriage, and to the apparently narrow principle of self-love,[15] which prompts each individual to exert himself in bettering his condition, we are indebted for all the noblest exertions of human genius, for everything that distinguishes the civilized from the savage state. A strict inquiry into the principle of population leads us strongly to the conclusion[16] that we shall never be able to throw down the ladder by which we have risen to this eminence; but it by no means proves that we may not rise higher by the same means. The structure of society, in its great features, will probably always remain unchanged. We have every reason to believe that it will always consist of a class of proprietors and a class of labourers; but the condition of each, and the proportion which they bear to each other, may be so altered as greatly to improve the harmony and beauty of the whole. It would indeed be a melancholy reflection that, while the views of physical science are daily enlarging, so as scarcely to be bounded by the most distant horizon, the science of moral and political philosophy should be confined within such narrow limits, or at best be so feeble in its influence, as to be unable to counteract the increasing obstacles to human happiness arising from the progress of population.[17] But however formidable these obstacles may have appeared in some parts of this work, it is hoped that the general result of the inquiry is such as not to make us give up the cause of[18] the improvement of human society in despair. The partial good which seems to be attainable is worthy of all our exertions; is sufficient to direct our efforts and animate our prospects. And although we cannot expect that the

---

[15] [In 1826 this was changed to 'self-interest'.
[16] [In 1806 Malthus amended this:
   A strict inquiry into the principle of population obliges us to conclude that we shall never ...
[17] [In 1806 this was altered to:
   ... unable to counteract the obstacles to human happiness arising from a single cause.
[18] [In 1806 the words *the cause of* were omitted.]

virtue and happiness of mankind will keep pace with the brilliant career of physical discovery yet; if we are not wanting to ourselves, we may confidently indulge the hope that, to no unimportant extent, they will be influenced by its progress and will partake in its success.

Appendix, 1806

[In 1806 this was headed simply 'Appendix'. A quarto version was published separately, for the convenience of those who possessed the edition of 1803, so that it could be bound in with the original work. This quarto version was entitled 'Reply to the Chief Objections which have been urged against the Essay on the Principle of Population, published in an Appendix to the Third Edition'.]

In the preface to the last[1] edition of this Essay, I expressed a hope that the detailed manner in which I had treated the subject and pursued it to its consequences, though it might open the doors to many objections, and expose me to much severity of criticism, might be subservient to the important end of bringing a subject so nearly connected with the happiness of society into more general notice. Conformably to the same views I should always have felt willing to enter into the discussion of any serious objections that were made to my principles or conclusions, to abandon those which appeared to be false, and to throw further lights, if I could, on those which appeared to be true. But though the work has excited a degree of public attention much greater than I could[2] have presumed to expect, yet very little has been written to controvert it; and of that little, the greatest part is so full of illiberal declamation, and so entirely destitute of argument, as to be evidently beneath notice. What I have to say therefore at present, will be directed rather more to the objections which have been urged in conversation, than to those which have appeared in print. My object is to correct some of the misrepresentations which have gone abroad respecting two or three of the most

---

[1] [In 1807 *last* was changed to 'second'.   [2] [In 1826 *could* was altered to 'should'.

important points of the Essay; and I should feel greatly obliged to those who have not had leisure to read the whole work, if they would cast their eyes over the few following pages, that they may not, from the partial and incorrect statements which they have heard, mistake the import of some of my opinions, and attribute to me others which I have never held.

The first grand objection that has been made to my principles is that they contradict the original command of the Creator, to increase and multiply and replenish the earth. But those who have urged this objection have certainly either not read the work, or have directed their attention solely to a few detached passages, and have been unable to seize the bent and spirit of the whole. I am fully of opinion, that it is the duty of man to obey this command of his Creator, nor is there in my recollection a single passage in the work which, taken with the context, can to any reader of intelligence warrant the contrary inference.

Every express command given to man by his Creator is given in subordination to those great and uniform laws of nature which he had previously established; and we are forbidden both by reason and religion to expect that these laws will be changed in order to enable us to execute more readily any particular precept. It is undoubtedly true that, if man were enabled miraculously to live without food, the earth would be very rapidly replenished; but as we have not the slightest ground of hope that such a miracle will be worked for this purpose, it becomes our positive duty as reasonable creatures, and with a view of executing the commands of our Creator, to inquire into the laws which he has established for the multiplication of the species. And when we find, not only from the speculative contemplation of these laws, but from the far more powerful and imperious suggestions of our senses, that man cannot live without food, it is a folly exactly of the same *kind* to attempt to obey the will of our Creator by increasing population without reference to the means of its support, as to attempt to obtain an abundant crop of corn by sowing it on the wayside and in hedges, where it cannot receive its proper nourishment. Which is it, I would ask, that best seconds the benevolent intentions of the Creator in covering the earth with esculent vegetables, he who with care and foresight duly ploughs and prepares a piece of ground, and sows no more seed than he expects will grow up to maturity, or he who scatters a profusion of seed indifferently over the land, without reference to the soil on which it falls, or any previous preparation for its reception?

It is an utter misconception of my argument to infer that I am an enemy to population. I am only an enemy to vice and misery, and consequently to that unfavourable proportion between population and food which produces these evils. But this unfavourable proportion has no necessary connection with the quantity of absolute population which a country may contain. On the contrary, it is more frequently found in countries which are very thinly peopled than in those which are populous.

The bent of my argument on the subject of population may be illustrated by the instance of a pasture farm. If a young grazier were told to stock his land well, as on his stock would depend his profits, and the ultimate success of his undertaking, he would certainly have been told nothing but what was strictly true. And he would have to accuse himself, not his advisers, if in pursuance of these instructions he were to push the breeding of his cattle till they became lean and half-starved. His instructor, when he talked of the advantages of a large stock, meant undoubtedly stock in proper condition, and not such a stock as, though it might be numerically greater, was in value much less. The expression of stocking a farm well does not refer to particular numbers, but merely to that proportion which is best adapted to the farm, whether it be a poor or a rich one, whether it will carry fifty head of cattle or five hundred. It is undoubtedly extremely desirable that it should carry the greater number, and every effort should be made to effect this object; but surely that farmer could not be considered as an enemy to a large quantity of stock, who should insist upon the folly and impropriety of attempting to breed such a quantity, before the land was put into a condition to bear it.

The arguments which I have used respecting the increase of population are exactly of the same nature as these just mentioned. I believe that it is the intention of the Creator that the earth should be replenished;[3] but certainly with a healthy, virtuous, and happy population, not an unhealthy, vicious, and miserable one. And if in endeavouring to obey the command to increase and multiply, we people it only with beings of this latter description, and suffer accordingly, we have no right to impeach the justice of the command, but our irrational mode of executing it.

In the desirableness of a great and efficient population, I do not differ from the warmest advocates of increase. I am perfectly ready to acknowledge with the writers of old, that it is not extent of territory but extent of

---

[3] This opinion I have expressed. [p. 214 of this edition]

population that measures the power of states. It is only as to the mode of obtaining a vigorous and efficient population that I differ from them; and in thus differing I conceive myself entirely borne out by experience, that great test of all human speculations.

It appears from the undoubted testimony of registers, that a large proportion of marriages and births is by no means necessarily connected with a rapid increase of population, but is often found in countries where it is either stationary or increasing very slowly. The population of such countries is not only comparatively inefficient from the general poverty and misery of the inhabitants, but invariably contains a much larger proportion of persons in those stages of life in which they are unable to contribute their share to the resources or the defence of the state.

This is most strikingly illustrated in an instance which I have quoted from M. Muret, in a chapter on Switzerland, where it appeared that, in proportion to the same population, the Lyonois produced 16 births, the Pays de Vaud 11, and a particular parish in the Alps only 8; but that at the age of 20 these three very different numbers were all reduced to the same. In the Lyonois nearly half of the population was under the age of puberty, in the Pays de Vaud one third, and in the parish of the Alps only one fourth. The inference from such facts is unavoidable, and of the highest importance to society.

The power of a country to increase its resources or defend its possessions must depend principally upon its efficient population, upon that part of the population which is of an age to be employed effectually in agriculture, commerce, or war; but it appears with an evidence little short of demonstration, that in a country, the resources of which do not naturally call for a larger proportion of births, such an increase, so far from tending to increase this efficient population, would tend materially to diminish it. It would undoubtedly at first increase the number of souls in proportion to the means of subsistence, and consequently[4] cruelly increase the pressure of want; but the number of persons rising annually to the age of puberty might not be so great as before, a larger part of the produce would be distributed without return to children who would never reach manhood; and the additional population, instead of giving additional strength to the country, would essentially lessen this strength, and operate as a constant obstacle to the creation of new resources.

We are a little dazzled at present by the population and power of

[4] [In 1826 *consequently* was changed to 'therefore'.

France, and it is known that she has always had a large proportion of births: but if any reliance can be placed on what are considered as the best authorities on this subject, it is quite certain, that the advantages which she enjoys do not arise from any thing peculiar in the structure of her population; but solely from the great absolute quantity of it, derived from her immense extent of fertile territory.

[5]●The effective population in this country, compared with the whole, is considerably greater than in France; and England not only can, but does, employ a larger proportion of her population in augmenting and defending her resources than her great rival.●[5] According to the *Statistique générale et particulière de la France* lately published, the proportion of the population under twenty is almost $\frac{9}{20}$; in England it is probably not much more than $\frac{7}{20}$.[6] Consequently, out of a population of ten millions,

[5] [In 1807 Malthus excised this sentence, and began the paragraph as follows:

Necker, speaking of the population of France, says that it is so composed, that a million of individuals present neither the same force in war, nor the same capacity for labour, as an equal number in a country where the people are less oppressed and fewer die in infancy.[a] And the view which Arthur Young has given of the state of the lower classes of the people at the time he travelled in France, which was just at the commencement of the revolution, leads directly to the same conclusion. According to the *Statistique générale et particulière* ...

[a] Necker sur les Finances, Tom. i, ch. ix, p. 263, 12mo.

[6] [In 1807 a long footnote was added here:

I do not mention these numbers here, as vouching in any degree for their accuracy, but merely for the sake of illustrating the subject. [a]●Unfortunately there are no data respecting the classifications of the population of different countries according to age on which any reliance can be placed with safety.●[a] I have reason to think that those which are given in the *Statistique Générale* were not taken from actual enumerations, and the proportion of the population under 20 mentioned in the text, for England, is entirely conjectural and certainly too small.[b] Of this however we may be quite sure, that when two countries, from the proportion of their births to deaths, increase nearly at the same rate, the one in which the births and deaths bear the greatest proportion to the whole population will have the smallest comparative number of persons above the age of puberty. That England and Scotland have, in every million of people which they contain, more individuals fit for labour, than France, the data we have are sufficient to determine; but in what degree this difference exists cannot be ascertained, without better information than we at present possess. On account of the more rapid increase of population in England than in France before the revolution, England ought, *cæteris paribus*, to have had the largest proportion of births, yet in France the proportion was $\frac{1}{25}$ or $\frac{1}{26}$, and in England only $\frac{1}{30}$.

The proportion of persons capable of bearing arms has been sometimes calculated at one fourth, and sometimes at one fifth, of the whole population of a country. The reader will be aware of the prodigious difference between the two estimates, supposing them to be applicable to two different countries. In the one case, a population of 20 millions would yield five millions of effective men; and in the other case, the same population would only yield 4 millions. We cannot surely doubt which

England would have a million more of persons above twenty than France, and would at least have three or four hundred thousand more males of a military age.[7] If our population were of the same description as that of France, it must be increased numerically by more than a million and a half in order to enable us to produce from England and Wales the same number of persons above the age of twenty as at present; and if we had only an increase of a million, our efficient strength in agriculture, commerce, and war, would be in the most decided manner diminished, while at the same time the distresses of the lower classes would be dreadfully increased. Can any rational man say that an additional population of this description would be desirable, either in a moral or political view? And yet this is the kind of population which invariably results from direct encouragements to marriage, or from that want of personal respectability which is occasioned by ignorance and despotism.

It may perhaps be true that France fills her armies with greater facility and less interruption to the usual labours of her inhabitants than England; and it must be acknowledged that poverty and want of employment are powerful aids to a recruiting serjeant; but it would not be a very humane project, to keep our people always in want for the sake of enlisting them cheaper, nor would it be a very politic project, to diminish our wealth and strength with the same economical view. We cannot attain incompatible objects; if we possess the advantage of being able to keep nearly all our people constantly employed either in agriculture or commerce, we cannot expect to retain the opposite advantage of their being always at leisure, and willing to enlist for a very small sum.[8] But we may rest perfectly assured that, while we have the efficient population,

---

of the two kinds of population would be of the most valuable description both with regard to actual strength, and the creation of fresh resources. Probably, however, there are no two countries in Europe in which the difference in this respect is so great as that between $\frac{1}{4}$ and $\frac{1}{5}$.

[a] [In 1826 this sentence was omitted.]

[b] [At the same time, Malthus altered the sentence which followed it:
   ... illustrating the subject. I have reason to think that the proportion given in the *Statistique Générale* was not taken from actual enumerations, and that mentioned in the text for England is conjectural, and probably too small. Of this, however, we may be quite sure ...

[7] [In 1807 Malthus changed this to:
   ... France, and would upon this supposition have at least three or four hundred thousand more males of a military age.

[8] This subject is strikingly illustrated in Lord Selkirk's lucid and masterly observations 'On the Present State of the Highlands, and on the Causes and Probable Consequences of Emigration', to which I can with confidence refer the reader.

we shall never want men to fill our armies if we propose to them adequate motives.

In many parts of the Essay I have dwelt much on the advantage of rearing the requisite population of any country from the smallest number of births. I have stated expressly that a decrease of mortality at all ages is what we ought chiefly to aim at; and as the best criterion of happiness and good government, instead of the largeness of the proportion of births, which was the usual mode of judging, I have proposed the smallness of the proportion dying under the age of puberty. Conscious that I had never intentionally deviated from these principles, I might well be rather surprised to hear that I had been considered by some as an enemy to the introduction of the vaccine inoculation, which is calculated to attain the very end which I have uniformly considered as so desirable. I have indeed intimated what I still continue most firmly to believe, that if the resources of the country would not permanently admit of a greatly accelerated rate of increase in the population (and whether they would or not, must certainly depend upon other causes besides the number of lives saved by the vaccine inoculation),[9] one of two things would happen, either an increased mortality of some other diseases, or a diminution in the proportion of births. But I have expressed my conviction that the latter effect would take place; and therefore, consistently with the opinions which I have always maintained, I ought to be, and am, one of the warmest friends to the introduction of the cow-pox. In making every exertion which I think likely to be effectual, to increase the comforts and diminish the mortality among the poor, I act in the most exact conformity to my principles. Whether those are equally consistent who profess to have the same object in view, and yet measure the happiness of nations by the large proportion of marriages and births, is a point which they would do well to consider.

It has been said by some that the natural checks to population will always be sufficient to keep it within bounds, without resorting to any other aids; and one ingenious writer has remarked that I have not deduced a single original fact from real observations to prove the

---

[9] It should be remarked, however, that a young person saved from death is more likely to contribute to the creation of fresh resources than another birth. It is a great loss of labour and food to begin over again. And universally it is true that, under similar circumstances, that article will come the cheapest to market which is accompanied by fewest failures.

inefficiency of the checks which already prevail.[10] These remarks are correctly true, and are truisms exactly of the same kind as the assertion that man cannot live without food. For undoubtedly, as long as this continues to be a law of his nature, what are here called the natural checks cannot possibly fail of being effectual. Besides the curious truism that these assertions involve, they proceed upon the very strange supposition that the *ultimate* object of my work is to check population, as if anything could be more desirable than the most rapid increase of population unaccompanied by vice and misery. But of course my ultimate object is to diminish vice and misery, and any checks to population which may have been suggested are solely as means to accomplish this end. To a rational being, the prudential check to population ought to be considered as equally natural with the check from poverty and premature mortality, which these gentlemen seem to think so entirely sufficient and satisfactory; and it will readily occur to the intelligent reader, that one class of checks may be substituted for another, not only without essentially diminishing the population of a country, but even under a constantly progressive increase of it.[11]

On the possibility of increasing very considerably the effective population of this country, I have expressed myself in some parts of my work more sanguinely, perhaps, than experience would warrant. I have said that in the course of some centuries it might contain two or three times as many inhabitants as at present, and yet every person be both better fed and better clothed.[12] And in the comparison of the increase of population and food at the beginning of the Essay, that the argument might not seem to depend upon a difference of opinion respecting facts, I have allowed the produce of the earth to be unlimited, which is certainly going too far. It is not a little curious therefore, that it should still continue to be urged against me as an argument, that this country might contain two or three times as many inhabitants; and it is still more curious, that some persons, who have allowed the different ratios of increase on which all my principal conclusions are founded, have still asserted that no diffi-

[10] I should like much to know what description of facts this gentleman had in view when he made this observation. If I could have found one of the kind which seems here to be alluded to, it would indeed have been truly original.

[11] Both Norway and Switzerland, where the preventive check prevails the most, are increasing with some rapidity in their population; and in proportion to their means of subsistence, they can produce more males of a military age than any other country of Europe.

[12] P. 512, 4to edit. [And p. 232 of this edition.]

culty or distress could arise from population, till the productions of the earth could not be further increased. I doubt whether a stronger instance could readily be produced of the total absence of the power of reasoning than this assertion, after such a concession, affords. It involves a greater absurdity than the saying that because a farm can, by proper management, be made to carry an additional stock of four head of cattle every year, that therefore no difficulty or inconvenience would arise if an additional forty were placed in it yearly.

The power of the earth to produce subsistence is certainly not unlimited, but it is strictly speaking indefinite; that is, its limits are not defined, and the time will probably never arrive when we shall be able to say, that no farther labour or ingenuity of man could make further additions to it. But the power of obtaining an additional quantity of food from the earth by proper management, and in a certain time, has the most remote relation imaginable to the power of keeping pace with an unrestricted increase of population. The knowledge and industry which would enable the natives of New Holland[13] to make the best use of the natural resources of their country must, without an absolute miracle, come to them gradually and slowly; and even then, as it has amply appeared, would be perfectly ineffectual as to the grand object; but the passions which prompt to the increase of population are always in full vigour, and are ready to produce their full effect even in a state of the most helpless ignorance and barbarism. It will be readily allowed, that the reason why New Holland, in proportion to its natural powers, is not so populous as China, is the want of those human institutions which protect property and encourage industry; but the misery and vice which prevail almost equally in both countries, from the tendency of population to increase faster than the means of subsistence, form a distinct consideration, and arise from a distinct cause. They arise from the incomplete discipline of the human passions; and no person with the slightest knowledge of mankind has ever had the hardihood to affirm that human institutions could completely discipline all the human passions. But I have already treated this subject so fully in the course of the work, that I am ashamed to add any thing further here.

The next grand objection which has been urged against me, is my denial of the *right* of the poor to support.

Those who would maintain this objection, with any degree of consist-

---

[13] [It is strange that Malthus never substituted 'Australia' for *New Holland*.]

ency, are bound to show that the different ratios of increase with respect to population and food, which I attempted to establish at the beginning of the Essay, are fundamentally erroneous; since on the supposition of their being true, the conclusion is inevitable. If it appear, as it must appear on these ratios being allowed, that it is not possible for the industry of man to produce sufficient food[14] for all that would be born, if every person were to marry at the time when he was first prompted to it by inclination, it follows irresistibly that all cannot have a *right* to support. Let us for a moment suppose an equal division of property in any country. If, under these circumstances, one half of the society were by prudential habits so to regulate their increase that it exactly kept pace with their increasing cultivation, it is evident that they would always remain as at first. If the other half, during the same time, married at the age of puberty, when they would probably feel most inclined to it, it is evident that they would soon become wretchedly poor. But upon what plea of justice or equity could this second half of the society claim a right, in virtue of their poverty, to any of the possessions of the first half? This poverty had arisen entirely from their own ignorance or imprudence; and it would be perfectly clear, from the manner in which it had come upon them, that if their plea were admitted, and they were not suffered to feel the particular evils resulting from their conduct, the whole society would shortly be involved in the same degree of wretchedness. Any voluntary and temporary assistance which might be given as a measure of charity by the richer members of the society to the others, while they were learning to make a better use of the lessons of nature, would be quite a distinct consideration, and without doubt most properly applied; but nothing like a claim of *right* to support can possibly be maintained till we deny the premises; till we affirm that the American increase of population is a miracle, and does not arise from the greater facility of obtaining the means of subsistence.[15]

---

[14] [In 1826 there was an insertion here:
... to produce on a limited territory sufficient food ...

[15] It has been said that I have written a quarto volume to prove that population increases in a geometrical, and food in an arithmetical ratio; but this is not quite true. The first of these propositions I considered as proved the moment that the American increase was related, and the second proposition as soon as it was enunciated. The chief object of my work was to inquire what effects these laws, which I considered as established in the first six pages, had produced, and were likely to produce, on society: a subject not very readily exhausted. The principal fault of my details is that they are not sufficiently particular; but this was a fault which it was not in my power to remedy. It would be a most curious, and to every

In fact, whatever we may say in our declamations on this subject, almost the whole of our *conduct* is founded on the non-existence of this right. If the poor had really a claim of *right* to support, I do not think that any man could justify his wearing broadcloth, or eating as much meat as he likes for dinner, and those who assert this right, and yet are rolling in their carriages, living every day luxuriously, and keeping even their horses on food of which their fellow creatures are in want, must be allowed to act with the greatest inconsistency. Taking an individual instance without reference to consequences, it appears to me that Mr. Godwin's argument is irresistible. Can it be pretended for a moment that a part of the mutton which I expect to eat today would not be much more beneficially employed on some hard-working labourer who has not perhaps tasted animal food for the last week, or on some poor family who cannot command sufficient food of any kind fully to satisfy the cravings of appetite?[16] If these instances were not of a nature to multiply in proportion as such wants were indiscriminately gratified, the gratification of them, as it would be practicable, would be highly beneficial; and in this case I should not have the smallest hesitation in most fully allowing the right. But as it appears clearly both from theory and experience, that if the claim were allowed it would soon increase beyond the *possibility* of satisfying it, and that the practical attempt to do so, would involve the human race in the most wretched and universal poverty, it follows necessarily that our conduct, which denies the right, is more suited to the present state of our being, than our declamations which allow it.

The great author of nature,[17] indeed, with that wisdom which is apparent in all his works, has not left this conclusion to the cold and speculative consideration of general consequences. By making the passion of self-love beyond comparison stronger than the passion of benevolence, he has at once impelled us to that line of conduct which is essential to the preservation of the human race. If all that might be born could be adequately supplied, we cannot doubt that he would have made the desire of giving to others as ardent as that of supplying ourselves. But since, under the present constitution of things, this is not so, he has

philosophical mind a most interesting piece of information, to know the exact share of the full power of increase which each existing check prevents; but at present I see no mode of obtaining such information.

[16] [In 1817 *appetite* was changed to 'hunger'.

[17] [In 1817 'Author' was spelt with a capital A.]

enjoined every man to pursue as his primary object his own safety and happiness, and the safety and happiness of those immediately connected with him; and it is highly instructive to observe that, in proportion as the sphere contracts, and the power of giving effectual assistance increases, the desire increases at the same time. In the case of children, who have certainly a claim of *right* to the support and protection of their parents, we generally find parental affection nearly as strong as self-love; and except in a few anomalous cases, the last morsel will be divided into equal shares.

By this wise provision the most ignorant are led to promote the general happiness, an end which they would have totally failed to attain if the moving principle of their conduct had been benevolence.[18] Benevolence indeed, as the great and constant source of action, would require the most perfect knowledge of causes and effects, and therefore can only be the attribute of the Deity. In a being so short-sighted as man, it would lead into the grossest errors, and soon transform the fair and cultivated soil of civilized society into a dreary scene of want and confusion.

But though benevolence cannot in the present state of our being be the great moving principle of human actions, yet, as the kind corrector of the evils arising from the other stronger passion, it is essential to human happiness; it is the balm and consolation and grace of human life, the source of our noblest efforts in the cause of virtue, and of our purest and most refined pleasures. Conformably to that system of general laws, according to which the Supreme Being appears with very few exceptions to act, a passion so strong and general as self-love could not prevail without producing much partial evil; and to prevent this passion from degenerating into the odious vice of selfishness,[19] to make us sympathise in the pains and pleasures of our fellow-creatures, and feel the same *kind* of interest in their happiness and misery as in our own, though diminished in degree, to prompt us often to put ourselves in their place, that

[18] In saying this let me not be supposed to give the slightest sanction to the system of morals inculcated in the *Fable of the Bees*, a system which I consider as absolutely false, and directly contrary to the just definition of virtue. The great art of Dr. Mandeville consisted in misnomers.

[19] It seems proper to make a decided distinction between self-love and selfishness, between that passion which under proper regulations is the source of all honourable industry, and of all the necessaries and conveniences of life, and the same passion pushed to excess, when it becomes useless and disgusting, and consequently vicious.

we may understand their wants, acknowledge their rights, and do them good as we have opportunity; and to remind us continually, that even the passion which urges us to procure plenty for ourselves was not implanted in us for our own exclusive advantage, but as the means of procuring the greatest plenty for all; these appear to be the objects and offices of benevolence. In every situation of life there is ample room for the exercise of this virtue; and as each individual rises in society, as he advances in knowledge and excellence, as his power of benefiting others[20] becomes greater, and the necessary attention to his own wants less, it will naturally come in for an increasing share among his constant motives of action. In situations of high trust and influence it ought to have a very large share, and in all public institutions be the great moving principle. Though we have often reason to fear that our benevolence may not take the most beneficial direction, we need never apprehend that there will be too much of it in society. The foundations of that passion on which our preservation depends are fixed so deeply in our nature, that no reasonings or addresses to our feelings can essentially disturb it. It is just therefore, and proper, that all the positive precepts should be on the side of the weaker impulse; and we may safely endeavour to increase and extend its influence as much as we are able, if at the same time we are constantly on the watch to prevent the evil which may arise from its misapplication.

The law which in this country entitles the poor to relief is undoubtedly different from a full acknowledgment of the natural right; and from this difference and the many counteracting causes that arise from the mode of its execution, it will not of course be attended with the same consequences. But still it is an approximation to a full acknowledgment, and as such appears to produce much evil, both with regard to the habits and the temper of the poor. I have in consequence ventured to suggest a plan of gradual abolition, which, as might be expected, has not met with universal approbation. I can readily understand any objections that may be made to it, on the plea that the right having been once acknowledged in this country, the revocation of it might at first excite discontents; and should therefore most fully concur in the propriety of proceeding with the greatest caution, and of using all possible means of preventing any sudden shock to the opinions of the poor. But I have

---

[20] [In 1817 Malthus changed *benefiting others* to 'doing good to others'.

never been able to comprehend the grounds of the further assertion which I have sometimes heard made, that if the poor were really convinced that they had no claim of right to relief, they would in general be more inclined to be discontented and seditious. On these occasions the only way I have of judging is to put myself in imagination in the place of the poor man, and consider how I should feel in his situation. If I were told that the rich by the laws of nature and the laws of the land were bound to support me, I could not, in the first place, feel much obligation for such support; and in the next place, if I were given any food of an inferior kind, and could not see the absolute necessity of the change, which would probably be the case, I should think that I had good reason to complain. I should feel that the laws had been violated to my injury, and that I had been unjustly deprived of my right. Under these circumstances, though I might be deterred by the fear of an armed force from committing any overt acts of resistance, yet I should consider myself as perfectly justified in so doing, if this fear were removed; and the injury which I believed that I had suffered might produce the most unfavourable effects on my general dispositions towards the higher classes of society. I cannot indeed conceive anything more irritating to the human feelings, than to experience that degree of distress which, in spite of all our poor laws and benevolence, is not unfrequently felt in this country; and yet to believe that these sufferings were not brought upon me either by my own faults, or by the operation of those general laws which, like the tempest, the blight, or the pestilence, are continually falling hard on particular individuals, while others entirely escape, but were occasioned solely by the avarice and injustice of the higher classes of society.

On the contrary, if I firmly believed that by the laws of nature, which are the laws of God, I had no claim of *right* to support I should, in the first place, feel myself more strongly bound to a life of industry and frugality; but if want, notwithstanding, came upon me, I should consider it in the light of sickness, as an evil incidental to my present state of being, and which, if I could not avoid, it was my duty to bear with fortitude and resignation. I should know from past experience, that the best title I could have to the assistance of the benevolent would be, the not having brought myself into distress by my own idleness or extravagance. What I received would have the best effect on my feelings towards the higher classes. Even if it were much inferior to what I had been accustomed to, it would still, instead of an injury, be an obligation; and conscious that I had no claim of *right*, nothing but the fear of absolute famine, which would overcome all other considerations, could morally justify resistance.[21]

I cannot help believing that if the poor in this country were convinced that they had no claim of *right* to support; and yet in scarcities and all cases of urgent distress were liberally relieved, which I think they would be, the bond which unites the rich with the poor would be drawn much closer than at present, and the lower classes of society, as they would have less real reason for irritation and discontent, would be much less subject to these uneasy sensations.

Among those who have objected to my declaration that the poor have no claim of *right* to support is Mr. Young, who, with a harshness not quite becoming a candid inquirer after truth, has called my proposal for the gradual abolition of the poor laws a horrible plan, and asserted that the execution of it would be a most iniquitous proceeding. Let this plan however be compared for a moment with that which he himself and others have proposed, of fixing the sum of the poor's rates, which on no account is to be increased. Under such a law, if the distresses of the poor were to be aggravated tenfold, either by the increase of numbers or the recurrence of a scarcity, the same sum would invariably be appropriated to their relief. If the statute which gives the poor a right to support were to remain unexpunged, we should add to the cruelty of starving them the extreme injustice of still *professing* to relieve them. If this statute were expunged or altered, we should virtually deny the right of the poor to support, and only retain the absurdity of saying that they had a right to a certain sum; an absurdity on which Mr. Young justly comments with much severity in the case of France.[22] In both cases the hardships which

---

[21] [In 1817 this sentence was altered:

... no claim of *right*, nothing but the dread of absolute famine, which might overcome all other considerations, could palliate the guilt of resistance.

[22] The National Assembly of France, though they disapproved of the English poor laws, still adopted their principle, and declared that the poor had a right to pecuniary assistance; that the Assembly ought to consider such a provision as one of its first and most sacred duties; and that with this view, an expense ought to be incurred to the amount of 50 millions a year. Mr. Young justly observes, that he does not comprehend how it is possible to regard the expenditure of 50 millions a sacred duty, and not extend that 50 to 100 if necessity should demand it, the 100 to 200, the 200 to 300, and so on in the same miserable progression which has taken place in England. Travels in France, c. xv. p. 439.

I should be the last man to quote Mr. Young against himself, if I thought he had left the path of error for the path of truth, as such kind of inconsistency I hold to be highly praiseworthy. But thinking, on the contrary, that he has left truth for error, it is surely justifiable to remind him of his former opinions. We may recall to a

they would suffer would be much more severe, and would come upon them in a much more unprepared state, than upon the plan proposed in the Essay.

According to this plan all that are already married, and even all that are engaged to marry during the course of the year, and all their children, would be relieved as usual; and only those who marry subsequently, and who of course may be supposed to have made better provision for contingencies, would be out of the pale of relief.

Any plan for the abolition of the poor laws must presuppose a general acknowledgment that they are essentially wrong, and that it is necessary to tread back our steps. With this acknowledgment, whatever objections may be made to my plan, in the too frequently short-sighted views of policy, I have no fear of comparing it with any other that has yet been advanced, in point of justice and humanity; and of course the terms iniquitous and horrible 'pass by me like the idle wind which I regard not'.

Mr. Young it would appear has now given up this plan. He has pleaded for the privilege of being inconsistent, and has given such reasons for it that I am disposed to acquiesce in them, provided he confines the exercise of this privilege to different publications, in the interval between which he may have collected new facts; but I still think it not quite allowable in the same publication; and yet it appears that in the very paper in which he has so severely condemned my scheme, the same arguments which he has used to reprobate it are applicable with equal force against his own proposal, as he has there explained it.[23]

He allows that his plan can only provide for a certain amount of families, and has nothing to do with the increase from them;[24] but in allowing this, he allows that it does not reach the grand difficulty attending a provision for the poor. In this most essential point, after reprobating me for saying that the poor have no claim of *right* to support, he is compelled to adopt the very same conclusion, and to own that 'it might be prudent to consider the misery to which the progressive population might be subject, when there was not a sufficient demand for them in towns and manufactures, as an evil which it was absolutely and

---

vicious man his former virtuous conduct, though it would be useless and indelicate to remind a virtuous man of the vices which he had relinquished.

[23] [In 1817 Malthus changed *as he has there explained it* to:
... his own proposal as there explained.

[24] Annals of Agriculture, No. 239, p. 219.

physically impossible to prevent'. Now the sole reason why I say that the poor have no claim of *right* to support is the physical impossibility of relieving this progressive population. Mr. Young expressly acknowledges this physical impossibility; yet with an inconsistency scarcely credible still declaims against my declaration.

The power which the society may possess of relieving a certain portion of the poor is a consideration perfectly distinct from the general question; and I am quite sure I have never said that it is not our duty to do all the good that is practicable. But this limited power of assisting individuals cannot possibly establish a general right. If the poor have really a natural right to support, and if our present laws be only a confirmation of this right, it ought certainly to extend unimpaired to all who are in distress, to the increase from the cottagers as well as to the cottagers themselves; and it would be a palpable injustice in the society to adopt Mr. Young's plan, and purchase from the present generation the disfranchisement of their posterity.

Mr. Young objects very strongly to that passage of the Essay,[25] in which I observe that a man who plunges himself into poverty and dependence, by marrying without any prospect of being able to maintain his family, has more reason to accuse himself than the price of labour, the parish, the avarice of the rich, the institutions of society, and the dispensations of Providence; except in as far as he has been deceived by those who ought to have instructed him. In answer to this, Mr. Young says, that the poor fellow is justified in every one of these complaints, that of Providence alone excepted; and that seeing other cottagers living comfortably with three or four acres of land, he has cause to accuse institutions which deny him that which the rich could well spare, and which would give him all he wants.[26] I would beg Mr. Young for a moment to consider how the matter would stand, if his own plan were completely executed. After all the commons had been divided as he has proposed, if a labourer had more than one son, in what respect would this son be in a different situation from the man that I have supposed?[27] Mr. Young cannot possibly mean to say, that if he had the very natural desire of marrying at twenty, he would still have a right to complain that the society did not give him a house and three or four acres of land. He has indeed expressly denied this absurd consequence, though in so doing

[25] Book iv. c. iii. p. 506, 4to. edit.   [26] Annals of Agriculture, No. 239, p. 226.
[27] In 1807 this was amended to:
     ... in what respect would the second or third be in a different situation ...?

he has directly contradicted the declaration just quoted.[28] The progressive population, he says, would, according to his system, be cut off from the influence of the poor laws, and the encouragement to marry would remain exactly in that proportion less than at present. Under these circumstances, without land, without the prospect of parish relief, and with the price of labour only sufficient to maintain two children, can Mr. Young seriously think that the poor man, if he be really aware of his situation, does not do wrong in marrying, and ought not to accuse himself for following what Mr. Young calls the dictates of God, of nature, and of revelation? Mr. Young cannot be unaware of the wretchedness that must inevitably follow a marriage under such circumstances. His plan makes no provision whatever for altering these circumstances. He must therefore totally disregard all the misery arising from excessive poverty, or if he allows that these supernumerary members must necessarily wait, either till a cottage with land becomes vacant in the country, or that by emigrating to towns they can find the means of providing for a family, all the declamation which he has urged with such pomp against deferring marriage in my system, would be equally applicable in his own. In fact, if Mr. Young's plan really attained the object which it professes to have in view, that of bettering the condition of the poor, and did not defeat its intent by encouraging a too rapid multiplication, and consequently lowering the price of labour, it cannot be doubted that not only the supernumerary members just mentioned, but all the labouring poor, must wait longer before they could marry than they do at present.

The following proposition may be said to be capable of mathematical demonstration. In a country, the resources of which will not permanently admit of an increase of population more rapid than the existing rate, no improvement in the condition of the people which would tend to diminish mortality could *possibly* take place without being accompanied by a smaller proportion of births, supposing of course no particular increase of emigration.[29] To a person who has considered the subject,

[28] Annals of Agriculture, No. 239, p. 214.

[29] With regard to the resource of emigration, I refer the reader to the 4th chapter, Book iii. of the Essay. Nothing is more easy than to say, that three fourths of the habitable globe are yet unpeopled but it is by no means so easy to fill these parts with flourishing colonies. The peculiar circumstances which have caused the spirit of emigration in the Highlands, so clearly explained in the able work of Lord Selkirk before referred to, are not of constant recurrence; nor is it by any means to be wished that they should be so. And yet without some such circumstances, people are by no means very ready to leave their native soil, and will bear much distress at home, rather than venture on these distant regions. I am of opinion that it is both

there is no proposition in Euclid which brings home to the mind a stronger conviction than this, and there is no truth so invariably confirmed by all the registers of births, deaths, and marriages that have ever been collected. In this country it has appeared that, according to the returns of the population act, the proportion of births to deaths is about 4 to 3.[30] This proportion with a mortality of 1 in 40,[31] would double the population in 83 years and a half; and as we cannot suppose that the country could admit of more than a quadrupled population in the next hundred and sixty-six years, we may safely say that its resources will not allow of a permanent rate of increase greater than that which is taking place at present.[32] But if this be granted, it follows as a direct conclusion that if Mr. Young's plan, or any other, really succeeded in bettering the condition of the poor, and enabling them to rear more of their children, the vacancies in cottages in proportion to the number of expectants would happen slower than at present and the age of marriage must inevitably be later. [33]●Those, therefore, who propose plans for bettering the condition of the poor, and yet at the same time reprobate later or fewer marriages, are guilty of the most puerile inconsistency; and I cannot but be perfectly astonished that Mr. Young, who once understood the subject, should have indulged himself in such a poor declamation about passions, profligacy, burning, and ravens. It is in fact a silly, not to say impious, declamation against the laws of nature and the dispensations of Providence.●[33]

With regard to the expression of later marriages, it should always be recollected that it refers to no particular age, but is entirely comparative. The marriages in England are later than in France, the natural consequence of that prudence and respectability generated by a better government; and can we doubt that good has been the result? The marriages in this country now are later than they were before the revolution, and I feel firmly persuaded that the increased healthiness

the duty and interest of government to facilitate emigration; but it would surely be unjust to oblige people to leave their country and kindred against their inclinations.

[30] [In 1817 Malthus inserted a footnote here:
    The returns of 1801.
[In 1826 he omitted the footnote and amended the text instead:
    ... it has appeared that according to the returns of the Population Act in 1801, the proportion of births to deaths was about 4 to 3.

[31] Table iii. p. 238, 4to. edit.

[32] [In 1826 this was altered to:
    ... a permanent rate of increase greater than that which was then taking place.

[33] [In 1817 this passage was expunged.]

observed of late years could not possibly have taken place without this accompanying circumstance.[34] Two or three years in the average age of marriage, by lengthening each generation, and tending, in a small degree, both to diminish the prolificness of marriages, and the number of born living to be married, may make a considerable difference in the rate of increase, and be adequate to allow for a considerably diminished mortality. But I would on no account talk of any limits whatever. The only plain and intelligible measure with regard to marriage is the having a fair prospect of being able to maintain a family. If the possession of one of Mr. Young's cottages would give the labourer this prospect, he would be quite right to marry; but if it did not, or if he could only obtain a rented house without land, and the wages of labour were only sufficient to maintain two children, does Mr. Young, who cuts him off from the influence of the poor laws, presume to say that he would still be right in marrying?[35]

Mr. Young has asserted that I have made perfect chastity in the single state absolutely necessary to the success of my plan; but this surely is a misrepresentation. Perfect virtue is indeed absolutely necessary[36] to enable man to avoid *all* the moral and physical evils which depend upon his own conduct; but whoever expected perfect virtue upon earth? I have said what I conceive to be strictly true, that it is our duty to defer marriage till we can feed our children, and that it is also our duty not to indulge ourselves in vicious gratifications; but I have never said that I expected either, much less both, of these duties to be completely fulfilled. In this, and a number of other cases, it may happen, that the violation of one of two duties will enable a man to perform the other with greater facility; but if they be really both duties, and both practicable, no power *on earth* can absolve a man from the guilt of violating either. This can only be done by that God who can weigh the crime against the temptation, and will temper justice with mercy. The moralist is still bound to inculcate the practice of both duties, and each individual must be left to

---

[34] [In 1826 Malthus added a footnote here:
  (1825) It appears from the three returns of the Population Act, in 1801, 1811, and 1821, that the proportion of marriages has been diminishing with the increasing health of the country, notwithstanding the augmented rate of increase in the population.

[35] The lowest prospect with which a man can be justified in marrying seems to be the power, when in health, of earning such wages as, at the average price of corn, will maintain the average number of living children to a marriage.

[36] [In 1817 the word *absolutely* was excised.]

act under the temptations to which he is exposed as his conscience shall dictate. Whatever I may have said in drawing a picture *professedly* visionary, for the sake of illustration, in the practical application of my principles I have taken man as he is, with all his imperfections on his head. And thus viewing him, and knowing that some checks to the population must exist, I have not the slightest hesitation in saying that the prudential check to marriage is better than premature mortality. And in this decision I feel myself completely justified by experience.

In every instance that can be traced, in which an improved government has given to its subjects a greater degree of foresight, industry, and personal dignity, these effects, under similar circumstances of increase, have invariably been accompanied by a diminished proportion of marriages. This is a proof that an increase of moral worth in the general character is not at least *incompatible* with an increase of temptations with respect to one particular vice; and the instances of Norway, Switzerland, England and Scotland, adduced in the last chapter of this Essay, show that, in comparing different countries together, a small proportion of marriages and births does not necessarily imply the greater prevalence even of this particular vice. This is surely quite enough for the legislator. He cannot estimate with tolerable accuracy the degree in which chastity in the single state prevails. His general conclusions must be founded on general results, and these are clearly in his favour.

To much of Mr. Young's plan, as he has at present explained it, I should by no means object. The peculiar evil which I apprehended from it, that of taking the poor from the consumption of wheat, and feeding them on milk and potatoes might certainly be avoided by a limitation of the number of cottages; and I entirely agree with him in thinking that we should not be deterred from making 500 000 families more comfortable, because we cannot extend the same relief to all the rest. I have indeed myself ventured to recommend a general improvement of cottages, and even the cow system on a limited scale; and perhaps, with proper precautions, a certain portion of land might be given to a considerable body of the labouring classes.

If the law which entitles the poor to support were to be repealed, I should most highly approve of any plan which would tend to render such repeal more palatable on its first promulgation; and in this view, some kind of compact with the poor might be very desirable. A plan of letting land to labourers, under certain conditions, has lately been tried in the parish of Long Newnton in Gloucestershire; and the result, with a general proposal founded on it, has been submitted to the public by Mr. Estcourt. The present success has been very striking; but in this, and every other case of the kind, we should always bear in mind that no experiment respecting a provision for the poor can be said to be complete till succeeding generations have arisen.[37] I doubt if there ever has been an instance of anything like a liberal institution for the poor which did not succeed on its first establishment, however it might have failed afterwards. But this consideration should by no means deter us from making such experiments, when present good is to be obtained by them, and a future overbalance of evil not justly to be apprehended. It should only make us less rash in drawing our inferences.

With regard to the general question of the advantages to the lower classes of possessing land, it should be recollected that such possessions are by no means a novelty. Formerly this system prevailed in almost every country with which we are acquainted, and prevails at present in many countries where the peasants are far from being remarkable for their comforts, but are, on the contrary, very poor, and particularly subject to scarcities. With respect to this latter evil, indeed, it is quite obvious that a peasantry which depends principally on its possessions in land must be more exposed to it than one which depends on the general wages of labour. When a year of deficient crops occurs in a country of any extent and diversity of soil, it is always partial, and some districts are more affected than others. But when a bad crop of grass, corn, or potatoes, or a mortality among cattle, falls on a poor man, whose principal dependence is on two or three acres of land, he is in the most deplorable and helpless situation. He is comparatively without money to purchase supplies, and is not for a moment to be compared with the man who depends on the wages of labour, and who will of course be able to purchase that portion of the general crop, whatever it may be, to which his relative situation in the society entitles him. In Sweden, where the farmers' labourers are paid principally in land, and often keep two or three cows, it is not uncommon for the peasants of one district to be almost starving, while their neighbours at a little distance are living in

---

[37] In any plan, particularly of a distribution of land, as a compensation for the relief given by the poor laws, the succeeding generations would form the grand difficulty. All others would be perfectly trivial in comparison. For a time everything might go on very smoothly, and the rates be much diminished; but afterwards they would either increase again as rapidly as before, or the scheme would be exposed to all the same objections which have been made to mine, without the same justice and consistency to palliate them.

comparative plenty. It will be found indeed generally that, in almost all the countries which are particularly subject to scarcities and famines, either the farms are very small, or the labourers are paid principally in land. China, Indostan, and the former state of the Highlands of Scotland furnish some proofs among many others of the truth of this observation; and in reference to the small properties of France, Mr. Young himself in his tour particularly notices the distress arising from the least failure of the crops; and observes that such a deficiency as in England passes almost without notice, in France is attended with dreadful calamities.[38]

Should any plan therefore of assisting the poor by land be adopted in this country, it would be absolutely essential to its ultimate success to prevent them from making it their principal dependence. And this might probably be done by attending strictly to the two following rules. Not to let the divisions of land be so great as to interrupt the cottager essentially in his usual labours; and always to stop in the further distribution of land and cottages when the price of labour, independent of any assistance from land, would not at the average price of corn maintain three, or at least two children. Could the matter be so ordered that the labourer, in working for others, should still continue to earn the same real command over the necessaries of life that he did before, a very great accession of comfort and happiness might accrue to the poor from the possession of land, without any evil that I can foresee at present. But if these points were not attended to, I should certainly fear an approximation to the state of the poor in France, Sweden, and Ireland; nor do I think that any of the partial experiments that have yet taken place afford the slightest presumption to the contrary. The result of these experiments is indeed exactly such as one should have expected. Who could ever have doubted that if, without lowering the price of labour, or taking the labourer off from his usual occupations, you could give him the produce of one or two acres of land and the benefit of a cow, you would decidedly raise his condition? But it by no means follows that he would retain this advantage if the system were so extended as to make the land his principal dependence, to lower the price of labour and, in the language of Mr. Young, to take the poor from the consumption of wheat and feed them on milk and potatoes. It does not appear to me so marvellous as it does to Mr. Young that the very same system, which in Lincolnshire and

---

[38] Travels in France, vol. i. c. xii. p. 409. That country will probably be the least liable to scarcities, in which agriculture is carried on as the most flourishing *manufacture* of the state.

Rutlandshire may produce now the most comfortable peasantry in the British dominions should, in the end, if extended without proper precautions, assimilate the condition of the labourers of this country to that of the lower classes of the Irish.

It is generally dangerous and impolitic in a government to take upon itself to regulate the supply of any commodity in request, and probably the supply of labourers forms no exception to the general rule. I would on no account therefore propose a positive law to regulate their increase; but as any assistance which the society might give them cannot, in the nature of things, be unlimited, the line may fairly be drawn where we please; and with regard to the increase from this point, everything would be left as before to individual exertion and individual speculation.

If any plan of this kind were adopted by the government, I cannot help thinking that it might be made the means of giving the best kind of encouragement and reward to those who are employed in our defence. If the period of enlisting were only for a limited time, and at the expiration of that time every person who had conducted himself well was entitled to a house and a small portion of land, if a country labourer, and to a tenement in a town and a small pension, if an artificer, all inalienable, a very strong motive would be held out to young men, not only to enter into the service of their country, but to behave well in that service; and in a short time there would be such a martial population at home, as the unfortunate state of Europe seems in a most peculiar manner to require. As it is only limited assistance that the society can possibly give, it seems in every respect fair and proper that, in regulating this limit, some important end should be attained.

If the poor laws be allowed to remain exactly in their present state, we ought at least to be aware to what cause it is owing that their effects have not been more pernicious than they are observed to be, that we may not complain of, or alter those parts, without which we should really not have the power of continuing them. The law which obliges each parish to maintain its own poor is open to many objections. It keeps the overseers and churchwardens continually on the watch to prevent new comers, and constantly in a state of dispute with other parishes. It thus prevents the free circulation of labour from place to place, and renders its price very unequal in different parts of the kingdom. It disposes all landlords rather to pull down than to build cottages on their estates; and this scarcity of habitations in the country, by driving more to the towns than would otherwise have gone, gives a relative discouragement to agriculture, and a relative encouragement to manufactures. These, it must be allowed, are no inconsiderable evils; but if the cause which occasions them were removed, evils of much greater magnitude would follow. I agree with Mr. Young in thinking that there is scarcely a parish in the kingdom where, if more cottages were built, and let at any tolerably moderate rents, they would not be immediately filled with new couples. I even agree with him in thinking that, in some places, this want of habitations operates too strongly in preventing marriage. But I have not the least doubt that, considered generally, its operation in the present state of things is most beneficial; and that it is almost exclusively owing to this cause that we have been able so long to continue the poor laws. If any man could build a hovel by the roadside, or on the neighbouring waste, without molestation, and yet were secure that he and his family would always be supplied with work and food by the parish, if they were not readily to be obtained elsewhere, I do not believe that it would be long before the physical impossibility of executing the letter of the poor laws would appear. It is of importance, therefore, to be aware that it is not because this or any other society has really the power of employing and supporting all that might be born, that we have been able to continue the present system; but because by the indirect operation of this system, not adverted to at the time of its establishment, and frequently reprobated since, the number of births is always very greatly limited, and thus reduced within the pale of possible support.

The obvious tendency of the poor laws is certainly to encourage marriage; but a closer attention to all their indirect as well as direct effects, may make it a matter of doubt how far they really do this.[39] They clearly tend, in their general operation, to discourage sobriety and economy, to encourage idleness and the desertion of children, and to put virtue and vice more on a level than they otherwise would be; but I will not presume to say positively that they tend to encourage population.[40] It is certain that the proportion of births in this country compared with others in similar circumstances is very small: but this was to be expected from the superiority of the government, the more respectable state of the people, and the more general spread[41] of a taste for cleanliness and

[39] [In 1817 *how far* was replaced by:
   ... to what extent ...
[40] [In 1817 this was altered to:
   ... but I will not presume to say positively that they greatly encourage population.
[41] [In 1817 *spread* was changed to 'diffusion'.

conveniences. And it will readily occur to the reader that, owing to these causes, combined with the twofold operation of the poor laws, it must be extremely difficult to ascertain, with any degree of precision, what has been their effect on population.[42]

The only argument of a general nature against the Essay which strikes me as having any considerable force is the following. It is against the application of its principles, not the principles themselves, and has not, that I know of, been yet advanced in its present form. It may be said that, according to my own reasonings and the facts stated in my work, it appears that the diminished proportion of births, which I consider as absolutely necessary to the permanent improvement of the condition of the poor, invariably follows an improved government, and the greater degree of personal respectability which it gives to the lower classes of society. Consequently, allowing the desirableness of the end, it is not necessary, in order to obtain it, to risk the promulgation of any new opinions which may alarm the prejudices of the poor, and the effect of which we cannot with certainty foresee; but we have only to proceed in improving our civil polity, conferring the benefits of education upon all, and removing every obstacle to the general extension of all those privileges and advantages which may be enjoyed in common, and we may be quite sure that the effect to which I look forward, and which can alone render these advantages permanent, will follow.

I acknowledge the truth and force of this argument, and have only to observe, in answer to it, that it is difficult to conceive that we should not proceed with more celerity and certainty towards the end in view, if the principal causes which tend to promote or retard it were generally known. In particular, I cannot help looking forward to a very decided improvement in the habits and temper of the lower classes, when their

---

[42] [In 1807 Malthus added a footnote here:

The most favourable light, in which the poor laws can possibly be placed, is to say, that under all the circumstances, with which they have been accompanied, they do not encourage marriage;[a] and undoubtedly the returns of the Population Act seem to warrant the assertion. Should this be true, many of the objections which have been urged in the Essay against the poor laws will of course be removed; but I wish to press on the attention of the reader, that they will in that case be removed in strict conformity to the general principles of the work, and in a manner to confirm, rather than to invalidate,[b] the main positions which it has attempted to establish. [In 1817 (Vol. III, p. 374 n.) Malthus made two significant alterations to this footnote, one near the beginning and one at the end:

[a] ... the poor laws ... do not much encourage marriage;

[b] ... in a manner to confirm, not to invalidate, the main positions ...

real situation has been clearly explained to them; and if this were done gradually and cautiously, and accompanied with proper moral and religious instructions, I should not expect any danger from it. I am always unwilling to believe that the general dissemination of truth is prejudicial. Cases of the kind are undoubtedly conceivable, but they should be admitted with very great caution. If the general presumption in favour of the advantage of truth were once essentially shaken, all ardour in its cause would share the same fate, and the interests of knowledge and virtue most decidedly suffer. It is besides a species of arrogance not lightly to be encouraged, for any man to suppose that he has penetrated further into the laws of nature than the great Author of them intended, further than is consistent with the good of mankind.

Under these impressions I have freely given my opinions to the public. In the truth of the general principles of the Essay I confess that I feel such a confidence that, till something has been advanced against them very different indeed from anything that has hitherto appeared, I cannot help considering them as incontrovertible. With regard to the application of these principles the case is certainly different; and as dangers of opposite kinds are to be guarded against, the subject will of course admit of much latitude of opinion. At all events, however, it must be allowed that, whatever may be our determination respecting the advantages or disadvantages of endeavouring to circulate the truths on this subject among the poor, it must be highly advantageous that they should be known to all those who have it in their power to influence the laws and institutions of society. That the body of an army should not in all cases know the particulars of their situation may possibly be desirable; but that the leaders should be in the same state of ignorance will hardly, I think, be contended.

If it be really true, that without a diminished proportion of births[43] we cannot attain any *permanent* improvement in the health and happiness of the mass of the pople, and secure that description of population which, by containing a larger share of adults, is best calculated to create fresh resources, and consequently to encourage a continued increase of efficient population; it is surely of the highest importance that this should be known, that if we take no steps directly to promote this effect, we should

---

[43] It should always be recollected that a diminished *proportion* of births may take place under a constant annual increase of the absolute number. This is, in fact, exactly what has happened in England and Scotland during the last forty years.
[This figure was never altered, although by 1826 another twenty years had elapsed.]

not at least,[44] under the influence of the former prejudices on this subject, endeavour to counteract it.[45] And if it be thought inadvisable to abolish the poor laws, it cannot be doubted that a knowledge of those general principles, which render them inefficient in their humane intentions, might be applied so far to modify them and regulate their execution, as to remove many of the evils with which they are accompanied, and make them less objectionable.

There is only one subject more which I shall notice, and that is rather a matter of feeling than of argument. Many persons, whose understandings are not of that description that they can regulate their belief or disbelief by their likes or dislikes, have professed their perfect conviction of the truth of the general principles contained in the Essay; but, at the same time, have lamented this conviction, as throwing a darker shade over our views of human nature, and tending particularly to narrow our prospects of future improvement. In these feelings I cannot agree with them. If, from a review of the past, I could not only believe that a

[44] [In 1817 the words *at least* were omitted.]

[45] We should be aware that a scarcity of men, owing either to great losses, or to some particular and unusual demand, is liable to happen in every country; and in no respect invalidates the general principle that has been advanced. Whatever may be the tendency to increase, it is quite clear that an extraordinary supply of men cannot be produced either in six months, or six years; but even with a view to a more than usual supply, causes which tend to diminish mortality are not only more certain but more rapid in their effects than direct encouragements to marriage. An increase of births may, and often does, take place, without the ultimate accomplishment of our object; but supposing the births to remain the same, it is impossible for a diminished mortality not to be accompanied by an increase of effective population.

We are very apt to be deceived on this subject by the almost constant demand for labour which prevails in every prosperous country; but we should consider that in countries which can but just keep up their population, as the price of labour must be sufficient to rear a family of a certain number, a single man would[(a)] have a superfluity, and labour would be in constant demand at the price of the subsistence of an individual. It cannot be doubted that in this country we could soon employ double the number of labourers if we could have them at our own price; because supply will produce demand as well as demand supply. The present great extension of the cotton trade did not originate in an extraordinary increase of demand, at the former prices, but it an increased supply at a much cheaper rate, which of course immediately produced an extended demand. As we cannot, however, obtain men at sixpence a day by improvements in machinery, we must submit to the necessary conditions of their rearing; and there is no man, who has the slightest feeling for the happiness of the most numerous class of society, or has even just views of policy on the subject, who would not rather choose that the requisite population should be obtained by such a price of labour, combined with such habits, as would occasion a very small mortality, than from a great proportion of births, of which comparatively few would reach manhood.

[(a)] [In 1817 *would* was changed to 'will'.

fundamental and very extraordinary improvement in human society was possible, but feel a firm confidence that it would take place, I should undoubtedly be grieved to find that I had overlooked some cause, the operation of which would at once blast my hopes. But if the contemplation of the past history of mankind, from which alone we can judge of the future, renders it almost impossible to feel such a confidence, I confess, that I had much rather believe that some real and deeply-seated difficulty existed, the constant struggle with which was calculated to rouse the natural inactivity of man, to call forth his faculties, and invigorate and improve his mind; a species of difficulty which it must be allowed is most eminently and peculiarly suited to a state of probation; than that nearly all the evils of life might with the most perfect facility be removed, but for the perverseness and wickedness of those who influence human institutions.[46]

A person who held this latter opinion must necessarily live in a constant state of irritation and disappointment. The ardent expectations, with which he might begin life, would soon receive the most cruel check. The regular progress of society, under the most favourable circumstances, would to him appear slow and unsatisfactory; but instead even of this regular progress, his eye would be more frequently presented with retrograde movements and the most disheartening reverses. The changes to which he had looked forward with delight would be found big with new and unlooked-for evils, and the characters on which he had reposed the most confidence would be seen frequently deserting his favourite cause, either from the lessons of experience or the temptation of power. In this state of constant disappointment, he would be but too apt to attribute everything to the worst motives; he would be inclined to give up the cause of improvement in despair; and judging of the whole from a part, nothing but a peculiar goodness of heart and amiableness of

---

[46] The misery and vice arising from the pressure of the population too hard against the limits of subsistence, and the misery and vice arising from promiscuous intercourse, may be considered as the Scylla and Charybdis of human life. That it is possible for each individual to steer clear of both these rocks is certainly true, and a truth which I have endeavoured strongly to maintain; but that these rocks do not form a difficulty independent of human institutions, no person with any knowledge of the subject can venture to assert.

[Malthus has forgotten his classical studies here. According to legend, Scylla was either a rock or a monster, but Charybdis was indubitably a whirlpool; they were on opposite sides of the narrow Straits of Messina. Ships that tried to avoid the one were liable to be destroyed by the other, and Odysseus' passage of these Straits is described in the twelfth book of Homer's Odyssey.]

disposition could preserve him from that sickly and disgusting misanthropy which is but too frequently the end of such characters.

On the contrary, a person who held the other opinion, as he would set out with more moderate expectations, would of course be less liable to disappointment. A comparison of the best with the worst states of society, and the obvious inference from analogy, that the best were capable of further improvement, would constantly present to his mind a prospect sufficiently animating to warrant his most persevering exertions. But aware of the difficulties with which the subject was surrounded, knowing how often in the attempt to attain one object some other other had been lost, and that though society had made rapid advances in some directions, it had been comparatively stationary in others, he would be constantly prepared for failures. These failures, instead of creating despair, would only create knowledge; instead of checking his ardour, would only[47] give it a wiser and more successful direction; and having founded his opinion of mankind on broad and general grounds, the disappointment of any particular views would not change this opinion; but even in declining age he would probably be found believing as firmly in the reality and general prevalence of virtue, as in the existence and frequency of vice; and to the last, looking forward with a just confidence to those improvements in society, which the history of the past, in spite of all the reverses with which it is accompanied, seems clearly to warrant.

It may be true that if ignorance is bliss, 'tis folly to be wise; but if ignorance be not bliss, as in the present instance; if all false views of society must not only impede decidedly the progress of improvement, but necessarily terminate in the most bitter disappointments to the individuals who form them; I shall always think that the feelings and prospects of those who make the justest estimates of our future expectations are the most consolatory; and that the characters of this description are happier themselves, at the same time that they are beyond comparison more likely to contribute to the improvement and happiness of society.[48]

---

[47] [In 1817 the word *only* was omitted.]

[48] While the last sheet of this Appendix was printing, I heard with some surprise that an argument had been drawn from the Principle of Population in favour of the slave trade. As the just conclusion from that principle appears to me to be exactly the contrary, I cannot help saying a few words on the subject.

If the only argument against the slave trade had been that, from the mortality it occasioned, it was likely to unpeople Africa or extinguish the human race, some comfort with regard to these fears might, indeed, be drawn from the Principle of Population; but as the necessity of the abolition has never, that I know of, been urged on the ground of these apprehensions, a reference to the laws which regulate the increase of the human species was certainly most unwise in the friends of the slave trade.

The abolition of the slave trade is defended principally by the two following arguments:

1st. That the trade to the coast of Africa for slaves, together with their subsequent treatment in the West Indies, is productive of so much human misery, that its continuance is disgraceful to us as men and as Christians.

2d. That the culture of the West-India islands could go on with equal advantage, and much greater security, if no further importation of slaves were to take place.

With regard to the first argument it appears, in the Essay on the Principle of Population, that so great is the tendency of mankind to increase, that nothing but some physical or moral check operating in an *excessive* and *unusual* degree, can permanently keep the population of a country below the average means of subsistence. In the West India islands a constant recruit of labouring negroes is necessary; and consequently the immediate checks to population must operate with *excessive* and *unusual* force. All the checks to population were found resolvable into moral restraint, vice, and misery. In a state of slavery moral restraint cannot have much influence; nor in any state will it ever continue permanently to diminish the population. The whole effect, therefore, is to be attributed to the *excessive* and *unusual* action of vice and misery; and a reference to the facts contained in the Essay incontrovertibly proves that the condition of the slaves in the West Indies, taken altogether, is most wretched, and that the representations of the friends of the abolition cannot easily be exaggerated.

It will be said that the principal reason why the slaves in the West Indies constantly diminish is that the sexes are not in equal numbers, a considerable majority of males being always imported; but this very circumstance decides at once on the cruelty of their situation, and must necessarily be one powerful cause of their degraded moral condition.

It may be said also, that many towns do not keep up their numbers, and yet the same objection is not made to them on that account. But the cases will admit of no comparison. If, for the sake of better society or higher wages, people are willing to expose themselves to a less pure air, and greater temptations to vice, no hardship is suffered that can reasonably be complained of. The superior mortality of towns falls principally upon children, and is scarcely noticed by people of mature age. The sexes are in equal numbers, and every man after a few years of industry may look forward to the happiness of domestic life. If during the time that he is thus waiting, he acquires various[a] habits which indispose him to marriage, he has nobody to blame except himself. But with the negroes the case is totally different. The unequal number of the sexes shuts out at once the majority of them from all chance of domestic happiness. They have no hope of this kind to sweeten their toils, and animate their exertion; but are necessarily condemned either to unceasing privation, or to the most vicious excesses; and thus shut out from every cheering prospect, we cannot be surprised that they are in general ready to welcome that death which so many meet with in the prime of life.

The second argument is no less powerfully supported by the Principle of Population than the first. It appears, from a very general survey of different

[a] [In 1807 *various* was changed to 'vicious'.

countries, that under every form of government, however unjust and tyrannical, in every climate of the known world, however apparently unfavourable to health, it has been found that population, with the sole exception above alluded to, has been able to keep itself up to the level of the means of subsistence. Consequently, if by the abolition of the trade to Africa, the slaves in the West Indies were placed only in a *tolerable* situation, if their civil condition and moral habits were only made to *approach* to those which prevail among the mass of the human race in the worst-governed countries of the world, it is contrary to the general laws of nature to suppose that they would not be able, by procreation, fully to supply the effective demand for labour; and it is difficult to conceive that a population so raised would not be in every point of view preferable to that which exists at present.

It is perfectly clear, therefore, that a consideration of the laws which govern the increase and decrease of the human species tends to strengthen, in the most powerful manner, all the arguments in favour of the abolition.

With regard to the state of society among the African nations, it will readily occur to the reader that, in describing it, the question of the slave trade was foreign to my purpose; and I might naturally fear that if I entered upon it I should be led into too long a digression. But certainly all the facts which I have mentioned, and which are taken principally from Park, if they do not absolutely *prove* that the wars in Africa are excited and aggravated by the traffic on the coast, tend powerfully to confirm the *supposition*. The state of Africa, as I have described it, is exactly such as we should expect in a country where the capture of men was considered as a more advantageous employment than agriculture or manufactures. Of the state of these nations some hundred years ago it must be confessed that we have little knowledge that we can depend upon: but allowing that the regular plundering excursions, which Park describes, are of the most ancient date; yet it is impossible to suppose that any circumstance which, like the European traffic, must give additional value to the plunder thus acquired, would not powerfully aggravate them, and effectually prevent all progress towards a happier order of things. As long as the nations of Europe continue barbarous enough to purchase slaves in Africa, we may be quite sure that Africa will continue barbarous enough to supply them.

[The rumour that Malthus approved of the slave trade was probably due to a malicious article by William Cobbett (1763–1835) in his *Political Register* for 16 February 1805. It was headed 'Jamaica Complaints', and in an oblique reference to homosexuality Cobbett wrote:

> But, as to the Africans, it is not pretended. I believe, that the constant fresh supply is rendered necessary by the destructiveness of the climate, so much as by the effects of *celibacy*, and other circumstances therewith connected. And, is this an *evil?* A question not to be settled without a discussion, into which, I should think, that even Mr Wilberforce would not be inclined to enter, at least not very minutely. If he were, however, it might be quite sufficient to refer him to the profound work of Mr Malthus, who has not scrupled to recommend *checks to population*, as conducive to the *good* of mankind.

Eleven months later, on 18 January 1806, Cobbett quoted Malthus's quotation from Mungo Park about the Africans voluntarily selling their children into slavery when food was short. This could well have been 'While the last sheet of this Appendix was printing'.

Just over a year after that, Malthus went up to London from Hertford, to the House of Commons, when the chief debate on the abolition of the slave trade took place on 23 February 1807. He was able 'to see Mr Wilberforce before he went into the house, and to furnish him with data to rescue my character from the imputation of being a friend to the slave trade'. (See Patricia James, *Population Malthus*, Routledge and Kegan Paul, 1979, p. 125.) In the editions of the *Essay* of 1817 and 1826 Malthus inserted '(1807)' at the beginning of this note 48, after 'While the last sheet of this Appendix was printing . . .' The date is presumably incorrect, and one must assume that Malthus jotted it down absent-mindedly, while he was recalling the year of this meeting with Wilberforce and the passing of the Act.]

Appendix, 1817

Since the publication of the last edition of this Essay in 1807, two Works have appeared, the avowed objects of which are directly to oppose its principles and conclusions. These are *the Principles of Population and Production*, by Mr. Weyland; and *an Inquiry into the Principle of Population*, by Mr. James Grahame.

I would willingly leave the question, as it at present stands, to the judgment of the public, without any attempt on my part to influence it further by a more particular reply; but as I professed my readiness to enter into the discussion of any serious objections to my principles and conclusions, which were brought forward in a spirit of candour and truth; and as one at least of the publications above mentioned may be so characterized, and the other is by no means deficient in personal respect, I am induced shortly to notice them.

I should not, however, have thought it necessary to advert to Mr. Grahame's publication, which is a slight work without any very distinct object in view, if it did not afford some strange specimens of misrepresentation, which it may be useful to point out.

Mr. Grahame in his second chapter, speaking of the tendency exhibited by the law of human increase to a redundance of population, observes that some philosophers have considered this tendency as a mark of the foresight of nature, which has thus provided a ready supply for the waste of life occasioned by human vices and passions; while 'others, of whom Mr. Malthus is the leader, regard the vices and follies of human nature, and their various products, famine, disease and war, as *benevolent remedies* by which nature has enabled human beings to correct the disorders that would arise from that redundance of population which the unrestrained operation of her laws would create'.[1]

[1] P. 100.

These are the opinions imputed to me and the philosophers with whom I am associated. If the imputation were just, we have certainly on many accounts great reason to be ashamed of ourselves. For what are we made to say? In the first place, we are stated to assert that *famine*[2] is a benevolent remedy for *want of food*, as redundance of population admits of no other interpretation than that of a people ill supplied with the means of subsistence, and consequently the benevolent remedy of famine here noticed can only apply to the disorders arising from scarcity of food.

Secondly, we are said to affirm that nature enables human beings by means of diseases to correct the disorders that would arise from a redundance of population – that is, that mankind willingly and purposely create diseases, with a view to prevent those diseases which are the necessary consequence of a redundant population, and are not worse or more mortal than the means of prevention.

And thirdly, it is imputed to us generally, that we consider the vices and follies of mankind as benevolent remedies for the disorders arising from a redundant population; and it follows as a matter of course that these vices ought to be encouraged rather than reprobated.

It would not be easy to compress in so small a compass a greater quantity of absurdity, inconsistency, and unfounded assertion.

The two first imputations may perhaps be peculiar to Mr. Grahame; and protection from them may be found in their gross absurdity and inconsistency. With regard to the third, it must be allowed that it has not the merit of novelty. Although it is scarcely less absurd than the two others, and has been shown to be an opinion not to be inferred from any part of it, it has been continually repeated in various quarters for fourteen years, and now appears in the pages of Mr. Grahame. For the last time I will now notice it; and should it still continue to be brought forward, I think I may be fairly excused from paying the slightest further attention either to the imputation itself, or to those who advance it.

If I had merely stated that the tendency of the human race to increase faster than the means of subsistence was kept to a level with these means by some or other of the forms of vice and misery, and that these evils were absolutely unavoidable, and incapable of being diminished by any human efforts; still I could not with any semblance of justice be accused of considering vice and misery as the remedies of these evils, instead of the very evils themselves. As well nearly might I be open to Mr. Grahame's imputations of considering the famine and disease necessarily

[2] [In 1826 the word *famine* was not italicised.]

arising from a scarcity of food as a benevolent remedy for the evils which this scarcity occasions.

But I have not so stated the proposition. I have not considered the evils of vice and misery arising from a redundant population as unavoidable, and incapable of being diminished. On the contrary, I have pointed out a mode by which these evils may be removed or mitigated by removing or mitigating their cause. I have endeavoured to show that this may be done consistently with human virtue and happiness. I have never considered any possible increase of population as an evil, except as far as it might increase the proportion of vice and misery. Vice and misery, and these alone, are the evils which it has been my great object to contend against. I have expressly proposed moral restraint as their rational and proper remedy; and whether the remedy be good or bad, adequate or inadequate, the proposal itself, and the stress which I have laid upon it, is an incontrovertible proof that I never can have considered vice and misery as themselves remedies.

But not only does the general tenour of my work, and the specific object of the latter part of it, clearly show that I do not consider vice and misery as remedies; but particular passages in various parts of it are so distinct on the subject, as not to admit of being misunderstood but by the most perverse blindness.[3]

It is therefore quite inconceivable that any writer with the slightest pretension to respectability should venture to bring forward such imputations; and it must be allowed to show either such a degree of ignorance, or such a total want of candour, as utterly to disqualify him for the discussion of such subjects.

But Mr. Grahame's misrepresentations are not confined to the passage above referred to. In his Introduction he observes that, in order to check a redundant population, the evils of which I consider as much nearer than Mr. Wallace, I 'recommend immediate recourse to human efforts, to the restraints prescribed by Condorcet, for the correction or mitigation of the evil'.[4] This is an assertion entirely without foundation. I have never adverted to the check suggested by Condorcet without the most marked disapprobation. Indeed I should always particularly reprobate any artificial and unnatural modes of checking population, both on account of their immorality and their tendency to remove a necessary

---

[3] [In 1826 the word *but* was excised, so that the sentence concluded:
. . . as not to admit of being misunderstood by the most perverse blindness.

[4] P. 18

stimulus to industry. If it were possible for each married couple to limit by a wish the number of their children, there is certainly reason to fear that the indolence of the human race would be very greatly increased; and that neither the population of individual countries, nor of the whole earth, would ever reach its natural and proper extent. But the restraints which I have recommended are quite of a different character. They are not only pointed out by reason and sanctioned by religion, but tend in the most marked manner to stimulate industry. It is not easy to conceive a more powerful encouragement to exertion and good conduct than the looking forward to marriage as a state peculiarly desirable; but only to be enjoyed in comfort by the acquisition of habits of industry, economy and prudence. And it is in this light that I have always wished to place it.[5]

In speaking of the poor-laws in this country, and of their tendency (particularly as they have been lately administered) to eradicate all remaining spirit of independence among our peasantry, I observe that 'hard as it may appear in individual instances, dependent poverty ought to be held disgraceful'; by which of course I only mean that such a proper degree of pride as will induce a labouring man to make great exertions, as in Scotland, in order to prevent himself or his nearest relations from falling upon the parish, is very desirable, with a view to the happiness of the lower classes of society. The interpretation which Mr. Grahame gives to this passage is that the rich 'are so to embitter the pressure of indigence by the stings of contumely, that men may be driven by their pride to prefer even the refuge of despair to the condition of dependence!!'[6] – a curious specimen of misrepresentation and exaggeration.

I have written a chapter expressly on the practical direction of our charity; and in detached passages elsewhere have paid a just tribute to the exalted virtue of benevolence. To those who have read these parts of my work, and have attended to the general tone and spirit of the whole, I willingly appeal, if they are but tolerably candid, against these charges of Mr. Grahame, which intimate that I would root out the virtues of charity and benevolence, without regard to the exaltation which they bestow on the moral dignity of our nature; and that in my view the 'rich are required only to harden their hearts against calamity, and to prevent the charitable visitings of their nature from keeping alive in them that virtue which is often the only moral link between them and their fellow-

[5] [In the present edition this passage in the chapter 'Of moral restraint' will be found on pp. 211–12.]

[6] P. 236.

mortals'.[7] It is not indeed easy to suppose that Mr. Grahame can have read the chapter to which I allude, as both the letter and spirit of it contradict, in the most express and remarkable manner, the imputations conveyed in the above passages.

These are a few specimens of Mr. Grahame's misrepresentations, which might easily be multiplied; but on this subject I will only further remark that it shows no inconsiderable want of candour to continue attacking and dwelling upon passages which have ceased to form a part of the work controverted. And this Mr. Grahame has done in more instances than one, although he could hardly fail to know that he was combating expressions and passages which I have seen reason to alter or expunge.

I really should not have thought it worth while to notice these misrepresentations of Mr. Grahame if, in spite of them, the style and tone of his publication had not appeared to me to be entitled to more respect than most of my opponents.

With regard to the substance and aim of Mr. Grahame's work, it seems to be intended to show that emigration is the remedy provided by nature for a redundant population; and that if this remedy cannot be adequately applied, there is no other that can be proposed which will not lead to consequences worse than the evil itself. These are two points which I have considered at length in the Essay; and it cannot be necessary to repeat any of the arguments here. Emigration, if it could be freely used, has been shown to be a resource which could not be of long duration. It cannot therefore under any circumstances be considered as an adequate remedy. The latter position is a matter of opinion, and may rationally be held by any person who sees reason to think it well founded. It appears to me, I confess, that experience most decidedly contradicts it; but to those who think otherwise, there is nothing more to be said, than that they are bound in consistency to acquiesce in the necessary consequences of their opinion. These consequences are that the poverty and wretchedness arising from a redundant population or, in other words, from very low wages and want of employment, are absolutely irremediable, and must be continually increasing as the population of the earth proceeds; and that all the efforts of legislative wisdom and private charity, though they may afford a wholesome and beneficial exercise of human virtue, and may occasionally alter the distribution and vary the

---

[7] Ibid.

pressure of human misery, can do absolutely nothing towards diminishing the general amount or checking the increasing weight of this pressure.

Mr. Weyland's work is of a much more elaborate description than that of Mr. Grahame. It has also a very definite object in view: and although, when he enters into the details of his subject, he is compelled entirely to agree with me respecting the checks which practically keep down population to the level of the means of subsistence, and has not in fact given a single reason for the slow progress of population, in the advanced stages of society, that does not clearly and incontrovertibly come under the heads of moral restraint, vice or misery; yet it must be allowed that he sets out with a bold and distinct denial of my premises, and finishes, as he ought to do from such a beginning, by drawing the most opposite conclusions.

After stating fairly my main propositions, and adverting to the conclusion which I have drawn from them, Mr. Weyland says: 'Granting the premises, it is indeed obvious that this conclusion is undeniable.'[8]

I desire no other concession than this; and if my premises can be shown to rest on unsolid foundations, I will most readily give up the inferences I have drawn from them.

To determine the point here at issue it cannot be necessary for me to repeat the proofs of these premises derived both from theory and experience, which have already so fully been brought forward. It has been allowed that they have been stated with tolerable clearness; and it is known that many persons have considered them as unassailable, who still refuse to admit the consequences to which they appear to lead. All that can be required therefore on the present occasion is to examine the validity of the objections to these premises brought forward by Mr. Weyland.

Mr. Weyland observes, 'that the origin of what are conceived to be the mistakes and false reasonings, with respect to the principle of population, appears to be the assumption of a tendency to increase in the human species, the quickest that can be proved possible in any particular state of society, as that which is natural and theoretically possible in all; and the characterizing of every cause which tends to prevent such quickest possible rate as checks to the natural and spontaneous tendency of population to increase; but as checks evidently insufficient to stem the

---

[8] Principles of Population and Production, p. 15.

progress of an overwhelming torrent. This seems as eligible a mode of reasoning, as if one were to assume the height of the Irish giant as the natural standard of the stature of man, and to call every reason, which may be suggested as likely to prevent the generality of men from reaching it, checks to their growth."[9]

Mr. Weyland has here most unhappily chosen his illustration, as it is in no respect applicable to the case. In order to illustrate the different rates at which population increases in different countries, by the different heights of men, the following comparison and inference would be much more to the purpose.

If in a particular country we observed that all the people had weights of different sizes upon their heads, and that invariably each individual was tall or short in proportion to the smallness or greatness of the pressure upon him; that every person was observed to grow when the weight he carried was either removed or diminished, and that the few among the whole people, who were exempted from this burden, were very decidedly taller than the rest; would it not be quite justifiable to infer that the weights which the people carried were the cause of their being in general so short; and that the height of those without weights might fairly be considered as the standard to which it might be expected that the great mass would arrive, if their growth were unrestricted?

For what is it, in fact, which we really observe with regard to the different rates of increase in different countries? Do we not see that, in almost every state to which we can direct our attention, the natural tendency to increase is repressed by the difficulty which the mass of the people find in procuring an ample portion of the necessaries of life, which shows itself more immediately in some or other of the forms of moral restraint, vice and misery? Do we not see that invariably the rates of increase are fast or slow, according as the pressure of these checks is light or heavy; and that in consequence Spain increases at one rate, France at another, England at a third, Ireland at a fourth, parts of Russia at a fifth, parts of Spanish America at a sixth, and the United States of North America at a seventh? Do we not see that, whenever the resources of any country increase, so as to create a great demand for labour and give the lower classes of society a greater command over the necessaries of life, the population of such country, though it might before have been stationary or proceeding very slowly, begins immediately to make a start

[9] P. 17.

forwards? And do we not see that in those few countries, or districts of countries, where the pressure arising from the difficulty of procuring the necessaries and conveniences of life is almost entirely removed, and where in consequence the checks to early marriages are very few, and large families are maintained with perfect facility, the rate at which the population increases is always the greatest?

And when to these broad and glaring facts we add, that neither theory nor experience will justify us in believing, either that the passion between the sexes, or the natural prolificness of women, diminishes in the progress of society; when we further consider that the climate of the United States of America is not particularly healthy, and that the qualities which mainly distinguish it from other countries are its rapid production and distribution of the means of subsistence – is not the induction as legitimate and correct as possible, that the varying weight of the difficulties attending the maintenance of families, and the moral restraint, vice and misery which these difficulties necessarily generate, are the causes of the varying rates of increase observable in different countries; and that, so far from having any reason to consider the American rate of increase as peculiar, unnatural and gigantic, we are bound by every law of induction and analogy to conclude that there is scarcely a state in Europe where, if the marriages were as early, the means of maintaining large families as ample, and the employment of the labouring classes as healthy, the rate of increase would not be as rapid, and in some cases, I have no doubt, even more rapid, than in the United States of America?

Another of Mr. Weyland's curious illustrations is the following: He says that the *physical tendency* of a people in a commercial and manufacturing state to double their number in twenty-five years is 'as absolutely gone as the tendency of a bean to shoot up further into the air, after it has arrived at its full growth'; and that to assume such a *tendency* is to build a theory upon a mere shadow, 'which, when brought to the test, is directly at variance with experience of the fact; and as unsafe to act upon, as would be that of a general who should assume the force of a musket-shot to be double its actual range, and then should calculate upon the death of all his enemies as soon as he had drawn up his own men for battle within this line of assumed efficiency'.[10]

Now I am not in the least aware who it is that has assumed the *actual*

[10] P. 126.

range of the shot, or the actual progress of population in different countries, as very different from what it is observed to be; and therefore cannot see how the illustration, as brought forward by Mr. Weyland, applies, or how I can be said to resemble his miscalculating general. What I have really done is this (if he will allow me the use of his own metaphor): having observed that the range of musket-balls, projected from similar barrels and with the same quantity of powder of the same strength, was, under different circumstances, very different, I applied myself to consider what these circumstances were; and, having found that the range of each ball was greater or less in proportion to the smaller or greater number of the obstacles which it met with in its course, or the rarity or density of the medium through which it passed, I was led to infer that the variety of range observed was owing to these obstacles; and I consequently thought it a more correct and legitimate conclusion, and one more consonant both to theory and experience, to say that the *natural tendency* to a range of a certain extent, or the force impressed upon the ball, was always the same, and the actual range, whether long or short, only altered by external resistance; than to conclude that the different distances to which the balls reached must proceed from some mysterious change in the *natural tendency* of each bullet at different times, although no observable difference could be noticed either in the barrel or the charge.

I leave Mr. Weyland to determine which would be the conclusion of the natural philosopher, who was observing the different velocities and ranges of projectiles passing through resisting media; and I do not see why the moral and political philosopher should proceed upon principles so totally opposite.

But the only arguments of Mr. Weyland against the *natural tendency* of the human race to increase faster than the means of subsistence are a few of these illustrations which he has so unhappily applied, together with the acknowledged fact, that countries under different circumstances and in different stages of their progress, do really increase at very different rates.

Without dwelling therefore longer on such illustrations, it may be observed, with regard to the fact of the different rates of increase in different countries, that as long as it is a law of our nature that man cannot live without food, these different rates are as absolutely and strictly *necessary* as the differences in the power of producing food in countries more or less exhausted; and that to infer from these different rates of increase, as they are actually found to take place, that 'population has a *natural tendency* to keep within the powers of the soil to afford it subsistence in every gradation through which society passes', is just as rational as to infer that every man has a *natural tendency* to remain in prison who is necessarily confined to it by four strong walls; or that the pine of the crowded Norwegian forest has no *natural* tendency to shoot out lateral branches, because there is no room for their growth. And yet this is Mr. Weyland's first and grand proposition, on which the whole of his work turns!!![11]

But though Mr. Weyland has not proved, or approached towards proving, that the *natural* tendency of population to increase is not unlimited; though he has not advanced a single reason to make it appear probable that a thousand millions would not be doubled in twenty-five years just as easily as a thousand, if moral restraint, vice and misery, were equally removed in both cases; yet there is one part of his argument which undoubtedly might, under certain circumstances, be true; and if true, though it would in no respect impeach the premises of the Essay, it would essentially affect some of its conclusions.

The argument may be stated shortly thus – that the natural division of labour arising from a very advanced state of society, particularly in countries where the land is rich, and great improvements have taken place in agriculture, might throw so large a portion of the people into towns, and engage so many in unhealthy occupations, that the immediate checks to population might be too powerful to be overcome even by an abundance of food.

It is admitted that this is a possible case; and, foreseeing this possibility, I provided for it in the terms in which the second proposition of the Essay was enunciated.

The only practical question then worth attending to, between me and Mr. Weyland, is whether cases of the kind above stated are to be considered in the light in which I have considered them in the Essay, as exceptions of very rare occurrence, or in the light in which Mr. Weyland has considered them, as a state of things naturally accompanying every stage in the progress of improvement. On either supposition, population would still be repressed by some or other of the forms of moral restraint, vice or misery; but the moral and political conclusions, in the actual state of almost all countries, would be essentially different. On the one

---

[11] [In 1826 Malthus reduced the number of exclamation marks here from three to one.]

supposition moral restraint would, except in a few cases of the rarest occurrence, be one of the most useful and necessary of virtues; and on the other, it would be one of the most useless and unnecessary.

This question can only be determined by an appeal to experience. Mr. Weyland is always ready to refer to the state of this country; and, in fact, may be said almost to have built his system upon the peculiar policy of a single state. But the reference in this case will entirely contradict his theory. He has brought forward some elaborate calculations to show the extreme difficulty with which the births of the country supply the demands of the towns and manufactories. In looking over them the reader, without other information, would be disposed to feel considerable alarm at the prospect of depopulation impending over the country; or at least he would be convinced that we were within a hair's breadth of that formidable point of *non-reproduction*, at which, according to Mr. Weyland, the population *naturally* comes to a full stop before the means of subsistence cease to be progressive.

These calculations were certainly as applicable twenty years ago as they are now; and indeed they are chiefly founded on observations which were made at a greater distance of time than the period here noticed. But what has happened since? In spite of the enlargement of all our towns; in spite of the most rapid increase of manufactories, and of the proportion of people employed in them; in spite of the most extraordinary and unusual demands for the army and navy; in short, in spite of a state of things which, according to Mr. Weyland's theory, ought to have brought us long since to the point of *non-reproduction*, the population of the country has advanced at a rate more rapid than was ever known at any period of its history. During the ten years from 1800 to 1811, as I have mentioned in a former part of this work, the population of this country (even after making an allowance for the presumed deficiency of the returns in the first enumeration) increased at a rate which would double its numbers in fifty-five years.

This fact appears to me at once a full and complete refutation of the doctrine that, as society advances, the increased indisposition to marriage and increased mortality in great towns and manufactories always overcome the principle of increase; and that, in the language of Mr. Weyland, 'population, so far from having an inconvenient tendency uniformly to press against the means of subsistence, becomes by degrees very slow in overtaking those means'.

With this acknowledged and glaring fact before him, and with the most striking evidences staring him in the face that, even during this period of rapid increase, thousands both in the country and in towns were prevented from marrying so early as they would have done, if they had possessed sufficient means of supporting a family independently of parish relief, it is quite inconceivable how a man of sense could bewilder himself in such a maze of futile calculations, and come to a conclusion so diametrically opposite to experience.

The fact already noticed, as it applies to the most advanced stage of society known in Europe, and proves incontrovertibly that the actual checks to population, even in the most improved countries, arise principally from an insufficiency of subsistence, and soon yield to increased resources, notwithstanding the increase of towns and manufactories, may I think fairly be considered as quite decisive of the question at issue.

But in treating of so general and extensive a subject as the Principle of Population, it would surely not be just to take our examples and illustrations only from a single state. And in looking at the other countries Mr. Weyland's doctrine on population is, if possible, still more completely contradicted. Where, I would ask, are the great towns and manufactories in Switzerland, Norway and Sweden, which are to act as *the graves of mankind*, and to prevent the possibility of a redundant population? In Sweden the proportion of the people living in the country is to those who live in towns as 13 to 1; in England this proportion is about 2 to 1; and yet England increases much faster than Sweden. How is this to be reconciled with the doctrine that the progress of civilization and improvement is always accompanied by a correspondent abatement in the natural tendency of population to increase? Norway, Sweden and Switzerland have not on the whole been ill governed; but where are the necessary 'anticipating alterations', which, according to Mr. Weyland, arise in every society as the powers of the soil diminish, and 'render so many persons unwilling to marry, and so many more, who do marry, incapable of reproducing their own numbers, and of replacing the deficiency in the remainder'?[12] What is it that in these countries indisposes people to marry, but the absolute hopelessness of being able to support their families? What is it that renders many more who do marry incapable of reproducing their own numbers, but the diseases generated by excessive poverty – by an insufficient supply of the necessaries of life? Can any man of reflection look at these and many of the other countries

[12] P. 124.

of Europe, and then venture to state that there is no moral reason for repressing the inclination to early marriages; when it cannot be denied that the alternative of not repressing it must necessarily and unavoidably be premature mortality from excessive poverty? And is it possible to know that in few or none of the countries of Europe the wages of labour, determined in the common way by the supply and the demand, can support in health large families; and yet assert that population does not press against the means of subsistence, and that 'the evils of a redundant population can never be necessarily felt by a country till it is actually peopled up to the full capacity of its resources'?[13]

Mr. Weyland really appears to have dictated his book with his eyes blindfolded and his ears stopped. I have a great respect for his character and intentions; but I must say that it has never been my fortune to meet with a theory so uniformly contradicted by experience. The very slightest glance at the different countries of Europe shows, with a force amounting to demonstration, that to all practical purposes the *natural tendency* of population to increase may be considered as a given quantity; and that the actual increase is regulated by the varying resources of each country for the employment and maintenance of labour, in whatever stage of its progress it may be, whether it is agricultural or manufacturing, whether it has few or many towns. Of course this actual increase, or the actual limits of population, must always be far short of the utmost powers of the earth to produce food; first, because we can never rationally suppose that the human skill and industry actually exerted are directed in the best *possible* manner towards the production of food; and secondly because, as I have stated more particularly in a former part of this work, the greatest production of food which the powers of the earth would admit cannot possibly take place under a system of private property. But this acknowledged truth obviously affects only the actual quantity of food and the actual number of people, and has not the most distant relation to the question respecting the *natural tendency* of population to increase beyond the powers of the earth to produce food for it.

The observations already made are sufficient to show that the four main propositions of Mr. Weyland, which depend upon the first, are quite unsupported by any appearances in the state of human society, as it is known to us in the countries with which we are acquainted. The last of these four propositions is the following: 'This tendency' (meaning the

[13] P. 123.

natural tendency of population to keep within the powers of the soil to afford it subsistence) 'will have its complete operation so as constantly to maintain the people in comfort and plenty in proportion as religion, morality, rational liberty and security of person and property approach the attainment of a perfect influence.'[14]

In the morality here noticed, moral or prudential restraint from marriage is not included: and so understood, I have no hesitation in saying that this proposition appears to me more directly to contradict the observed laws of nature than to assert that Norway might easily grow food for a thousand millions of inhabitants. I trust that I am disposed to attach as much importance to the effects of morality and religion on the happiness of society, even as Mr. Weyland; but among the moral duties I certainly include a restraint upon the inclination to an early marriage when there is no reasonable prospect of maintenance for a family; and unless this species of virtuous self-denial be included in morality, I am quite at issue with Mr. Weyland; and so distinctly deny his proposition as to say that no degree of religion and morality, no degree of rational liberty and security of person and property, can under the existing laws of nature place the lower classes of society in a state of comfort and plenty.

With regard to Mr. Weyland's fifth and last proposition;[15] I have already answered it in a note which I have added, in the present edition, to the last chapter of the third book,[16] and will only observe here that an illustration to show the precedence of population to food, which I believe was first brought forward by an anonymous writer, and appears so to have pleased Mr. Grahame as to induce him to repeat it twice, is one which I would willingly take to prove the very opposite doctrine to that which it was meant to support. The apprehension that an increasing population would starve[17] unless a previous increase of food were procured for it, has been ridiculed by comparing it with the apprehension that increasing numbers would be obliged to go naked unless a previous increase of clothes should precede their births. Now however well or ill-founded may be our apprehensions in the former case, they are certainly quite justifiable in the latter; at least society has always acted as

---

[14] C. iii. p. 21.

[15] C. iii. p. 22.

[16] Pp. 205–6.

[17] This I have never said; I have only said that their condition would be deteriorated, which is strictly true.

if it thought so. In the course of the next twenty-four hours there will be about 800 children born in England and Wales; and I will venture to say that there are not ten out of the whole number, that come at the expected time, for whom clothes are not prepared before their births. It is said to be dangerous to meddle with edged tools which we do not know how to handle; and it is equally dangerous to meddle with illustrations which we do not know how to apply, and which may tend to prove exactly the reverse of what we wish.

On Mr. Weyland's theory it will not be necessary further to enlarge. With regard to the practical conclusions which he has drawn from it in our own country, they are such as might be expected from the nature of the premises. If population, instead of having a tendency to press against the means of subsistence, becomes by degrees very slow in overtaking them, Mr. Weyland's inference, that we ought to encourage the increase of the labouring classes by abundant parochial assistance to families, might perhaps be maintained. But if his premises be entirely wrong, while his conclusions are still acted upon, the consequence must be that universal system of unnecessary pauperism and dependence which we now so much deplore.[18] Already above one-fourth of the population of England and Wales are regularly dependent upon parish relief;[19] and if the system which Mr. Weyland recommends, and which has been so generally adopted in the midland counties, should extend itself over the whole kingdom, there is really no saying to what height the level of pauperism may rise. While the system[20] of making an allowance from the parish for every child above two is confined to the labourers in agriculture, whom Mr. Weyland considers as the breeders of the country, it is essentially unjust, as it lowers without compensation the wages of the manufacturer and artificer: and when it shall become just by including the whole of the working classes, what a dreadful picture does it present! What a scene of equality, indolence, rags and dependence, among one-half or three-fourths of the society! Under such a system to expect any essential benefit from *saving banks* or any other institutions to promote industry and economy is perfectly preposterous. When the

[18] [In 1826 this was altered:
    ... still acted upon, the consequence must be a constantly increasing amount of unnecessary pauperism and dependence. ...

[19] [In 1826 this sentence was changed:
    Already above one-fourth of the population of England and Wales have been dependent upon parish relief; and if the system ...

[20] [In 1826 *the system* was changed to 'the practice'.

wages of labour are reduced to the level to which this system tends, there will be neither power nor motive to save.

Mr. Weyland strangely attributes much of the wealth and prosperity of England to the cheap population which it raises by means of the poor-laws; and seems to think that, if labour had been allowed to settle at its natural rate, and all workmen had been paid in proportion to their skill and industry, whether with or without families, we should never have attained that commercial and manufacturing ascendancy by which we have been so eminently distinguished.

A practical refutation of so ill-founded an opinion may be seen in the state of Scotland, which in proportion to its natural resources has certainly increased in agriculture, manufactures and commerce, during the last fifty years, still more rapidly than England, although it may fairly be said to have been essentially without poor-laws.

It is not easy to determine what is the price of labour most favourable to the progress of wealth. It is certainly conceivable that it may be too high for the prosperity of foreign commerce. But I believe it is much more frequently too low; and I doubt if there has ever been an instance in any country of very great prosperity in foreign commerce, where the working classes have not had good money wages. It is impossible to sell very largely without being able to buy very largely; and no country can buy very largely in which the working classes are not in such a state as to be able to purchase foreign commodities.

But nothing tends to place the lower classes of society in this state so much as a demand for labour which is allowed to take its natural course, and which therefore pays the unmarried man and the man with a family at the same rate; and consequently gives at once to a very large mass of the working classes the power of purchasing foreign articles of consumption, and of paying taxes on luxuries to no inconsiderable extent. While, on the other hand, nothing would tend so effectively to destroy the power of the working classes of society to purchase either home manufactures or foreign articles of consumption, or to pay taxes on luxuries, as the practice of doling out to each member of a family an allowance, in the shape of wages and parish relief combined, just sufficient, or only a very little more than to furnish them with the mere food necessary for their maintenance.

To show that, in looking forward to such an increased operation of prudential restraint as would greatly improve the condition of the poor, it is not necessary to suppose extravagant and impossible wages, as Mr.

Weyland seems to think, I will refer to the proposition of a practical man on the subject of the price of labour; and certainly much would be done, if this proposition could be realized, though it must be effected in a very different way from that which he has proposed.

It has been recommended by Mr. Arthur Young so to adjust the wages of day-labour as to make them at all times equivalent to the purchase of a peck of wheat. This quantity, he says, was earned by country labourers during a considerable period of the last century, when the poor-rates were low, and not granted to assist in the maintenance of those who were able to work. And he goes on to observe that 'as the labourer would (in this case) receive 70 bushels of wheat for 47 weeks' labour, exclusive of five weeks for harvest; and as a family of six persons consumes in a year no more than 48 bushels; it is clear that such wages of labour would cut off every pretence of parochial assistance; and of necessity the conclusion would follow, that all right to it in men thus paid should be annihilated for ever'.[21]

An adjustment of this kind, either enforced by law, or used as a guide in the distribution of parish assistance, as suggested by Mr. Young, would be open to insuperable objections. At particular times it might be the means of converting a dearth into a famine. And in its general operation, and supposing no change of habits among the labouring classes, it would be tantamount to saying that, under all circumstances, whether the affairs of the country were prosperous or adverse; whether its resources in land were still great, or nearly exhausted; the population ought to increase exactly at the same rate – a conclusion which involves an impossibility.

If, however, this adjustment, instead of being enforced by law, were produced by the increasing operation of the prudential check to marriage, the effect would be totally different, and in the highest degree beneficial to society. A gradual change in the habits of the labouring classes would then effect the necessary retardation in the rate of increase, and would proportion the supply of labour to the effective demand, as society continued to advance, not only without the pressure of a diminishing quantity of food, but under the enjoyment of an increased quantity of conveniences and comforts; and in the progress of cultivation and wealth the condition of the lower classes of society would be in a state of constant improvement.

[21] Annals of Agriculture, No. 270, p. 91, note.

A peck of wheat a day cannot be considered in any light as excessive wages. In the early periods of cultivation, indeed, when corn is low in exchangeable value, much more is frequently earned; but in such a country as England, where the price of corn, compared with manufactures and foreign commodities, is high, it would do much towards placing the great mass of the labouring classes in a state of comparative comfort and independence; and it would be extremely desirable, with a view to the virtue and happiness of human society, that no land should be taken into cultivation that could not pay the labourers employed upon it to this amount.

With these wages as the average minimum, all those who were unmarried, or, being married, had small families, would be extremely well off; while those who had large families, though they would unquestionably be subjected sometimes to a severe pressure, would in general be able, by the sacrifice of conveniences and comforts, to support themselves without parish assistance. And not only would the amount and distribution of the wages of labour greatly increase the stimulus to industry and economy throughout all the working classes of the society, and place the great body of them in a very superior situation, but it would furnish them with the means of making an effectual demand for a great amount of foreign commodities and domestic manufactures, and thus, at the same time that it would promote individual and general happiness, would advance the mercantile and manufacturing prosperity of the country.[22]

Mr. Weyland, however, finds it utterly impossible to reconcile the necessity of moral restraint either with the nature of man, or the plain dictates of religion on the subject of marriage. Whether the check to population, which he would substitute for it, is more consistent with the nature of a rational being, the precepts of revelation, and the benevolence of the Deity, must be left to the judgment of the reader. This check, it is already known, is no other than the unhealthiness and mortality of towns

---

[22] The merchants and manufacturers who so loudly clamour for cheap corn and low money wages, think only of selling their commodities abroad, and often forget that they have to find a market for their returns at home, which they can never do to any great extent, when the money wages of the working classes, and monied incomes in general, are low. (a)●One of the principal causes of this check which foreign commerce has experienced during the last two or three years, has been the great diminution of the home market for foreign produce.●(a)

(a) [In 1826 this sentence was omitted.]

and manufactories.[23] And though I have never felt any difficulty in reconciling to the goodness of the Deity the necessity of practising the virtue of moral restraint in a state allowed to be a state of discipline and trial; yet I confess that I could make no attempt to reason on the subject, if I were obliged to believe, with Mr. Weyland, that a large proportion of the human race was doomed by the inscrutable ordinations of Providence to a premature death in large towns.

If indeed such peculiar unhealthiness and mortality were the proper and natural check to the progress of population in the advanced stages of society, we should justly have reason to apprehend that, by improving the healthiness of our towns and manufactories, as we have done in England during the last twenty years, we might really defeat the designs of Providence. And though I have too much respect for Mr. Weyland to suppose that he would deprecate all attempts to diminish the mortality of towns, and render manufactories less destructive to the health of the children employed in them; yet certainly his principles lead to this conclusion, since his theory has been completely destroyed by those laudable efforts which have made the mortality of England – a country abounding in towns and manufactories, less than the mortality of Sweden – a country in a state almost purely agricultural.

It was my object in the two chapters on *Moral Restraint*, and its *Effects on Society*, to show that the evils arising from the principle of population were exactly of the same nature as the evils arising from the excessive or irregular gratification of the human passions in general; and that from the existence of these evils we had no more reason to conclude that the principle of increase was too strong for the purpose intended by the Creator, than to infer, from the existence of the vices arising from the human passions, that these passions required diminution or extinction, instead of regulation and direction.

If this view of the subject be allowed to be correct, it will naturally follow that, notwithstanding the acknowledged evils occasioned by the principle of population, the advantages derived from it under the present constitution of things may very greatly overbalance them.

A slight sketch of the nature of these advantages, as far as the main object of the Essay would allow, was given in the two chapters to which I have alluded; but the subject has lately been pursued with considerable

---

[23] With regard to the indisposition to marriage in towns, I do not believe that it is greater than in the country, except as far as it arises from the greater expense of maintaining a family, and the greater facility of illicit intercourse.

ability in the Work of Mr. Sumner on the Records of the Creation; and I am happy to refer to it as containing a masterly development and completion of views of which only an intimation could be given in the Essay.

I fully agree with Mr. Sumner as to the beneficial effects which result from the principle of population, and feel entirely convinced that the natural tendency of the human race, to increase faster than the possible increase of the means of subsistence, could not be either destroyed, or essentially diminished, without diminishing that hope of rising and fear of falling in society, so necessary to the improvement of the human faculties and the advancement of human happiness. But with this conviction on my mind, I feel no wish to alter the view which I have given of the evils arising from the principle of population. These evils do not lose their name or nature because they are overbalanced by good: and to consider them in a different light on this account, and cease to call them evils, would be as irrational as the objecting to call the irregular indulgences of passion vicious, and to affirm that they lead to misery, because our passions are the main sources of human virtue and happiness.

I have always considered the principle of population as a law peculiarly suited to a state of discipline and trial. Indeed I believe that, in the whole range of the laws of nature with which we are acquainted, not one can be pointed out which in so remarkable a manner tends to strengthen and confirm this scriptural view of the state of man on earth. And as each individual has the power of avoiding the evil consequences to himself and society resulting from the principle of population by the practice of a virtue clearly dictated to him by the light of nature, and sanctioned by revealed religion, it must be allowed that the ways of God to man with regard to this great law of nature are completely vindicated.

I have, therefore, certainly felt surprise as well as regret that no inconsiderable part of the objections which have been made to the principles and conclusions of the Essay on Population has come from persons for whose moral and religious character I have so high a respect, that it would have been particularly gratifying to me to obtain their approbation and sanction. This effect has been attributed to some expressions used in the course of the work which have been thought too harsh, and not sufficiently indulgent to the weaknesses of human nature and the feelings of Christian charity.

It is probable that, having found the bow bent too much one way, I was induced to bend it too much the other, in order to make it straight. But I shall always be quite ready to blot out any part of the work which is considered by a competent tribunal as having a tendency to prevent the bow from becoming finally straight, and to impede the progress of truth. In deference to this tribunal I have already expunged the passages which have been most objected to, and I have made some few further corrections of the same kind in the present edition. By these alterations I hope and believe that the work has been improved without impairing its principles. But I still trust that whether it is read with or without these alterations, every reader of candour must acknowledge that the practical design uppermost in the mind of the writer, with whatever want of judgment it may have been executed, is to improve the condition and increase the happiness of the lower classes of society.

Note, 1825

Since the last edition of this work was published an answer from Mr. Godwin has appeared, but the character of it both as to matter and manner is such that I am quite sure every candid and competent inquirer after truth will agree with me in thinking that it does not require a reply. To return abusive declamation in kind would be as unedifying to the reader as it would be disagreeable to me, and to argue seriously with one who denies the most glaring and best attested facts respecting the progress of America, Ireland, England, and other states,[1] and brings forward Sweden, one of the most barren and worst supplied countries of Europe, as a specimen of what would be the natural increase of population under the greatest abundance of food, would evidently be quite vain with regard to the writer himself, and must be totally uncalled for by any of his readers whose authority could avail in the establishment of truth.

[1] See article *Population* in the Supplement to the 'Encyclopædia Britannica'.
[This anonymous article was written by Malthus himself.]

Index

Cambridge Texts in the History of Political Thought